Special Category States of India

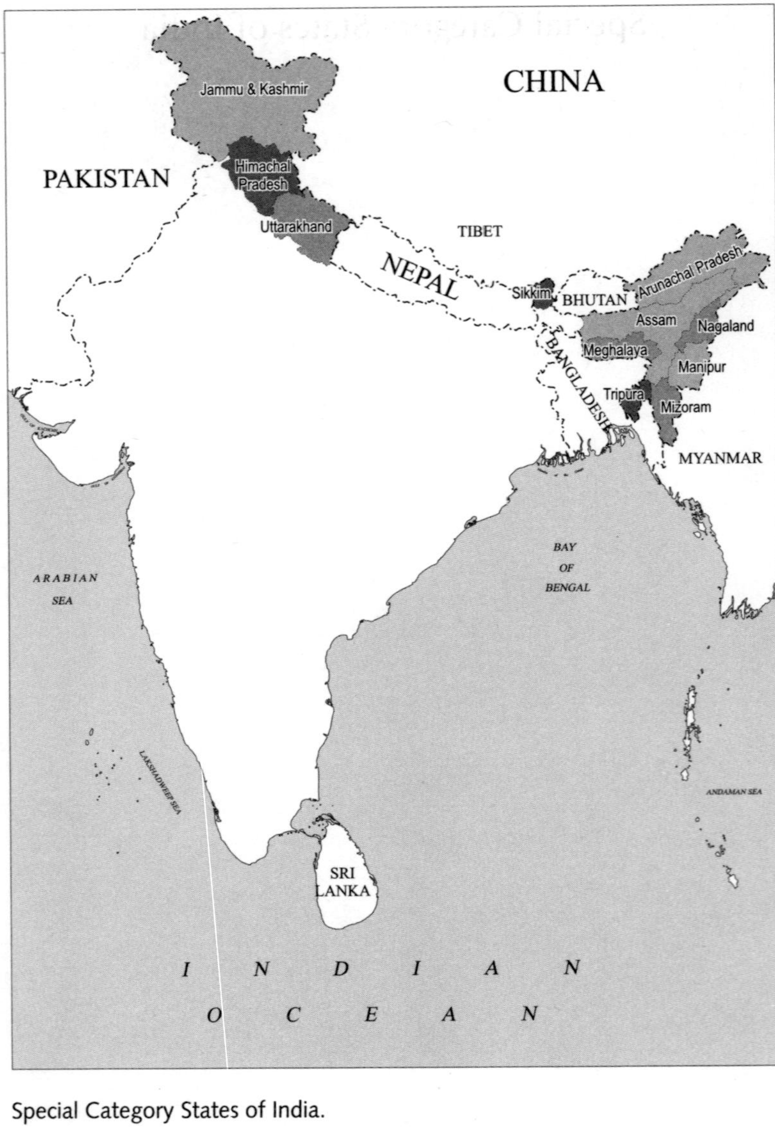

Special Category States of India.

Note: All maps in this book are courtesy of the author. These maps do not claim to represent the authentic domestic or international boundaries of India. These maps are not to scale and are provided for illustrative purposes only.

Special Category States of India

GOVIND BHATTACHARJEE

OXFORD
UNIVERSITY PRESS

OXFORD
UNIVERSITY PRESS

Oxford University Press is a department of the University of Oxford. It furthers the University's objective of excellence in research, scholarship, and education by publishing worldwide. Oxford is a registered trademark of Oxford University Press in the UK and in certain other countries.

Published in India by
Oxford University Press
YMCA Library Building, 1 Jai Singh Road, New Delhi 110 001, India

First Edition published in 2016

ISBN-13: 978-0-19-946083-0
ISBN-10: 0-19-946083-3

Typeset in ITC Giovanni Std 9.5/13
by The Graphics Solution, New Delhi 110 092
Printed in India by Rakmo Press, New Delhi 110 020

To all those who fought for the rights
of the marginalized and the dispossessed

Contents

Tables, Maps, and Boxes

Tables

Maps

Boxes

Preface

Eleven economically backward hill states of India sharing international boundaries comprise the group of 'Special Category States'. They lie at the periphery of the consciousness of mainstream India, to which they are no more than a striking demonstration of the exotic elements of a composite Indian culture. These states suffer from many drawbacks that arise from their remoteness and geographical isolation, historical circumstances, and demographic peculiarities. The state of their infrastructure was pathetic, resources scanty, and human potential unrealized; factors that could propel economic growth were all equally stymied. Economic backwardness seemed their only inheritance from the past, which was otherwise rich and colourful. They represent the asymmetrical elements of our federation, marginalized minorities in a majoritarian nation.

The centre sought to address this asymmetry, partly through constitutional provisions and partly through the mechanism of endowing them the 'special category status', which was designed to solve the problems of their economic backwardness only by providing them liberal access to central funds. This was rather an unimaginative solution that relied solely upon the use of funds, ignoring the inherent structural weaknesses and capacity constraints of these states, without any emphasis on the creation of necessary institutional architecture; neither did it envisage any structure for monitoring and accountability. In the absence of all this, any flow of funds is liable to become a drain of resources, perpetuating lethargy, inefficiency, and corruption, which it did. Like many of our national policies regarding backward areas, this too was an ad-hoc solution, applied without insight into the nature of the problems and that too without the involvement of stakeholders—the people of these states. This approach had many other weaknesses as well, as discussed in this book.

It is not that the mechanism had failed to deliver altogether. While some of the special category states gradually developed the necessary capacity over time and could use the central resources to their advantage, others could not do so for various reasons. In some states, militant insurgency and political instability obstructed the implementation of development schemes, which further stoked the fire of insurgency, while endemic corruption and lack of good governance coupled with the absence of visionary leadership rendered the state machinery dysfunctional and irrelevant in others. The unabated flow of central funds, unlinked to any performance expectations, produced an overwhelming dependence on the centre and led to complacence, an attitude that culminated in just seeking more and more funds from centre as a magic solution to any problem faced by these states, to the exclusion of looking for other alternatives. Still some states did manage to come out of such debilitating dependency and improve the living standards of their people in very significant measures.

Till now, there has not been any objective assessment of the impact of central assistance for the special category states; in fact, academic literature on special category states itself is scarce. There is little awareness or clarity about why they have been created, what the expectations were at the time of creating them, and whether they will permanently remain as special category states for all times to come. Now that fresh demands are being raised by some other states for this status, these questions are assuming increasing importance.

The primary objective of the book is to explore the reality of the special category states, to go into the roots of their backwardness, to examine their distinct ethnic, cultural, and historical identities within the framework of asymmetric federalism in India, and finally, to assess the impact of continued central financial assistance upon their socio-economic development over time. In the process, a whole range of issues covering their history and geography, their creation and evolution as separate states, problems of their political economy and their public financial management systems, and planning had to be extensively researched and examined on the basis of analysable statistics.

Specifically, the book deals with the circumstances under which the special category status was accorded to these states and undertakes a close scrutiny of their economy and public finances. Examination of the process of devolution of central resources to these states exposed the larger weaknesses and aberrations in the system of fiscal and financial relations between the centre and states in general. In particular, the role played by the Planning Commission, which determined how and when special category status was to be accorded, also came under critical scrutiny. Finally, an attempt has been made to assess and rank the performance of individual states within this category and compare them not only with each other but also to the pan-Indian situation to see where they stand in relation to the rest of the country.

The mechanism of special category status has been in place for a long time, since 1969, with little change in its configurations. No society is ever static, and no political or socio-economic institution or mechanism can remain permanently in place without losing vitality. Renewal is an essential prerequisite for progress and growth. It is perhaps time to review the entire arrangement of special category status, correct the distortions that have crept in over the course of time, replace the existing institutional devices that have become obsolete, and install an edifice of strong accountability. The dynamic forces of society are unravelling the past at an ever-accelerating rate, making people and especially the youth impatient for change, and unless these expectations can be reasonably met, the resulting turbulence may be highly unsettling. This is a challenge for Indian federalism as a whole. This book is a humble attempt towards taking a relook at these issues in trying to redefine the developmental pathways for the special category states.

Four years of research that went into this book has taken me to the past of these states while trying to understand their present. It has not only been an interesting journey, but also immensely enriching and no less a humbling experience in making me realize the extent of my ignorance about much of my own country.

Govind Bhattacharjee
New Delhi
March 15, 2015

Acknowledgements

I am deeply grateful to Dr N. K. Chaudhary, Professor, Department of Economics, Patna University, and Dr Shaibal Gupta and Dr P. P. Ghosh of the Asian Development Research Institute, Patna, for inspiring me to undertake this study. Without their constant encouragement, this book would perhaps never have been written.

This work would not have been completed without the support and help provided by the North Eastern Council, Shillong. I am grateful to them for providing me a workspace with unrestricted access to their enormously rich library—a library that contains almost all published works on the north-eastern states and many more. I thank Dr Shantanu Mitra, Dr Shyamananda Bhattacharjee, and Shri Mohitosh Chakravarty for all the help extended to me. I also thank my brother, Shri J. P. Bhattacharjee, Deputy Director General of the National Sample Survey Organisation, for providing the national accounts statistics pertaining to the pre-1970 period that was essential for this study. My wife, Dr Rakhee Bhattacharjee, Associate Professor at Jawaharlal Nehru University (JNU) and an authority on the northeastern states, provided me valuable suggestions and ideas throughout.

I would like to record my immense appreciation for colleagues in the Indian Audit and Accounts Department, especially those who were posted in the special category states, for providing finance accounts and planning-related data, besides supplying me with additional materials that they thought would be useful for the work, as indeed those were. To name all of them would take pages, but I must record my gratitude to Principal Accountants General Dr S. C. Pandey of Jammu & Kashmir, Shri L. Tochhawng of Mizoram, Shri L. A. C. Singh of Sikkim and

Shrimati Mahua Pal of Uttarakhand; Accountants General Shri C. H. Kharshiing of Assam, Shri A. P. Chophy of Meghalaya, Shri S. A. Bathew of Arunachal Pradesh, Shri V. K. Girijavallaban and Shri R. Naresh of Nagaland, Shri L. Hangsing of Manipur, Shri K. Srinivasan of Tripura, and Shri Manish Kumar of Jammu & Kashmir; Shri S. Garg, Senior Deputy Accountant General in Tripura and Deputy Accountants General Shrimati Nirmalamati Maisnam in Manipur and Shri G. S. Chawla in Himachal Pradesh. Without the data supplied by them from their old archives dating back to four decades, this work would never have seen the light of the day.

I am grateful to my senior colleague Shri Niranjan Pant, former Deputy Comptroller & Auditor General, for being a continuous source of inspiration and support. I am especially grateful to Dr Nagesh Singh, the then Advisor to the Planning Commission for facilitating my understanding of the process relating to the creation of special category states, without which I could not have developed the perspective necessary for this work. I am grateful to Dr Balveer Arora, retired professor of JNU, for going through the entire manuscript and offering his insightful guidance.

Last but not the least, I am grateful to the editors at Oxford University Press for their patience to see the work through; their efforts led to vast improvements in the book. To them and many others I have not named, I am deeply indebted and shall always remain so.

Abbreviations

AASU	All Assam Students' Union
ACA	Additional Central Assistance
AC	Autonomous Community
ADC	Autonomous District Council
AFSPA	Armed Forces (Special Powers) Act
AL&RR	Assam Land and Revenue Regulations
ARC	Administrative Reforms Commission
ATPLO	All Tripura People's Liberation Organization
ATTF	All Tripura Tiger Force
BN	Barisan Nasional
BNCT	Borok National Council of Tripura
BRGF	Backward Region Grant Fund
BSP	Bahujan Samaj Party
CHT	Chittagong Hill Tracts
CSS	Centrally Sponsored Schemes
EITU	Eastern India Tribal Union
EOU	Export Oriented Units
FC	Finance Commission
FGN	Federal Government of Nagaland
FRBMA	Fiscal Responsibility and Budget Management Act
GBS	Gross Budgetary Support
GFD	Gross Fiscal Deficit
GFR	General Financial Rules
GSDP	Gross State Domestic Product
HRPM	Himachal Riyasti Praja Mandal
ICT	Information and Communications Technology

IGC	Industrial Growth Centre
IIDC	Integrated Infrastructural Development Centre
KCP	Kangleipak Communist Party
KSU	Khasi Students' Union
LEP	Look East Policy
LCS	Land Custom Station
MDONER	Ministry of Development of North Eastern Region
MLA	Member of Legislative Assembly
MNF	Mizo National Front
MNREGP	Mahatma Gandhi National Rural Employment Guarantee Program
MNFF	Mizo National Famine Front
MP	Member of Parliament
MPF	Modernization of Police Force
MSC	Meitei State Committee
MU	Mizo Union
NCA	Normal Central Assistance
NCAER	National Council of Applied Economic Research
NCDBA	National Committee on the Development of Backward Areas
NDC	National Development Council
NDFB	National Democratic Front of Bodoland
NEC	North Eastern Council
NEFA	North East Frontier Agency
NER	North Eastern Region
NFG	Naga Federal Government
NHTA	Naga Hills Tuensang Area
NLCPR	Non-lapsable Central Pool of Resources
NLFT	National Liberation Front of Tripura
NNC	Naga National Council
NPC	Naga People Convention
NSCN	Nationalist Socialist Council of Nagalim
ONGC	Oil and Natural Gas Corporation
PEPSU	Patiala and East Punjab States Union
PLA	People's Liberation Army
PRI	Panchayat Raj Institutions
PREPAK	People's Revolutionary Party of Kangleipak
PULF	People's United Liberation Front

SAFTA	South Asian Free Trade Area
SATP	South Asia Terrorism Portal
SITCO	Sikkim Time Corporation
SPA	Special Plan Assistance
SP	Samajwadi Party
SSU	Small Scale Units
TNLF	Tripura National Liberation Front
TNV	Tripura National Volunteers
TTAADC	Tripura Tribal Areas Autonomous District Council
TUJS	Tripura Upajati Juba Samity
TwFC	Twelfth Finance Commission
UCM	United Committee of Manipur
UKD	Uttarakhand Kranti Dal
ULFA	United Liberation Front of Assam
UMFO	United Mizo Freedom Organization
UMNO	United Malays National Organization
UNLF	United National Liberation Front
UT	Union Territory
VAT	Value Added Tax

Introduction to the Special Category States

Eleven of the twenty-nine states of India comprise what is collectively called the 'Special Category States'. These states are: Arunachal Pradesh, Assam, Himachal Pradesh, Jammu & Kashmir, Manipur, Meghalaya, Mizoram, Nagaland, Sikkim, Tripura, and Uttarakhand. Eight of these states constitute the northeastern part of India; the three that lie outside that region are Jammu & Kashmir, Himachal Pradesh, and Uttarakhand. By and large, these impoverished and mostly resource-starved states lay at the periphery of India's economic development. They were created at different points of time in the history of independent India[1] to accommodate the socio-economic as well as the ethno-cultural aspirations of their respective peoples who were handicapped in various ways. These handicaps did not simply arise from the remoteness of their locations or the inaccessibility of their hilly terrains with sparsely populated habitation, nor due to their historical circumstances alone. They were also constrained by the shortage of capital and natural resources within their boundaries and lack of any viable physical and social infrastructure for economic growth and development. High cost of production with low availability of resources and hence low economic base, coupled with high transport costs led to high delivery cost of public services within these states. Centuries of economic deprivation and neglect combined with isolation from the mainstream of Indian states had resulted in widespread poverty, unemployment, and economic backwardness of the people living within their territories. They have in fact been victims of the combined burden of history, geography, economics, and governance. Even the resources that Nature has endowed them with could not be harnessed and utilized for their development due to the pathetic state of their infrastructure and their continued neglect over decades.

Advent of Information and Communications Technology (ICT) that was transforming life and living in other parts of India could make little inroads within these states. As pointed out by Ahluwalia (2000a: 1637–48), inter-state disparities in growth rates of Gross State Domestic Product (GSDP) had in fact increased after the reforms of 1991 across the states in India. The reforms had of course given a much needed push to accelerate the growth of the country and propel its economy into a high growth economy, but as shown by various authors, the process of economic reform had not promoted balanced regional development (Ahluwalia 2000b), but had mostly benefited the already prosperous or well governed states rather than the laggards. The reform-orientated states had generally performed better than the other states since the process started in 1991 (Bajpai & Sachs 1999). The poorer states have always been ill-equipped to profit from the reforms because of various impediments like their 'less attractive social, economic, and probably, political conditions' (Baddeley, McNay, & Cassen 2006). Kurian (2000: 538–50) noticed widening regional disparities among the states in general and between the forward and the backward states in particular. The forward states, by virtue of their higher income, better physical and social infrastructure, higher per capita transfers and private investments, were much better placed to take advantage of the globalization and liberalization processes and move ahead. As a result, richer states became even richer, while poorer states could not make much headway. All these indicate that whenever the disparity level increases across the states, the special category states can be expected to be the worst sufferers in terms of economic growth and development. Sachs, Bajpai, and Ramiah (2002) also found that there was marked divergence in the growth and income levels among the Indian states during the period 1980–98, as well as during both the pre-reform and post-reform subperiods. This divergence was most noticeable within the poorer group of states.

Economic neglect and lack of development create inequality and disparity; these in their extremes stages often lead to violence and militancy. Predictably, the development-disparity paradigm had stoked the sinister fire of insurgency in many of these states, leading to decades of political unrest followed by mindless violence and bloodshed that were tearing apart their social fabric, driving them to the fringes of existence and further impeding their growth and development. A few states like Himachal Pradesh, Sikkim, and Uttarakhand were spared this sinister cycle of violence and disruption where visible economic progress and other mitigating factors did not allow militancy and terror to raise their ugly heads. But, as Bhattacharjee (2014a) pointed out, most of the other special category states, at some point during their history, had to struggle against militancy and violence that had stubbornly kept their development at bay; some, like Tripura and Mizoram, were able to resolve these problems and marched ahead, while others still continue to struggle against an enemy that is largely invisible. They are actually paying for the neglect, deprivation, and exploitation of the past. Jammu & Kashmir is of course another story, perhaps more complex than the other states due to reasons associated with the history of its accession to India and due to the international dimensions involved.

Special Category Status

The Special Category Status is granted to a state by the National Development Council (NDC) on the recommendation of the Planning Commission. The Planning Commission had laid down the criteria according to which the special category status is granted to states characterized by certain common features that demand special considerations. A Planning Commission note[2] details these criteria: 'These features include: (1) hilly and difficult terrain, (2) low population density and/or sizeable share of tribal population, (3) strategic location along borders with neighbouring countries, (4) economic and infrastructural backwardness, and (5) non-viable nature of state finances. States under this category have a low resource base and are not in a position to mobilize resources for their developmental needs' irrespective of their per capita income. Many of these states were previously administered as small Union Territories (like Manipur, Mizoram, Tripura, Arunachal Pradesh, and Himachal Pradesh which was earlier a part of erstwhile Punjab) or constituted from one or more districts of erstwhile states (like Nagaland and Meghalaya carved out of Assam and

Uttarakhand carved out of Uttar Pradesh); thus 'necessarily involving creation of overheads and administrative infrastructure that was out of proportion to their resource base'. The note further adds that 'The decision in this regard is taken by the NDC which is the sole body competent to do so. This decision is based on the integrated consideration of all the factors listed above and the peculiar situation of the State and cannot be reduced into a mechanically applied formula.' It may be mentioned that the special category status does not find any mention in the Indian Constitution. Like the Planning Commission and the subsequent invention of non-lapsable pool of resources for the states in the northeast, this is an extra-constitutional arrangement.

These 'Special Category States' are special primarily as far as their plan assistance from the Government of India is concerned. The Constitution of India provides for uniform rule in all the states, while making special provisions for the protection of distinct cultural identities, traditions, and customs of certain ethnic groups and for accommodating the economic interests and political aspirations of the indigenous peoples. Special category states naturally come under these provisions. Most of these states are inhabited by tribal people who have their own distinct social institutions, economic relations, languages, traditions, and customs. Though the Constitution of India does not provide for the creation or categorization of any state as a 'Special Category State', yet, recognizing that certain regions in the country were historically more disadvantaged than the others in terms of socio-economic development and therefore were in need of additional assistance the 'Special Category' status was bestowed upon three states—Assam, Jammu & Kashmir, and Nagaland—for the first time in 1969, after the Fifth Finance Commission had recommended a liberal dose of central assistance for them under the five year plans.[3]

Before discussing the issues related to the special category states, it would be useful to describe the structure of federal financial relations in the country including institutional mechanisms for transfer of resources from the centre to the states.

State Finances

The Seventh Schedule to the Indian Constitution outlines the distribution of legislative powers between the centre and the states through the three lists: Union List, State List, and Concurrent List. To discharge their socio-economic responsibilities, the state governments require adequate resources which can come from both tax and non-tax revenues. Resources of the state governments come from three major sources: (1) revenues the state raises through taxes, (2) revenues it collects from non-tax sources, and (3) resources that are transferred to the state from the centre. The Union List enumerates the taxes to be raised by the centre, like the income tax and wealth tax, union excise duty, customs duty, service tax, etc. The State List in the same schedule includes subjects on which the state government can impose and collect taxes, these taxes include taxes on sales within the state or VAT, state excise, stamp and registration fees, taxes on motor vehicles, taxes on goods and railway passengers terminating within a state, entertainment tax, electricity duty, etc. The Concurrent List that contains subjects of concurrent jurisdiction under both the Union and the States does not have any taxing entry.

As per Article 266 of the Constitution, all revenues received by the state government, all loans raised by it, and all money received by it as recovery of loans are credited to the Consolidated Fund which is to be maintained for the purpose by every union and state government. No money can be spent from this fund except with the approval of the legislature, obtained through the mechanism of annual budget. Other than this, there are two separate funds managed by the state government. The first is the Contingency Fund which is in the nature of an impress with a fixed corpus that can be created by the legislature under Article 267 of the Constitution to meet unforeseen expenditure, pending their subsequent authorization by the legislature and recoupment of the amount spent from the Consolidated Fund. All other money received by or on behalf of the government is credited to the Public Account, constituted under Article 266(2) of the Constitution. The Public Account contains funds that the government holds in trust on behalf of the public—like small savings and provident fund, civil deposits, reserve funds, etc. from which governments can borrow. No legislative authorization is required to withdraw any money from the Public Account, the balances of which stand merged with the cash balance of the government.

Under Article 275 of the Constitution, every state is entitled to a share of all central taxes in the Union List which are pooled together to form what is known as the divisible pool of central taxes. These are shared between the centre and the states as per recommendation of the Finance Commission constituted once in five years under Article 280 of the Constitution. Article 275 thus provides a mechanism, in fact, the only mechanism for automatic devolution of resources of the centre to the states. The Finance Commissions also determine the inter-se share of each individual state depending on a number of factors with the objective of removing inter-regional disparities and promoting better fiscal management. Currently, under recommendations of the Thirtenth Finance Commission, 32 per cent all sharable Central taxes are transferred to the states and the shares of individual states are determined by a formula that gives appropriate weightage to the population and area of each state, differences in fiscal capacities between states, and the discipline exercised by them in managing their finances.

The state's non-tax revenues include interest receipts from loans and advances made to various government companies, public sector undertakings and other bodies, dividends and profits from them, and receipts from different services rendered by the state. These services are classified under three categories: (1) general services concerned with running the day-to-day administration of the state, like legislative, executive, and judiciary, police, fiscal services like collection of taxes and duties, subsidy, pension, etc.; (2) social services which include education, public health, sanitation, welfare of the backward classes, etc.; and (3) economic services like agriculture and animal husbandry, fisheries, plantations and forestry, irrigation, power, industries and minerals, transport, communication and tourism services, etc. Expenditure on social and economic services is classified as developmental expenditure while expenditure on general services is known as non-developmental expenditure since it does not contribute directly towards development, though it enables the creation of conditions without which no development can take place.

Apart from the revenue receipts from tax and non-tax sources, states also receive money by way of grants from the centre. The grants from the centre are given for both plan and non-plan purposes, among the plan grants there are separate grants for state's own plan schemes, central plan schemes, and centrally sponsored schemes. The non-plan grants are covered by recommendations of the Finance Commissions under Article 275 and include the statutory grants to finance the non-plan revenue deficit of the states as well as for various other public purposes. Plan transfers do not have any such statutory authority and are often discretionary in nature. These are made under Article 282 of the Constitution which enables grants to be given for any public purpose. The other source of funds for the state is of course borrowing; states borrow from the public by floating bonds that carry fixed interest rates, they also borrow from financial institutions. These constitute the internal debt of the states. Besides, they also borrow from the centre, though of late such borrowings have much been reduced. Such borrowings constitute the state's external debt. These borrowings are made on the security of the Consolidated Fund of the state, which is the repository of all resources—taxes, non-tax receipts, and public debt—of the state government.

The resources raised by the state are applied to meet government expenditure. The government incurs expenditure to run the administration of the state, i.e., on general services, and for the development of the state through various social and economic services. It also has to pay interest on its outstanding debt, besides repaying instalments pertaining to the principal amounts of outstanding debt. Government accounts are classified into two accounts—revenue and capital. While receipts into the revenue account include all tax and non-tax revenues and grants, expenditure from the accounts is made to maintain the assets already created by the state. But if the government wants to create a new asset, it needs capital for that purpose which is generally raised through borrowings. Hence, receipt into the capital account mainly comes from borrowings, while expenditure from the capital account is made for the capital outlay to create capital assets and also to repay the principal amounts of the past debt. Interest is paid from the revenue account.

Deficits are important indicators of the government's finances; they represent excess of expenditure over receipts in any account. Thus, we have the revenue and capital deficits in the respective accounts. The total resource gap in the finances of a state government is measured by the gross fiscal deficit (GFD) which is composed of the revenue deficit, capital outlay, and the lending made by the government net of recoveries of past loans given by it. GFD is financed by the net borrowings made by the state in its Consolidated Fund plus the net borrowings from its Public Account balances as well as by drawing down the cash balance available with the RBI, if needed. The Fiscal Responsibility and Budget Management Legislations (FRBML) enacted by every state (and also by the centre) limit the borrowings to a percentage (generally 3 per cent) of the total state income, known as the Gross State Domestic Product or GSDP, which is the state equivalent of GDP (Gross Domestic Product) of the country.

Transfer of Resources from the Centre to the States: Finance Commission and Planning Commission Conundrum

To integrate the economic and social fabric of the country as a whole, it is essential to reduce disparities that exist between different regions and within regions, among the different states in the country. Drivers of growth differ from state to state, though certain key drivers—like fiscal policy, credit availability, and therefore the existence of financial markets, capital investments on physical infrastructure that implies a reasonable savings rate, investments in social infrastructure, etc.—can possibly be identified and fitted into a consistent framework of development. Both the constitutional mechanism of the Finance Commission and extra-constitutional mechanism of the Planning Commission, which was created by a resolution of the Government of India in March 1950, sought to address the problem of striking an equitable balance between the socio-economic growth of individual states and the disparity that exists between them. The Finance Commission strove to achieve this by transferring resources from the richer to the poorer states through the agency of the Central Government, while the Planning Commission addressed this problem by allocating central resources through its five year plans to meet the growth needs of the individual states—by ensuring higher per capita allocation to the poorer states. During the 1950s and 1960s, about two thirds of the central resources was thus used to be transferred to the states through the Planning Commission, but gradually its share in resource transfer got reduced (Vaidya 2005).

The Finance Commission recommendations cover both the vertical transfer from the centre to the states as well as horizontal transfers among the states, from the richer to the poorer states; hence these are equalization transfers. Rangarajan and Srivastava (2011: 134–7) pointed out that in the vertical transfer of resources from the centre to the states, there has been a long term stability. While the relevant shares and ratios have undergone changes, the relative shares of the centre and the states have more or less remained stable, especially since the Seventh Finance Commission (1979–84). They further pointed out that prior to the transfers, the centre collected about 63–64 per cent of the combined revenue receipts, while after transfers states get about 64 per cent of the combined revenue receipts. The states spend nearly 57 per cent of the combined revenue expenditure of the centre and the states, while centre spends only 43 per cent of the combined revenue expenditure by retaining only 36 per cent of the revenues, and is hence forced to borrow relatively more.

Finance Commissions, constituted once in every five years under Article 280 of the Constitution of India, recommend transfer of central resources to the states by two mechanisms: transfer through devolution of taxes and transfer through grants, keeping in mind the redistributive considerations as well as fiscal needs of the states, while giving adequate importance to the consideration for incentives to be given to the states that perform better in terms of fiscal and financial management. The transfers are determined by three guiding principles of ensuring equalization, equity, and efficiency. The mechanism for automatic devolution of high-yielding union taxes to the states has been provided in the Constitution itself in the taxing powers of the union and the states as defined in Articles 270 and 272,[4] while grants are to be given to the states under Article 275. While the devolution of taxes is made to reduce both the vertical imbalance between the centre and the states in terms of availability of resources for development as well as the horizontal imbalance between the rich and the poor states, the central grants-in-aid to the states are recommended for bridging their non-plan revenue deficits, for local bodies and Panchayati Raj institutions, for disaster relief, management of environment and sustainable development, for upgradation of standards of services and outcomes, for special purposes like health, education, etc. as well as for state-specific purposes. These are all non-plan transfers, while the transfers made at the behest of the Planning Commission are referred to as plan transfers. The Constitution does not distinguish between plan and non-plan expenditure, it only provides for yearly transfers to the states in aid of their revenues from the Consolidated Fund of India in Article 275 and recognizes the need for different states requiring different amounts in respect of such transfers. Plan transfers do not have any such statutory authority and are often discretionary in nature. These are made under Article 282 of the Constitution which only enables grants to be given for any public purpose by the union or the states, even if that purpose may not be within their legislative jurisdictions.

It has remained a matter of debate whether the plan grants are covered under Article 275 mentioned earlier or under Article 282.[5] As pointed out by Paranjape (1988: 1953–54), Article 282 derived from Section 150 of the Government of India Act 1935 that was mainly used to enable the special central assistance to Bengal in the wake of the famine of 1943; later ad-hoc grants were also made under this section to provide for special contingencies and to meet unforeseen expenditure needs. This is further supported by the fact that while Article 275 is included under part XII of the constitution under the sub-title 'Distribution of Revenues between the Union and the States' indicating the regular nature of such distribution, Article 282 is included under the sub-title 'Miscellaneous Financial Provisions', indicating the non-regular nature of transfers under this provision. Legally, therefore, a plan transfer that includes transfer of revenue from the union on a regular basis should be covered under Article 275 in keeping with the spirit of the constitution, and not under Article 282 which gives unfettered discretion to the centre. Legal and constitutional experts have opined from time to time that it was not intended by the Constitution to be a channel for regular transfers and hence was illegal (Vithal and Sastry 2001: 229–30). But generally the accepted practice has been that the Finance Commissions would look into the non-plan side of the revenue expenditure and make recommendations for grants to bridge the non-plan revenue deficits of the states. Plan grants, revenue as well as capital, was recommended by the Planning Commission; while plan revenue expenditure pertained to the revenue component of the different plan projects under execution, capital expenditure was overwhelmingly plan expenditure. The Central Government has also largely limited the role of the Finance Commissions to the examination of only the non-plan part of the revenue expenditure.

Distinction of expenditure into plan and non-plan components has again been a subject of debate during the last few decades, and to resolve it the Planning Commission had appointed a 'High Level Expert Committee on Efficient Management of Public Expenditure, headed by

Dr. C Rangarajan which has since submitted its report in July 2011[6] in which they had recommended removal of this distinction between plan and non-plan expenditure, leaving the Planning Commission only with the task of formulating the five year plans. The government is yet to accept this report.

It must be pointed out that states were more dependent on non-statutory transfers of a discretionary nature made by the Planning Commission than on the statutory resource transfers made by the Finance Commission, as non-statutory transfers earlier used to constitute the bulk of total transfers to the states. George and Gulati (1985), in their study for the period from 1956–84, had pointed out that the states' dependence on the centre had increased over time as a major part of the total devolution of fiscal resources was dependent on the centre's discretion; further, the nature of such dependence was also undergoing a change which was not keeping with the spirit of constitutional devolution. About 60 per cent of the gross transfers to the states were affected by the Planning Commission during 1951–84, and the increase in the discretionary component was leading to increasing inequality in such transfers. As shown by Khemani (2003) in his studies of inter-governmental transfers during 1972–95, allocation of resources by the Planning Commission was often influenced by political rather than rational economic considerations, with the result that the states ruled by the same political party that ruled at the centre was often favoured with higher allocations. In the statutory transfers by Finance commissions, however, no such discriminations were noticed. Unlike the statutory transfers by Finance Commissions, Planning Commission transfers, being discretionary in nature, were more vulnerable to political considerations. Singh and Vashishta (2004) also echoed similar observations in their study of inter-governmental transfers during 1983–93, where they noticed states with more political relevance to the ruling dispensations at the centre wielding greater bargaining powers with the central government. Paranjape (1988: 1957) rightly argued that the role of the Planning Commission as the most important extra-constitutional allocator of resources was jeopardizing the centre–state relations in the matter of development planning and financing. Garg (2006: 4977) pointed out that central assistance for the state plans has been used as the principal instrument of control of states by the centre for influencing them and for interfering with their autonomy.

Central Plan Assistance and Gadgil Formula

It can thus be said that expenditure of the states (or the union) is classified as plan and non-plan expenditure; plan expenditure pertains to expenditure allocated by the Planning Commission to meet the requirements of the states' annual and five year plans which are supported by central assistance. Plan assistance given to states is discretionary in the sense that there is no obligation on the part of the centre to provide plan grants to any state. Plan expenditure of the centre may take any of the three forms: (1) plan grants for central sector schemes—these usually relate to subjects in the Union List. There are more than 40 central sector schemes; (2) plan grants for centrally sponsored schemes which are formulated by the centre for implementation by the states, for which a major part of the expenditure is borne by the centre, but the states also have to finance between 10 per cent and 35 per cent of the total expenditure. As of March 2014, there were 66 such schemes; and (3) plan grants for state plans which usually relate to subjects in the State List. States are entitled to get the following types of Central Assistance for their annual plans and five year plans[7]:

(a) Normal Central Assistance (NCA) for Central Plans and State Plans
(b) Additional Central Assistance (ACA) for implementation of externally assisted projects
(c) ACA for Centrally Sponsored Schemes like Mahatma Gandhi National Rural Employment Guarantee Programme (MNREGP), Sarva Shiksha Aviyan (SSA), National Rural Health Mission (NRHM), Integrated Child Development Scheme (ICDS), Total Sanitation Campaign (TSC), Prime Minister's Gram Sadak Yojna (PMGSY), Indira Awas Yojna (IAY), Mid-Day Meal Scheme (MDM), National Rural Drinking Water Mission (NRDWM), etc., which are operated throughout India
(d) ACA for special programmes funded by the Ministry of Finance but implemented by other Departments/Ministries, like Jawaharlal Nehru National Urban Renewal Mission (JNNURM), Accelerated Irrigation Benefits Programme (AIBP), National e-Governance Plan, Backward Region Grants Fund (BRGF), MP Local Area Development Programme (MPLAD), etc

(e) Special Central Assistance (SCA) for special programmes operated in some states, e.g., Border Areas Development Programme
(f) Advance Central Assistance given in special, usually exceptional, situations

The NCA is given as per a formula which is known as Gadgil Formula since 1969, after Dr D R Gadgil, the then Deputy Chairman of the Planning Commission. Apparently the Gadgil formula was adopted to introduce into the discretionary nature of the plan assistance some semblance of rationality that effectively curbed the absolute discretion the centre enjoyed over such transfers. This formula has been revised from time to time and is now called the modified Gadgil Formula or the Gadgil/Mukherjee formula for determining the central assistance to a state (after Dr Gadgil and Shri Pranab Mukherjee, the then Deputy Chairman of the Planning Commission). Under this formula, adopted since 1991, the central plan assistance is given to states based on a combination of criteria having different weightage that varied from plan to plan. The successive stages of evolution of the formula with the different weightage allotted to its criteria are summarized in Table 1.1.

The latest criteria used in Table I.1 for plan assistance to non-special category states are explained as follows:

1. **Population Criterion: 60 per cent weightage** is given to 1971 population, adopted on the basis of a Statement of Policy issued in June 1977.
2. **Income criteria: 25 per cent weight** has been assigned to this. This has two components based on the way they are calculated:

(a) Deviation Method—Weight 20 per cent

States are categorized on the basis of per capita comparable State Domestic Product (average of per capita SDP for the latest three years) compared to the corresponding national average. 20 per cent of the assistance is allotted to the states whose per capita incomes are below the national average. The relative weight of a state is determined on the basis of distance of its per capita income from the state with the highest per capita income, multiplied by its 1971 population and divided by the total product for all states.

Table I.1 Criteria and Weightage under Original Gadgil Formula and its Revisions for Allocation of Central Assistance for States' Plans

Criteria (Weightage %)	Original Gadgil Formula (1969)	Modified Gadgil Formula (1980)	NDC Revised Formula (1990)	NDC Revised Formula (1991)
A. Special Category States	30% share of 3 States excluding North Eastern Council	30% share of 8 States excluding North Eastern Council	30% share of 10 States excluding North Eastern Council	30% share of 11 States excluding North Eastern Council
B. Non-Special Category States				
(i) Population (1971)	60.0	60.0	55.0	60.00
(ii) Ongoing major irrigation and power projects.	10.0	0.0	0.0	0.0
(iii) Per Capita Income of which:	10.0	20.0	25.0	25.0
(a) According to the deviation method covering only the states with per capita income below the national average	10.0	20.0	20.0	20.0
(b) According to the distance method covering all the states.	0.0	0.0	5.0	5.0
(iv) Performance of which:	10.0	10.0	5.0	7.5
(a) Tax effort	10.0	10.0	0.0	2.5
(b) Fiscal Management	0.0	0.0	5.0	2.0
(c) National Objectives	0.0	0.0	0.0	3.0
1. Population Control	0.0	0.0	0.0	1.0

2. Elimination of Female illiteracy	0.0	0.0	0.0	1.0
3. On-time Completion of Externally Aided Projects	0.0	0.0	0.0	0.5
4. Success in Land Reforms.	0.0	0.0	0.0	0.5
(v) Special Problems	10.0	10.0	15.0	7.5
TOTAL	**100.0**	**100.0**	**100.0**	**100.0**

Source: The criteria and their explanation have been quoted from a background note appended to Demi-Official letter No.4/9/96-FR/DCH/3670 dated 24 February 1997 forwarded by S hri Madhu Dandavate, the then Deputy Chairman, Planning Commission to Shri Prakash Singh Badal, the then Chief Minister of Punjab.

(b) Distance Method—Weight 5 per cent

In this, the comparable per capita State Domestic Product is used to measure the distance of per capita income of each state from the highest per capita income state. These values are multiplied by the population of each state and percentage share of each state is then calculated.

3. **7.5 per cent weightage** is given to **Performance of the State** assessed on the basis of:
   a. **Tax Effort** criterion, based on the Tax: SDP ratio of a state, calculated on the annual average tax receipts and comparable SDP of the state for the latest 3 consecutive years;
   b. **Fiscal Management** criterion, based on the difference between the target and actual resources mobilized by the state during the last five years (including net small savings and provident funds receipts in the Public Account, besides resources on the Consolidated Fund);
   c. **Population Control** criterion, based on the difference between desired and actual performance in relation to birth rate and infant mortality rate which are worked out for each state and the distance of each state from the lowest performing state is calculated. Since both the considerations are given equal weights, the average of the two shares for each state determines its share in the total distribution;
   d. **Elimination of Illiteracy,** for which the factors taken into consideration are female literacy rate and decennial growth rate of female literacy. For both factors, the share of each state for each factor is determined as proportion of each state's performance to the total of all states, and average of the two shares for each state determines its share in the total distribution;
   e. **On-Time Completion of Externally Aided Projects,** considering the utilization of external aid as a percentage of available finances for each state and then converting these ratios as percentages to the total to determine the shares of individual states; and
   f. **Land Reforms criterion** assigns equal weights to two indicators, viz., the area distributed as a percentage of surplus land declared by the state and the area distributed by a state as a percentage

of total area distributed by all states. Average of the two shares calculated for each state determines its share in the total distribution.

4. The balance 7.5 per cent weightage is allotted to **special problems of the states.**

Under this formula, during the 11th Plan, within the general category states, the individual state's shares in total NCA varied between 0.495 per cent for Goa to 19.481 per cent for UP; Bihar (11.062 per cent), West Bengal (8.814 per cent), MP (6.922 per cent) also received higher shares than the other states. Within the special category states, the share of individual states varied between 3.771 per cent for Sikkim to 19.532 per cent for Assam and 19.148 per cent for Jammu & Kashmir, followed by 9.656 per cent for Himachal Pradesh, 9.535 per cent for Uttarakhand, 8.243 per cent for Tripura, 7.928 per cent for Arunachal Pradesh, 5.908 per cent for Nagaland, 5.840 per cent for Manipur and 4.849 per cent for Meghalaya.[8]

Origin of the Gadgil Formula and Special Category Status

The origin of the formula can be traced back to 1965, when the need for a set of principles was emphasized by some chief ministers for the allocation of central assistance to states for the Fourth Five Year Plan. The minutes of the National Development Council (NDC) Meeting on December 1967 noted that though there was lack of unanimity among the chief ministers of various states about the criteria, yet 'there was a general feeling that States like Assam, Jammu & Kashmir and Nagaland would, in any way, have to receive special treatment.'[9] It may be mentioned here that even Article 275(1A) of the Constitution recognized the need for special treatment to Assam and made provisions for separate grants to be given to that state. The summary record of the NDC meeting further notes that in the light of the views expressed by the NDC, the Planning Commission evolved the following guidelines:

(i) Every State should receive first a quantum of 70 per cent of the total amount to be distributed in proportion to its population.

(ii) The balance should again be distributed but after taking into account (i) the special needs of Jammu & Kashmir, Assam and Nagaland to

> enable them to have a modest and reasonable Plan, and (ii) the special needs of some States which are required to contribute large amounts of expenditure on continuing schemes of irrigation and power of national importance, and (iii) the need for accelerated development of certain backward regions like hill areas, etc.
>
> After making tentative allocations of the Central assistance on the above principles, the allocations of the entire amount were finally determined after detailed discussions with the Chief Minister of each State. The overall Plan outlay for each State was thus finalised taking into account its own resources position, the third plan outlays and the necessity to provide adequately for programmes of national importance, e.g., agricultural production, continuing irrigation and power schemes, rural electrification, the need for accelerating development of certain specially backward regions like hill areas, etc.[10]

It is interesting to note that the resources of all the states taken together at that time were estimated to be only Rs 826 crore against the proposed outlay of Rs 2103 crore, thus leaving a gap of nearly Rs. 1280 crore to be financed by the centre during the Second Five Year Plan (1956–61), against which the actual normal central assistance given was Rs 1058 crore. Assam and Jammu & Kashmir claimed only Rs 51 crore out of this, i.e., 4.8 per cent of the total share. Nagaland did not exist then and would be created only in 1963. The share including that of Nagaland went up to 6.8 per cent of total central assistance during the third plan (1961–66). During 1968–69, at the time of creation of the special category states, however, these three states together claimed a share of 9 per cent of the total normal central plan assistance provided to all the states during that year. It was 19.3 per cent during the entire fourth plan period. The share of the special category states in total central assistance thus was doubled immediately after their creation; this share would gradually rise further to one third of the total normal central assistance for all states.

Till 1957, the Naga Hills was a district of Assam. In response to the demands of the Naga People's Convention, the chief political party in Nagaland, in December 1957, the Naga Hills district was brought under the union administration as Naga Hills Tuensang Area (NHTA) under the Ministry of External Affairs. Demand for its statehood gradually started getting stronger since then, and finally, by virtue of the sixteen-point agreement between the Naga People's Convention and the then Prime Minister of India in July 1960, the administration of Naga Hills was placed under an interim Regional Council under the Nagaland (Transitional Provision) Regulation 1961. This interim body was dissolved and Nagaland was formally declared as the sixteenth state of the Indian Union on December 1 1963 (Upadhyay: 2005a). In the 16 point agreement, it was mentioned that:

> To supplement the revenues of Nagaland, there will be a need for the Government of India to pay out of the Consolidated Fund of India grants in aid as follows:
>
> (1) Lump-sums as may be necessary each year for the development programme in Nagaland;
>
> (2) A fixed recurring sum (annual subvention) for meeting the cost of the administration of Nagaland.[11]

Thus plan transfer was not specifically mentioned in the agreement. But after formation of the state, it started receiving plan assistance along with Assam and Jammu & Kashmir. It was long recognized that such assistances were inadequate to address the problems of these states, and in response to such recognition, all three were accorded the special category status in 1969. Article 275(1A) of the Constitution also recognized the need for special assistance for these states.

In 1968, the Fifth Finance Commission was constituted by the Government of India to recommend the devolution of taxes and grants to the states for the period 1969–74. It submitted its report in 1969, where it noted huge disparities existing among the 17 Indian states. The richest state had a per capita income of Rs 619 and the poorest Rs 292 only; the largest had a population of 9 crore and the smallest only 4 lakh. It expressed concern that the need for equalization among the states demanded a more positive redistributive policy then simply dividing the grants on the basis of population—by taking the reality of the rich and poor states into account. In this context it correctly observed,

> Where the general level of economic development of the country is not high, the degree to which backward States can be assisted to come up to the average level of services is a matter for detailed assessment but there can be no doubt that Article 275 of the Constitution is designed to help the States which are less developed and have less capacity to raise resources of their own. How far such transfers can be made available to enable States with low per capita income to improve their level of services

and the stages by which that should be done are matters to be decided not merely on fiscal considerations but with due regard also to the promotion of a sense of national unity.

The transfer of funds recommended by the Finance Commission can only partially fulfil the objective of equalization in view of the division of functions which now exists between the Planning Commission and the Finance Commission whereby the former looks after developmental needs and gives plan grants for this purpose. As the language of Article 275 stands, there is nothing to exclude from its purview grants for meeting revenue expenditure on Plan schemes nor is there any explicit bar against grants for capital purposes.

We are not, however, able to agree with this view as it would blur the entire division of functions between this Commission and the Planning Commission.'[12]

Hence in considering the Finance Commission transfers, this Commission, for the first time, also considered the Planning Commission transfers to look at the totality of funds at the disposal of the states, and recommended much higher amounts of transfers in respect of Assam, Jammu & Kashmir and Nagaland:

we wish to indicate that we have, in assessing the revenue receipts and expenditure of the states and applying the principles and general conditions explained in the preceding paragraphs, particularly kept in view the special problems of the states of Assam, Jammu & Kashmir and Nagaland. We have tried to treat their needs and requirements, with as much care and consideration as possible. The grants which we are recommending for these States are of a much larger magnitude that would ordinarily be justified in case of other States of similar size or having similar resources. We hope that these three states also will, on their part, make efforts to increase their resources and exercise better fiscal management and proper economy consistent with efficiency and take steps to improve the returns on their investments so that their financial position may steadily improve and in course of time they may be enabled to have more adequate revenues to improve their social and administrative services.[13]

Of the total Finance Commission grants of Rs 637.85 for the entire period 1969–74, these three states claimed a share of 39.75 per cent of the total; Assam was allotted Rs 101.97 crore, Jammu & Kashmir Rs. 73.68 crore, and Nagaland Rs. 72.62 crore. Except Odisha, and to some extent West Bengal, no other state received as high a grant.[14] Thus, in respect of non-plan grants, these three states became rather 'special'.

Planning Commission would soon follow suit. The twenty-sixth meeting of the National Development Council held in April 1969 noted:

> ...since the report of the Fifth Finance Commission was still awaited a clear picture of Centre's own liabilities was not available, but notwithstanding this, the Central Government had agreed, on the recommendation of the Planning Commission, to keep their contribution to the State Plans at Rs. 3,500 crore.[15]

Minutes of the same meeting further noted that the

> Deputy Chairman *(Dr Gadgil)* referred to the principles for the distribution of central assistance to States which had been evolved at the meeting of the NDC Committee of State Chief Ministers held in September 1968. It was agreed that the requirements of the States of Assam, Jammu & Kashmir, and Nagaland be met through an ad hoc lump assignment out of the total central assistance and that the balance should be distributed as follows: 60 per cent on the basis of population, 10 per cent on the basis of per capita income only to the States below the national average, 10 per cent on the basis of tax effort in relation to per capita income, 10 per cent on account of continuing major irrigation and power schemes and the remaining 10 per cent on consideration of the special problems of the States.[16]

Thus, the needs of these three states: Assam, Jammu & Kashmir, and Nagaland—were given priority over the needs of other states by the Planning Commission as well. Hence, both in respect of plan as well as non-plan grants, these states received much higher amounts compared to the other Indian states and in that sense these states were treated as special. This, then, was the genesis of the Gadgil formula and of the special category status accorded to these three states in 1969.[17]

The Fifth Finance Commission's report did raise some criticism about the Central Government restricting the role of the Finance Commission into examining only part of the total expenditure, and also about the jurisdiction of Finance Commission vis-à-vis that of the Planning Commission. From the Fourth Finance Commission onwards, Finance Commissions were asked to restrict their recommendation regarding the grants-in-aid to states in respect of their non-plan requirements only. The Centre reacted to these concerns by initiating the practice of appointing a member of the Planning Commission, generally as a part time member, into the Finance Commission, from the Sixth Finance Commission onwards.

The Administrative Reforms Commission (ARC) appointed in 1966 constituted a 'Study Team for the Machinery of Planning' to address the concerns raised in various quarters about the centralizing tendencies seen in the planning process and the adoption of uniform pattern of priorities, as determined by the Planning Commission, by the states resulting from the manner in which central assistance was administered. The remedies it suggested were: (i) improving the planning capability in the states, and (ii) ensuring that central assistance was used only to provide direction to the states and not to influence states' planning priorities. In their final report submitted in 1968, the team recommended that states should receive untied block grants from the centre, which they should be free to use at their discretion, except in case of a few programmes of crucial importance. These suggestions were, however, not accepted (Paranjape 1988: 1953–55).

After 1967, non-Congress parties had come to power in quite a few states. These states stared asserting increasingly against the way plan assistance was being provided and also against the proliferation of Centrally Sponsored Schemes (CSS). As a result, some objectivity was introduced into the hugely discretionary transfers through the Gadgil formula and the number of CSS also came down. This began a process of decentralization of the planning process, which was reversed after the Congress secured power not only at the centre and also in a number of states after 1970–71. The centralizing tendency was again briefly halted during the short-lived Janata rule at the centre during 1977–80, but reasserted itself with ever greater force after 1980 (Paranjape 1988: 1953–55).

It is to be noted that before the Gadgil formula was applied, the states used to get more resources from the centre as loans and less as grants, plan and non-plan combined, leading to their increasing indebtedness of the states. This situation was substantially changed since the fourth plan onwards, after central assistance started getting distributed as per the Gadgil formula (Goswami 2007: 69–70).

When the Gadgil formula was applied for the first time in 1969, there were altogether 17 states, and only three among them were treated as special category states. During the Fifth Plan period, the total number of states had increased to 22, and all but the original 14 were treated as special category states. As and when new states were created, by carving them out of Assam or by giving statehood to erstwhile Union

Territories, all, except Goa, were created as special category states. The reasons were obvious; all these states were small states and had small populations. Therefore they will not enjoy the advantage a state with a large population would get from the higher weightage given to population in the Gadgil Formula. This practice of adding the newly created states to the list of special category states continued till 2001, when only one state, viz., Uttaranchal (now Uttarakhand) out of the three states created in 2000 was added to the list of special category states by a decision of the 49th meeting of the NDC on September 01 2001, 18 months after its creation; but the other two, viz., Jharkhand and Chhattisgarh, were treated only as general category states. The agenda note for meeting had detailed the case for Uttaranchal:[18]

> The predominantly hill districts account for about 90 per cent of the total area of the newly created state of Uttaranchal, while more than 2/3 of the population of the state resides in the hill areas. Almost 1/3 of the total area in Uttaranchal is either rocky/ snow covered/ glaciated, or otherwise unproductive degraded land. About 3 per cent of the population of the state is tribal.' It further adds that, 'Uttaranchal is a geo-politically sensitive area. While in the North the state has international borders with China, in the East the region is bound by Nepal. Uttaranchal is a difficult area in terms of geography, accessibility, and sustainable growth rates. The mountain environment is fragile although it is rich in bio-diversity. Unit expenditure of initially providing an average standard of services in such hill regions is higher, and unit cost of operation and maintenance is also very high. The Uttaranchal region is vulnerable to many types of disasters. Special arrangements would be necessary to improve administrative, organizational, and technical capabilities in the area of disaster preparedness and disaster management.

Examining the finances of the state, the agenda papers noted that the state had a non-plan revenue deficit of Rs 1738 crore in 2000–01 while its interest liability alone was Rs 450 crore. It did not have enough resources to meet the committed expenditure on accounts of salary, pension, and interest payments and would require heavy investments to make it financially viable in the long run, as the benefits of such investments would flow only after a sufficiently long time interval.[19]

Himachal Pradesh was a Union Territory that was accorded full statehood in 1971. Meghalaya was carved out from Assam and made a Special Category State in 1972. Two more Union Territories in the northeast—Manipur and Tripura— were made into full-fledged states and accorded Special Category status also in 1972. Sikkim became an Indian state and a Special Category state in 1975. Mizoram and Arunachal Pradesh which hitherto were union territories were accorded full statehood along with Special Category Status in 1987 and Uttarakhand was carved out of Uttar Pradesh in 2000, and was made the 11th Special Category state of India in 2001.

It is to be mentioned that even though the number of special category states increased from only three in 1969 to 11 in 2001, their kitty of 30 per cent of the central plan funds, after setting aside funds for externally aided projects and special area programmes in certain states, remained unchanged—there was no proportionate increase in resources set out for this category as new states were added on. As a result, the share of individual states within the category had declined. Even when a decision was taken in 1969 to include Assam among one of the three initial states belonging to this category, it was given the benefit of 90 per cent grants and 10 per cent loans available to special category states only from April, 1990. From time to time various states, including Bihar, Odisha, Rajasthan, Punjab, Chhattisgarh, and even Delhi has demanded to be included in this category, but with so many states sharing the same 30 per cent of plan funds, addition of more states would defeat the purpose of creation of this category altogether.

Aberration of Plan Transfers: Transfers Outside State Budgets

As we shall see, creating the institution of the Planning Commission without an appropriate accountability structure and vesting it with extra-constitutional powers of recommending plan transfers to states from the public exchequer—something without any parallel in the history of parliamentary democracy—has been a perpetual source of distortions in federal finances in India. The willingness of the Planning Commission which actually was a political body of the ruling dispensation to play to their political masters has also resulted in diluting the original intention behind according special category status to help states that are in need of special financial assistance.

The major contribution of the Gadgil formula has been to bring in discipline, transparency, and objectivity in the plan transfers by limiting the arbitrary discretion of the centre over these transfers. Of course the Centre would devise another way of exercising its discretion through the mechanism of the CSS we shall discuss later. As Vithal and Sastry (2001: 281) correctly observed:

> the Gadgil formula gave to the states the same amount of transparency and objectivity as the transfers through the Finance Commissions. This has, however, been seriously compromised severely by the intrusion of Centrally Sponsored Schemes. The system, therefore, has come under strain not so much due to two institutions being present but by the nature of the plan financing itself. Plan revenue deficits have outrun the balance from current revenues, resulting in overall revenue deficits. This is a virus that enters the system through Plans and persists later through committed expenditure, resulting in non-Plan revenue deficits......Subtracting a negative from a negative is not a zero-sum game.

As pointed out earlier, Article 282 has often been misused by the centre to make discretionary transfers which were against the spirit of the Constitution. The centre often used the plan transfers to control the recalcitrant states that were not willing to abide by its dictates. This was in itself a violation of the principles of fiscal federalism. The transfers under this Article often lacked transparency. The intrusion of an extra-constitutional authority like the Planning Commission into the working of Finance Commission in respect of transfer of resources from the centre to the states through the means 'discretionary transfers' as opposed to 'statutory transfers' violates the principles of federalism implicit in the financial relations between the union and the states as defined in the Constitution of India. The situation is made murkier by the implementation of numerous centrally sponsored schemes which include the flagship schemes of the Central Government on which astronomical sums are spent each year, often with questionable justifications. All these constitute a politically manoeuvred aberration in the Indian financial system and in fact, an assault on the fiscal federalism principles.

As if this was not enough, this aberration was further eroded by the direct fiscal transfers by the centre outside the states' budgets and accounts, bypassing the internal controls that are inherent in budget execution and accounting. They not only render the process illegal and unconstitutional, they dilute and undermine the authority of the states. These direct transfers under the CSS have been burgeoning since the last few decades and now constitute between one-half and two-thirds of the total central grants going to the states. The amount of such transfers during 2008–13, are shown in Table I.2, from which it can be seen that the total amount of Gadgil formula transfers form a miniscule part of the total central plan transfers to states, barely amounting to 10 per cent

Table I.2 Central Plan Assistance to States (Excludes UTs) Rs Crore

	2008–09 Actuals	2009–10 Actuals	2010–11 Actuals	2011–12 RE	2012–13 BE
Central Assistance for State Plans, of which	73,611	79,157	89,747	101,105	124,249
NCA as per Gadgil formula	**15948**	**17,442**	**20,008**	**21,831**	**25,589**
Additional Central Plan Assistance to States for Central and Centrally Sponsored Schemes passed through State Budgets	50,319	49,604	55,163	61,275	78,507
Special Plan Assistance including Special Central Assistance for Hill and Border Areas etc.	7,344	12,111	14,576	17,999	20,153
Direct Transfer of Central Plan Assistance to State/District Level Autonomous Bodies/ Implementing Agencies outside budget	83224	90,520	118,740	112,803	133,358
Percentage of Direct Transfers in Total Transfers	51.92	51.72	56.06	51.74	50.64
Percentage of Gadgil formula Transfers in Total Transfers	9.95	9.97	9.45	10.01	9.72

Source: Union Budget 2011–12 and 2012–13: Expenditure Budget, Vol I, Statements 16 to 18.

Note: RE – Revised Estimates; BE – Budget estimates

of the total transfers during the last five years. Direct transfers far exceed the central assistances for state plans; the transfers in respect of Central Plan and CSS that are routed through the state budgets constitute a small part, barely 30 per cent, of the total transfers under the plans. It makes a mockery of the principles of federalism in fiscal and financial relations between the union and the states. There also seems to be a pattern in systematically and deliberately increasing the extra-budgetary transfers at the cost of budgetary transfers. The transfers under Gadgil formula have suffered the most; their share in total transfers over the last three plans (ninth to eleventh) has gradually fallen from 35 per cent during Ninth Plan to only 10 per cent during Eleventh plan, while the share of direct transfers has increased from 20 per cent to 52 per cent over the same period (Table I.3). Gadgil transfers that limited the discretion of the centre was thus rendered ineffective. The plan funds routed through the state budgets have fallen from 80 per cent to only 48 per cent of the total transfers over the periods of these three plans, in another glaring example of undermining the autonomy of states. This naturally restricted the amounts of funds that could otherwise flow to the special category states (and other states as well) through normal central assistance.

As noted earlier (in the section titled '**Central Plan Assistance and Gadgil Formula**'), the Central plan assistance comes to the states through various forms: Normal Central Assistance (NCA), and various types of Additional Central Assistance (ACA). NCA received by the special as well as the non-special category states for their plans during various plan periods is shown in Table I.3. Before the Gadgil Formula was applied to determine the NCA, states which would later become the special category states used to receive less than 10 per cent of the total NCA for all the states; after the formula was applied, their share gradually increased over the successive plan periods to reach more than a third of the total NCA for all the states during the Eleventh Plan. Side by side their numbers also increased, but in respect of the NCA, Gadgil formula did make a difference to the special category states (Table I.4).

But to put the things in proper perspective, we need to consider not only the NCA, but the Total Central Assistance (TCA) which includes, besides assistance for the Externally Aided Projects (EAP) which forms a small part of the TCA, the assistance for CSS also. In Table I.5, the TCA received by the special and non-special category of states have been

Table I.3 Details of Central Plan Assistance to States and Union Territories[20] (Rs Crore)

	NCA–States	SCA	UT	ACA–States	Total Central Assistance to States and UTs (Through Budget)	Direct Transfer (Off Budget)	Direct Transfer/ Total Transfer (%)	Gadgil Transfer in total Transfer (%)	Transfer through State Budget/ Total Transfer (%)
1997–98	12888	1398	904	11811	27001	6998	20.58	37.91	79.42
1998–99	14120	1790	1067	13130	30107	7772	20.52	37.28	79.48
1999–2000	15417	2021	1208	17089	35735	8696	19.57	34.70	80.43
2000–01	15561	2019	1302	19087	37969	8827	18.86	33.25	81.14
2001–02	17120	2476	1285	17997	38878	9797	20.13	35.17	79.87
9th Plan Total	**75106**	**9704**	**5766**	**79114**	**169690**	**42090**	**19.87**	**35.46**	**80.13**
2002–03	18711	3237	1514	22408	45870	8849	16.17	34.19	83.83
2003–04	20000	3362	1335	23963	48660	9477	16.30	34.40	83.70
2004–05	23070	4401	1469	24448	54858	10998	16.70	35.03	83.30
2005–06	25675	4459	1927	24328	56389	14249	20.17	36.35	79.83
2006–07	14016	5658	2147	24399	46220	45166	49.42	15.34	50.58
10th Plan Total	**101472**	**21117**	**8392**	**119546**	**251997**	**88739**	**26.04**	**29.78**	**73.96**
2007–08	15358	4424	2938	36135	58855	54776	48.21	13.52	51.79
2008–09	15948	7344	3464	50319	77075	83224	51.92	9.95	48.08
2009–10	17442	12111	5333	49604	84490	90520	51.72	9.97	48.28
2010–11	20008	14576	3331	55163	93078	118740	56.06	9.45	43.94

2011–12 RE	21831	17999	4093	61275	105198	112803	51.74	10.01	48.26
11th Plan Total	**90587**	**56454**	**19159**	**252496**	**418696**	**460063**	**52.35**	**10.31**	**47.65**
2012–13 BE	25589	20153	5749	78507	129998	133358	50.64	9.72	49.36

Source: Union Budget 2011–12 and 2012–13: Expenditure Budget, Vol I, Statements 16 to 18. The data quoted in the table have been taken from the Budget documents and earlier these documents reported the RE figures only. Hence the data may be at variance with actual accounts figures reported elsewhere.

Table I.4 Normal Central Plan Assistance (Under Gadgil Formula) to States

	No of Special Category States[21]	Special Category States		Non-Special Category States	
		NCA (Rs Cr)	As Percentage of Total NCA	NCA (Rs Cr)	As Percentage of Total NCA
1st Plan (1951–56)	2	22	6.63	310	93.37
2nd Plan (1956–61)	2	50	4.73	1008	95.27
3rd Plan (1961–66)	3	172	6.84	2343	93.16
Annual Plans (1966–69)	3	161	8.97	1634	91.03
4th Plan (1969–74)	7	682	19.29	2853	80.71
5th Plan (1974–78)	8	846	16.95	4145	83.05
Annual Plan (1978–80)	8	866	16.61	4347	83.39
6th Plan (1980–85)	8	3547	19.44	14702	80.56
7th Plan (1985–90)	10	9625	24.85	29104	75.15
Annual Plans (1990–92)	10	5485	23.41	17944	76.59
8th Plan (1992–97)	10	21705	23.31	71419	76.69
9th Plan (1997–2002)	11	36738	48.29	39335	51.71
10th Plan (2002–07)	11	60453	42.37	82228	57.63
11th Plan (2007–12) (Figures till 2009–10)	11	64787	36.44	112998	63.56

Source: Data for 1st to 4th Plan have been taken from the Report of the Seventh Finance Commission and the Minutes of the Twenty-fifth meeting of the National Development Council, Annexure II, Planning Commission, Govt. of India, May 1968; for 4th–8th Plans, data have been taken from 'The Gadgil Formula', Vithal, B P R, and M L Sastry, Manohar, 2002. 9th, 10th and 11th Plan data have been compiled from the Combined Finance and Revenue Accounts of the Union and States by the Comptroller & Auditor General of India for the respective years.

Table I.5 Total Central Plan Assistance Received by States (Figures in bracket indicate percentage to total transfer of resources)

Plan Periods	Statutory Transfers (Revenue + Non-Plan Grants)	Plan Transfers (NCA and Other Central Assistance)	Discretionary Transfers (CSS)	Total Transfer of Resources from Centre
1st Plan	447	332	548	1,327
(1951–56)	(33.7)	(25.0)	(41.3)	
2nd Plan	918	1058	892	2,868
(1956–61)	(32.0)	(36.9)	(31.1)	
3rd Plan	1,590	2,515	1,495	5,600
(1961–66)	(28.4)	(44.9)	(26.7)	
Annual Plans	1,782	1,795	1798	5,375
(1966–69)	(33.2)	(33.4)	(33.5)	
4th Plan	5421	3,535	6,145	15,101
(1969–74)	(35.9)	(23.4)	(40.7)	
5th Plan	8,395	4,991	1,546	14,932
(1974–78)	(56.2)	(33.4)	(10.4)	
Annual Plan	6,142	5,213	1,390	12,745
(1978–80)	(48.2)	(40.9)	(10.9)	
6th Plan	24,998	18,249	7,498	48,504
(1980–85)	(49.3)	(36.0)	(14.8)	
7th Plan	54,388	38,729	15,579	108,841
(1985–90)	(50.1)	(35.6)	(14.3)	
Annual Plans	35437	23,429	10,248	71,672
(1990–92)	(51.3)	(33.9)	(14.8)	
8th Plan(1992–97)	162,777	93,124	38,089	293,990
	(55.4)	(31.7)	(13.0)	
9th Plan	265,647	185,259	99,001	549,907
(1997–2002)	(48.3)	(33.7)	(18.0)	
10th Plan	537,201	249,763	229,763	1,016,727
(2002–07)	(52.8)	(24.6)	(22.6)	
11th Plan[22]	12,13,544	425,617	660,506	2,299,667
(2007–12)	(52.8)	(18.5)	(28.7)	

(Cont'd)

Table I.5 (*Cont'd*)

Source: 1st Plan to 8th Plan data have been taken from Planning Commission database, 7th Finance Commission Report; Vithal B P R and M L Sastry, *The Gadgil Formula*, 2002, 153–164; and 'Centre-State Resource Transfers, 1951-84' (Vithal and Shastry 2002), Data for Discretionary transfers for 9th to 11th Plan are from the Report of the Committee on Restructuring of CSS, Sept, 2011, pp. 19 and 22. Other data for 9th Plan is based on Finance Ministry figures at www.finmin.nic.in/reports/IPFStat200708.pdf and the 10th Plan document, Vol-I, 118. 10th Plan data have been computed from 11th Plan document, Vol I 163 and the Union Government Expenditure Budget, Statements 16 for the respective years. Data for 11th Plan are taken from *Report on the Committee on Restructuring CSS*, pp 18-19 and Economic Survey, GoI, 2011–12, 48–50.

shown along with the statutory transfers under Finance Commission (FC) recommendations.

Some interesting trends are noticed here. First, the statutory transfers under Finance Commissions' recommendations constituted about one third of the total transfers during the first plan period, this proportion has gradually increased to 53 per cent during the tenth and eleventh plan periods. Still about half the total transfers took place through non-statutory mechanism of the Planning Commission. Second, the non-discretionary plan assistance to states (under Gadgil Formula and other transfers tied to specific projects) used to dominate the total plan transfers, but the proportion of such transfers in the total transfers have declined progressively, with the result that presently the discretionary transfers, most of which are extra budgetary, account for the bulk of such transfers.

Thankfully, extra-budgetary transfers have been discontinued with effect from the union budget of 2013–14. Henceforth all plan funds will be routed through the state budgets, giving the states more access and control over these funds. Distortions that have so long characterized the plan transfers will hopefully stand corrected.

Plan and Non-Plan Transfers to Special and Non-Special Category States

The special category states not only received special consideration from the Planning Commission but also from the successive Finance

Commissions which went on increasing their shares in total devolution of resources, both under grants and shares of the divisible pool of central taxes, starting with the second Finance Commission (Table I.6).

The Ninth Finance Commission stated:

> The states of Arunachal Pradesh, Himachal Pradesh, Jammu and Kashmir, Manipur, Meghalaya, Mizoram, Nagaland, Sikkim and Tripura and also Assam form a distinct group requiring somewhat different treatment from what we have accorded to the non-special category states..... Keeping in view the special features of the special category states and the historical background in which these states came to be constituted, we have adopted a liberal approach in assessing their receipts as well as expenditures.

The share of the special category states in the total transfers increased till the sixth Finance Commission's award period, but then remained more or less at that level, before falling to 12.48 per cent under Thirteenth Finance Commission's recommendations.

Table I.6 Transfer of Resources by Finance Commission Recommendations (Rs Crore)

Finance Commissions (FC)	Period	Transfers to non-SCS (Rs Crore)	Transfers to SCS (Rs Crore)	% of total transfers to SCS	Statutory transfer as % of total transfers[23]
1st FC	1952–57	394	18	4.37	28.9
2nd FC	1957–62	979	70	6.67	31.6
3rd FC	1962–66	1,230	81	6.18	39.9
4th FC	1966–69	1,583	163	9.34	35.9
5th FC	1969–74	4,796	521	9.80	35.9
6th FC	1974–79	8,249	1,359	14.14	44.2
7th FC	1979–84	18,816	2,026	9.72	43.1
8th FC	1984–89	33,906	5,546	14.06	60.1
9th FC	1989–95	101,014	18,684	15.61	61.5
10th FC	1995–2000	191,648	34,995	15.44	68.6
11th FC	2000–05	376,263	58,642	13.48	69.4
12th FC	2005–10	646,773	108,978	14.42	68.0
13th FC	2010–15	1,493,689	212,988	12.48	NA

Source:: Calculated on the basis of reports of various Finance Commissions.

Table I.7 Share of Total Central Assistance (TCA) under Different Plans to Special and Non-Special Category States

Plan Periods	TCA (Rs Crore) given to		Percentage of TCA received by	
	Special Category States	Non-Special Category States[24]	Special Category States	Non-Special Category States
1st Plan (1951–56)	31	849	3.52	96.48
5th Plan (1974–79)	1005	5532	15.37	84.63
Annual Plan (1979–80)	924	5679	13.99	86.01
6th Plan (1980–85)	4347	21400	16.88	83.22
7th Plan (1985–90)	11577	42731	21.31	78.69
Annual Plans (1990–92)	6461	27216	19.19	80.81
8th Plan (1992–97)	26988	104225	20.57	79.43
9th Plan (1997–2002)	62872	144831	30.27	69.73
10th Plan (2002–07)	123568	251368	32.96	67.04
11th Plan (2007–12) till 2009–10	118130	279030	29.74	70.26

Source: Data for 1st Plan from *The Gadgil Formula* (2002: 153–64) and the rest from Combined Finance and Revenue Accounts of the CAG of India for the respective years.

It is also seen that the share of special category states in Total Central Assistance including non-plan grants recommended by the Finance Commissions has increased from a meagre 3.52 per cent to about 30 per cent during the 11th Plan (Table I.7).

Aberration of Centrally Sponsored Schemes

CSSs have always been characterized by bewildering varieties. As of 2005–06, there were 112 CSS under Category I funded through state budgets and 43 CSS under category II, i.e., partially funded by the state budgets. The total allocation under these two categories amounted to little more than Rs. 20000 crore. Besides, there were 41 other CSS funded by the central budget but operating outside the state budgets having an allocation of more than Rs 34000 crore. They formed 24 per cent of the total Gross Budgetary Support (GBS) for the annual plan for the year (104 per cent of the central assistance to state plans and 253 per cent of Normal Central Assistance)(Garg 2006: 4982).

As pointed out earlier, the CSS which were initiated by the centre *de facto* constituted a ploy by the centre to make grants to states by exercising its discretion—a discretion that the Gadgil formula apparently took away. As at the end of 2011–12, there were as many as 147 CSS operating in the country, despite transferring a large number of CSS to the states from time to time.

It may be argued that the CSS followed from the Directive Principles in the Constitution that enjoins upon the state to 'secure a social order for the promotion of welfare of the people' (Article 38), or, to provide for 'early childhood care and education to children below the age of six years' (Article 45), or the 'right to work, to education and to public assistance in certain cases' (Article 41). In fact the Government of India Resolution of 1950 establishing the Planning Commission mentioned the Fundamental Rights as well as the Directive Principles of State Policy in the Constitution that 'the State shall try to promote the welfare of the people' and asserted that the objective behind setting up of the Commission was to further the 'declared objective of the Government to promote a rapid rise in the living standards of the people by efficient exploitation of the resources of the country, increasing production and offering employment opportunities'.[25] However, no transfer of resources from the centre to meet the needs of above is envisaged in the Constitution; besides, the ad-hoc manner in which these schemes were allowed to proliferate without any rhyme or reason, or the way many of these were being run, raises legitimate doubts about the sincerity of their purpose and in their actual and potential use more for meeting the political ends of the powers that be than for the stated purpose of improving standards of public services provided to the citizens.

Till the Fourth Five Year Plan, central assistance was given to states for implementation of the plan schemes within the state's jurisdiction. Funds were allocated scheme-wise and the system lacked the requisite flexibility and efficiency for effective implementation of these schemes. A separate classification for CSS was introduced in the Fourth Plan. Before that, most schemes for which funds were given in the Central Plan but which were implemented by the states were transferred to the states as part of the state plans. At the end of the Third Plan, there were

92 such plan schemes which were, so to say, 'assisted' or 'sponsored' by the centre. A sub-committee of the NDC had considered the need for harmonizing their structure and funding patterns with the schemes run by the states in 1967 and recommended a reduction in their number. But instead the draft Fourth Plan included as many as 147 such schemes which were finally cut down to 90, with varying funding patterns by the centre and the states (between 50 per cent to 100 per cent funding by centre). Another NDC Committee appointed in 1968 recommended for the CSS a ceiling of $1/6^{th}$ of total central plan assistance to states, which were never heeded by the central ministries; they merrily went on increasing their numbers and bypassed this recommendation cleverly by treating them as 'Central Sector Schemes' though they were very much in the nature of CSS. This committee also laid down the criteria for selection of a CSS, which mainly stipulated that they should relate to pilot projects, surveys, and research; should have regional and inter-state character and an overall significance from all India angle. From time to time, a large number of these schemes were transferred to the states and the resultant savings to the centre were also transferred to the states as 'Additional Block Assistance' based on the 'Income Adjusted Total Population Formula' (Vithal and Sastry 2002: 55–60).

During the Fourth and Fifth Plan periods, the administrative ministries went on introducing one CSS after another, ignoring the advice of the NDC Committee or the criteria for CSS laid down earlier, often without any justification. States did not object as all these were 100 per cent financed by the centre. When after the Emergency, the Congress Government was replaced by the Janata Government at the centre, they terminated the Fifth Plan (1974–79) prematurely in 1978 while preparing to launch the 'Rolling Plan' and appointed a Committee to re-examine the running of CSS. At that time there were 116 CSSs, besides 74 other schemes of the same nature but called the Central Sector schemes in order to bypass the $1/6^{th}$ limit for CSS. The committee consulted the states which argued that a proliferation of these schemes run by the centre had effectively shrunk the amount of central assistance available for state plans, while centre argued that for these innovative schemes, the states' development would not be uniform. The Committee recommended that the CSS should be financed 100 per cent by the centre in respect of certain health, family planning schemes, and power projects, while in respect of CSS for rural and agricultural development and for weaker sections, the cost should be shared by the centre and the states. These recommendations were adopted in the Sixth Plan (1978–83) and 70 CSSs were transferred to the state plans (Vithal and Sastry 2002: 59).

The Sixth Plan was reformulated by the newly elected Congress Government for 1980–85, treating the previous two plans as annual plans. But the number of CSS continued to proliferate. An Expert Committee was appointed in 1984 under the chairmanship of Shri K Ramamurthi to examine their scope and role and to re-examine the laid down criteria of CSS prescribed by the NDC Committee in 1968 and followed since then, as mentioned earlier.

The report of the Expert Committee submitted in 1985 highlighted that:

(i) There was no centralised agency in the Government of India which had complete information regarding the CSS under implementation.
(ii) Though decisions were taken from time to time to reduce the number of CSS, the schemes, in actual practice, had been increasing over the years.
(iii) In 1969, their number was 45. At the time of finalization of the Sixth Plan (1978-83) it was 190, which was decided to be reduced to 75 by the NDC in 1979. (Vithal and Sastry 2002: 64).

However, by the end of the Sixth Plan, their numbers had risen to 201. Their allocation which was Rs 1238 crore in 1980–81, was also increased to Rs 9318 crore for the revised Sixth Plan (1980–85) representing 35 per cent of the Total Central Assistance for state plans, far exceeding the $1/6^{th}$ limit that was laid down earlier. Details of all the CSS operated during the Sixth Plan are indicated in the Table I.8.

It was also seen that developed states gained from CSS in terms of per capita plan assistance while, backward states like Bihar, Rajasthan, UP, and Odisha received much lesser per capita assistance than they otherwise would have got under the Gadgil formula due to the large number of CSS eating up a substantial chunk of the total plan funds. Since most schemes required a matching grant from the states, states that were in a position to afford these grants reaped the benefits; some states of course gave its own contribution so as to attract the funds which they later diverted towards meeting their non-plan expenditure, sometimes for paying salaries to their staff (Vithal and Sastry, 2002: 64–5).

Table I.8 CSS during the Sixth Plan

Ministry	No of Schemes	Allocations during Sixth Plan (1980–85) in Rs Crore
Agriculture	53	879
Health	21	1924
Home Affairs	12	852
Industry	11	889
Rural Development	12	2772
Works and Housing	7	910
Irrigation	7	378
Others	78	715
Total	201	9319

Source: Vithal and Sastry (2002: 65).

The Committee recommended for the continuance of the CSS more or less on the existing lines. However, since the states demanded further reduction in the numbers of CSS, the NDC formed another Committee headed by Shri P V Narsimha Rao, the then Minister for HRD, in 1985 which added to the existing criteria of the condition that any CSS selected for implementation must fulfil an important national objective like poverty alleviation or providing the minimum standards of education, besides retaining 149 of the 262 schemes from the 6th Plan period and removing any limit for outlay on the CSS (Vithal & Sastry 2002: 65–6). But the criteria recommended were so broad that it instead facilitated the continued proliferation of the CSS as shown in Table I.9:

Even within a plan their numbers have greatly varied, for example during the tenth and Eleventh Plans, as shown in Table I.10.

Following the elections and the subsequent change in Government in November 1989, a reconstituted Planning Commission had prepared a note stating that the schemes to be transferred to the states would carry with them block grants and loans in the ratio of 85 per cent: 15 per cent. The 42nd meeting of the NDC that considered this note emphasized that the CSS should not only be decentralized from the centre to the state, but the decentralization should be carried down to the PRIs. In December 1990, following another change of government at the centre, the Planning Commission was again reconstituted. For the CSS to be taken up during the Ninth Plan (1992–97), the NDC

Table 1.9 Number of CSS: From Fourth to Eleventh Plan

Plan Period	No. of CSS at the end of the Plan	Total Allocation of Central Funds (Rs Crore)
4th Plan (1969–74)	90	6,145
5th Plan (1974–79)	190	6,357
Annual Plan (1979–80)	201	9,318
6th Plan (1980–85)	262	15,757
7th Plan (1985–90)	125	14,104
8th Plan (1992–97)	236	29,483
9th Plan[28] (1997–2002)	360	99,001
10th Plan (2002–07)	188	2,29,762
11th Plan (2007–12)	147	6,60,506

Source: 4th to 8th Plan: Vithal and Sastry (2002), p. 19; 9th Plan onwards: B K Chaturvedi Committee Report on the Restructuring of CSS, Planning Commission (2011), p. 18.

Table I.10 Year-wise Number of CSS during Tenth to Twelfth Plan

Year	Plan Period	No. of CSS
2002–03	Tenth Plan	188
2003–04		213
2004–05		207
2005–06		204
2006–07		155
2007–08	Eleventh Plan	99
2008–09		133
2009–10		138
2010–11		139
2011–12		147
2012–13	Twelfth Plan	137
2013–14		66

Source: B K Chaturvedi Committee Report on Restructuring of CSS, para 5.1, p. 18, 2011 and budget documents.

appointed another sub-committee in 1999. As observed by Vithal and Sastry (2002: 76):

> And thus the charade of appointing committees, sub-committees and working groups, goes on. The logical flaw in all these exercises is that the total limit on allocation of central funds for the CSS is sought to be derived from the list of schemes finalized. The original exercise at the time of the Gadgil formula first set a limit of 1/6 of total central assistance for State Sector Plan and then specified what type of schemes could be formulated within this limit. What all needed is now to reiterate their limit and ask some groups to decide schemes within that limit……
>
> Where does this reluctance to reduce such schemes come from? ….. Basically the resistance comes from Central Ministries dealing with State List. These Ministries have grown in size essentially on schemes implemented by the States.

And there lies the crux of the problem. These ministries do want to see any shrinking of their turfs; these are mainly the ministries of Agriculture, Health, HRD, and Rural Development. These are the ministries that handle thousands of crores of rupees of allocations under the CSS that they can dole out to the rural electorates, creating a niche vote-bank for their political masters. No government, irrespective of the political dispensation in power, would be likely to give up these privileges. The system was also playing havoc with state budgets since almost 60–70 per cent of the total grants received by the states from the centre were transferred outside their budgets directly to the executing agencies of the CSS, which could be autonomous government organizations, NGOs, or a combination of the two. In the process, the normal budgetary and accounting controls that regulate any government expenditure were done away with, since any expenditure that is not passing through the treasuries would not be captured in the accounts prepared by the Accountant General of a state. Since these funds were not routed through the state budget, the legislators had no chance to vote for these, and the drawing and disbursing officers could not exercise any controls over these funds. In fact till today, there is no database in existence which would give up-to-date information about all the CSS operating within a state—their number, the money spent on them or the benefits that have been accrued to the people from them. It is a typical case where public money is spent ostensibly on public purposes, but outside the machinery of public accountability system ensured and enforced by the instruments of state budget, accounts and legislative, or parliamentary committees—and all this in the name of economic and social welfare of the weaker sections of our society. Thankfully, such 'centralized' welfare has now been stopped.

The 360 CSS at the end of Ninth Plan consumed about 60 per cent of total central assistance provided to the states. For the 10th Plan, the Planning Commission, under a zero base budgeting exercise, had weeded out 48 schemes, besides merging 161 schemes into 53 and retaining the remaining 135 schemes, making a total of 188. For the 11th Plan, of the total allocation of Rs 6.6 lakh crore for 147 schemes, the 9 flagship schemes (IAY, MNREGA, PMGSY, TSC, NRDWM, NRHM, ICDS, SSA, and MDM)[26] alone consumed Rs 5.24 lakh crore or 79.4 per cent of the total allocation.[27] Consequently, as a result of much higher allocation to CSS, and also due to the fact that after the Twelfth Finance Commission recommendations, the centre was only giving grants and not grants as well as loans as it used to give to the states earlier, NCA to states came down to 6.74 per cent of the centre's GBS. 'The pattern of assistance varied from 100 per cent to 90:10 for NE States, 65:35 in SSA, 75:25 in IAY and 75:25 in a number of other schemes.'[28] Two more bodies were appointed on the issue of CSS, one an Expert Group headed by Shri Arvind Varma in October 2005 which recommended, *inter alia,* that the Planning Commission should take up the zero base budgeting exercise once every five years in consultation with the states and that all CSS funds should be routed through the state budgets and hence subjected to the usual checks exercised by the Accountants General (Audit). This was, of course, found unacceptable by the Planning Commission which recommended establishment of a scheme-wise reliable information system with the help of the Chief Controller of Accounts attached to the Ministries (Central Plan Schemes Monitoring System, or CPSMS, introduced in 11th Plan). What was not mentioned was that the ministries would not accept any independent authority exercising oversight functions over what they considered their exclusive turf. It accepted the other recommendation of reducing the CSS to 82 in 2007–08 from 155 existing in 2006–07.[29]

There was also the problem that most CSS guidelines were based on 'one size fits all' presumption. Guidelines were issued by the Centre in which states had very little say. For example, under the flagship scheme of PMGSY, funds are released for construction of roads, bridges, etc., only when all the criteria such as width, length, etc. are met. But unlike the plains regions in most parts of India, based on which the guidelines were framed to allow for construction of wider roads, narrow roads are more suited for mountainous terrains of the northeastern states. Naturally, these states could not utilize most of the funds allocated under PMGSY because of this guideline-imposed constraint. Same was true for many other schemes.

The B K Chaturvedi Committee, set up in April 2011 to review the CSS, submitted its report in September 2011. Its major recommendations were:[30]

- **Restructuring of CSS**
  - (i) Since administering a large number of CSS makes their implementation and monitoring difficult, their number should be reduced to 59 under three categories:
    Category I:Flagship schemes to address major gaps in health, education, irrigation, rural and urban development, etc;
    Category II: Sub-sectoral schemes to address sub-sectors of major sectors like agriculture, education etc. and to improve the effectiveness of plan expenditure; and
    Category III: Sector umbrella schemes to address sectoral gaps for improving the effectiveness of plan expenditure.
  - (ii) CSS with outlays less than Rs 100 crore made no national impact and hence should be weeded out or merged with other schemes;
- **Flexi Funds**
  - (iii) Given the widely diversified socio-economic, demographic, and geographical coverage of the CSS across the country, a certain amount of flexibility is needed to cater to the state-specific needs. Hence Category-II and III CSS must have 20 per cent funds as 'Flexi Funds' to be used by states for their own schemes. In Flagship Schemes, which have large budgetary outlays, these flexi-funds may constitute 10 per cent of annual outlay.
- **Flexibility in physical and financial norms**
  - (iv) Given the divergent requirements of different states, there should be appropriate norms for different CSS. States will have the flexibility to modify these norms. Similarly, in respect of financial norms, an automatic revision after two years of the plan should be made on the basis of Wholesale Price Index.

- **Funding Pattern**
  - (v) NCA should not fall below 10 per cent of GBS; except in case of new flagship schemes, all CSS would be 100 per cent centrally funded; and
  - (vi) Instead of direct transfers, there should be a gradual move to transfers only through state budgets during the 12th Plan period.

- **Independent Evaluation and Monitoring**
  - (vii) In addition to regular monitoring by ministries, independent evaluation of CSS should be carried out through professional institutions and experts.

As stated earlier, the High Level Expert Committee on 'Efficient Management of Plan Expenditure' headed by Shri C Rangarajan, also set up by the Planning Commission, had submitted its report in July 2011 recommending abolition of the distinction between plan and non-plan expenditure. Government is yet to accept the recommendations of this Committee.

In June 2013, the Union Cabinet decided to restructure the existing CSS and Additional Central Assistance (ACA) schemes in the Twelfth Five Year Plan into 66 schemes, including 17 Flagship programmes with significant outlays. For state-specific requirements, it also approved that a scheme may have state specific guidelines to be recommended by an Inter-Ministerial Committee constituted for this purpose. All financial assistance to the states in these schemes would henceforth be provided through the Consolidated Funds of the states, eliminating direct off-budget transfers, and 10 per cent of the scheme outlays would be treated as flexi-funds. For each new CSS/ACA/Flagship scheme, at least 25 per cent of funds may be contributed by the general category states and 10 per cent of funds by the special category states. These arrangements will come into force for the remaining years of the Twelfth Five Year Plan. In the BE of 2013-14, budgetary provision had been made for 137 CSS and 5 Scheme-based ACA excluding block grants.[31]

Plan Assistance to Special Category States

The special category states have been getting higher per capita central plan assistance than the non-special category states. During the Fifth Plan, the per capita transfer for special category states was Rs 415 compared to only Rs 84 for non-special category states. During the Tenth Plan period (2002–07), these states had received per capita central assistance of Rs 2403.85 (Rs 2574.98 for the NER states) compared to all India average of only Rs 683.94; it was 9.65 per cent of their GSDP compared to only 1.94 per cent for the non-special category states in 2007.[32]

As already stated, 30 per cent of the centre's gross budgetary support for plan expenditure goes to the special-category states. Earlier, plan assistance was given to the general category states by way of grants and loans in the ratio of 30 per cent and 70 per cent respectively. In the case of special-category states, however, 90 per cent of plan assistance was given as grants, and only 10 per cent as loans.

The Twelfth Finance Commission rightly pointed out that the central plan assistance to states had a counterpart in the interest rate charged by the central government on the plan loans given to the states, which was much higher (by about 3 to 4 per cent) than the cost of funds to the Centre, that is, the market rate of interest, and hence could become a source of funds to the centre at the cost of the states. It therefore recommended that plan grants should be given as genuine grants and states should be encouraged to borrow directly from the market whenever they need additional resources, subject to their repaying capacities, thus delinking grants from loans for plan assistance. This, according to the Twelfth Finance Commission, would 'facilitate determination of grants according to needs and loans according to capacities'. The plan size of each state should also take into account its sustainable level of debt. In other words, the considerations for grants should be different from those of loans. This has bearings also on the fiscal deficit of the centre, since it borrows almost the entire funds needed for meeting the plan expenditure. It therefore recommended that the

> Planning Commission should confine itself to extending plan grants to the states, and leave it to the states to decide how much they wish to borrow and from whom, i.e., from the centre or from the open market. This dis-intermediation of the centre in the borrowing process of the states would go a long way in ensuring greater fiscal discipline on the part of the states by removing the structural obligation to borrow from the centre. This would, of course, benefit the centre as well, because it would bring down its own fiscal deficit.[33]

History has proved that the Commission was absolutely right in its premises as well as in its conclusions on this aspect. This measure has restored the fiscal balances of the centre as well as of the states to a large measure and has brought down their fiscal deficits. The Twelfth Finance Commission's recommendations of which the above was a major one had transformed the fiscal landscape of the country and if most states today are able to generate revenue surpluses and out of the debt trap into which they were falling earlier, the credit undoubtedly goes to the Commission. After the Twelfth Finance Commission, the centre now gives only grants, and leaves it to the states to raise loans as they need. The 90 per cent grants: 10 per cent loans formula for special-category states is now restricted only to CSS and externally aided projects. For general category states, external aid is passed on in the exact mixture of loan and grants in which it is received at the centre. For them, in the case of CSS, 70 per cent of the central funding is given as grants. Today states borrow insignificant amounts from the Centre and in about another fifteen years of time, most states will cease to be indebted to the Centre.

Evaluation of the Role of Planning Commission

The Planning Commission was disbanded in August 2014, soon after the new NDA Government came to power. In January 2015, the Government announced its replacement it by NITI (National Institution for Transforming India) Aayog.

The role and need of a Planning Commission, which was being seen as a relic of Nehruvian socialism, were increasingly being questioned for quite some time. Doubts have also been cast over the classification of expenditure under plan and non-plan categories which has created an intrinsic bias towards plan expenditure at the cost of non-plan maintenance expenditure, often to the neglect of the latter. Even the Independent Evaluation Office attached to the Planning Commission and established to assess the impact of Government's flagship programmes castigated the Planning Commission for acting rather like a 'Control Commission' that had blocked all attempts to reform itself, and suggested that its functions be transferred to the Finance Commission.[34] The Economic Survey of 2013–14 admitted sub-optimal utilization of resources and diffused accountability in the existing budgetary practices and stressed the need to unify the process of budget making only at the Finance Ministry (Bhattacharjee 2014b).

The mechanism of centralized planning has proved to be ineffective in the Indian context in addressing the problems of poverty, inflation, and unemployment even after six decades of planning. Planning Commission, a body that usurped that function of the State by allocating public funds not only without legitimate authority, but also without any accountability, has become rather irrelevant in today's scenario. For the past several decades, it has become the major driving force behind doling out national resources in the form of ill-conceived and poorly implemented CSS. This has not only defeated the spirit of fiscal federalism in our Constitution by compromising the autonomy of the states, but its role as the most important extra-constitutional allocator of huge public resources has inevitably led to shrinking of the states' fiscal space, besides creating strains upon the centre-state relations.

Planning Commission was not a constitutional but a political body—with every change in the central government, its constitution also changed. Its allegiance therefore was always to the ruling dispensation. The discretionary nature of the transfers made by it has made these transfers vulnerable to political rather than economic considerations. Other aberration followed in course, like continued proliferation of the CSS and off-budget transfers to states. Plan transfers became tied to populist schemes and their allocations took quantum jumps in recent years. In the process, state autonomy suffered and their flexibility to launch schemes specific to their own needs almost completely disappeared. Private sector investment naturally went to states having better infrastructure, further widening economic imbalance and disparity among states.

The first seven plans could not arrest falling outputs, soaring prices, and rising unemployment. Poverty remained undented and growth continued to languish within the Hindu rate of 3.5 per cent till 1991 when the economy was poised precariously on the verge of failure. But all through, as more and more ambitious plans were introduced with ever increasing allocation of public funds, Yojna Bhavan bureaucracy had also flourished, becoming ever more powerful. Its style of functioning, however, became more and more curious, increasingly falling out of sync with a modern economy.

It determined what the economy should produce as well as the quantity and mode of production. After surveying the available resources, a growth target for each sector of the economy was fixed and investments allocated to each sector, specifying the type of projects and sometimes even the specific production techniques. Naturally, it led to an economy characterized by extensive regulation, protectionism and a public sector supposed to dominate the 'commanding heights of the economy'. The government size also grew in tandem. The extensive control only fuelled pervasive corruption all around and stifled growth. Vital sectors of economy were nationalized, and the rest regulated by an elaborate system of licenses and red-tapism that discouraged entrepreneurial initiative and inhibited private investment, making the economy reel under this License-Permit Raj. This tyranny of the State only benefited certain entrenched groups but smothered individual entrepreneurship.

In such a collectivized, centralized planned economy, economic democracy, growth, and productivity became the ultimate casualties, and market—the driver of growth in a modern economy, was not allowed to flourish. As Professor P R Brahmananda (1977: 13) had insightfully observed, instead of attacking poverty through a wage-goods model, the authorities chose a number of anti-poverty and pubic distribution measures, which were simply in the nature of fire-fighting exercises with large leakages. The result was a forced impoverishment of the nation that earned the nickname of 'Sick Man of Asia'.

The economic reforms came after realization dawned that it was the market and not the government that should drive the economy. In recognition of this fact, the Eighth Plan stated in its preface that the plan was only 'indicative' in nature and that the state could at best be a facilitator for investment by the private sector. As the Commission on Centre-State Relations observed in its report (March 2010), 'Following the introduction of economic reforms in the country, the role of central planning seemed to have lost much of its relevance. There was a shrinking of the share of the public sector investment. States saw an opportunity to regain ground lost to the Planning Commission. However, this hope was belied.' Despite the declining share of public investment post-reforms and promotion of public-private partnership mode of investment, the role and importance of the Planning Commission did not diminish.

Command economies invariably tend to get corrupt as by concentrating economic power and authority, the normal decision-making process is given a go-by. Thus, plans drawn on the basis of insufficient information were approved and implemented with disastrous results. As growth slugged, inequality amplified, rural-urban divide widened, resource allocation to different sectors remained lopsided, and ad-hocism reigned supreme. The evils that distress the common man—inflation, poverty, and unemployment—remained unfettered.

As global experiences show (Bhattacharjee 2014c), a central over-arching body is not a necessary prerequisite for development; in fact in a diverse country such as ours, where skill, talent, and entrepreneurship are abundantly available, centralized planning is unlikely to work. The 73rd Amendment to our Constitution provides for planning at the grassroots level of villages and consolidation of these plans all the way up. This way a realistic plan can be made by considering the local needs and addressing the implementation bottlenecks, since people actually responsible for implementation will be involved in this bottoms-up planning process. Planning must be a responsibility of states, which cannot be relegated to technocrats and experts on any pretext. It should be the responsibility of the elected representatives who should drive the process through consensus, with the involvement of all stakeholders including experts. The process of consensus-based planning will ensure efficiency of the plan, and involvement of elected representatives will strengthen the accountability mechanism.

The newly formed NITI Aayog is to replace the erstwhile one-way flow of policy from the centre to states by 'a genuine and continuing partnership' while acknowledging that we need to find and adopt our own strategy for growth, without depending on imported models. The stated objectives of NITI Aayog include providing a framework 'national agenda' to 'foster cooperative federalism through structured support initiatives and mechanisms with the states on a continuous basis, recognizing that strong States make a strong nation'. The Ayyog is to develop mechanisms to formulate credible plans at the village level and aggregate these plans progressively at higher levels of government. The thirteen stated objectives also include designing strategic and long-term policies and programmes, monitoring and evaluating their implementation and progress, and identification of required resources for strengthening delivery while focussing on technology upgradation and capacity building for implementation of programmes and initiatives.

Chaired by the Prime Minister, it will have a Governing Council comprising Chief Ministers of all the states and Lt. Governors of all union territories; that will automatically render the existing National Development Council defunct. There will also be regional councils to address issues and contingencies specific to different regions.

However, like its predecessor, NITI Aayog also does not have any constitutional status and will therefore remain a think tank of the Government. What role it will discharge and what purpose it will serve remain to be seen.

* * *

The special category status refers mainly to the plan assistance to these states given by the centre—but it also entitles a state to preferential treatment in federal assistance and tax breaks by giving significant excise duty and income tax concessions to industries that would be set up within their territories. The status is bestowed by the Planning Commission. There is no formal declaration, but it is made apparent by the pattern of assistance provided to the special category state so selected; neither is there any formal agreement with the state. Once the status is awarded, the specific assistance pattern follows to the state in perpetuity. There is no stipulation as to what is intended to be achieved by such a status, or the time period within which this is to be achieved. The status once bestowed upon a state carries only rewards but no obligation on the part of the state, since there is no performance expectation. The status is also neutral to the scale of backwardness and limited only to the funding pattern, without any consideration of state's capacity to utilize these funds. There is no coherent strategy envisaged for its development, nor any institutional set-up for guiding and overseeing the utilization of funds by states or for monitoring their progress. A singular absence of accountability structure debilitates the mechanism, which concerns only the transfer of funds. These certainly are not the ideal mechanisms for upliftment and empowerment of a state.

Since 1969, the number of such states has increased to 11, and the last state to have been accorded this status was Uttarakhand in 2001. Since then, there have been demands from all the newly formed states as well as from Bihar, Rajasthan, Odisha, and Andhra Pradesh (after creation of Telangana) for this status, claiming that the criteria devised by the Planning Commission were arbitrary. Such claims had started finding favour with the ruling dispensation in the era of coalition politics and wafer-thin majorities in Parliament.

Without a shadow of doubt, the criteria devised by the Planning Commission were indeed arbitrary. The Planning Commission ought not to have been vested with such extra-constitutional powers without accountability. It is through the Planning Commission that the ruling dispensation used to get extra-legislative access to public funds to be dispensed to favoured states, presumably under Article 282 which should be used only to deal with extra-ordinary situations.

A body created by an executive resolution like the Planning Commission should not have been given the authority to decide whether a state should or should not be a special category one—such decision should be left to only the elected representatives of people as befits a democratic system and not to technocrats enjoying the rewards of their office at the pleasure of the ruling dispensation. Its power to channel public funds without accountability has led to arbitrary decisions being imposed upon the nation from time to time, and such arbitrariness and ad-hocism have permeated our entire financial apparatus, creating aberrations all along. That the Planning Commission criteria for according the special category status to a state was of no real significance—something that could be easily junked when it came to politics of convenience—had been amply demonstrated in the case of Bihar and Andhra Pradesh (after the creation of Telangana), when the status was denied by the UPA Government to the former, but was promised to the latter because it had suited the ruling dispensation—regardless of the fact that none of these states fulfilled the Planning Commission-defined criteria for special category status.

The special category status was devised primarily to empower the peripheral, marginalized states and bring them to the fold of mainstream states in the country. As we shall see in the next chapter, similar ideas are applied in every asymmetrical federation. But instead of empowering the states by giving them real economic advantage, it had only created states increasingly dependent on central doles, unable to negotiate their economic future on their own strength and carve out a path of progress for themselves. Whatever little hope was there for real economic empowerment was obscured by the gradual incursion of centrally sponsored schemes and direct transfers, creating a structure that bred unchecked corruption in the absence of an effective accountability structure.

However, over the years, perception about the role of the government has also undergone a remarkable transformation. From being the controller of all economic activities, it became a facilitator of those activities. Side by side, the principles of federalism in Indian democracy has taken stronger roots; with the hitherto sacrosanct concept of a single party with absolute majority of its own ruling at the centre becoming mostly a thing of the past, the balance of power that was skewed earlier in favour of the centre has now shifted towards the states, increasing their bargaining power. This facilitated increasing resources to be transferred to the states, some of which have been able to leverage these resources to their advantage and developed faster, in the process lifting a significant proportion of their population above the poverty levels. As the states thus started becoming more powerful, their people's expectation for development and a higher standard of living also grew. This ultimately led to demands for and creation of smaller states by breaking up of the larger and largely ungovernable states to smaller ones in response to the aspirations and agitations of people inhabiting areas within these states that hitherto were neglected for various reasons. From 1972 onwards, the creation of more special category states followed as a result of the increasing aspirations of people. Some special category states thus created have indeed registered much higher rates of growth than were ever thought to be possible under their earlier dispensations. An investigation into this aspect remains an important objective of this study at the end of which we shall revisit the question whether it is time to take a relook at the whole arrangement regarding the award of special category status to a state in the present form and its continuation in perpetuity.

Notes

1. Assam, Jammu & Kashmir, and Nagaland were accorded the special category status in 1969, Himachal Pradesh in 1971, Manipur, Meghalaya, and Tripura in 1972 when they were created, Sikkim in 1975, Arunachal Pradesh and Mizoram in 1987, and Uttarakhand in 2001.

2. Note submitted by the Adviser, Financial Resource Division, Planning Commission dated 16 November 2006 to the Member (AS) and Dy Chairman of the Commission. Also stated in the Rajya Sabha in response to Unstarred Question No 1614 dated 3 December 2009.

3. It is to be noted that the Finance Commission never used the term Special Category in relation to any of these states; further, allocating plan grants is the job of the Planning Commission—not of the Finance Commission.

4. Art 272 has since been repealed by 80th Amendment to the Constitution enacted for giving effect to the recommendations of the 10th Finance Commission.

5. Terms of Reference of the Ninth Finance Commission required it to adopt a normative approach in assessing the receipts and expenditures on the revenue account of the States and the Centre and also to look into the revenue account as a whole, including plan and non-plan expenditure. These raised the legal issue of whether Grants under both Articles 275 and 282 can be recommended by the Finance Commission and whether these grants can be given for capital purposes also. It took legal opinion and expressed the view that the plan transfers were very much within the purview of the Finance Commission and covered under Article 275.

6. Report of the High Level Expert Committee on Efficient Management of Public Expenditure, Planning Commission, July 2011. Available at http://planningcommission.nic.in/reports/genrep/rep_hle.pdf; accessed 9 February2013.

7. http://cpsms.nic.in/Static/ accessed 15 December 2014.

8. Eleventh Plan document, Vol I, 142.

9. Twenty-fourth Meeting of the NDC, Summary Record, Planning Commission, Government of India, December 1967.

10. Twenty-fourth Meeting of the NDC, Summary Record, Planning Commission, Government of India, December 1967.

11. Para 11, 16-Point Agreement, July 1960.

12. *Report of the Fifth Finance Commission, Para 2.9.*

13. *Report of the Fifth Finance Commission, Para 6.46.*

14. *Report of the Fifth Finance Commission, Para 6.50.*

15. Minutes of the Twenty-sixth meeting of the National Development Council, April1, 1969, Para 9, Planning Commission, Govt. of India.

16. Minutes of the Twenty-sixth meeting of the National Development Council, April1, 1969, Para 10, Planning Commission, Govt. of India..

17. Central Assistance was provided to special category states as 90 per cent grant and 10 per cent loan from the beginning of the Fourth Five Year Plan except Assam and Jammu & Kashmir which were covered under the pattern of Central Assistance of 30 per cent grant and 70 per cent loan as in the case of non-special category states; the 10 per cent–90 per cent formula was applied only in respect of the hilly areas of Assam and Ladakh region of Jammu & Kashmir. This was extended to the entire area of these two states by a decision of the NDC in October, 1990 only. (File No 12/1/2005-FR, Financial Resources Division, Planning Commission, Govt. of India and also Letter No. 19(2)/PF.I/92 dated

21 December1992 of the Ministry of Finance, Dept. of Expenditure, Plan Finance- I Division, Govt. of India.)

18. Agenda Item No 4: Placing Uttaranchal on the List of Special Category States, 49th Meeting of NDC dated 01/09/2001.

19. The issue of Uttaranchal was examined by the full Planning Commission in its meetings held on 27 and 29 June 2001, chaired by the Prime Minister.

20. Source of data: *Ibid.* The data quoted in the table have been taken from the Budget documents and earlier these documents reported the RE figures only. Hence the data may be at variance with actual accounts figures reported elsewhere.

21. Till 1969, there was no special category state. But the states that would later become so have been indicated in this column till 1969.

22. Figures include actual for 2007-10, Revised Estimates for 2010–11 and Budget Estimates for 2011–12.

23. For data relating to 1st to 6th Finance Commissions, Report of the Seventh Finance Commission, 172–175; for the rest, Reports of 8th to 13th Finance Commissions.

24. UT grants are not included, unlike in Table 3.

25. Resolution No. I.P(C)/50 dated March 15, 1950 constituting the Planning Commission, Paragraphs 3 and 4.

26. MNREGA, IAY and PMGSY fall under the Ministry of Rural Development, NRHM and ICDS under the Ministry of Health and Family Welfare, TSC and NRDWP under Ministry of Drinking Water Supply, SSA and MDM under the Dept. of School Education and Literacy.

27. *B K Chaturvedi Committee Report on the Restructuring of CSS*, September 2011, 19.

28. *B K Chaturvedi Committee Report on the Restructuring of CSS*, September 2011, 19.

29. *B K Chaturvedi Committee Report on the Restructuring of CSS*, September 2011, 19.

30. *B K Chaturvedi Committee Report on the Restructuring of CSS*, September 2011, 19. 35–44.

31. PIB Notification GoI, 20 June 2013.

32. *Eleventh Five Year Plan*, GOI, 152.

33. *Report of the Twelfth Finance Commission, Chapter X.*

34. *Times of India*, New Delhi, 10 July 2014

1 Special Category States in the Framework of Asymmetrical Federalism in India

Unity in Diversity

The creation of special category states for according them special privileges in terms of liberal plan assistance is nothing extraordinary in a federal set-up; such an arrangement easily fits into the framework of federal structure in a diverse country like India. There are two articles in our constitution, Articles 370 and 371—besides Schedules V and VI dealing with tribal areas of the country and the northeastern states—that grant special privileges to certain states or treat certain disadvantaged regions of the country in a special manner. While Article 370 deals exclusively with the state of Jammu & Kashmir, the omnibus Article 371 deals with certain other states. Both are included under Part XXI of the Constitution called 'Temporary, Transitional and Special Provisions'; The word 'Special' was later added by the Constitution (Thirteenth Amendment) Act in 1962, reversing the original intention of the constitution makers that such provisions were only transitional in nature, to be dispensed with after suitable time. While there were no amendments to Article 370 (though it was much diluted through administrative mechanisms), Article 371 was expanded and amended time and again through various Constitution Amendment Acts.

Article 371 empowers the Governors in certain states to exercise special powers and responsibilities for the benefit of the people without giving them a separate flag and a separate constitution, unlike Article 370. Initially Article 371 had provided for some special arrangements like separate development boards and equitable allocation of developmental expenditure in respect of certain regions of Andhra Pradesh,[1] Gujarat, and Maharashtra. Subsequently, a series of special provisions were added to this article, providing special arrangements in respect of other disadvantaged states or certain regions therein. Thus Article 371A created special provision in respect of Nagaland, 371B for Assam, 371C for Manipur, 371D, and E for Andhra Pradesh, 371F for Sikkim, 371G for Mizoram, 371H for Arunachal Pradesh, 371(I) for Goa and the latest, 371(J) for granting special status to Hyderabad consequent upon the creation of Telangana state by the 118th Constitution Amendment Act, 2012. By and large, these provisions allowed special administrative or judicial mechanisms to be created in these states, or protected their autonomy by guaranteeing non-interference in their indigenous social, religious, or cultural practices and in their customary laws or procedures, in the administration of civil and criminal justice systems in accordance with those laws for the protection of ownership and transfer rights to their land and other resources. There was no provision, however, to grant special financial assistance to address the problems of their remoteness, historical and geographic isolation, and backwardness. It was to address this, presumably, that the mechanism of special category status was invented. But as we have already seen in the last chapter, the mechanism was considerably diluted by the politics of discretion and convenience.

Many federations have learnt to accommodate diverse socio-economic and ethno-religious realities as well as cultural-linguistic differences between their constituent units—especially in large federations where differences between the constituent units are serious enough to breed and nurture the seeds of future potential conflicts. It is in this context that the framework of asymmetric federalism assumes importance. All federal systems have to provide for independence, autonomy, and self-determination of their constituent units within a broader political union. In symmetric federalism, there is no distinction between the constituent units in terms of their powers or autonomy within the federation. In contrast, in asymmetric federal systems, different sub-national entities are given differential constitutional status and are allowed to exercise differential powers, with some entities enjoying higher degrees of autonomy than the others. According to Burgess and Gress (1999: 43), 'Federal political systems are consciously and purposively designed to facilitate flexible accommodation for the many diversities which acquire political salience.' The idea is unity in diversity, rather than uniformity.

Of course, there is a strong argument that symmetry in a federation goes hand in hand with harmony and unity within it, and asymmetry and decentralization succeed only in increasing tension and instability (Tarlton 1965). However, this view has gradually changed over time in favour of asymmetry which has been recognized as a purposeful instrument to address not only difference and diversity, but also imbalance and inequity within a multinational federal state and to control dissatisfaction of certain entities within a federal unit where such imbalances are very pronounced.

Asymmetric Federalism

A large body of literature exists in respect of asymmetric federalism, the idea of which was introduced by Charles. D. Tarlton of the University of California, Berkley, in 1965 and practised in many countries across the world. In the Indian context, both Articles 370 and 371 capture the spirit of asymmetric federalism by giving special powers to certain states to promote democratic justice, especially in states lying at the northeastern border of our country where 'loyalty and sense of belonging to the Indian state-nation is thin' (Hausing 2014: 87). As Hausing notes, 'the debate on asymmetric federalism is primarily about the politics of recognition that undergird multinational states' responses to competing nationalist claims of territorially concentrated sub-state nations. Out of the many possible responses like coercive assimilation, ethnic cleansing, genocide, internal colonization, partition, territorial/non-territorial autonomy, consociationalism, devolution, decentralization, and cantonization, a quick survey of selected cases from Canada, Belgium, Spain, United Kingdom, Russia, and India shows that asymmetric federalism has emerged as one of the most popular and defensible responses to recognize and accommodate sub-state nations within multinational states' (Hausing 2014: 87-111). Both symmetric and asymmetric federalism are essential elements of any federal democratic system and they coexist for cohesion in every federation.

Historians and political scientists have often cited India's case as a successful example of unity in the midst of extreme diversity, holding together groups and communities that exhibit wide divergence in respect of language, custom, culture, region, etc. that display strong centrifugal tendencies. Indian experience with regard to its special category states is a valuable case study in a successful federal democracy that has to deal with abundant asymmetry. The Indian Constitution's makers were fully aware of the constraints and limitations in dealing with the many divergent tendencies that existed in a newborn 'majoritarian' nation, but decided to accommodate these fissiparous tendencies in a harmonious manner through Articles 370 and 371. Arora *et al* (2013: 125), in their survey of the pluricultural foundations and multicultural tendencies of Indian society, have observed, 'The institutional celebration of 'unity in diversity' by envisioning an asymmetric federal framework is not only a deliberate choice, but it is also an ineluctable outcome of India's long-standing experience as a pluricultural society. This framework facilitates public recognition of cultural differences and allows certain territorially concentrated ethno-cultural minorities to have extensive self-rule within the framework of a shared rule.'

Federal asymmetry can either be *de jure* asymmetry, i.e., giving differential constitutional status and powers only to few states in a federation, as distinguished from political or *de facto* asymmetry that derives from variations in size, geography, wealth, history, and culture of constituent states. Asymmetry occurs due to the combination of various factors in federations—which are referred to as conditions of asymmetry by Watts and Burgess. Burgess classifies them as socio-economic or cultural-political; there could be various sub-categories like political culture and traditions, social cleavages arising from religious, linguistic or ethnic nationalistic origins, territoriality or relationship between different regions affecting politics, socio-economic factors, or demographic patterns (Watts 2005; Burgess 2006: 215–7; Burgess and Gress 1999: 48–50). Degree of asymmetry also varies from federation to federation. *De jure* asymmetry addresses the problems of divergence by conferring differential powers to different regions through the Constitution and political processes. *De facto* asymmetry is present in every federation–'there is no federal system in the world in which all the component units are even approximately equal in size, population, political power, predominance of either urban or rural interests, social structures, traditions or relative geographical location'(Duchacek 1971: 53–71). Obviously, if a bigger unit is in a position to dominate a smaller unit in a federation that is left powerless and dissatisfied, the federation as a whole is likely to be destabilized and endangered. Both these types of asymmetry are present in the special category states of India.

Burgess contends that fiscal or taxing power and autonomy is one type of *de facto* asymmetry—a richer unit can claim a higher degree of autonomy since it has to depend less on federal resources and on their devolution (Burgess 2006: 218–19), but in India, the federal fiscal transfers ensure that the poorer states stand to gain more from such devolution. Representation in Parliament is another consideration. 'In Canada, for example, Québec feels that it lacks sufficient parliamentary representation to properly represent its majority Francophone population in a predominantly Anglophone Parliament, and this province must seek additional ways to protect its minority identity'(Burgess and Gress 1999: 52). There are several ways to protect such identity—through political parties, or through *de jure* asymmetry, i.e., through constitution by creating what Swenden calls 'formal asymmetric institutional devices' implying Constitutional or legal processes (Swenden 2006: 63). Asymmetry occurs when constituent units of a federation are separated along cultural or linguistic basis, 'creating units of varying size and distinct populations' (Watts 1999: 34). *De jure* asymmetry is then used to counteract the *de-facto* asymmetry and to create harmonizing conditions between different constituent units. Gagnon and Gibbs (1999: 78–92) indicate three principles behind asymmetric federalism that might lead to some form of asymmetry: a communitarian principle (preserving political communities within a country), a functional principle (managing a large and diverse territory efficiently), and a democratic principle (ensuring liberty, equality, and political participation of all citizens and nationalities within a country).

Asymmetrical Federalism in India

Quoting several experts, Arora *et al* have argued that while India displays abundant features of *de facto* asymmetry, it has a rather limited *de jure* asymmetry, which is seen in the exercise of 'varying degrees of power and autonomy enjoyed by J & K under Article 370 and the eight states of India's Northeast by the omnibus Article 371' (Arora *et al* 2013: 125). Asymmetric powers as embodied in these articles were envisaged within the centralized federal structure of the Indian Union to accommodate the conflicting demands of language, religion, caste, and tribe in diverse and sometimes peripheral communities living in these states. Such practices have been tried in other countries also, as we shall see. The ability to accommodate these diversities is indeed an indicator of the strength of the Indian federation. Conferring special category status to some states can be seen as an extension of this logic by incorporating an additional element of financial assistance into the asymmetrical arrangement. This was intended to help the backward states which were marginalized to the point of being economically unviable to survive as separate independent entities and achieve a level of development comparable with the other states.

The makers of our Constitution were acutely aware of the destabilizing tendencies that might arise from asymmetrical federalism in a majoritarian country and evolved the centralized federal structure to act as a bulwark against such destabilizing and centrifugal tendencies. Many experts, like Tarlton, have pointed out that asymmetric federalism has a 'secessionist potential' by encouraging social and political disintegration of the federation or of certain parts within it. Tarlton suggested that while symmetry promotes unity within a federation, asymmetry generates disunity; 'the degree of harmony or conflict within a federal system can be thought of as a function of the symmetrical or asymmetrical pattern prevailing within the system' (Tarlton 1965: 871). Where too much of asymmetry might create 'a great cessation potential', a unitary system with a coercive central authority might be the most appropriate response 'for achieving unity in the presence of highly diverse components', as Tarlton believed (Tarlton 1965: 874).

In fact, it is logical to presume that the institutional recognition of different identities within a federation would have the potential to magnify and widen those differences to foster 'inegalitarian citizenship' which in the long run might constitute 'the building blocks for separatist movements'. But as Hausing (2014: 89) observes, 'Granting differential constitutional status and powers to territorially concentrated sub-state nations under this rubric as a means to recognize their distinctiveness and to extend "self-rule" within the framework of "shared-rule" has, as Jan Erk and Lawrence Anderson reminded us in a different context, an inherent paradox, that is: it can be both "secession-inducing and secession-preventing"'. We see examples of both secession preventing and secession inducing tendencies among the special category states—especially in Jammu & Kashmir (J&K) and among the states in the Northeast; while separatist movements have strong followings in Nagaland and J&K, Arunachal Pradesh, Himachal, and Uttarakhand do not exhibit any such tendencies. As Rudolph and Rudolph (2001: 36–65) indicated, if a way could be found to leverage federalism 'to share and negotiate divided sovereignty', it might lead to the emergence of a 'polycentric polity' as had happened in the case of India and thereby address the destabilizing factors and help resolve potential conflicts. It is, in fact, in the manner of resolution of conflicts within the existing politico-legal boundaries that the strength of a multinational federation is always tested. It is no wonder that all durable multinational states also happen to be federal democratic states (Stepan 1999: 19–34; McGarry 2005: 302–24) in which conflict-resolution mechanisms are inherently stronger than in any other system..

Tillin (2007: 45–67) argued that the special status enjoyed by J&K under Article 370[2] did not stem from the recognition of the unique ethnic identity of 'Muslim-majority' in Kashmir, but from the 'unique circumstances' in which the state was incorporated into the Indian Union, as aspect we shall explore in the next chapter. Integration of Nagaland into the Indian Union was a similar case. In the case of Arunachal Pradesh, Himachal, and Uttarakhand, the circumstances of according them the special category status were quite different. While the need to maintain the integrity of the nation by accommodating different ethno-cultural identities of the tribal people led to the creation of several states in the northeast as special category states with certain special privileges during 1970s and 1980s, creation of Jharkhand, Uttaranchal (now Uttarakhand), and Chhattisgarh in 2000 was in response to the overriding requirements of development and governance (Mawdsley 2002: 34–54; Tillin 2008: 23–33). Between the 1970s and 2000, this was the paradigm shift that had happened in our political and economic landscape.

Federalism cannot have a fixed and rigid structure—it has to be a flexible, evolving, and dynamic process involving multi-layered governmental functioning, integrating, and accommodating within a larger entity various sub-units, some of which may display a fair degree of homogeneity while some others may exhibit extraordinary degrees of heterogeneity. Nowhere is this divergence more manifest than in the Northeast of the country which is home to more than 200 tribes with different languages, traditions, religions, and culture. Historically, as argued by Arora (1995: 80–85), in India, asymmetries have arisen due to the dual federalizing processes: (i) through decentralization of power within the provinces directly administered by the British and (ii) the accession of former princely states with a previously sovereign or quasi-sovereign existence to India at independence. In the northeast, creation of the hill states out of Assam during the 1970s was due to the former process, while in Tripura and J&K, it was due to the latter. Bhargava (2012: 245–75) argues that the complexity and size of India needed a deeper asymmetrical federalism. Though the Indian Union was inclusive enough to recognize the differences between communities, it 'fell short of grasping the precise form of recognition for which some societies increasingly yearned. This was a political as much as a conceptual failure.' The subsequent failure of the Indian state to successfully integrate the states in the northeast and also J&K may rightly be attributed to Bhargava's argument: 'Instead of responding even more democratically to multi-layered difference, the Indian state, which had recognised difference pretty early, responded to it with force. Furthermore, it could not imagine that the organisational principle of different states could itself be very different. The crisis of border states in India must also be accounted in terms of this deeper conceptual failure.' The response of the Indian state to the assertion of individual nationalistic identities and the right to self-determination by different groups among the special category states have been dealt with at appropriate places in the subsequent chapters, which will vindicate the argument to a large extent that instead of recognizing and dealing with the 'multinational' character of these claims, the Indian state treated them as 'sub-national' and dismissed these merely as regional or cultural differences, relying exclusively on the use of coercive power and law and order machinery to resolve them (Hausing 2014: 95; quoting Bhargava) and in the process, further alienating their people from the Indian federation. Arora has quoted several scholars to point out that there is an academic consensus that 'sustained counter-insurgency strategies, epitomized by the Armed Forces (Special Powers)' Act, have failed to restore 'law and order' and have rather spawned 'militarized democracy' in the North-East' (Arora 2013: 134). Had the centre displayed little more pragmatism and tried to address the problems with a proper understanding of the demographic and ethnic issues arising from the questions of identity of various groups, much of the later conflicts in north-eastern region could have been avoided.

Bordoloi Committee and the Sixth Schedule

According to Hausing (2009), the issue of accommodating diverse tribal groups in the Northeast within India's larger federal framework has proceeded along two routes: (a) socio-cultural and political route and (b) economic and financial route. The first one is evident in the constitutional arrangements of Schedule V and VI and in the omnibus Article 371 discussed earlier. Schedule V deals with the administration and control of scheduled areas and tribes, while Schedule VI deals with special provisions for administration of tribal areas in Assam, Meghalaya, Tripura, and Mizoram. Under the Government of India Act 1935, the habitats of the tribes were administratively divided into 'partially excluded areas' and wholly 'excluded areas'[3]—excluded from normal administration mainly for the purpose of maintaining law and order. The areas notified as partially excluded areas under the 1935 Act were later declared as Schedule V areas and the wholly excluded areas mostly became Schedule VI areas under the Constitution.

No criteria were specified in the Constitution to bring in any area under these schedules, and as pointed out by the Scheduled Areas and Scheduled Tribes Commission 1961, under the chairmanship of Mr. U N Dhebar, law and order continued to remain the primary consideration for this purpose even after independence. However, over a period of time a specific set of criteria has evolved. These are: (i) preponderance of tribal population; (ii) compactness and reasonable size of the area; (iii) under-developed nature of the area, and (iv) marked disparity in economic standard of the people.[4] These criteria embodied the principles followed in declaring 'Excluded' and 'Partially-Excluded' Areas under the Government of India Act, 1935, recommendations of the Excluded and Partially Excluded Areas Sub Committee of Constituent Assembly (Bordoloi Committee) and the Scheduled Areas and Scheduled Tribes Commission. It can be recognized that some of these were also included in the set of criteria determined by the Planning Commission to accord the special category status to a state.

The Fifth Schedule, *inter alia*, provided for constitution of the Tribes Advisory Council with 20 members, of whom three-fourth should be the Scheduled Tribe members of the state legislature, to advice on such matters pertaining to the welfare and advancement of the Schedule Tribes as may be referred to them by the Governor who also has the power to direct, under Presidential assent, that a particular Act of the Parliament or of the State Legislature shall not apply to a Scheduled Area or to its parts, with exceptions as considered necessary. These powers are somewhat extraordinary, possible only within the ambit of an asymmetrical federal arrangement.

The Sixth Schedule had its origin in the Cabinet Mission of 1946 that had discussed the political status of the hill districts of Assam and suggested the constitution of an 'Advisory Committee on the Rights of Citizens, Minorities, Tribals and Excluded Areas', which was formed by the Constituent Assembly. The Advisory Committee appointed a sub-committee with Gopinath Bordoloi as its Chairman, which became known as the Bordoloi Committee. The Bordoloi Committee had made wide-ranging recommendations including the constitution of regional and autonomous district councils with specific powers to administer these areas, allocation of certain taxes, and financial powers to these councils and only tribal representation from these areas to the state legislature. The recommendations generated angry debates in the Constituent Assembly in 1949, with members from Assam, like Brajeshwar Prasad, warning that, 'To vest wide political powers into the hands of tribals is the surest method of inviting chaos, anarchy and disorder throughout the length and breadth of this country'; some, like Kuladhar Chaliha, even going a step ahead and pointing to the seeds of separatism inherent in this scheme: 'If you see the background of this Schedule you will find that the British mind is still there. There is the old separatist tendency and you want to keep them away from us. You will thus be creating a Tribalstan just as you have created a Pakistan. The ultimate result will be that you will create a Communistan.' But the scheme had the staunch support of Dr. B R Ambedkar, Chairman of the Drafting Committee for the Constitution, who strongly defended the rationality of having a separate order for the tribal people of Assam:

> I am speaking of Assam and other areas for the moment. The difference seems to be this. The tribal people in areas other than Assam are more or less Hinduised, more or less assimilated with the civilization and culture

> of the majority of the people in whose midst they live. With regard to the tribals in Assam that is not the case. Their roots are still in their own civilization and their own culture. They have not adopted, mainly or in a large part, either the modes or the manners of the Hindus who surround them. Their laws of inheritance, their laws of marriage, customs and so on are quite different from that of the Hindus. I think that is the main distinction which influenced us to have a different sort of scheme for Assam from the one we have provided for other territories.[5]

Ambedkar compared the situation of the tribals of Assam to those of the Red Indian in USA who 'by their laws and modes of living, their habits and manners of life were so distinct that it would be dangerous to bring them at one shot, so to say, within the range of the laws made by the white people for white persons and for the purpose of the white civilization.'[5] This was another example of *de jure* asymmetrical federalism enshrined in our Constitution. The Bordoloi Committee recommendations, adopted with some minor amendments, became the Sixth Schedule to the Constitution of India.

The Sixth Schedule envisaged Autonomous District Councils (ADCs), of which there are currently 16 in the Northeast. Apart from these, there are five autonomous councils in Assam and five ADCs in the 'hill areas' of Manipur created outside the ambit of the Sixth Schedule. The ADCs and the Regional Councils under the Sixth Schedule have powers to make laws in respect of areas under their jurisdiction, which cover allotment, occupation and use of land for agricultural and non-agricultural purposes, management of forest, control of jhuming or other forms of shifting cultivation, establishment of town councils or village councils, appointment of chiefs, their succession, inheritance of property, marriage, preservation social customs etc. The working of the Sixth Schedule will be discussed later, but the purpose of the Constitution makers in creating this arrangement was not fulfilled to the desired extent. In the first place, it provided for a limited autonomy and self-rule and these too were much diluted later due to other inherent administrative incapacities and inefficiencies as well as financial weaknesses, since the councils were perpetually dependent on grants from the state and the union. Like Article 370 which also has been diluted by administrative machinations and lost much of its original purpose, the Sixth Schedule has also remained ineffective in addressing the concerns and aspirations of the tribals, which in the first place had led to demands for separate hill states in the region, culminating in carving out of some states out of the erstwhile composite state of Assam. It was just a case of not too much but too little asymmetric federalism. As Hausing (2014: 91) has pointed out, 'More than six decades of making ADCs work under the Sixth Schedule, however, leverages a tenuously negotiated sovereignty regime, since ADCs are *not* endowed with the plenary power to transfer land, although they can regulate on its actual occupation…The powers of ADCs can also be clipped by the Governor who wields the Damocles' Sword to dissolve or suspend ADCs on the advice of the Council of Ministers of the State, which is normally controlled by the majority community against whom the tribals are sought to be protected. Yet, the Sixth Schedule puts in place a useful 'system of cascading linkages joining together various units of the federal polity in a complex system of coordination.' It served a purpose, howsoever limited, to hold together these units in the Indian federation, as, by and large, the tribal communities in these states have learnt to accept the self-determination privileges envisaged in the Sixth Schedule.

Fifth Schedule and Tribal Land Alienation

Tribal land alienation has been one major cause of the conflicts and conflagrations within the northeastern region. Land is basic to the livelihood of tribals, but actually it is much more than mere livelihood for them. A tribal's culture and life, his identity—indeed his entire existence is deeply embedded in land. As Bhaumik (2010: 64) has observed, whenever his intimacy with the land is threatened, either due to manipulation by non-tribal outsiders or real estate sharks, or due to large government projects like dams, his world is shattered and he is alienated and angry, and his anger often finds expression in violence. Almost the entire northeast has seen this sinister cycle of alienation and violence repeat itself time and again, and will probably see this many more times till the questions of land and tribal identity which entwine and reinforce the 'mainstream sub-stream' divide are resolved and integrated within the broader context of federalism, nationalism, and economic development.

Identity politics of the region stems from the historical experiences of various communities living within this region and their traditions

(Fernandes 2012). Most tribes regulate their community and social affairs according to their customary laws which are integral to their culture and identity (Fernandes and Bharali 2008: 93). Traditionally, among the northeastern tribes, land has been community property (a Common Property Resource). As Fernandes and Bharali (2008) observed, community ownership is basic to intra- and inter-generational equity. 'When a community controls the resource, every family is able to use it according to its need since it cultivates land according to the number of mouths to feed. Community ethos ensured inter-generational equity' (Fernandes and Bharali 2008: 96).

Land ownership patterns in the region had started changing since colonial times as a result of revenue administration needs and laws like Assam Land and Revenue Regulation (AL&RR) of 1886 that had created the conditions for shift of ownership from the communal to the individual, since formal law recognizes only individual ownership. Taking a cue from AL&RR, other laws promulgated in the region even in the post-Independence period, like the Manipur Land Revenue and Land Reform Act, 1960 and the Tripura Land Reform and Land Revenue Act, 1960, which recognized individual ownership of land, further facilitated tribal land alienation in the name of development. Migration to the region from outside as well as increasing urbanization triggered by the changing nature of economy only accelerated the pace of land alienation. Government's developmental projects, especially dams, also needed large tracts of agricultural land, which pushed the process further. Marginalzation of tribes was the natural consequences of all these processes, which also seriously impacted their culture, values, and identity. Individual ownership altered not only the ingrained equity in the tribal societies, but also the existing power structure within them by leading to the formation elite classes in an otherwise equal and egalitarian society, once land became subject to control by few men instead of the whole community. Added to these processes was encroachment and occupation of tribal land by immigrants, mainly from across the borders, which the states were not in a position to control. The Fifth and Sixth Schedules had provisions for protecting tribal land, but they could do little to halt the changing patterns of ownership triggered by economic processes and driven by powerful interests.

Other than interfering in the tribal culture, land alienation issues have often engendered violent conflicts in the region. As Fernandes

(2012) has pointed out, 'imposition of an individual-based legal system on their community-centred customary law creates a disjunction between their legal and social realities. This ambiguity makes it easy for the immigrants to encroach on tribal and other CPRs without the consent of the communities whose sustenance it has been for centuries. 'This pitted the immigrants against the indigenous tribals who viewed them as usurpers of their land and destroyers of their livelihood. In a society that is predominantly dependent on land and agriculture for sustenance, land alienation naturally leads to shortages and increases competition for the remaining scarce resources. Bhaumik (2003: 83–5) has pointed out that in Tripura, the state had acquired tribal land to resettle the immigrants from the then East Pakistan, and by the 1970s, indigenous tribals had lost more than 60 per cent of their land to immigrants. The state then decided to build the Dumbur dam, ignoring the protests of tribals, displacing as many as 2,611 tribal families, and excluding 6,000 CPR-dependent families from the rehabilitation benefits. This was one of the causes behind the violent tribal insurgency that began in early 1970s in Tripura. Land alienation has caused violent ethnic conflicts in Bodoland and Karbi Anglong areas from time to time and the cycle of violence continues unabated, spilling the blood of hundreds of innocents, including children and women, even now. It had been at the root of Kuki-Naga conflict of the 1990s, Meitei-Naga conflict of 2001, Karbi-Kuki conflict in 2003 (Fernandes and Barbora 2008: 4), and many other violent conflicts.

It would thus seem that in the post-colonial times, the Indian nation-state had indeed failed to address the pastoral concerns of indigenous people while planning for development projects. The local tribes often seemed to be out of tune and out of place with the new socio-economic order and political milieu. With changes in modes of production and the structure of economic and social relationships and identities 'which were inscribed in stone for colonial administrators' needed to be forged anew. As Fernandes and Barbora (2008:12) have observed, 'It is true that in the space of a generation, traditional institutions and structures disappeared. Worlds ceased to exist. Yet, they are continuously being re-created.'

Localized resistance had developed within and outside the special category states, with people opposing hydroelectric power dams in Sikkim, Uttarakhand, Himachal Pradesh, Arunachal Pradesh, Assam,

Jharkhand, and in many other states. Notwithstanding the laws like Panchayat (Extension to Scheduled Areas) Act (PESA) 1996, Forest Rights Act 2006, or even the Fifth Schedule, attempts at alienation of lands of the indigenous people have continued, with consequent loss of their traditional means of livelihood, without equipping and empowering them with any alternative set of skills.

More than 80 per cent of all coal reserves and around 50 per cent of other minerals besides forest, water, and other natural resources lie in regions inhabited predominantly by tribal people. The tribal peoples who constituted eight per cent of the total population of India at 1991 census made up 55 per cent of the total displaced persons due to development projects up to 1990. According to the Ministry of Tribal Affairs, nearly 85 lakh tribals were displaced until 1990 on account of mega developmental projects like dams, mining, industries, and conservation of forests, etc.[6] And a lakh more had been displaced since then, after liberalization and privatization of economy. As Fernandes and Paranjpye (1997) pointed out, large dams have been the single most important factor behind such displacement, accounting for an estimated 75 per cent of all the displaced people, followed by mining and large industrial projects. Tribals, thus, had to pay a heavy price for development from which they themselves benefited very little, while the State acted like a predator.

Wherever development causes displacement, land becomes an emotive issue. Thus, sustained agitations were built around projects like Posco or Vedanta in Odisha or Koel Karo in Jharkhand. Provisions of the Fifth Schedule prohibit transfer of tribal lands, but after liberalization of economy, both the central and several state governments have undermined the Fifth Schedule provisions to allow industries to take over tribal and forest lands. In violation of the Fifth Schedule, private mining has been taking place in almost all the nine states within Fifth Schedule areas, most notably in Chhattisgarh, Jharkhand, MP and Odisha.

In the early nineties, Samata (also referred as Samatha), an advocacy and social-action group working on the rights of tribal communities in Andhra Pradesh took up the case of leasing of tribal lands to private mining industries by the government, reducing the tribals to work as wage labourers in mining operations in their own lands. The protracted legal battle ultimately led to a historic judgment by the Supreme Court in 1997 which restored the right of tribals to their own land. It permitted mining activities as long as it was undertaken by the government, or through 'the instrumentality of state or a cooperative society of the tribals' (Samatha v. State of Andhra Pradesh, 1997 8 SCC 191). All lands leased by the government or its agencies to private mining companies were rendered null and void by the judgment, which upheld the transfer of land to government or its instrumentalities in public interest but prohibited transfer of land in Scheduled Areas to non-tribals or corporates to prevent their exploitation in any form. The verdict reiterated the provisions of the 73rd Amendment Act of 1992 to prevent alienation of land in the scheduled areas and seeking to restore any unlawful alienation of land of scheduled tribes. It asserted that minerals should be exploited by tribals themselves, either individually or through cooperative societies.[7]

The judgement pleased neither the central nor the state government who appealed against it, but the appeal was firmly rejected by the Supreme Court in 2000. The centre then contemplated amending the Fifth Schedule itself. However, following widespread agitations, it was forced to shelve its plan to reverse the judgment in 2001.[8] The Right to Fair Compensation and Transparency in Land Acquisition, Rehabilitation and Resettlement Act, 2013, has now provided that 'no land shall be transferred by way of acquisition, in the Schedules Areas, in contravention of any law (including any order or judgment of a Court which has become final) relating to land transfer, prevailing in such Schedules Areas.'[9] However, the powerful nexus between politicians, bureaucrats, lobbies of multinational and domestic private industries will always try to undermine the spirit of the Constitution and the court judgments, which calls for increased vigilance by all stakeholders.

Insufficient Asymmetrical Powers

No large society in the world is wholly integrated or wholly diversified. All societies fall somewhere in the wide spectrum between these two extremities. Similarly, all federal countries thrive on the basis of a compromise between union on the one hand and autonomy and independence of all constituent subunits on the other, combining 'the advantages of the large state—peace, order and general well-being—with those of the small state—the full development and autonomy of the individual citizen' (Edward Freeman cited in Burgess 2006: 13). However, in the case of northeast, there was neither peace, nor an empowering autonomy of the states in this region, despite the *de jure* asymmetrical powers given to them through Article 371 and Schedule VI. The policy and interventions of the central government were largely responsible for this, though the failure of the constitutional mechanism to accord them a higher level of asymmetry cannot also be ignored. Smallness of their size or population should be of no consequence; what matters in a federation is the degree of differentiation in terms of culture or identity or economic backwardness and the federation's ability to accommodate the diverse interests and identities of different groups. Tillin's view that these states, being 'peripheral units' were relatively inconsequential in the larger federal set-up of the Indian Union does not hold good as an argument. First, due to its strategic location along international borders, India's northeast could no longer be treated as peripheral. Besides, the *du jure* asymmetry and their special category status were, in fact, meant to address their incapacities and differences and bring them from the periphery into the core of mainstream India. If there was a failure to do this, it was because of subsequent policies and insufficient understanding by the Indian political system of the problems of the region and aspirations of their people. The spark that ignited the flames of insurgency that would later engulf and singe almost the entire region were born in the insufficient asymmetrical powers given to these states, as many scholars have argued.

Sanjib Baruah (1999) pointed out that central policy towards the border region was more dictated by national security interests than a rational understanding of the problems of this region. This has resulted in proliferation of economically unviable 'mini-states' within the region which have fulfilled the tribal aspirations for self-rule but resulted in these states becoming perpetually dependent on central grants for their economic sustenance and hence vulnerable to direct and constant central interference in their affairs (Baruah 2003a: 915–39; Sachdeva 2000a: 60–1). As we shall see later, without liberal financial support from the centre, most of these states would have been embroiled in perpetual turmoil as they had no means of survival on their own resources. Such support without a concomitant obligation on the part of the states to effect visible improvements in the physical and social infrastructure and deliver on performance within an accountability structure has spawned a culture of unbridled corruption in the entire region and led to colossal leakages of public funds to the unholy nexus of politician-contractor-businessmen trinity, but has not advanced the cause of growth and development in the region. As a result, despite continued inflow of massive central funds, the region still languishes in backwardness with practically no industry, and lag far behind the rest of the country in terms of infrastructure and growth, though the living standards of people have improved over the years. Rather than breaking the core-periphery barrier and inculcating among the people of this region a strong sense of belongingness to the larger federation, the short-sighted policies of the centre have only succeeded in strengthening the identity mindset, leading to their further isolation from the rest of the country. As Sachdeva (2000b) had argued, the 'inappropriate economic policy framework' has created 'an unbalanced and unsustainable economy' in the region. The image of the state as a 'development-giver' has produced all-round dependency, making these states demand central funds as their right instead of being forced to address their own inefficiencies. Such 'cosmetic federalism' hardly serves the purpose of real empowerment and integration. As Arora has rightly pointed out (2013: 137), it has 'resulted in the reinvention of the traditional dependency relationship as states clamour for patronage under various schemes funded by a resurgent economy'.

Weiner (1978) and Baruah (1999) argued that non-Assamese minorities were alienated due to the lack of sufficient constitutional asymmetry in Assam that could not prevent the migration of people from outside in the absence of enabling constitutional provisions. Unrestrained migration naturally led to an altered demographic profile of the state, with consequent impact on jobs and livelihood for indigenous people. There were similar failures of the Indian state elsewhere, for example in Nagaland, where, instead of trying to negotiate a shared sovereignty through conferring more asymmetric powers, the Indian state took a rigid stand, willing to concede only a 'sub-State autonomy under the Sixth Schedule'. All these had repercussions not only in the fragmentation of the region into a number of unviable smaller entities, but also in breeding resentment and discontent among various groups that escalated into secessionist demands, which were fuelled by the continued economic backwardness and absence of any visible development. The miasma of despair and denial experienced by the people of this region would eventually excite a conflagration that enveloped the entire region in an unceasing spiral of disorder, violence, and instability, seriously hindering any further prospect of growth and progress. This also completely alienated the non-tribal population of the region and reduced them to the status of second-class citizens. The conundrum still continues, and some out-of-box solution may be helpful to resolve it, like what Baruah (2003b) suggested by introducing a system of '*de facto* two-tiered citizenship'—one of the federation and another of the state that would not discriminate between tribals and non-tribals—an arrangement not unknown in other federal systems. As Baruah (2003b) rightly says, 'The time has come to consider ways of breaking away from the ethnic discourse of the existing protective discrimination regime that, in effect, involves the state forever categorising groups of people in ethnic terms and making descendants of immigrants into perpetual outsiders.' If this solution seems impracticable in the current politico-economic discourses in India, we need to think about other radical alternatives people might not object to.

Example of Other Countries

Let us briefly discuss how other countries have attempted to deal with similar 'nationalist' and 'sub-nationalist' claims within their own territories. The oft-quoted examples are of Belgium, Canada, Spain, Italy, and Switzerland. For the sake of brevity, we shall restrict our discussion only to the essential asymmetrical features in Belgium, Canada, and Spain. To put things in the proper perspective, as Moreno and Colino (2010a: 8–10) point out, of the 65 countries in the world that exhibit substantial diversity, i.e., where ethno-cultural, linguistic, or religious minorities account for more than five per cent of population, only 15 have federal systems; of these again, there are only nine countries where the minorities are non-territorially concentrated. Countries have devised different institutional arrangements to deal with their own configurations of diversities for their integration and accommodation—through legal, political, and constitutional processes, political participation, fiscal federalism, or other institutional means and consociational arrangements to deal with the multiple divergences arising from economic disparity, migration, religion, language, culture, race, or ethno-national identities.

Belgium

Belgium is a small country in Western Europe inhabited by little over ten million people. Fifty-eight per cent of its population are Dutch speakers who live in the northern part of the country in the Flemish Region (Flanders). About 32 per cent are French-speakers who live in Wallon Region (Wallonia) in the south. There is also the Brussels capital region which is located just inside the Flemish boundary with Wallonia, where about 10 per cent Belgians live. There is a tiny population of about 72,000 German-speaking Belgians living inside Wallonia in the south-eastern part of the country. Belgium has to deal with a complex setting of linguistic, cultural, political, economic, and religious divides, made more complex by the absence of national political parties. But it is the linguistic divide that has shaped the Belgian federalism and public policies in the country, which is described as a 'consociational democracy' (Delmartino, Hugues and Drooghenbroeck 2010: 48–51). As Burgess (2006: 115) points out, these policies are a 'judicious combination of constitutional, legal and political procedures, mechanisms and devices that furnish a battery of checks and balances which guarantee respect for the integrity of entrenched cultural identities and protect minority rights' that has evolved into the peculiar institutional arrangements imparting a unique character to the Belgian federation.

Though territorially, Belgium is divided into three regions, linguistically it is divided into three communities: Dutch, French, and German, as seen above. Each of the regions and communities has its own parliament and executive, with their constitutionally-assigned powers. But since the Dutch-speaking community and the northern Flemish region overlap substantially, the institutions have merged in this region and there is only one Flemish Government and Parliament. But the French Community has no authority over the minority of French-speakers inhabiting the Flemish region and the Flemish community has no say over the still smaller minority of Dutch-speakers inhabiting the Walloon region. As Swenden (2003) observed,

> In sum, the frequently made assumption that Belgium is a major example of asymmetric federalism primarily pertains to the incomplete congruence between Regional and Community borders: Brussels is a Region but not a Community, and the German-speakers have been recognised as a Community but not as a Region. However, unlike in Spain or the

> United Kingdom, the competences which have been assigned to each of the Regions or each of the Communities are almost identical. For example, although the German-speaking Community is almost hundred times smaller than the Flemish Community, both Communities share similar powers in educational or cultural policies. (Swenden 2003: 7)

The executive and legislative powers are also divided evenly among the three regions and communities. The federal parliament is bicameral, comprising the Chamber of Representatives and the Senate. The federal government has equal number of ministers from the Dutch and the French-speaking communities (excluding the Prime Minister) and must have a majority within both the linguistic groups in parliament. The Cabinet decides by consensus. Constitutional amendments which pertain to regional interests require not only a two-thirds majority in both houses of Parliament, but also a majority within both linguistic groups in each of the legislative chambers. A detailed set of regional competences, including the financing mechanisms of communities and regions is laid out in the 'special majority laws' which cannot be passed without two-third majorities within each of the linguistic groups in both parliamentary chambers (Swenden 2003: 5–11). Belgian party system is bipolar—structured along the two major linguistic groups. Both houses of parliament are divided into linguistic groups. The 71-member Senate has 41 members from the Dutch, 29 from the French, and 1 member from the German speaking communities. In the lower house, there are 150 representatives who get elected from the respective political parties through the method of proportional representation.[10] Thus there is no scope for over or under-representation by any linguistic group.

There is also substantial measure of 'intra-state federalism' exhibited in the institutional arrangement that has evolved in Belgium. Regions have a say in federal policymaking and can effectively block the federal government from enacting legislation that affect the interests of the minority French-speakers. Article 131 of the Constitution prohibits 'all forms of discrimination for ideological or philosophical reasons', for which communities are placed under the supervision of the federal legislative assemblies. There is a unique parliamentary 'alarm-bell procedure' that gives two-thirds of a linguistic group the right to temporarily suspend the adoption of certain language laws. The 'double majority' required to enact a law and this 'alarm-bell' procedure together provide sufficient guarantee for the protection of the rights of each community.

As Burgess (2006: 117) observes, 'The upshot of the 'complex ambiguity' that constitutes the Belgian federation can be crisply summarized: while "the logic of Belgian federalism is bipolar, several solutions designed to respond to different tensions are multipolar"'. Bipolarity thus exists in the Belgian federation along with multi-polarity through interactions between the federal, regional, and community governments, requiring a co-operation between all of them, or at least between two of them, for major policy decisions.

Canada

Unity and diversity are two sides of the same coin, as Gagnon and Simeon (2011) have remarked. This is exhibited by the Canadian federation, which like the Belgian federation, is unique in several respects. Canada is a large country spread over nearly 10 million sq. kms of area with a population of only 33 million (2008), divided into two major linguistic groups: 59 per cent of its citizens speak English while 23 per cent speak French, of whom 80 per cent live in Québec alone. It is a federal country characterized by the division between predominantly francophone Québec, 85 per cent of whose population are French-speakers, and the Rest of Canada (ROC). Canada is often described as a bi-national federation, with Québec seeking constitutional recognition 'as a distinct society or nation', or aspiring to become an independent country while retaining its 'economic and political association with Canada'. As observed by Gagnon and Simeon (2010: 110–11),

> Canadians have debated their differences—even the possibility that one constituent unit (Québec) might wish to secede from the country—in ways that are peaceful, civil, and respectful of democratic values……both Canadian law and historical political practice (conventions) have been generally based on the premise that unity is best achieved through the recognition and accommodation of difference rather than through its rejection or denial.

Political tension between the British and French immigrants into Canada was a historical legacy dating back to the eighteenth century, when French and British immigrants came together to settle in Canada. Québec (Lower Canada) became home to the largely Catholic French settlers, while the largely Protestant English settled in Ontario (Upper Canada). But the relationship between the two entities remained strained, and even in 1840, they were like 'two nations warring in the bosom of a single state' (Gagnon and Simeon 2010: 114) which ultimately led to their separation. But the declining British support and threat perception from an increasingly powerful United States forced them to come together again in 1867 in a confederation of 'equal partnership', with both having rights to their language and religion guaranteed by the Constitution Act of 1867. The Act recognized the 'unique character' of Québec, permitting the Québecers to practise their own civil law as distinguished from the common law system prevailing in the rest of Canada and strengthening it further by ensuring that at least three of the nine judges of Supreme Court came from Québec. The Canadian Constitution ensures that the Canadian Parliament is bilingual, that each province is sufficiently represented and that provincial autonomy is fully protected (Funk 2011: 23–4). According to a landmark Supreme Court Judgment in 1998, 'democracy, federalism, constitutionalism and the rule of law, and respect for minority rights were and must remain the guiding principles of the Canadian federation' (Gagnon and Simeon 2010: 111).

There had been consistent struggles between centralizing and decentralizing tendencies in Canadian society during the subsequent centuries, especially in the 1960s and 1970s, when Québec nationalist movement was intensified by the separatist and nationalist political party, Parti Québecois, that demanded independence for the Québec 'nation' with an association of equal partnership with the Rest of Canada. Ever since, the French-speaking Québec remained steadfast in its determination to retain exclusive control over its language, culture, and social life and would not allow any domination by a federal government, whose laws, by and large, prevail over nine of the ten English speaking provinces in Canada save Québec. Québec retains extensive authority over employment and immigration issues within its borders, issues that are prerogatives of the federal government in all other provinces. It follows its own plan, objectives, standards, and criteria in respect of healthcare, different from those in the other provinces covered by the federal scheme. It operates its own pension plan, while the other nine provinces are covered by the federal/provincial Canada Pension Plan. Such asymmetry naturally created tension between Québec and the rest of Canada which demanded more symmetry and feared that too much of asymmetry could 'lead to slippery slope, ending in secession'(Gagnon and Simeon 2010: 116). Much of the twentieth century has seen attempts by Québec to maximize its autonomy, and to limit incursion into what it considers 'its own spheres of exclusive jurisdiction'. Gagnon and Simeon (2010: 116) feel that, 'In good part, it is this consistent resistance to centralizing pressures that helps account for the decentralized character of the contemporary Canadian federation.' This decentralizing character is reinforced by the Canadian Charter of Rights and Freedoms of 1982, which *inter alia*, prescribes a procedure for amending the Constitution, but stipulates that an amendment would not be applicable to a province without the consent of its own legislature, and federal government will compensate the province to carry out its own programmes within its territory. There is also a so-called 'notwithstanding clause' which permits any provincial legislature, within a specified time frame, to supersede the Charter in matters involving fundamental freedoms, legal, and equality rights. Québec was the only province to exercise this right in 1988 (Funk 2011: 26–27).

But the asymmetry in Canadian federation actually goes much deeper than the issues of autonomy and rights, and addresses the fundamental question whether two distinct societies or nations can co-exist within a federation with an option to exit it at a time of their choosing. It was a question of whether Québec can be constitutionally recognized as a distinct society within Canada and has the right to secede. At the height of the separatist movement in 1995, in a provincial referendum allowed by the Canadian Constitution which was held to decide the question of secession, less than 1 per cent (about 50000) of votes separated a 'Yes'-vote from a 'No'-vote. It prompted the federal government to refer the matter to the Supreme Court, asking it whether Québec had the right to secede unilaterally under Canadian or international law. In a landmark judgment, the Court, while ruling that such a right did not exist under the Constitution, asserted that if Québec decides to secede on the basis of a 'clear question' and 'majority vote' then the other federal partners would have the constitutional obligation to 'negotiate a new pact', making Canada one of the few countries to recognize the right of secession by a constituent unit and rendering it, at least in theory, 'divisible'. In a subsequent development, through a simple motion in the House of Commons in 2006, the federal government recognized Québec as a distinct society and assured that it would not support any constitutional change without the support of Québec and other regions of Canada. It 'resolved that Québec, at least sociologically, constitutes a 'nation' within Canada' (Gagnon and Simeon 2010: 119).

Asymmetrical federalism is not a panacea for all conflicts, but it certainly prevents marginalization of communities within a federation. Canadians have so far failed to evolve a constitutional formula to resolve their differences, but it has not prevented them from holding together as a strong, multi-national, multi-cultural federation committed to the constitutional principles of federalism, democracy, rule of law, and respect for minority rights. As Gagnon and Simeon (2010: 114) observe, 'The debate within Québec is not about whether Québec is a nation, but whether that nation can best be preserved and developed within Canada or as an independent country.' Asymmetrical federation has certainly helped in diffusing tension to the extent that majority of Québecers retain strong and positive attachments to Canada; Québec has provided prime ministers to the nation during most of the post-1968 period. Canadian experiment is an example of a fine balance between unity and diversity, symmetry and asymmetry, and of peaceful and democratic management of multiple diversities through negotiation, accommodation, and renegotiation.

Spain

Complex societies that display remarkable diversities are often the products of their complex histories. Spain is a multinational state—a 'nation of nations' or to some, a 'plurinational state' with a long and complex history, unlike Canada. Spain which is often described as 'a federation all but in name' was a dictatorship under General Francisco Franco till his death in 1975; in 1978 when its present Constitution came into force, Spain became an Autonomic State—*Estado de las Autonomias*—comprising 17 Autonomous Communities (AC) through an extensive asymmetric decentralization of 'competences'—i.e., powers and responsibilities. It was based on the concept of a 'sub-state *nacionalidade*' evolved as a result of 'historical interpretations and identity politics' (Moreno and Colino 2010b: 289–91). As Agranoff (1999: 96) observed, 'The constitutional design in the post-Franco period (1975–1978) legally constructed shared rule by creating autonomy, largely to gain the support of the historically and ethnically nationalistic territories.'

During its long history, Spain which has been a dominant colonial power has experimented with republicanism, dictatorship, democracy and had to contend with anarchy, violence, civil war, and periods of prolonged political instability. It has a multilingual population which is widely divergent—economically, territorially, demographically, ethnically as well as culturally. A strong Castilian majority exists with a number of minority nationalities—Catalonia, Galicia, and the Basque Country—each with its distinctive history, culture, and language. The four largest ACs—Andulasia, Catalonia, Madrid, and Valencia—share among themselves about 58 per cent of the national population of 46 million, and nearly 60 per cent of Spain's GDP. Catalonia and the Basque Country, regions that have histories dating back to several centuries regard themselves more as 'historical nations', and demand recognition as such in the international fora (Funk 2011: 40–2). In many ways the special category states of India resemble the Basque Country which is similarly isolated in the Pyrenees Mountains, and is inaccessible with limited economic potential—this seclusion had marginalized them to resist assimilation into the Spanish mainstream and Christianity for a long time (Ivanov 2011).

The 1978 Constitution, while asserting the 'indissoluble unity of the Spanish nation', recognizes multiple nationalities and their right to self-govern themselves. Article 143 of the Constitution guarantees the fundamental right of ACs to autonomy and Article 151 outlines the procedures for implementation of this right. Self-governance of ACs and their representation in the central institutions of the country are guaranteed in constitution which lays down two major routes to regional autonomy through Statutes of Autonomy—'a kind of constitution by itself in stipulating the name, organization, division of powers and rights in every AC' (Ivanov 2011). First is a 'fast track route' (Article 151) for 'historic regions' that already have their Statutes of Autonomy passed by a regional referendum and approved by the Constitutional Committee of the Congress; the Basque Country, Catalonia, and Galicia, deemed 'nationalities with a historic past' became ACs through this route. The second is a 'slow track route' (Article 143) applicable to other regions 'with common historic, cultural and economic characteristics, insular territories and provinces with a historic regional status'; they need five years to exercise their right to self-governance after their statutes have been approved by all provincial councils and two-thirds of all municipal councils. The Constitution also prescribes some 'exceptional' routes that allow regions without any recognized historic past claim full autonomy through a somewhat complex procedure followed by a referendum. Andulasia, the largest and the most populous province, managed its autonomy through this exceptional route in 1981, and caught up with the fast track 'historic regions'. Constitution also has the provision to expand regional powers, making use of which Valencia gained more autonomy than the three 'historic regions' in 1982. Navarra was given the status through a Parliamentary law, recognizing it as a community with historical rights, or, *'fueros'* in 1983 (Swenden 2006, 64).[11]

The procedure defined in Article 151 requires a majority of the population in a region to assert their right to be called an 'Autonomous Community' through a referendum, after which the regional assembly drafts the provisions of the Statute that is negotiated in the Constitutional Commission involving the national legislature and the regional assembly, followed by another regional referendum and final ratification by both chambers of the legislative. Re-affirmation at the regional level at multiple points and involvement of the state not only imparts legitimacy to the Statute, but also eliminates the threats 'that ACs were designed to combat in the first place—separatism and political extremism' (Ivanov 2011).

A homogenous standard is applied to governance in all 17 ACs: each AC has a legislative assembly, elected directly through proportional representation; the Government Council is headed by a President with legislative and executive powers and each AC has a Supreme Court of Justice under the jurisdiction of Spain's Supreme Court. Castilian is the official language, but Article 3 of the Constitution recognizes the existence of, and accords co-official status to, other Spanish languages in their respective Statutes through which five languages have official status, besides Castilian. However, as regards financial autonomy, two ACs, Navarre and the Basque Country, which are recognized *'fueros'*, have additional competencies not enjoyed by the other ACs—they can collect some of the state taxes like income tax and pay to the state for the services they receive from it, while the other communities follow a uniform tax regime based on collection by the state and their redistribution and devolution to the Communities (Funk 2011: 48).

Distributing legislative competences between the centre and the ACs is rather complicated and ambiguous. According to Swenden (2006:

55), 'Such complexity stems in part from the lack of agreement on where the Spanish state should be heading: a federal, a regionalized or unitary decentralized state?' The Spanish constitution lays down separate lists of competences for the centre (Constitution uses the word State) and the regions (ACs), much like the Seventh Schedule of the Indian Constitution. Article 149 lists 32 areas under exclusive legislative competence of the State. Matters not falling within the jurisdiction of the State belong to the regions by virtue of their specific statutes. Further, each region also has a 'Statute of Autonomy' that must contain, 'the competences assumed within the framework of the Constitution and the bases for the transfer of the corresponding services to them' (Article 147). Article 148 lists 22 subject areas of competence in which the regions may assume responsibilities; these competences, *de facto*, are not exclusive to the regions but shared with the State, since framework legislation in these matters can be worked out by the State Parliament, making these concurrent legislative areas. But the most striking feature of the Constitution is that the regional list of competences as prescribed in Article 148 is not static; it can be expanded by amendment of the regional Statutes which of course is a complex process, involving the consent of the State and regional legislatures as well as majority of the concerned regional electorates; regions can even encroach upon 'exclusively central' competences of Article 149 (Swenden 2006: 55–6). This opens a road for bilateral negotiations between the State and the ACs, and some ACs may wrest more powers from the State than others. As Swenden (2006: 56) observes, 'By keeping the allocation of powers and responsibilities open to negotiation, the Spanish process of devolution contained a high degree of inbuilt flexibility. In this way a definitive settlement on the scope of regional autonomy was foreclosed and constitutional asymmetry was almost made inevitable.' This asymmetry arose not as a response to any majoritarian nationalism, but from a fragile central authority trying to bring together, and hold together, diverse nationalities which are in themselves powerful enough to demand additional competences needed to serve their respective interests. The conflicts and clashes of interests which are bound to arise from such an ambiguous arrangement are to be addressed by the Spanish Constitutional Court.

The high degree of *de jure* asymmetry was subsequently sought to be reduced and more symmetry brought in through the so-called policy of '*cafe para todos*'—coffee for everyone instead of 'champagne for the *nacionalidades*', through two agreements. The first one called LOAPA (Law for the Harmonisation of Autonomous Process) was signed between the State and the major national parties (UCD and PSOE), in 1981 challenging the preferential status of some ACs even though these were ratified earlier, which naturally brought these ACs, especially Catalan and the Basque Country, into conflict with the state (Börzel 2002: 95). The Constitutional Court finally nullified a large number of its provisions as unconstitutional reinforcing the autonomy of the ACs, but the agreement still managed to bring in more uniformity and symmetry in the process. A second agreement, *Pacto Autonomico*, was signed in 1992 by the State with the two largest national parties (PP and PSOE) for removing the asymmetry between the fast-track and slow-track ACs, by equalization of their competences through an Organic Law that was passed in December 1992 and followed by necessary reforms of the Statutes of the disadvantaged ACs. This allowed major competences in education, health and some social services to be transferred to them. The progressive transfer of competences to the ACs enabled the Spanish system to reduce the extensive asymmetry and to introduce substantial symmetry in the original constitutional arrangement. Demands for renegotiation of the Statutes for greater autonomy were subsequently raised by the Basque Country and Catalonia, inspired by their nationalistic movements. The extremist and separatist group called ETA in the Basque Country has been seeking total independence.

Spanish Constitution does not recognize the right of self-determination by Spain's nationalities or regions. However, both Basque and Catalan Parliaments have already voted for recognition of the right to self-determination for their ACs. Permitting referendum is the exclusive prerogative of the Spanish Parliament and hence a referendum by an AC would be invalid without its consent. In June 2008, the Basque Parliament passed a law for conducting a referendum, which was contested by the Central Government before the Constitutional Court which confirmed the unconstitutionality of this law. The Basque government consequently abandoned the idea of holding this referendum (Moreno and Colino 2010b: 306).

While the Basque Country wanted to be 'a free state associated with Spain'—and wanted to increase its autonomy, a demand that was rejected by the Spanish Congress in 2004, Catalonia demanded recognition as a nation and higher levels of competences, most of which demands met with overwhelming approval of the Congress in 2006. However, Spain's Constitutional Court ruled in 2010 that parts of Catalonia's revamped statute of autonomy, approved in a popular referendum in 2006, were unconstitutional; it also did not recognize Catalonia as a nation—a ruling that fired up nationalist sentiments in Catalonia demanding independence from Spain.[12]

Spain probably has to find a new way to negotiate and restructure itself to accommodate its multinationality. The constraints are the inadequacy of the existing 'integrating and co-ordinating mechanisms' as well the effect of past confrontations and political violence, particularly in the Basque Country (Moreno and Colino 2010b: 314).

If the foundation of belief of an autonomous society is threatened, it may unravel the federation, just as 'an overabundant use of asymmetrical federalism' may result in secession. A fine-tuning of balance is needed for stability and solidarity of the federation, an important lesson we have to learn in the Indian context of special category states. Cultural norms and identities cannot be ignored in any federation to the disadvantage of the minorities. As the examples in Belgium, Canada, and Spain show, the highly asymmetrical systems have not resulted in disintegration of the federation or degenerated in the kind of violence and instability we have witnessed in India; they have rather cemented the edifice of democracy and rule of law in these countries. In the northeast, the inadequacy of the existing constitutional arrangements may have fostered secessionist sentiments. Multiple identities are natural in large and complex societies, as in these countries. The essence of a cohesive federation is to capture the complexity of society as a whole, to integrate unity with diversity while allowing distinct cultural identities to flourish, and to provide an inbuilt mechanism to deal with the tension and conflicts which are parts of the natural order of things in every society. Only in doing so, a common identity is forged which does not subsume the individual identities of the constituent units, but helps them blossom further. Diversities are also not fixed in time but evolve continuously. As Burgess (2006: 156) observes, 'Federations emerge, then, because of the imperative to structure and institutionalise difference and diversity. Their genius lies in their capacity, via constitutional entrenchment, to accommodate and reconcile different forms of unity with different forms of diversity.'

Malaysia

Let us briefly focus on a federation closer to us—Malaysia, whose constitutional mechanism shows quite a few similarities to India's and which also exhibits a high degree of diversity. Malaysia is a union of 28.6 million people (2010) living in thirteen states: eleven in peninsular Malaysia and two in the northern part of Borneo—Sabah and Sarawak, separated by 640 kms from the peninsula by the South China Sea. Malay and other indigenous people, called *Bumiputeras* (Sons of the Soil), together constitute nearly 62 per cent of its population; among the rest, 23 per cent are Chinese and seven per cent are Indians, besides eight per cent non-citizen immigrants.[13] Islam is the official religion, though the constitution gives fundamental right to all citizens to profess, practice, and propagate (subject to legal proviso like restrictions on the distribution of religious materials, etc. in some areas) their own religion (Burgess 2006: 128). Muslims constitute just above 60 per cent of the population (2010) and Buddhists 19 per cent, Christians, Hindus and other religionists comprise the rest. Like India, as Burgess (2006: 125) observed, 'Malaysia has to be understood largely in terms of its overriding concern for order, stability and national unity in a society that can be described as multiethnic, multiracial, multilingual, multicultural and multinational.'

Malaysia was formed in 1963 by the merger of the independent Federation of Malaya and the formerly British colonies of Singapore, Sabah, and Sarawak. Singapore was a part of Malaysia until 1965, but the union was rocky from the beginning. The political and ethnic tensions between the ethnic Malays of Malaysia and the largely ethnic Chinese population of Singapore caused several racial riots. These tensions and differences over economic policies ultimately led to the secession of Singapore from the federation in 1965 and its emergence as an independent sovereign country under Lee Kuan Yew, after the Malaysian Parliament voted 126–0 to expel it from the federation (Bhal 2008).

Burgess (2006: 126–8) identifies three major ethnic-social cleavages and political conflicts inherent in the Malaysian society: between the *Bumiputeras* and non-Malays largely based in peninsular Malaysia, between fundamental Islamists and moderate Muslims and also among the *Bumiputeras*—between Muslims based largely in the peninsula and non-Muslim natives of Sarawak and Sabah. The communal nature of these conflicts has close parallels in India. Malaysia addresses these conflicts by granting significant autonomy to Malays and indigenous peoples of Sabah and Sarawak, much in excess of the autonomy exercised by the other eleven states. The Constitution of Malaysia, while guaranteeing that 'there shall be no discrimination against citizens on the ground only of religion, race, descent, place of birth or gender in any law' (Article 8), provides for positive discrimination by safeguarding 'the special position of the Malays and natives of any of the States of Sabah and Sarawak and the legitimate interests of other communities'(Article 153). It protects and promotes their interests in the four main areas of reservation: land, quotas for admission into certain sectors of federal public service, the issuing of licences and permits for the operation of certain businesses and the provision of scholarships and other forms of educational assistance. The Constitution made Malaya the 'national language' while providing for use of English and native languages in Sabah and Sarawak.

Malaysia is a highly centralized federation where powers are strongly concentrated in the central government rather than being evenly distributed between the centre and the states, much like in India. The Ninth Schedule of its Constitution enumerates the distribution of legislative powers and responsibilities between the federal and state governments, besides specifying the areas of concurrent jurisdiction. Taxation is almost an exclusive monopoly of the federal government, except in only a few relatively insignificant indirect taxes on land, mine, and forest where the Tenth Schedule gives the states some powers (Yeoh 2010). But Sabah and Sarawak are allowed to make laws for imposing taxes under Article 89; they are also exempted from the provisions of Article 76 that allows the federal government to encroach upon state subjects as enumerated in the State List. While the right to secede from the federation is denied, some constitutional safeguards (known as Twenty Points) for Sabah and Sarawak for their participation in the federation include the following (Huat and Chin 2011: 217):

- Islam's status as the official religion is not applicable to Sarawak and Sabah.
- Immigration control is vested in the state governments of Sabah and Sarawak.

- No specific safeguard granted under the Twenty Points can be amended by the federal government without the concurrence of Sabah and Sarawak state governments.
- Sabah and Sarawak are also given special powers for raising revenues and receiving grants.

These special privileges have since generated enough tension in the federal-state relations in Malaysia that still remain to be resolved.

The Malay Federation gained independence from the British in 1957, and special privileges and rights of these communities emerged from its imperial legacy as they had enjoyed these rights also under the British administration. The Independent Constitutional Commission appointed in 1956 prior to the independence of the Federation of Malaya, while deciding to continue with these privileges, recommended that with the gradual integration of these communities into a common nationality, the need for these special preferences would gradually disappear, and, 'in due course the present preferences should be reduced and should ultimately cease so that there should then be no discrimination between races or communities'. Their Constitution finally rejected their stipulation of a time limit of fifteen years for this purpose, and made the Head of State (the King) 'responsible for activating a periodic review of any revised proposals' (Burgess 2006: 127).

Because of concentration of powers in the federal government, Malaysia is often seen as a 'minimalist federation'. For almost its entire existence, the federal as well as the provincial governments have been ruled by a single coalition, the Barisan Nasional (BN), dominated by a single political party, the United Malays National Organization (UMNO), much like India's Congress Party. Virtually, like India, Malaysian nation has been mostly controlled by a single party, the UMNO, for most of its existence until the 2008 elections, when the opposition wrested control in five of the 13 state legislatures for the first time in history. However, the inadequate *de jure* asymmetry in Malaysia has not helped the cause of 'moderating ethnic conflict', but has rather led to 'constant tension from UMNO's ethno-nationalism' (Huat and Chin 2011: 210). The political process that allowed a single party to dominate national policy for five decades led to further weakening of the spirit of federalism in this highly centralized nation. In the name of national security and ethno-religious harmony, BN started to dictate the pace and direction of development in the states. Local authority elections were abolished in the 1970s, allowing the ruling coalition to appoint councillors in the municipalities, town councils, and district councils and thereby to penetrate the third tier of government. States were arm-twisted whenever they dared to challenge the central prerogatives. Opposition leaders calling for greater autonomy for Sabah were detained without trial on the grounds of fomenting secession; even within the UMNO, dissenting voices were silenced (Loh 2008). In these, one can find some uncanny parallels with India. Burgess (2006: 138) points out that in both India and Malaysia, 'the priority of state security—of internal order and external threat—has shaped the structure of the federation. And it has been the overriding objective that has served in practice to enhance the growth of executive power over and above increasing concerns for liberal democratic constitutionalism.' The pretext of internal and external threats has often been used in India to unleash state terrorism, as during the emergency in 1975–77 and in many special category states, in the Northeast and Jammu & Kashmir, as we shall see later.

* * *

The cases of Sabah and Sarawak in many respects resemble the northeastern states in India—in their remoteness and geographical isolation, in their economic dependence, and in their cultural differences from the mainstream. While Malaysia incorporated protective provisions in their Constitution for these provinces, provisions which were much stronger than similar provisions in the Indian Constitution, these have proved inadequate in the Malaysian context, since, while ensuring preservation and sustenance of their ethno-cultural identities, they did not allow sufficient political autonomy to these provinces. Perhaps for us, there is a lesson to be learnt here. A constitutional mechanism can be successful only when accompanied by an empowering political process as well as an enabling economic process. In Malaysia's case, none of these processes were initiated with sufficient thrust and energy, and in the case of special category states in India too, the assured constitutional protection proved inadequate to address the genuine concerns of the people in the absence of sufficiently empowering, concomitant political and economic processes. In India's case the emergence of coalition governments at the centre and changed configurations of political power structure have eroded the centralized federalism and given the states more bargaining power, but the special category states were not in a position to use this increased power to their economic and political advantage is the absence of sufficient autonomy. The situation was made worse by increasing economic centralization, politics of convenience indulged in by the coalition partners and reckless economic indiscretion used to further the political interests of the ruling dispensations, subverting the true spirit of federalism and eroding the ability of intergovernmental institutions and mechanisms to bring in stability through rule-based systems.

In heterogeneous societies, like in the European countries we have discussed, the higher extent of diversities and differences determined the level of *de jure* asymmetry necessary to bring in equilibrium to dissipate discontent and thwart potential conflicts. All federal processes depend on the bargaining strengths of their constituent units, and necessarily generate various degrees of asymmetry depending on the degree of existing diversity. More accommodation does not necessarily mean weakening of the federation to the point of disintegration, but rather contributes to assimilation and stability within the democratic structure and within the limits defined by the rule of law. In a centralized federation like India, this stability can be reinforced only if the process is guided not by considerations of political expediency of a powerful centre, but by national interests determined by the legal and constitutional framework, howsoever asymmetrical that might be.

In a diversified federation where diversity does not remain limited only to the issues of culture and identity, but acquires a much more complex character in the presence of extreme economic disparities between its sub-units, their integration and assimilation into the federation becomes all the more difficult. For this, certain prerequisites are essential—existence of an effective legal and constitutional framework, devolution of adequate resources to disadvantaged units, and creation of enabling institutions to transform those resources into concrete development, in the absence of which these resources tend to get misused through vested interests that develop automatically. In the case of special category states, especially in the northeast and J&K, first, there was insufficient *de jure* asymmetry, which inadequacy was further exacerbated by short-sighted policies, unjustified use of raw state power, poor understanding, unwillingness for accommodation, and lack of faith in the sacrosanct principle of 'unity in diversity' that has always been a hallmark of Indian culture since ancient times. Second, as we have noted in the last chapter, a mechanism for financial devolution through higher plan assistance was indeed brought in which was subsequently subverted through the incursion of CSS that were not ideally suited for these states. Lastly, institutions to channelize these resources and oversee their use were either not created, or, created—like the North Eastern Council or the Ministry of Development of North Eastern Region (MDONER)—with limited structure and inadequate capabilities. The result was the protracted economic and political imbroglio from which most of these states are yet to emerge.

Notes

1. A separate provision for the state of Andhra Pradesh was created by the Constitution (Thirty Second Amendment) Act for Andhra Pradesh in 1973, inserting article 371D.
2. Article 370 will be discussed in details in the next chapter.
3. There were actually three categories of tribal habitat under the British, apart from 'excluded' and 'partially excluded' areas, there was also a third category called frontier areas. The excluded areas were the Naga hills, the Lushai hills, and the North Cachar hills. The Garo Hills, the Mikir Hills, and Khasi and Jaintia Hills other than the Shillong Municipality and Cantonment were partially excluded areas. The frontier areas included Balipara, Sadiya, and Lakhimpur Tracts.
4. Ministry of Tribal Affairs, Govt. of India, http://tribal.nic.in/WriteReadData/CMS/Documents/ 201212270546272500000File1489.pdf accessed 1 June 2014.
5. Constituent Assembly Debates, *Official Report*, Vol. 9 (New Delhi: Lok Sabha Secretariat, 1949), September 6, 1949, http://164.100.47.132/LssNew/constituent/vol9p11.html, accessed 1 June 2014.
6. Available at http://socialissuesindia.wordpress.com/2012/09/06/the-samatha-judgment-and-the-fifth-schedule-of-the-constitutionaccessed 6 January 2015.
7. Available at http://www.samataindia.org.in/documents/SAMATA_EDIT1.PDF, accessed 29 December 2014.
8. Available at http://www.samataindia.org.in/documents/SAMATA_EDIT1.PDF, accessed 29 December 2014
9. Proviso under Section 2(2) of the Act.

10. Articles 43, 63, and 67 of Belgian Constitution.

11. Articles 137–151 of Constitution of Spain.

12. Available at http://www.nationalia.info/en/news/764, also AFP Report dated 10 June 2014.

13. Available at http://www.statistics.gov.my/portal/images/stories/files/LatestReleases/population/RingkasanPenemuan-SummaryFindings_2010-2040.pdf accessed 22 June 2014.

2 Assam, Nagaland, and Jammu & Kashmir

The First Special Category States

As discussed in the beginning, a state is accorded the 'special category status' by the National Developmental Council (NDC) at the behest of the Planning Commission. After approval by the NDC, the Finance Ministry processes the necessary grants, etc. to the concerned state. In this and the next few chapters, we shall explore the socio-economic conditions prevailing at each of the special category states before they were accorded this status, and try to identify the infirmities and handicaps arising from their history since developments occur within the context created and shaped by history. We shall also explore how their socio-economic circumstances have transformed over the last few decades after getting the benefits accruing from their special category status. Finally, we shall see where these states stand today in comparison to each other and also in relation to the country as a whole in terms of their socio-economic achievements.

At Independence, the northeastern region of India comprised the state of Assam, the princely states of Manipur and Tripura, as well as the excluded areas of Lushai Hills (present day Mizoram) and North East Frontier Tract (present day Arunachal Pradesh). Nagaland was formed in 1963 by carving the Naga Hills district out of Assam. Others became Union Territories first before attaining full statehood. In this chapter, we undertake an examination of the first three special category states, viz., Assam, Nagaland, and Jammu & Kashmir.

Assam—Legacy of Obstacles Created by History[1]

Assam is one of the oldest regions in India and home to ancient civilizations contemporaneous to the times of the Vedas, Ramayana, and Mahabharata. Its existence dates back to pre-historical times, to the Paleolithic period of which several sites have been discovered in the region. Being old, the region has attracted people from all over and was an experimental melting pot of humanity—the Indo-Aryan, Austro-Asiatic, and Tibeto-Burman cultures mingled here since ancient times, giving rise to a composite and largely homogeneous culture of the Ahoms who ruled this region for six centuries before the arrival of the British who annexed the state into the British Empire in India in 1826. Even after Independence it had continued to attract people from outside, from neighbouring West Bengal, Bihar, Bangladesh, and Myanmar.

Assam had essentially a riverine civilization flourishing all around the mighty Brahmaputra which meanders across the state, unparalleled in natural beauty. This beauty, many surmise, had given the state its name of Assam (from Asom or unrivalled); others hold that the name had come from the 'Ahom' rulers of the Tai-Mongoloid race who had ruled over most of the Brahmaputra valley for six centuries before the advent of the British.

The recorded history of Assam, or Kamrupa as it was called then, began in the fourth century AD with the Barman dynasty which attained the zenith of its glory in the seventh century AD during the rule of Bhaskar Barman, who ruled at the same time that Harsha Vardhan was reigning in north India. A lively account of his kingdom and its people is left by none other than the famous Chinese pilgrim Xuangxang who had visited the court of Bhaskar Barman in 640 AD. After twelfth century AD, the Kamrupa kingdom disintegrated into a number of smaller and independent kingdoms. Around the same time, the Ahoms, a Tai-Mongoloid group, migrated and settled in Assam from the present-day Yunan Province of China. Gradually, combining military might with a policy of conciliation and assimilation, Ahoms extended and consolidated their rule over the entire Brahmaputra valley. From the sixteenth century, however, Mughals started to make inroads into Ahom territory. But in 1671, in a fierce battle at Saraighat near Guwahati, Mughals were inflicted a crushing defeat by the Ahoms, and from then on, the

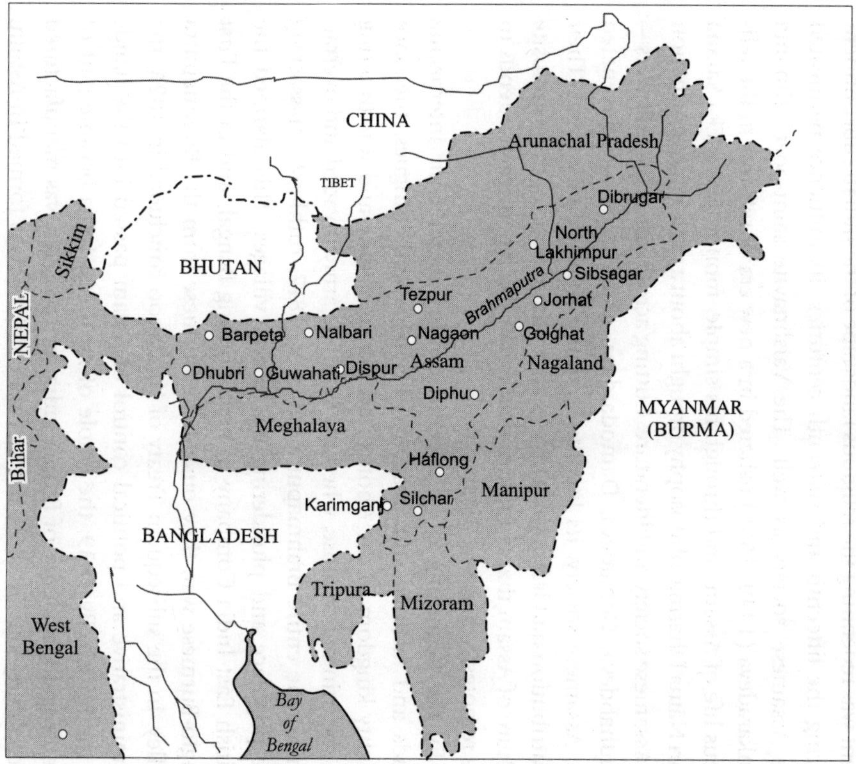

Map 2.1 Map of Assam

Manas river became the boundary between the Ahom and Mughal territories, an arrangement that was to continue until the British conquest of Assam in 1826.

Over the centuries, the rich natural resources of Assam had attracted many migrant groups from neighbouring China, Myanmar, and other countries in South-East Asia. Culturally, before the sixteenth century, Tantrik practices had flourished in Assam but when the Bhakti movement was redefining the religious landscape of the Indian subcontinent during the fifteenth and sixteenth centuries, its influence permeated the Assamese society as well. The Vaishnavite saint-poet Srimanta Sankaradeva (1449–1568) ushered in a new era of reforms in the religious life of Assam, and through his simple, monotheistic 'Eka Sarana Hari Nāma Dharma' philosophy brought about a radical transformation in Assamese society and literature. Cutting across castes, his followers—Madhabdeva, Gopaldeva, Damodardeva, and Harideva—rejuvenated the Assamese society, its literature, culture, and life in general. Their contribution had left an indelible mark in the mosaic of the composite culture of Assam that continues even today and its outreach extends to the remotest villages of Assam.

By the beginning of nineteenth century, beset with internecine feuds and factions and weakened by fights and intrigues, the once mighty kingdom of the Ahoms had lost its vitality and was tottering on the brink of collapse, when the Burmese army invaded and overran almost the entire Brahmaputra Valley in 1817, ruthlessly massacring the populace and plundering towns and villages. This alarmed the British East India Company in neighbouring Bengal, and in the First Anglo-Burmese war, they ousted the Burmese from the Brahmaputra Valley. In the subsequent Treaty of Yandaboo concluded in 1826, the administrative and political control of Assam passed into the hands of the British. By 1839, the whole of northeast India became part of the Bengal Presidency of British India. In 1837, tea was manufactured successfully and in 1839, the first tea company was formed in Assam. Ahom administrative structure was dismantled, Bengali was made the official language and instead of the local people, Bengali Hindus were recruited for various posts. Contract labourers were brought from Bihar, Orissa, and Andhra Pradesh. 'By the turn of the century, one and a half million of such coolies were employed on 700 plantations producing 145 million pounds of tea annually.'[2] The demographic patterns gradually started changing and outsiders began to occupy important positions, alienating the locals.

Before the advent of the British, for most part of its history, Assam was an independent kingdom. The freedom loving people of Assam could never embrace the British rule and there were many rebellions and revolts against it. In 1857, when the whole country rose in revolt against the British, Assam was no exception, but the uprising in Assam was ruthlessly suppressed. In 1874, Assam was finally separated from Bengal, Sylhet district of East Bengal was added to it and Assam was made into a separate Chief Commissioner's province, with its capital in the beautiful hill town of Shillong. In 1825, oil was discovered at Digboi in upper Assam, but the commercial production of oil began in 1899 with the formation of the Assam Oil Company. With the taking over of the Assam Oil Company by Burma Oil Company in 1921, the petroleum production got a boost. With the growth of tea and oil industries, ancillary industries were also getting set up—timber, plywood, river, and railway transport and coal mining among them.

The British had set up tea, oil, and timber-based industries and also created the basic railway infrastructure in Assam, but could not win over the hearts of the Assamese people who continued to fight for freedom. Gopinath Bordoloi, Tarun Ram Phukan, Nabin Chandra Bordoloi, Ambikagiri Roychoudhury, Kuladhar Chaliha, and many others gave leadership to the national freedom struggle. Gandhiji visited Assam in 1912, and in that year, Assam was made into a separate province of the British empire of India. But that did little to quell the nationalistic spirit that was gaining momentum and Assam participated in the non-cooperation movement of 1919–20, Civil Disobedience Movement of 1930, and Quit India Movement in 1942. Probably to punish Assam for its intransigence and also for its own commercial interests, early in the twentieth century, the British had brought in and settled the predominantly Muslim farmers from the provinces of East Bengal and Nepalis into Assam. They were encouraged to colonize vast tracts of land in Assam for cultivation. Subsequently Marwaris and Sikhs brought in capital and trading. In the process, the demography of Assam was changing perceptibly, and the seeds for future conflicts and subsequent balkanization of the state into several smaller entities were being sown along with it in the fertile soil of Assam.

During the Second World War (WWII), Assam became a major theatre of action for the Allied forces. The Indian National Army of Netaji Subhas Chandra Bose reached within the boundary of British India before being driven away. The Battle of Nagaland and Manipur turned the scale in favour of the Allied forces and Assam emerged as a major supply corridor in the eastern theatre of WWII. The Stilwell road (named after General Joseph W. Stilwell) connecting Ledo, the easternmost railhead in Assam, with Kunming in China (Yunan province), covering a distance of 1079 miles was completed in record time, allowing for large-scale Allied troop movements through Assam; it would become the most important supply link for the Allied forces in China, bypassing mainland Burma (Myanmar) which was then under Japanese occupation. The arms and ammunitions left behind by the Japanese and the Allied Armies would also eventually find their way into the hands of the first generation of underground Naga separatists in the 1950s when Nagaland was still a district of Assam, giving birth to the intractable problem of insurgency in the Northeast, a problem that would continue to bleed the entire region for decades on end.

The British did precious little to improve infrastructure, communication, or transport within Assam to improve accessibility and to bring in industrial capital to the state, except when it served their strategic and commercial interests, as in the case of Stilwell Road. As a result, at the time of independence, though the per capita income in Assam was comparable to that of India, the state was among the poorest in India in terms of infrastructure, power, transport, and communication, industry and consequently in its capacity to generate employment. It was a rich land but without any scope to harness its richness. Floods ravaged the land every year, and ethnic and linguistic riots also took their tolls at regular intervals, tearing asunder the fragile social fabric of the multi-ethnic state. With the partition of the country and consequent loss of road and railway transit routes through erstwhile East Bengal, Assam's tale of woe would now really begin. As the state became geographically isolated and secluded from the rest of the country the traditional trade relations between Assam and the neighbouring countries suffered irrevocably. The partition also brought in millions of refugees from the erstwhile East Bengal, stoking the fire of hatred and ethnic conflict. In 1950, a massive earthquake—one among the 10 largest recorded earthquakes in history till that time—changed the topography of the region and altered the course of the Brahmaputra, bringing in untold misery and suffering to its people, besides claiming more than 1500 lives. This dealt a severe body blow to the fragile economy of the state from which it would never recover completely.

A decade later, the state would again have to bear the full brunt of the nation's war with China in 1962, when Chinese forces overran almost the entire upper Assam till Tezpur on the northern bank of Brahmaputra before withdrawing. After this, it would be very difficult to convince any prospective investor that Assam was a safe place for investment. The 1965 war with Pakistan sealed all the waterways through East Pakistan. 1971 saw the heightening of Assam's problems due to its geographical location: millions of East Pakistani people displaced by the liberation war that would create Bangladesh crossed the border and sought refuge in Assam and West Bengal; many stayed on and never went back. The presence of so many alien refugees in Assam sowed the seeds for future ethnic conflicts; side by side demands for reassertion of the 'pre-eminence of Assamese culture in the region' and improvement of 'employment opportunities for native Assamese' also grew. This in turn alienated the tribal districts in Assam which started demanding their own states, leading to progressive balkanization of Assam into smaller states to fulfil the aspirations of their tribal populations.

In 1947, undivided Assam was a diverse collection of a number of hill tribes, plain tribes, and non-tribal people mostly inhabiting the plains. As ethnic consciousness gradually grew among the different groups, demands for independent states started rising from many quarters. To appease them, central government went on conceding to their demands without considering the financial viability of these newly created small states. The tribal state of Nagaland was created in 1963. By the North-Eastern Assam Reorganisation Act 1971, Meghalaya was carved out of Assam in 1972 when Assam lost its British-era capital of Shillong to Meghalaya; in 1974, its capital was shifted to Guwahati.[3] Manipur was given full statehood in 1972. Tripura , a former princely state, also got full statehood in the same year. A new union territory (UT) of Mizoram was created in 1972, comprising the territories of Mizo Hills district and the hill tracts under the North East Frontier Agency (NEFA) were also constituted into a new UT in the same year, called Arunachal Pradesh. Both these became full-fledged states in 1987. These states, together with Sikkim that merged with India in

1975, would comprise the northeastern region of India. All these states would be accorded the special category status upon their creation.

From 1979 to 1985, Assam was again convulsed by an agitation led by the All Assam Students Union (AASU) against large scale infiltration by illegal immigrants from Bangladesh that was changing the demography of Assam, threatening its culture and economic relationship patterns within its society. The agitation was called off after the signing of the Assam Accord in 1985 with the Government of India, but not before perpetrating some of the worst instances of post-partition genocides in the country like the Nellie massacre of 18th February 1983 in 14 villages in the Nagaon district of central Assam, in which more than 2000 people, mostly Muslim women and children allegedly from Bangladesh, were brutally murdered. In fact, the Assam agitation also sowed the seeds for the sinister rise of ULFA in the 1980s, followed by violent movement in the Bodo areas of Karbi Anglong and North Cachar districts of Assam. These separatist, militant movements led by outfits that survived and thrived on violence and extortion, killings and genocides, fear and retribution, also stoked similar movements all over the northeastern region of India, making the entire region appear as a permanent trouble spot in the socio-political map of India. The destructive potential of these movements is still alive in parts of the region. These movements drove away whatever little capital was available within the state along with its indigenous talents, bringing the process of industrialization and development initiatives in the region to a grinding halt. Even the natural resources the state abounds in could not be harnessed efficiently during the turbulence created by the Assam agitation. However, despite occasional strikes by militant outfits in Bodo and some other areas, agitation and militancy are no longer major problems for the state.

Because of poor infrastructure and other bottlenecks the state inherited from its past history, governance has never been particularly strong in the state. There are so many invisible enemies: lack of development, income, opportunities and employment, natural calamities like the devastating floods that rage and ravage every year, insurgency and terrorism, ethnic clashes and violence, all of which have created an extremely depressing, despondent environment dominated by a sense of insecurity and hopelessness , turning a potentially prosperous state into one of the most impoverished, underdeveloped, and problem-ridden states of India. As the Planning Commission (2002) had observed,

> At the time of Independence, Assam was one of the richer states and its per capita income was 4 per cent above the national average. Today, Assam ranks among one of the poorest states of the country and its per capita income is less than 60 per cent of the national average. What is even more disturbing is that the gap between Assam and rest of the country in terms of per capita income has been widening continuously during the last fifty years and if the present trend continues, then by 2020 the per capita income of Assam will be only about 40 per cent of the national average.[4]

Multiple debilitating factors had plagued the economy of Assam for decades and are still doing so. Inadequacy of quality infrastructure has of course been the largest bottleneck inhibiting industrialization and higher growth through diversification of income-generating activities. The primary sector was the mainstay of its economy, but it was growing at a sluggish rate due to primitive methods of cultivation. The turbulence, discord and disharmony that the state had gone through was a combined effect of all these. As the Assam Human Development Report 2003 notes,

> Development, or the lack of it, has contributed to the disquiet that has characterised much of the North East for several decades. The region continues to be marked by low agricultural productivity, poor infrastructure, tenuous communications and nascent levels of industrial activity. Conscious of its exceptional features (and of its strategic significance), the Centre has traditionally considered the North East region as deserving of singular treatment. There has also been recognition, in theory, of the fact that Government would need to play a special role in promoting development, creating infrastructure and stimulating economic activity.
>
> Despite these measures, there is evidence based on objective criteria to show that the gap between the North East and the rest of the country has widened. More importantly, the region continues to perceive itself as distant and distinct, and unable to participate in the benefits of an expanding, growing economy.[5]

Bordering six states of the northeastern region (NER) of India and two countries, Bangladesh and Myanmar, Assam today accounts for about 2.4 per cent of the country's geographical area. Its 31.17 million people (2011 Census) account for 2.58 per cent of the country's population, of which nearly 86 per cent live in the rural areas (*It was 92 per cent as per the Census Report of 1961*)—Assam, with its 26395 villages and less than 100 towns spread amongst its 27 districts, is, in fact, one of the most ruralized states in India. Density of population in Assam (397) is higher than that of India (382); but most of its population are concentrated in the fertile and green valleys of its two major rivers, the Brahmaputra and the Barak, and in the low-lying hill districts of Karbi Anglong and North Cachar Hills separating the two valleys.

Socio-Economic Landscape of Assam: 1969–2011

Between the years 1901 and 1971, Assam's population had increased by 4.44 times, while the country's population increased by only 2.30 times (Table 2.1). The decadal variation in population in Assam has always been higher than the country's, but after 1950, the rate of population growth hugely accelerated—one reason being the huge influx of illegal immigrants from Bangladesh. This was altering the demographic and income distribution patterns, and the State Government could do very little to prevent this. This ultimately led to the Assam agitation orchestrated by All Assam Students' Union (AASU) in the 1980s, which received overwhelming support of the Assamese people who had started feeling threatened in their own state. As density of population increased phenomenally due to uncontrolled immigration, land naturally came under pressure. In 1971, population density among the plains districts was eightfold compared to the hills districts. As the build-up of pressure on land started spilling over to the hills areas, people belonging to those areas also started demanding their own states.

Failing economic health of the state accompanied its changing demography. In 1960–61, Assam's per capita income of Rs 315 was higher than Rs 306 for all India; in 1970–71, it was only Rs 528 compared to India's average of Rs 637. The difference in per capita income has been widening ever since. NSDP growth rates in Assam have also almost always lagged behind those of India.[6]

Annexure 2.1 at the end of this chapter shows the progress of socio-economic indicators of Assam during the four decades since 1970–71, just after it had become a special category state. Though it had registered moderate achievements in terms of NSDP (at current prices) which grew at an average rate of 12.9 per cent annually during this

Table 2.1 Trends in Population: Assam and India

Year	Population (in thousands)		Percentage decadal variation		Population Density		
	Assam	India	Assam	India	Assam	Hill Districts	Plains Districts
1901	32,90	23,83,37	–	–			
1911	38,49	25,20,05	16.99	05.73	49.07	1.76	60.56
1921	46,37	25,12,39	20.47	00.30	59.12	1.89	73.00
1931	55,61	27,88,67	19.92	11.00	70.88	2.15	87.57
1941	66,94	31,85,39	20.37	14.23	85.35	8.68	103.97
1951	80,29	36,09,50	19.94	13.31	102.36	10.77	124.60
1961	1,08,37	43,90,72	34.97	21.64	138.16	18.21	167.28
1971	1,46,25	54,79,49	34.95	24.80	186.45	27.70	224.51
1981[7]	1,80,41	68,33,30	23.36	24.71	230.00	NA	NA
1991	2,24,14	84,64,22	24.24	23.87	285.75	53.13	342.23
2001	2,66,55	1,02,87,38	18.92	21.54	340.00	65.20	406.00

Source: Reports of the Census of India, various years.

period, the structure of its economy had not undergone much change till 1991. After economic reforms were started, NSDP growth accelerated, shares of services and manufacturing increased, and importance of the primary sector diminished somewhat, but the shift away from the agricultural sector did not lead to increased urbanization in the state which still remains almost as ruralized as it was four decades ago. Even at the turn of the century, more than half the working population of the state was employed in agriculture which contributed only 36 per cent to the state income, implying low wage rates and high underemployment. Agriculture in Assam is dependent mainly on tea and is heavily dependent upon rains—and lags behind the other parts of the country in modernization, irrigation, and mechanization; as a result, agricultural productivity is low.

Agriculture had also remained dependent on primitive practices leading to poor or negative growth and low productivity per worker—the yield per hectare was much less compared to national averages in respect of almost every produce except jute (Barua 1992: 27). Less than one fifth of the gross cropped area had access to irrigation even in 2009.

The special category status at least seems to have succeeded in containing rising poverty in the state. In 1973–74, more than half (51 per cent) of Assam's population were poor, but since then the poverty ratio has been improving. Most of the poor are concentrated in rural areas; urban poverty in Assam had decreased significantly after 1973–74. The urban poverty ratio (7.47 per cent) in 1999–2000 was also much lower than the national average of 23.62 per cent. The rural poverty ratio of 40 per cent in Assam in 1999—2000 was of course much higher than the national average of 27 per cent. The overall poverty ratio of 36 per cent in 1999–2000 (26 per cent for all India) further improved to 32 per cent in 2010–11. Special category status had also helped the state to register marked improvement in social indicators in respect of literacy, sex ratio, expansion of educational and health infrastructure as well as rural electrification. Per capita expenditure on education and health had multiplied several times over the period, which would have been impossible without the support of liberal central grants the state could access by virtue of its special category status. As a result, physical infrastructure had expanded significantly since 1970–71, but Assam is still way behind the rest of the country in terms of quality infrastructure. Road infrastructure remained among the poorest in the country; the density of surfaced road in 2010–11 was only 0.24 km per sq. km of area, against the national average of 1.43.[8] Power situation has remained dismal in the state throughout. About 40 per cent of the state's total cultivated area remains flood prone, and only half of this has some kind of flood protection. The pathetic lack of infrastructure results in substantial damages to livestock, agriculture, and property, besides human lives, due to the recurring annual floods of the Brahmaputra and the Barak.

As regards the financial infrastructure, in June 1969, there were only 74 bank offices in Assam, their coverage of population being 1.88 lakh per bank branch (national average 65000). But the banking infrastructure had expanded phenomenally after nationalization of banks, and in 2011, the number of bank branches had increased to 1563. However, the Credit-Deposit (CD) Ratio in Assam has remained dismal throughout; in 1973 it was 30 per cent; but in the hill districts it was not even 10 per cent.[9] The CD ratio of Assam could not be improved beyond 36 per cent even in 2011, compared to the national average of about 76 per cent. However, the CD ratio depends on demand for bank credit which in turn depends on a number of factors like industrial climate, availability of capital, power, and market, etc—factors which are conspicuous by their absence in Assam. The phenomenal expansion of bank branches within the state could do little to usher in a climate that could turn this scenario around, in the absence an enabling environment and adequate governmental support. The sad effect of this was evident in the bleak industrial situation in the state.

In 1969, Assam had only 1536 registered factories employing 67000 workers and producing total output of Rs 176.23 crore. The total public sector employment in Assam in 1974 was Rs 2.63 lakh, out of which the State Government alone employed 1.07 lakh workers. Railways and Central Government together employed about 74 thousand workers, and the rest were employed by local governments and quasi government bodies.[10] After 1981, the number of registered factories actually declined for the next two decades. While the factory employment continued to decline even after 1981, the number of government employees swelled four-folds during the three decades since 1971. Continuous agitations and militancy convulsed the state during the 1980s and 1990s, causing huge stagnation in the industrial scenario that continued till 2001. Only after 2001, there were some signs of revival of industrial activities in the state with a significant expansion in the number of factories, employment as well as increase in the value of output. However, the profits were modest, as was the gross fixed capital formation within the state. The manufacturing sector's growth in 2010–11 was only 4 per cent.[11] Even the benefit of tax holidays for new units in the special category states was not enough to attract new industries into the state.

Unlike the other states in the North Eastern Region (NER), Assam is a resource rich state, but like Bihar, it presents a paradox of poverty in the midst of plenty. Assam is also a major producer of crude oil and natural gas in India. Most of the oilfields of Assam are located in the Brahmaputra Valley. Apart from four oil refineries, there is no major industry, even though Assam is a major producer of silk. Weak transportation infrastructure, geographical isolation, lack of markets, vulnerability to floods, and militant extremism—all these together have conspired to hinder the growth of industry. Major industries in Assam in the beginning of 1970s were tea and petroleum, plywood, paper, fertilizer, jute, sugar, cotton, cement, and coal. Of these industries, tea and petroleum and petro-products employed the maximum number of workers. But the share of Assam in the total net national output from manufacturing was only 1.62 per cent in 1968–69, down from 2.35 per cent in 1960–61. Apart from a few public sector undertakings in the oil sector, rest of the industries in the state comprise only small-scale units, mostly family based. Handlooms, handicrafts, and silk are the major agro and sericulture-based industries. Lack of industries and hence employment opportunities are driving away most of the capital as well as talent away from the state.

Public Finance in Assam—Continued Dependence on Central Grants

Annexure 2.2 shows the state of public finances in Assam since 1969–70, just when it had become a special category state, through 2010–11. In 1969—70, state's own revenues, contributed only 35 per cent to total revenues and the rest 65 per cent came from central grants (47 per cent) and the state's share of central taxes (18 per cent). More than forty years down the line, the situation remains the same, only with some changes in the share of central grants and state's share of central taxes. In 1969–70, total central transfers including loans accounted for 53 per cent of the state's aggregate disbursements (revenue plus capital); by 2010-11, it had increased to 57 per cent. The contribution of the state's own revenue to total revenue had also remained constant at around 35 per cent over these 41 years. The special category status could not make the state more self-reliant, probably it had made it more dependent on the central grants. There had been no major structural changes in the public finance of Assam during the last four decades. It could meet only 36 per cent of its revenue expenditure needs from its own revenues in 2010–11, and this ratio was 31 per cent in 1969–70.

But there has been a remarkable change in the relative shares of revenue and capital receipts of the state; while revenue receipts (including central transfers) contributed 41 per cent to total receipts in 1969–70, its share had increased to 79 per cent in 2000–01 and 92 per cent in 2010–11. This was because of the state's better management of its public debt subsequent to the 12th Finance Commission (FC) recommendations (2005–10). As a result, debt servicing charges, or repayment of outstanding debt including interest thereon had declined from nearly 50 per cent of total expenditure till 2001 to only 11 per cent in 2011.

Consequently, almost the entire capital receipts could be utilized in 2010–11 for the purpose of creation of capital assets, an essential pre-requisite for development, compared to only 11 per cent in 1969–70. Post 12th FC, there was hardly any borrowing from the centre now. The ratio of outstanding public debt to GSDP had also declined from a high level of 41 per cent to a manageable 18 per cent during this period.

Structure of the tax revenues of Assam, however, did not undergo any radical shift after the special category status was awarded. The share of sales tax (VAT) in the state's own taxes increased from 43 per cent to 73 per cent during the period, indicating its overwhelming importance in the total state taxes; state excise, taxes on vehicles, land revenues, stamp and registration fees are the other major taxes. Receipts from petroleum are the major contributor to the state's non-tax revenue, apart from receipts from forest produces and interest. Both tax and non-revenues grew at an average rate that was higher than the growth rate of state during these four decades.

During this period, the share of non-developmental expenditure increased from 29 per cent of the state's total revenue expenditure in 1969–70 to 34 per cent in 2010–11, implying that the State was now spending substantially higher amounts on running its own administration, using resources that could have been better used for developmental purposes in the social and economic sectors. However, the share of interest payment in total revenue expenditure, a major component of the non-developmental expenditure, had declined from 12 per cent to 8 per cent during the period, though in absolute terms, the interest payments had increased from only Rs 15 crore to Rs 1912 crore. Salary and pension payments alone accounted for 51 per cent of its total expenditure in 2010–11; together with interest payment, the committed revenue expenditure of the state consumed 60 per cent of its total expenditure, leaving the rest for debt repayment (principal) and all other developmental expenditure. Expenditure on education increased from 3.5 per cent to 5.7 per cent of the state GSDP while the expenditure on health remained constant at around only 1 per cent of GSDP. State's own revenues increased marginally from 5.7 per cent to 7.4 per cent of its GSDP during this period, while its tax: GSDP moved only from 4.1 per cent to 5.3 per cent. These are much lower compared to the all India level.

Subsequent to the enactment of FRBMA in 2005–06, the state could generate a small surplus in its revenue account which had a huge deficit of Rs 780 crore in 2000–01 and was able to avail the debt relief of Rs 421 crore during the period covered by 12th FC. It has successfully reduced its Gross Fiscal Deficit from 5.4 per cent of GSDP in 1969–70 to only 1.8 per cent in 2010–11, well within the Fiscal Responsibility and Budget Management Act (FRBMA) limits. Thus it was a tale of some successes and many failures in the management of its public finances.

Debt Problems of Special Category States

Among all the Indian states, the special category states have always been the most heavily indebted, their indebtedness arising from their inherent lack of capacity and infrastructure as well as their inability to attract investments or to use central funds for creation of assets. Even in 1968–69, they were carrying a very heavy debt burden as seen in Table 2.2. Nagaland and Jammu & Kashmir had very small populations, but their debt: NSDP ratios and per capita debt figures were way above that of any other state in India; even Assam with its relatively small population had a higher per capita debt than most states. Loans and advances (of which more than 60 per cent were given to the various State Electricity Boards) made by these three states were very almost negligible, as were their capital outlays. The high indebtedness on the one hand and the lack of productive capital assets on the other hand compounded their problems, for this meant that the borrowings could not be utilized to create capacity for generating additional income in the economy—income that could have been utilized to discharge the rising levels of debt. The reason for such heavy borrowing again was the high cost of delivery of public services, given the problems of inaccessibility to remote areas in these states.

Planning in Assam

Table 2.3 shows the planning scenario in Assam from the fourth plan onwards when the state was accorded the special category status till the end of the eleventh Plan period. We notice a trend that will be repeated in the case of other special category states also—much higher outlay on economic services during the first few plans and the gradual increase in the share of social services during the later plans. Thus, during the Fourth and Fifth plans, the share of economic services was as much 70 per cent

Table 2.2 Debt Position of the States: 1968–69

States	Population* (Lakh)		Outstanding Public Debt (Rs Crore)	Per capita Debt (Rs)	Loans and Advances by State (Rs Crore)	Total Capital Outlay (Rs Crore)	NSDP (Rs Crore)	Per Capita NSDP (Rs)	Debt: NSDP Ratio (per cent)
	1961	1971							
Andhra Pradesh	360	435	613	146	205	384	2,043	495	30
Assam	**119**	**146**	**240**	**159**	**96**	**18**	**696**	**514**	**35**
Bihar	465	564	620	111	212	280	2,004	376	31
Gujarat	206	267	307	120	132	179	1,511	605	20
Haryana	76	100	160	165	38	37	596	635	27
J & K	**36**	**46**	**152**	**384**	**18**	**39**	**193**	**446**	**79**
Kerala	170	213	262	127	152	53	994	496	26
MP	324	417	466	118	196	157	1,646	420	28
Maharashtra	396	504	651	134	348	316	3,323	700	20
Mysore	236	293	386	136	156	319	1,631	588	24
Nagaland	**4**	**5**	**15**	**344**	**2**	**3**	**24**	**478**	**63**
Odisha	175	219	414	197	55	240	965	464	43
Punjab	111	136	250	177	268	251	1,166	903	21
Rajasthan	202	258	500	197	165	177	981	414	51
Tamil Nadu	337	412	485	126	358	146	1,926	499	25

(Cont'd)

Table 2.2 *(Cont'd)*

States	Population* (Lakh)		Outstanding Public Debt (Rs Crore)	Per capita Debt (Rs)	Loans and Advances by State (Rs Crore)	Total Capital Outlay (Rs Crore)	NSDP (Rs Crore)	Per Capita NSDP (Rs)	Debt: NSDP Ratio (per cent)
	1961	1971							
UP	737	883	812	92	560	315	3,829	453	21
West Bengal	349	443	591	136	198	179	2,748	660	22
Total	**4,303**	**5,415**	**6,924**	**133**	**3,160**	**3,093**	**26,252**	**552**	**26**

Source: Table 40: Statistical Tables, *Report of the Fifth Finance Commission*, 1969 and *Census reports* 1961 and 1971. NSDP figures are taken from *Estimates of State Domestic Product: 1960-61–1983-84*, CSO, November, 1985.

Note: In 1971, areas under Manipur had a population of 11 lakh, Meghalaya 10 lakh, Sikkim 2 lakh, and Tripura 16 lakh. These are not included in Assam's population. Mysore was renamed as Karnataka. Also, Nagaland's NSDP relates to 1970–71 when it was first measured there.

Table 2.3 Plan Outlay / Expenditure of Assam: Fourth to Eleventh Plan[12] (per cent)

Major Heads of Development	4th plan	5th plan	6th plan	7th plan	8th plan	9th plan	10th plan	11th plan
	1969–74	1974–79	1980–85	1985–90	1992–97	1997–02	2002–07	2007–12
Economic Services	**70**	**70**	**66**	**61**	**48**	**46**	**59**	**55**
Agriculture and Allied Activities	17	27	31	23	12	11	6	8
Rural Development	0	1	0	5	9	7	10	11
Special Areas Programme	0	0	0	2	2	4	11	6
Irrigation and Flood Control	34	21	0	10	10	9	5	10
Energy	0	0	14	3	0	1	6	4
Industry and Minerals	18	5	4	9	6	4	3	3
Transport and Communications	1	14	11	6	6	9	11	10
Science and Technology	1	0	0	0	0	0	0	0
General Economic Services	0	3	6	2	3	2	7	3
Social Services	**30**	**27**	**33**	**37**	**50**	**53**	**39**	**42**
Education	19	10	9	12	7	23	12	10
Medical and Public Health	10	6	6	6	1	6	3	4
Water supply and sanitation	0	5	9	8	1	6	7	5
Housing	0	2	2	2	0	1	0	0
Urban Development	0	1	0	0	0	1	2	4
Other Social Services	0	4	0	0	0	0	0	0
General Services	**0**	2	2	2	1	1	2	3
Total (Rs Crore)	**124**	**353**	**1,118**	**2,595**	**4,991**	**8,054**	**12,788**	**31,558**

Source: Records of the Accountant General of Assam.

which came down to 55 per cent during the Eleventh Plan. This was due to the needs of much higher plan outlay for building the almost non-existent physical infrastructure of roads, bridges, power, transport, and communication networks in the beginning. Only when some improvements could be made in these areas, focus could be shifted towards the social infrastructure of education, health, etc. But centralized planning was a dismal failure in India—it was an ill-conceived model in a widely diversified country like India—and had little touch with ground realities. So instead of helping the special category states, it rather increased their dependence on the plan funds which were frequently diverted towards non-plan purposes like payment of salaries.

Summing up

In the beginning of the 1970s Assam was a highly ruralized state starved of infrastructure and sustained by agriculture. Although gifted with rich natural resources like tea, petroleum, and forests, it lacked the basic conditions necessary for harnessing these resources optimally for industrial development with generation of income, and employment to reduce widespread poverty. While the country's partition had left its own scar on the state's economy, post-partition migration made the scenario much more complex, leading to unprecedented explosion of population. Ravaged by recurring floods and other natural disasters, limited by the use of primitive methods like shifting cultivation and constrained by the lack of irrigation and mechanization, its agricultural productivity was low. Incapacitated by the historical, geographical, and locational factors that gave rise to violent militancy stymied its economic growth, the state had to spend large parts of its scarce resources on running the administration alone, and had to depend on borrowings for meeting the needs of social and economic development, which again could not be utilized optimally for the above reasons. Savings being poor, the rate of capital formation was also poor. More than half of the total receipts of its government were coming by way of resource-transfers from the centre. The First Finance Commission in its report had noted: 'Assam is another State (*other than Punjab*) for which the suggested allocation of revenue will, in our view, be inadequate. It is also a state with special difficulties resulting from partition and it is necessary to allow it some margin for development.' Thus, it was perceived correctly at that time that the special category status was urgently needed to be given to Assam to develop its potential for economic growth—without such status it would not possibly have survived as a state. The liberal central assistance mitigated its endemic poverty and expanded its infrastructure during the last four decades, but as a state it has become overwhelmingly dependent upon the centre. Naturally it lagged way behind the other states which have since marched ahead.

Nagaland—Unyielding Reality

Nagaland's situation was no different from Assam being a part of which, it had inherited almost all the problems that had beset the growth and development of Assam. The erstwhile Naga Hills district of Assam and Tuensang Frontier Division of NEFA were brought together to form a separate administrative unit called Naga Hills Tuensang Area (NHTA) in 1957. In 1963, it was given full statehood and became known as Nagaland. Except for a small area in its west, the state has mountainous terrains with altitudes ranging from 900 to 3000 metres and with total area of 16579 sq kms. It is almost entirely populated by about 20 scheduled tribes, among them Angami, Ao, Chakhesang, Chang, Khiamniungan, Kuki, Konyak, Lotha, Phom, Pochury, Rengma, Sumi, Sangtam, Yimchungru, Zeliang, etc. More than one third of its difficult terrain used to be unadministered before independence. Except some primary schools run by the missionaries, there was practically no development of the area till 1947. Its backwardness thus was a legacy from its history and geography.

The ancient history of Nagaland is shrouded in obscurity, though Dimapur, one of its major towns situated on the banks of the River Dhansiri, was the ancient capital of the Dimasa kings who used to rule over the Brahmaputra Valley of Assam. The present Naga tribes are believed to be descendants of the Sino-Mongoloids who came in waves during the great migration that took place in South Asia in the first century AD (Iralu 2002: 9–10). Naga areas that were then inhabited by a number of heterogeneous tribes, all speaking different dialects, came under the British rule by the end of nineteenth century. By the beginning of twentieth century, Nagaland had embraced Christianity and Christian missionaries had brought education and civilization to the indigenous tribes. Nagas basically derived their sustenance from

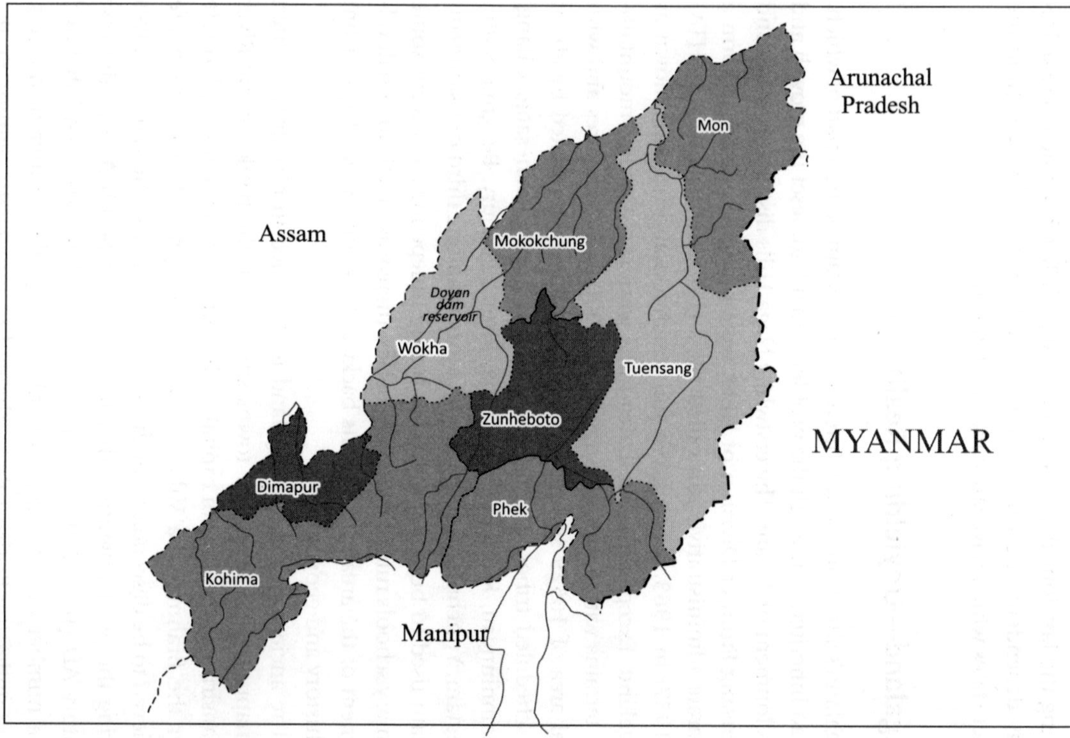

Map 2.2 Map of Nagaland.

agriculture and their social customs and economic relations were shaped by the soil. Like other tribal societies of the northeast, the tribes evolved something like an egalitarian society free from the rigid class and caste structures that had plagued the other regions of India since ancient times. The British did very little to uplift their standards of living or integrate them into their empire in India, they exercised political control over them only to prevent them from raiding and plundering the British controlled areas of Assam, Manipur, and Burma. But under the British rule, the traditional barter economy of Naga tribes was slowly replaced by the modern monetized market economy. Along with the influence of Christianity, this began to alter the structure of traditional Naga societies (Iralu 2002: 14).

Separatist movements started in Naga Hill areas soon after independence and the first two decades thereafter were turbulent times—especially the period between 1954 and 1964. The state hardly benefited from the first three five-year plans; in fact the total plan outlay for Nagaland during the third plan was only Rs 11 crore (Rs 287 per capita) out of a total plan outlay of Rs 4366 crore for the entire country. The separatist movement of Nagaland dating from the British Raj can be regarded as the mother of all subsequent secessionist movements that would spring up in almost all northeastern states of India and impede their growth and developments for decades.

Insurgency in Nagaland

Nagas, a race of fiercely independent tribes, could never reconcile themselves to the British rule. In March 1946, the firebrand leader of the Nagas, the Angami Zapu Phizo, who had fought for the liberation of India from the British rule by joining the INA led by Netaji Subhash Chandra Bose, had established the Naga National Council (NNC) to fight for the formation of an independent nation of Nagaland, comprising all Naga-inhabited areas in Assam, Manipur, and Burma. In June 1947, the NNC had signed a 'Nine-Point Agreement' with the Indian government represented by Sir Akbar Hydari, the then governor of Assam. Clause 9 of the agreement provided for review of the political status of Naga Hills as an independent entity after ten years, giving them an option to secede. Aware of the internecine rivalries within Naga tribes, and unviability of a small unit wedged between two large nations of India and China, the Indian state later disregarded Clause 9 and instead claimed Nagaland as integral part of India, having its autonomy guaranteed and protected under the Sixth Schedule and Article 371 of the Constitution. It took the position that since the Naga Hills were ruled by the British as part of India, the question of their sovereignty was absurd.

Naga independentists, on the other hand, contested that the British had never directly ruled their country; rather they protected their autonomy under Inner Line Regulation (1873), Chin Hills Regulation (1893), Backward Tract Act (1919), and Excluded and Partially Excluded Areas Act (1935), and refused to accept 'a shared and negotiated sovereignty'. They further pleaded that 'Nagas had never been integrated into Assam proper and had never been wedded to India's freedom struggle', and as such 'the Indian state does not have the moral and legitimate right to subsume their sovereignty rights' (Hausing 2014: 90–1). These positions were mutually irreconcilable and the best course perhaps would have been to negotiate exclusive asymmetrical terms with the Nagas to accommodate their demands for independence within an asymmetrical federal framework. But both were unrelenting in their respective positions, and the seeds of a long-drawn and violent conflagration were sown that would later threaten to tear asunder this beautiful and tranquil hill state.

NNC declared an Independent Naga Hills on 14 August 1947—which was celebrated with great euphoria among the Nagas and later endorsed in a plebiscite in 1951 conducted by NNC (Upadhyay 2005a). Phizo became the President of NNC in 1950 and met Prime Minister Nehru in 1952, but the meeting failed to resolve the problem. Repression by the Indian state followed and after the boycott of first general election in Naga Hills, it was declared as a disturbed area. After the NNC had formed its underground Naga Federal Government (NFG) and waged a war against the Indian state; the Indian army, along with Assam Rifles, marched into Nagaland in October 1956 to contain the unrest and to track down Phizo. Phizo managed to escape to London via East Pakistan, where he lived in exile till his death in 1990, remotely controlling the armed rebellion at home.

The Union Territory of Naga Hills Tuensang Area (NHTA) was formed in 1957 and following the 16-point Agreement reached between the Union of India and the Naga People Convention (NPC)—which included representatives from different Naga tribes—in July 1960, Nagaland was finally granted full-fledged statehood by the enactment of the State of Nagaland Act, 1962 in Indian Parliament. The state of Nagaland was formally inaugurated as the 16th state of Indian Union on December 1, 1963 with Kohima as the capital, and after elections in January, 1964, the first Nagaland Legislative Assembly was constituted on 11 February 1964.

The beginning of electoral politics and liberal central grants that started pouring into the state after its formation, coupled with strong counter-insurgency operations by the Indian Army, somehow managed to contain the insurgency, but 'the virus of power politics and lust for money gave birth to political vices and corruption that badly affected the desired economic development in the state' (Upadhyay 2005a). A ceasefire agreement between the two sides followed in April 1964, mediated by a Peace Mission, of which Rev. Michel Scott (a Baptist Church leader and British National who was instrumental in the escape of Phizo), Bimala Prasad Chaliha, the then Chief Minister of Assam, and Jai Prakash Narayan were the members. The Peace Mission was subsequently dissolved after Mr. Scott's expulsion from the country in 1966 for supporting the independence of Nagaland. Though some section of the NNC leadership had joined the mainstream electoral politics, the insurgency and counterinsurgency operations by the army continued unabated. In 1975, an agreement that came to be known as the Shillong Accord was reached between the Indian Government and the insurgent groups which agreed to accept the Indian Constitution, but the hardcore among the NNC leadership condemned it as 'total betrayal'; they included leaders like Isak Swu, Th Muivah, and S. S. Khaplang. These disgruntled leaders now formed the underground Nationalist Socialist Council of Nagalim (NSCN). NSCN established an underground Naga Federal government and adopted guerrilla warfare for fighting the Indian Union to claim their independent State.

Ethnic rivalry plagued the Naga insurgency all throughout. As Sashinungla (2005) notes, 'The entire Naga insurgency has been dominated by inter-tribal rivalry and a struggle for hegemony. Life in Nagaland begins with the tribe and the village. History shows that tribal and ethnic rifts predate all peace processes in Nagaland.' The ethnic rivalry would also split the NSCN into two factions—the NSCN (IM) led by Isak and Muivah and the NSCN (Khaplang)—during the late

1980s; between them, these two factions were estimated to command a cadre of about 5000 armed insurgents. Their budget (IM faction had a budget of Rs 44 crore in 2002-03) was financed by extortion in the name of tax collection, drug trafficking from Myanmar, international funding, and sale of arms to other insurgent groups. NSCN (IM) signed a cease fire agreement with Government of India (GoI) in 1997 that is still prevailing, but meetings between the GoI and their leaders in 2004 and 2005 could hardly make any headway towards finding a solution to the problem, also due to non-participation by the Khaplang group (Upadhyay 2005a) which signed a ceasefire agreement with GoI in 2001, but abrogated it unilaterally in 2015, followed by attack on army personnel and subsequent retaliation by the army. The ceasefires would never be able to bring abiding peace and resolution to the problem of insurgency.

Today the political scenario in Nagaland presents a strange, contradictory, and perplexing landscape with several splinter insurgent groups seen to be warring amongst themselves, some driven by the grand vision of a Nagalim or Greater Nagaland including all Naga inhabited areas of Assam, Manipur, Arunachal Pradesh, and also Myanmar. Naga people and people from other states working in Nagaland, whether for central or state governments, in private business or trade—all are subjected to extortion payments and taxes collected by the insurgent groups. Corruption level is among the highest in the country, and a significant part of the central funds flow into the hands of various insurgent groups. People in Nagaland today are subjected to 'tax' payments simultaneously to several parallel 'governments'—those run by the NSCN(IM), NSCN (K), FGN (Federal Government of Nagaland initially formed by Phizo), besides the democratically elected and the only legitimate government of the state. It is an extortion economy—any intransigence or non-compliance is met by torture or death. Inevitably, the widespread use of extortion machinery has also created a cadre of 'fake insurgents' by misguided youths who have become parasites on society.

The Naga intelligentsia wants both the liberal financial assistance as well as political freedom from the Indian Government. Naga academicians continue to indulge in the romanticism of a non-existent Naga nationalism, thereby providing intellectual support to an insurgency that is slowly fading away after running its course during the last six decades. They ignore the fact that the national and state elections today draw a majority of voters out to cast their votes, thereby confirming their faith in the democratic process within the Indian Union. No one questions the financial and economic viability of a state that requires central funds for meeting 80 per cent of its expenditure needs, and no one cares for the thousands of innocent lives lost—civilians members of insurgent groups and security forces alike. Vested interests—the politician-contractor-insurgent nexus—keep the insurgency alive; after all, insurgency begets money to the state in the name of security and some of this money finances the luxurious lifestyles of people with vested interests masquerading as leaders. In fact, in Nagaland, insurgency had acquired the status of an industry; without it the fragile extortion economy would completely collapse. Central funds were financing the insurgency in an indirect way. And this political game continues while the Naga imbroglio refuses to get resolved.

Pre-1970 Socio-Economic Scenario in Nagaland

Data about Nagaland's economy till the decade of the 1970s are scanty, partly due to the fact that the ongoing insurgency made it dangerous for central and state level data collections machineries to operate in the state. What is known is that at independence, Nagaland practically had no physical or social infrastructure in existence; it was mostly an un-administered wilderness lying outside of civilization. Most of the state had remained inaccessible for a long time—there was hardly any electricity, roads, schools, and healthcare facilities available within the state. It was a tribal society subsisting on agriculture carried out with the help of primitive methods of shifting cultivation (jhoom), with low productivity and low yield of crops. Agriculture employed 80 per cent of its total working population even during the decade of the 1990s, but with low food grain productivity (1.22 MT in 1996) and crop yield (1.85 MT per hectare in 1990 as against average all India figure of 22 MT), agriculture in Nagaland was clearly of the subsistence kind—and lacked the potential to contribute to economic growth. The secondary sector was equally hopeless, comprising only a few light, small, and cottage industries. During the 1970s some sugar, paper, and plywood factories were established, but most of these ceased to operate due to insurgency, adverse law, and order situation and lack of any market, power and infrastructure. The economic activities remained lopsided;

like all other northeastern economies, Nagaland was also a largely agrarian economy, with low level of industrialization, poor infrastructure, cost-inefficient service sector, and unsuccessful state-sponsored attempt at industrialization through the public sector. Even the potential of agriculture remained unrealized due to the use of primitive methods, lack of modernization and sub-optimal use of technology, besides the absence of economies of scale.

At Independence, Nagaland had a total of 102 kms of surfaced and 74 kms of un-surfaced roads, only 5 hospitals with total 40 beds, besides six dispensaries. It had 101 primary schools, three middle schools, only one high school, and no college. In 1962–63, on the eve of gaining full statehood, it had only 837 kms of roads, 603 schools and18 per cent literacy ratio. Only six of its 966 villages were electrified. Only two scheduled commercial bank branches operated in Nagaland in 1961, each served nearly two lakh people. As per the 1961 Census, Nagaland (then Naga Hill areas) had a population of only 3.69 lakh, of which 95 per cent lived in the rural areas, and 93 per cent belonged to the scheduled tribes (ST). As of March 1967, Nagaland had one km of railway and two kms of surfaced road per 100 sq km of its area. In April 1968, it had only 1.75 hospital beds per 1000 population.[13]

By the time of the 1971 census, the population had increased to 5.16 lakh, and 90 per cent of it was still rural. Only 27.4 per cent of the population were literate. In 1973–74, more than 50 per cent of its population lived below poverty line, like the other northeastern states. The per capita consumption of electricity in 1970–71 was only 8 KWH, compared to the national average of 90 KWH. Only 38 small scale industrial (SSI) units operated in the state, and this was all the industrialization that had been achieved till 1970-71. This was the situation when Nagaland was accorded the special category status in 1969; clearly, it would not have survived otherwise.

Progress since Special Category Status

Socio-economic indicators of Nagaland since 1980–81 through 2010–11 can be seen in Annexure 2.3 to this chapter. In 1970–71, primary sector constituted 52 per cent of Nagaland's NSDP, secondary sector contributed 10 per cent (manufacturing 2 per cent and construction 8 per cent) and the tertiary sector's share in NSDP was 38 per cent (public administration 17 per cent). However, the share of agriculture started declining soon afterwards till it stabilized at 33 per cent of NDSP and continued at that level till 2001; it further declined to 26 per cent during the present century. But the secondary sector continued to languish, the only activity driving growth being construction whose share increased from 8 per cent to 9 per cent during the period 1981–2011, while the share of manufacturing remained negligible. In the services sector also, most of the income was generated by the government through delivery of public services and goods. Government expenditure has, in fact, always been the major driving force in Nagaland's economy, with the total government expenditure accounting for almost the entire GSDP in 1980–81 and 47 per cent of GSDP in 2010–11.

Compared to the dismal economic scenario that prevailed during the 70s and 80s, Nagaland had made remarkable progress since then. Poverty ratio had decreased from 39 per cent in 1983 to only 19 per cent in 2011–12, less than the national average of 27.5 per cent, despite the state still remaining predominantly dependent on agriculture and engaging 68 per cent of the main workers even at the turn of the century. Thus the reduction in poverty was not due to generation of income from productive economic activities, but the result of expansion in government activities. Nagaland is still an agricultural economy, and the abundance of its natural resources and richness of its social capital still remain unharnessed. It remains caught up in a time warp, without any visionary leadership to help overcome its deep sense of historical alienation and to push it forward by recognizing enduring peace as the only way to development.

In terms of social infrastructure, Nagaland has registered remarkable progress. As per the 2011 census, 80 per cent of its population of 20 lakh were literate. Educational and health networks have expanded manifolds. But the physical infrastructure had not kept pace with this social progress. Only 45 per cent of its roads were surfaced, generation of electricity in fact had declined from the 1981 level and the state's own installed capacity was only 30 MW in 2011, though from the central agencies it received an additional 75 MWs. The per capita consumption of electricity was far below the national level. Only 63 per cent of its villages had access to electricity, as of 2011.To improve the performance of public utilities, in 2002, Nagaland Government had introduced the unique concept of 'communitization of public institutions and services' in areas of health, education, power, rural tourism, rural water supply, etc, by building partnerships between government and people through delegation of management responsibilities to the community through institutions like Village Councils and Village Development Boards, and becoming a facilitator and an enabler rather than a provider.[14]

In 1985, Nagaland had only 64 branches of scheduled commercial banks and its CD ratio was only 35 per cent. During the next quarter of a century, the number of bank branches increased marginally to 96, but the CD ratio declined to 26 per cent—a result of violent militancy. The low CDR also reflected insufficient demand for credit due to lack of industry, and industries would not come because of remoteness and lack of other prerequisites. To halt and reverse this vicious cycle, expansion of infrastructure was essential, which could not be done due to the lack of resources, and also due to the protracted insurgency. The slow rate of expansion of infrastructure could not help the process of industrialization. As protracted insurgency hindered the execution of all developmental projects, the money that was flowing in by way of additional central grants to a special category state fuelled unbridled corruption. Various CAG reports provide ample proof of this.

CAG reports have been attracting wide media coverage and debates in recent times, but they still do not occupy much space in serious academic literature in the country. They are highly technical in nature, have an extreme obsession for facts and figures and follow a standard templatized style of reporting. But beneath the veneer of their objectivity, they capture and reflect the trends and practices in contemporaneous society rather accurately.

A random check of CAG reports pertaining to the Government of Nagaland during the three years 2009–12 revealed repeated instances of fraudulent withdrawals from treasury running into several crore of rupees each year by most government departments, giving an impression of almost complete breakdown of the usual control mechanisms in the government apparatus. There were rampant withdrawals of money against fictitious bills, glaring instances of excess or wasteful expenditure, and blatant violations of rules with almost total impunity, and often with the active encouragement and involvement of those who are responsible for maintaining the integrity and probity of public expenditure. Almost every state in the northeast mirrors this picture.

The state remained industrially barren, with only 84 registered factories at the end of 2010–11. In 1991, it had 509 small scale units (SSUs) employing 2513 people; though the number of SSUs have increased since then, many of these units have become sick over time and the total employment has actually decreased. The state is conspicuous by the absence of any medium or large industries.

Public Finance in Nagaland

Tables 2.4 and 2.5 depict the revenue receipts and revenue expenditure of Assam, Nagaland, and Jammu & Kashmir in 1967—68, before they became special category states. It can be seen that 92 per cent of Nagaland's total revenue came by way of transfers from the centre, compared to much lesser ratios for the other two states. The per capita tax revenue in Nagaland was only Rs 5.75 compared to the all-India average of Rs 21.92 or Assam's average of Rs 18.66. But while Jammu & Kashmir had a revenue surplus, both Nagaland and Assam had substantial revenue deficits. The state had to borrow heavily to finance its revenue expenditure from the very beginning.

Five years after becoming a special category state, in 1974–75, Nagaland's revenue expenditure had increased to Rs 39.80 crore, of which only 9 per cent came from its own tax and non—tax revenues, the rest 91 per cent came from the centre by way of grants (88 per cent of total receipts) and only 3 per cent as state's share of central taxes. Rs 1.41 crore came by way of central loan. Central transfers including loans were paying 78 per cent of its aggregate disbursements in 1974–75. It was as if the rest of India was paying for keeping the insurgency alive and the insurgency-affected state within its fold.

Even in 2010–11, the situation had not changed much. The state's own revenues contributed only 8.2 per cent to the total revenue, the rest coming from the centre. Sales tax was practically the only revenue earner for the state, contributing 74 per cent of the state's taxes. Its Tax: GSDP ratio of 1.9 per cent was among the lowest in the country; in fact the ratio had come down from 3 per cent in 1974–75. It was one of the few states where the growth of taxes lagged behind the growth of state income.

The state is heavily indebted, and its outstanding debt has been increasing at a compound rate of 14.5 per cent annually. Interest payments were growing at an even higher annual rate of 16.7 per cent. The debt servicing charges including payment of interest in fact had exceeded the total borrowing in 2011 by Rs 193 crore, forcing the

Table 2.4 Revenue Receipts of Assam, Nagaland, and Jammu & Kashmir: 1967–68 (Rs Crore)

States	Share of Taxes	Central Grants	Total Central Transfer	Own Tax Revenue	Non-Tax Revenue	Total Own Revenue	Per Capita Tax Revenue (Rs)	Total Revenue Receipts	Own Revenue: Total Revenue (per cent)
Assam	12.31	16.52	28.83	26.31	8.59	34.90	18.66	63.73	54.76
Nagaland	4.59	7.07	11.66	0.23	0.76	0.99	5.75	12.65	7.83
Jammu & Kashmir	6.38	6.57	12.95	7.58	12.85	29.40	19.44	42.35	69.42
All India	384.08	140.61	572.60	1086.63	624.22	1710.85	21.92	2283.45	74.92

Source: Statistical Tables, *Report of the Fifth Finance Commission.*

Table 2.5 Revenue Expenditure of Assam, Nagaland, and Jammu & Kashmir: 1967—68 (Rs Crore)

States	Non-Developmental				Developmental					Total Revenue Expenditure
	General Admn.	Debt Services	Others	Total	Education	Medical & Public Health	Agriculture/ Animal Husbandry	Others	Total	
Assam	2.13	11.32	14.72	28.17	17.77	5.82	6.28	37.00	66.87	95.04
Nagaland	1.81	0.50	5.42	7.73	2.36	1.34	1.09	7.60	12.39	20.12
Jammu & Kashmir	1.20	0.72	6.38	8.30	7.36	3.84	2.33	22.64	36.17	44.47

Source: Statistical Tables, *Report of the Fifth Finance Commission.*

state to use that much of its own scarce revenues to discharge its debt obligations. One disturbing feature of its public finances was the high proportion of expenditure incurred on non-developmental general services that constituted 48 per cent and 44 per cent of its total revenue expenditure respectively during 2000–01 and 2010–11—a major chunk of this on the police. The per capita expenditure incurred for policing this insurgency-riddled state has been the highest in the country. However, the money was not as well spent as desired, as CAG's Performance Audit Report on the Modernization of Police Force (MPF) in Nagaland conducted during 2008–09 amply demonstrates. For the purpose of MPF, Nagaland was categorized as 'A' category state for facing the maximum internal security threat, which made it eligible for 100 per cent grants from the centre. CAG had identified serious deficiencies in the running of the scheme. Norms for vehicles were blatantly violated, there was more than 90 per cent shortfall in respect of sophisticated weapons in the police stations and huge quantities of ammunition remained unaccounted for. At one Police Central Store, more than 3 lakh rounds of ammunition were found missing; it is anybody's guess where these missing ammunitions could have gone. As against the norm of 80 vehicles for SP, Kohima, 160 vehicles were allotted, of which 93 were deployed for VIP and other duties, 40 were retained at Police Headquarters and only 14 vehicles were provided to five Police Stations against the norm of 50. These are only a few tell-tale examples about the efficiency of expenditure on police.

Nagaland had enacted the FRBMA in 2005-06 and was able to generate revenue surpluses since then. With FRBMA, its finances have been looking up. The GSDP ratio declined from double digits till 1991 to only 2.7 per cent, i.e., within the FRBMA limits in 2010–11. Debt: GSDP ratio had also been going down. In 1974–75, the ratio had increased to an unsustainable 77 per cent, but had gradually come down to 41.6 per cent in 2010–11, which was still a dangerous level. But the state appears to have emerged from the most vicious debt trap into which it was falling almost irrevocably.

Planning in Nagaland

Table 2.6 shows the plan outlay/expenditure in Nagaland since the fourth plan, i.e., since becoming a special category state. As in the

Table 2.6 Plan Outlay / Expenditure in Nagaland: Fourth to Eleventh Plan (per cent)

Major Heads of Development	4th Plan	5th Plan	6th Plan	7th Plan	8th Plan	9th Plan	10th Plan	11th Plan
	1969–74	1974–78	1980–85	1985–90	1992–97	1997–02	2002–07	2007–12
Economic Services	**71.1**	**67.5**	**64.7**	**60.4**	**69.1**	**62.9**	**61.3**	**63.2**
Agriculture & Allied Activities	13.5	18.2	12.4	14.1	7.2	7.7	11.5	8.3
Rural Development	2.9	2.6	8.0	7.9	10.4	13.2	8.1	5.2
Special Area Programmes	0.0	0.0	2.4	1.9	1.6	1.9	2.0	9.7
Irrigation and Flood Control	1.5	2.5	4.6	3.1	13.0	13.2	1.8	2.5
Energy	7.5	5.6	8.2	7.1	10.1	7.0	11.2	10.8
Industry and Minerals	12.6	8.9	6.1	6.3	3.5	6.4	8.6	6.3
Transport & Communications	32.0	29.0	22.3	17.9	9.5	11.1	7.6	13.7
Science and Technology	0.0	0.0	0.0	0.1	0.1	0.1	0.2	0.9
General Economic Services	1.0	0.7	0.8	1.9	13.7	2.4	10.2	5.7
Social Services	**28.9**	**32.5**	**30.2**	**30.5**	**26.9**	**34.6**	**33.1**	**31.0**
Education	10.5	8.2	5.7	7.7	7.1	7.3	8.6	8.4
Medical and Public Health	4.9	2.5	5.9	4.5	6.9	6.8	3.6	4.2
Water Supply and Sanitation	7.8	7.7	7.7	6.3	4.0	7.4	7.4	4.4
Housing	2.0	11.3	5.5	4.3	3.7	8.4	7.5	5.1
Urban Development	2.6	1.3	2.6	3.9	3.4	2.1	2.6	6.6
Others Social Services	1.1	1.6	2.8	3.7	1.9	2.5	3.5	2.3
General Services	**0.0**	**0.0**	**5.1**	**9.1**	**4.0**	**2.6**	**5.6**	**5.8**
Total (Rs Crore)	**39**	**70**	**227**	**465**	**937**	**1433**	**2228**	**5978**

Source: Records of the Accountant General of Nagaland.

case of Assam, the share of economic services in plan expenditure has declined gradually over the successive plans, from 71 per cent in the fourth plan to 63 per cent in the eleventh plan. But the share of social sector has only increased marginally from 29 per cent to 31 per cent during this period, while the share of administrative general services increased from nil to 6 per cent. Among the economic services, focus has gradually shifted from transport and communication during the initial plan periods to other sectors like energy, rural development, and special area programmes. Among the social services, emphasis remained on education, public health, water supply, and sanitation. During the later periods, more emphasis was also given on housing and urban development sectors.

Summing Up

We have seen that before 1969, Nagaland's position was far worse than Assam's. Characterized by almost total absence of any industry and heavy dependence on agriculture that employed most of its working population who could only eke out a mere subsistence from it, there was nothing to generate any surplus from this sector to provide any impetus to growth. The infrastructure was pathetic, and most of the state was inaccessible and hence largely unadministered, More than 80 per cent of its population lived in rural areas without roads, schools, health facilities, and electricity. With very little resources of its own that could be economically exploited and used for its growth, the state was absolutely dependent on the central grants for meeting more than 90 per cent of its expenditure needs; even after the infusion of liberal central funds, it had to borrow heavily to finance its revenue expenditure. It had no resources to invest in capital assets for improving physical and social infrastructure necessary for economic growth. On top of all these debilitating factors, there was the intractable problem of insurgency that was ravaging the state, stalling all development work.

In the absence of any other avenues for employment, government was the biggest employer, employing about 10 per cent of the population of the state, and their salaries accounted for nearly three quarters of its budgetary provisions, leaving little to spend on development. The huge salary liability was, in fact, a cause for the heavy indebtedness of the state. It was clearly economically unviable and needed heavy support—the 16 point agreement between the Government of Nagaland and the Union Government in 1963 for this reason had enjoined upon the Central Government the responsibility to pay the cost of meeting the needs of administrative and developmental expenditure of the Nagaland from the Consolidated Fund of India.

The Indian state's response to the Naga people's nationalistic aspirations was to use force instead of attempting a resolution to this complex issue through negotiated asymmetrical arrangements. This compounded the problem affecting all developmental activities within the state. It was only after the 1990s when insurgency started waning that Nagaland's socio-economic parameters started showing improvements. The state started reaping the benefits of special category status quite late; but much of these benefits that flowed in by way of higher central grants never reached the people. Instead these continued to feed endemic corruption and insurgency that had almost become a career for many in the state. The liberal grants from the centre have also miserably failed to increase the state's self-reliance by promoting productive economic activities and entrepreneurship; all it has succeeded in promoting was a culture of extortion and total lack of accountability at each level. The story for most other northeastern states is not much different.

Jammu & Kashmir—The Weight of History

The situation of Jammu & Kashmir was quite different from that of Assam or Nagaland. Kashmir is unique in many respects and its situation is incredibly more complex than the other two states. The luxuriant Valley of Kashmir lying on the north of India has rightly been known as the 'Paradise on Earth'. Surrounded by the snow-capped peaks of the Himalayas, its emerald lakes, and blue skies have an irresistible charm and seductive power that had attracted seekers of knowledge and beauty from all over since times immemorial. But then its ethereal beauty was lost in terror, terror was sought to be contained by the inquisition of an architecture of coercion mounted by the state. The unfortunate state rolled in a bloodbath for more than two decades. And the memories of all that distrust and violence, of all those unhappy years, of all the unfulfilled promises and dead dreams, still linger on. Old wounds reopen, and an unintended spark ignites the flames of

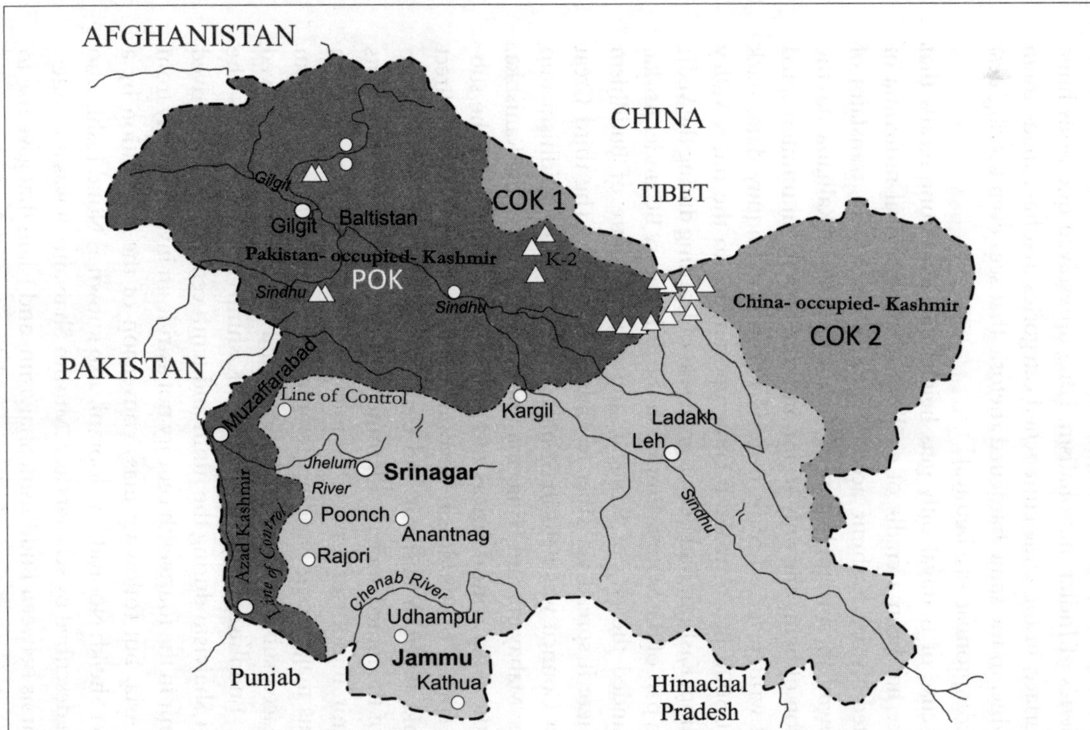

Map 2.3 Map of Jammu & Kashmir

Notes: POK: Pakistan Occupied Kashmir

COK: China Occupied Kashmir

hatred all over again. The fire of hatred and suspicion refuses to die, as Mehta (2011: 5) says, 'as if the entire weight of modern Indian history had once again chosen to explode in the valley: the green flags of Pakistan, militant sub-nationalism, the failures of Indian democracy, the anxieties of Indian nationalism. Long unresolved questions burst to the surface, in the same entrenched categories that have made them irresolvable, in the same hardened rhetoric that sees even the slightest hint of compromise as a betrayal.'

The sense of betrayal only gets heightened when one recalls that this place has been a cradle of civilization since several millennia of antiquated history. Kashmir, according to Sir Aurel Stein, translator of *Rajatarangini*, the ancient history of Kashmir written by Kalhana, has the distinction of being the only region in India having 'an uninterrupted series of written record of its history'. Kashmir's antiquity dates back to about 3000 BC, to make it contemporaneous to the Indus Valley Civilization. Kashmir had been a great seat of learning during the Vedic period, a part of the Maurya Empire in the 3rd century BC under Asoka, who founded the city of Srinagar, and a great centre of Buddhism from where it spread via Tibet to China and Japan. The third Great Buddhist Council was held in Srinagar that had split Buddhism into two sects: Mahayana and Hinayana under the Kushana king Kanishka. One of the most critical factors of Kashmir's prosperity (and the subsequent spread of Buddhism beyond India's borders) was the direct trade links between Kashmir and Central Asia—in fact the southern branch of the famed ancient silk route reached Ladakh and other parts of Kashmir. Buddhism survives till today in Ladakh which abounds in numerous magnificent Buddhist temples and monasteries. Buddhism was replaced subsequently by Shaivism and a synthesis was achieved between Buddhism and Shaivism in Kashmir to create Trika—the Kashmiri Shaivism during the ninth and tenth centuries. Islam arrived to Kashmir in the fourteenth century not astride an invading army from Central Asia, but following mass conversion of the population by a local poet Sheikh Nooruddin Noorani, also known as Nund Rishi, who has been described by scholars as a 'Muslim Shaivaite'. It was a wonderful synthesis between Buddhism, Shaivisim, and Islam that gave rise to the unique variety of Islam in Kashmir. 'Islam in Sufi form thus came to Kashmir not as a destroyer of the tradition, …but as its preserver, consolidator and perpetuator….The Kashmiri Muslim has remained a Kashmiri as well as a Muslim and rarely suffers from schizophrenic pangs which Islamic links and local patriotism often generate among Muslims elsewhere' (Puri 2011: 118–9). Thus a syncretic Sufiana culture evolved in Kashmir—it was a harmonious blend of all the three religions that through the ages had shaped Kashmiri life and Kashmiri culture and where their respective practices were assimilated into a composite ethos. Elphistone described Kashmir as 'the clearing house of several civilizations'. It had dominated the intellectual life of the country for almost two millennia, becoming a focus of Asiatic civilizations, akin to what ancient Greece was for the entire European civilization (Puri 2011: 118).

Kashmir was annexed into the Mughal Empire by Akbar in 1586 and then came under Pathan rule under Ahmed Shah Abdali in 1752. The ruthless Pathans were finally evicted from the valley by the Sikh ruler Ranjit Singh of Lahore in 1819. The kingdom of Jammu was subjugated by the Sikhs in 1780, who ruled Kashmir till their defeat by the British in the First Anglo-Sikh War in 1845.[15] In 1946, King Gulab Singh of the Dogra dynasty of Jammu bought Kashmir Valley from the East India Company paying 75 lakh rupees. In 1858, when the administration of British territories in India had passed onto the British Crown, Jammu & Kashmir became a princely state. It presented a conglomeration of many races and religions: Buddhist Ladakh in the east which was ethnically and culturally Tibetan; Jammu in the south with Hindus, Muslims, and Sikhs; the Sunni-dominated Kashmir valley in the centre with a small but influential Hindu minority, the Kashmiri Brahmins or Pandits; and the sparsely populated Baltistan in the northeast dominated by the Shias, who also live in Gilgit in the north and Poonch in the west. There are many distinct ethnic groups: Dards, Ladakhis, Paharis, Dogras, and nomadic tribes like Gujjars, Bakarwals, and many others. It was, and still is, a mosaic of geographical, ethnic, religious, tribal, and linguistic diversities, layer upon layers of overlapping identities forged by history.

Kashmir's Accession to India

Article 370 still generates acrimonious debates and inflames passions among Kashmiris and non-Kashmiris alike. Kashmiris regard the article as something sacrosanct, while the rightist political parties want it to be abrogated. Many political thinkers have quoted this article as an example of asymmetrical federalism in India. But as we shall see, the article was incorporated in the Indian Constitution as a direct consequence of the conditions under which Kashmir was forced to accede to India.

At independence, Kashmir was one among the 562 princely states left by the British, but it had the unique distinction of being a princely state where a Hindu king, Maharaja Hari Singh, ruled over a predominantly Muslim population—something similar to Junagad where a Muslim king ruled over a Hindu majority, but unlike any other disputed princely state, Kashmir with a huge territory of 222,236 sq. kms, was contiguous to both India and Pakistan and shared its borders with Afghanistan and China (Tibet) too.

Hari Singh, the last Dogra ruler, had ascended the throne in 1925, by which time, a young Muslim from the valley named Sheikh Mohammed Abdullah was emerging as a popular leader of the Muslims in the Valley. He had founded the National Conference and became its undisputed leader during the 1930s. At independence, all princely states were given the option of joining either India or Pakistan; but Hari Singh acceded to neither—instead he was flirting with the idea of independence for Kashmir. In September 1947, Sheikh Abdullah demanded complete transfer of power to the people in Kashmir under a secular government that would decide on his future. Meanwhile, to force the wavering Maharaja into making up his mind for acceding to Pakistan, on 22 October 1947, over several thousand armed Pathan tribesmen supported by the Pakistan army regulars had invaded the state from across the border. Occupying the unguarded northern reaches, and moving swiftly into the Jhelum valley, the unruly army of invaders captured the town of Muzaffarabad and plundered the town of Baramulla on the way to Srinagar on 24th October, when the Maharaja sought military assistance from the Indian government. On 26th October, the Maharaja signed the Instrument of Accession to India which was accepted by the Viceroy Lord Mountbatten on the next day, thus sealing its legality. In the same morning, the first planes—28 Dakotas in all—carrying Indian soldiers arrived in Srinagar. They drove the invaders out from Baramulla and other small towns by early November, but by this time, the harsh Kashmir winter had set on, making further military progress in the snowbound valley impossible.

While accepting the Instrument of Accession on 27 October 1947, Lord Mountbatten had said 'it is my government's wish that, as soon as law and order have been restored in Kashmir and her soil cleared of invaders, the question of state's accession should be settled by a reference to the people'. The words, 'Plebiscite under the UN auspices' were mentioned in radio broadcast made on the next day (Jagmohan 2011: 102), thus committing India to plebiscite, so that 'destiny of Kashmir is finally to be decided by the people who live in it'.[16]

Pakistan had claimed Kashmir on the ground that it was a Muslim majority state. Nehru and Sheik Abdullah, both of whom had strongly rejected the two-nation theory,[17] were equally opposed to this. India took the Kashmir dispute to the United Nations on 1 January 1948. By November 1948, Indian forces had recaptured Poonch, Dras, and Kargil, but the northern and western parts were still under occupation of the Pakistan Army, where a Government of Azad (independent) Kashmir was formed with Muzaffarabad as capital—it still remains so. With the onset of another winter, hostilities had to cease. In January 1949, UN mediated a ceasefire, subject to the United Nations Security Council Resolution 47. That resolution, adopted on 21 April 1948, recommended that in the interest of 'a free and impartial plebiscite', Pakistan must withdraw from J&K of all 'tribesmen and Pakistani nationals' who had 'entered the region for the purpose of fighting' and that India leave only the minimum number of troops needed for 'the maintenance of law and order'.[18] Subsequently India refused to implement the plebiscite claiming the withdrawal of Pakistan forces was a prerequisite as per this resolution. In 1990, after nearly four decades, the United States changed its position and was no longer urging for plebiscite in Kashmir, holding instead that the dispute should be settled through direct negotiations between India and Pakistan. A Special Commission of UN appointed for settlement of the Kashmir issue had visited Srinagar, Delhi, and Islamabad, without succeeding to offer any solution acceptable to all sides.

India today controls about 48 per cent of the former princely state of Jammu & Kashmir, with Pakistan controlling 33 per cent of the region in Gilgit-Baltistan and Azad Kashmir. China controls the rest 19 per cent, in Aksai Chin since the Sino-Indian War in 1962.[19] In addition, an adjoining region, the Trans-Karakoram Tract was ceded by Pakistan to China in 1963. After 1948, India had fought three more wars with Pakistan: in 1965, 1971, and the Kargil War in 1999, and except in 1971, all other wars with that country had been fought on Kashmir.

Article 370

Till the end of 1953, Government of India was not unwilling to conduct the plebiscite, which could not be held because Pakistan did not withdraw its forces from the POK as implied in the Security Council Resolution No. 47. Meanwhile, in 1956, the Constituent Assembly of Jammu & Kashmir ratified the accession of the State to India. Besides, the already strained Indo-Pak relations became even more so due to the involvement of superpowers bringing cold war into the region. Encouraged by its friendship with USA, Pakistan took an aggressive approach, forcing the Indian Government to take the stand that Kashmir's accession to India had become a settled fact and that plebiscite was no longer an option in view of the demographic changes effected by Pakistan settling thousands of non-native Pakistanis to the region in POK,[20] and also in view of the political changes in the region and in Kashmir. 'Since then, so far as India is concerned, Kashmir has been an irrevocable part of the nation. However, without openly saying so, Nehru and his successors have been willing to accept the status quo, that is to accept the ceasefire line or the line of control (LoC) as the permanent international border' (Chandra, Mukherjee, and Mukherjee 2000: 417). The Indian public stand has since remained unchanged that the entire Kashmir, including the POK, is an integral part of India.

The Instrument of Accession was identical for all princely states, and required them to surrender without any financial liability to the Union Government. The Union Parliament alone could make laws on only three subjects—defence, external affairs, and communication—the first two because the states were individually incapable of dealing with it, and the third, communication, which included road, waterways and rail transport, posts and telegraphs, was too important to be left to the individual rulers (Menon 1956: 74–6). The Instrument allowed a state to retain along with internal autonomy, its own flag as well as own Constitution. But by November 1949, all Princely States, saving Jammu & Kashmir, had accepted the Constitution of India. The representative of Jammu & Kashmir to the Constituent Assembly, however, wanted their state to abide by their own Constitution Act of 1939 instead of the Indian Constitution as per terms of the Accession (Anand 1998: 98–9). The genesis of Article 370 lies in this paradoxical situation and the Constituent Assembly had to incorporate Article 370 in the

Constitution (Article 306 A in the Draft Constitution) to resolve this. Gopalaswami Ayyangar, who moved the bill for a special constitutional provision for Jammu & Kashmir, stated, in response to a question by Maulana Hasrat Mohani explaining the reasons for this discrimination,

> The discrimination is due to the special conditions of Kashmir. That particular State is not yet ripe for this kind of integration. It is the hope of everybody here that in due course even Jammu and Kashmir will become ripe for the same sort of integration as has taken place in the case of other States. (Cheers) At present it is not possible to achieve that integration. There are various reasons why this is not possible now....

These reasons he elaborated as:

> In the first place, there has been a war going on within the limits of Jammu & Kashmir State. There was a ceasefire agreed to at the beginning of this year and that ceasefire is still on........ Part of the State is still in the hands of rebels and enemies. We are entangled with the United Nations in regard to Jammu and Kashmir and it is not possible to say now when we shall be free from this entanglement.....Again, the Government of India have committed themselves to the people of Kashmir in certain respects. They have committed themselves to the position that an opportunity would be given to the people of the State to decide for themselves whether they will remain with the Republic or wish to go out of it.... We have also agreed that the will of the people, through the instrument of a constituent assembly, will determine the constitution of the State as well as the sphere of Union jurisdiction over the State.[21]

The matter having reached the international stage, there was hardly any other option, and without much debate, Article 370 of the Constitution relating to 'Temporary Provisions with respect to the State of Jammu & Kashmir' under Part XXI called 'Temporary, Transitional and Special Provisions' was adopted by the Indian Constitution Assembly In 1949. It guaranteed a special status and internal autonomy for J&K with Indian Parliament's jurisdiction being limited only to the three areas mentioned earlier—defence, external affairs, and communication, the state retaining its autonomy in all other matters. The Union can make laws with respect to the state only with its concurrence. The state was authorized to have its own flag, Constitution, and Constituent Assembly, elect its Head of State Sadr-e-Riyasat, and to designate its Chief Minister as Prime Minister. The fundamental rights guaranteed in the Indian Constitution did not extend to the state neither did the emergency provisions under Articles 352 or 356 of the Indian Constitution. The Supreme Court of India, Comptroller & Auditor General of India, or the Election Commission of India did not have any jurisdiction over the State. It is to be noted that Article 370 was meant to serve as a temporary interim measure till the final integration of the State into the Union, 'for the continuance of the state with the Union on the existing basis', as Sardar Patel had said.[22] Thus, as Tillin (2007: 45–67) observed, 'differential autonomy had not been granted to Jammu & Kashmir as a final settlement of ethno-political conflict by recognizing a distinct religious or regional identity. The Indian government regarded Article 370 as a prelude to the state's full integration.' Tenor of the debate in the Constituent Assembly also had left no doubt that Article 370 was conceived only as a temporary measure.

Over the years, however, the State's special status under article 370 has been undermined significantly by increasing central intervention into its democratic process and polity. The first post-Independence election in the State returned Sheikh Abdullah and his National Conference almost unopposed since the main opposition party Praja Parishad had boycotted the election. In July 1952, an agreement, known as the Delhi Agreement, was signed between the Indian Government and Sheikh Abdullah by which provisions of the Indian Constitution regarding fundamental rights, jurisdiction of the Supreme Court of India, Indian Parliament's authority to make laws for the State and the President's authority over the State Government including the power to impose President Rule under article 356—all these were extended to the state. Hereditary rule was abolished, a separate flag for the state along with the national tricolour was allowed and the 'State subjects' were allowed to continue with special citizenship rights of the Indian Union. Nomenclature of the 'Sadr-e-Riyasat' was also changed to Governor and that of the Prime Minister of Jammu & Kashmir to Chief Minister. The state civil services have also since been integrated with the Indian civil services. Some of these were resented by the Kashmiris, but it gave rise to a strongly popular agitation in the Jammu region, led by the Jammu Praja Parishad, demanding full accession to India. An unfortunate incident that happened in the wake of this agitation was the arrest of the Jan Sangh MP Mr Shyama Prasad Mukherjee and his death by heart attack in the Srinagar jail on 23 June 1951, causing 'huge national anger against Sheikh Abdullah' (Jagmohan 2011: 196–7; Chandra,

Mukherhee and Mukherjee 2000: 418). The Constitution (Application to Jammu & Kashmir) Order, 1954 further eroded the autonomy of Kashmir, by empowering the Union Government to legislate on most subjects in the Union List. Bose (2003: 69) rightly observed, 'Article 370 has been a cipher for decades and its formal retention is an irrelevance.'

Kashmir since 1947

Sheikh Abdullah had a huge following and was a man of courage and integrity, but he was also a wily autocrat. Even after the Delhi Agreement, he was playing his own politics for 'full autonomy'—a 'euphemism for complete independence'. His autocratic ways alienated his own party, the National Conference, which demanded 'his dismissal on the charges of corruption, malpractices, disruptionism and dangerous foreign contacts'—he was in fact toying the idea of independence with the Americans. By July 1953, he started demanding independence for Kashmir. He was subsequently dismissed and Bakshi Ghulam Mohammad was installed as Chief Minister who immediately put him under arrest. Under pressure from Nehru, he was released in June 1958, only to be rearrested three months later. Nehru got him released in April 1964, but the wily Sheikh again started clamouring for Kashmir's right to self-determination when he had to be put under house arrest in May 1965, to be freed only in 1968.

After the 1971 war between India and Pakistan that culminated in the defeat of Pakistan and the emergence of Bangladesh as an independent nation, India and Pakistan signed the Shimla agreement in July 1972, recognizing the Line of Control (LoC). Both the nations agreed to respect LoC and also resolved to settle the Kashmir issue bilaterally. The break-up of Pakistan had significantly weakened the demand for secession in Kashmir and the Sheikh now discarded his idea of self-determination, settling for greater autonomy within the Indian Union. Finally in 1975 he became the Chief Minister once again and would remain so till his death in 1982, with his son Farooq Abdullah succeeding him as Chief Minister.

Ever since the first election in 1951, when Sheikh Abdullah's National Conference (NC) had won all but 2 seats in the Assembly till the 1990s, almost every election in the state was heavily rigged with the active connivance of the Congress governments at the Centre, barring only the 1977 elections conducted under the short-lived Janata rule after Emergency (Kak 2011: 37). But the worst rigging took place in the 1987 elections which returned Farooq Abdullah to power in alliance with the Congress, with the NC and Congress together winning 66 out of total 76 assembly seats. Many militant groups had participated in this election, but the results truly shook people's faith in the electoral process altogether. The 1987 election was indeed a turning point in the history of Kashmir. The rigging caused widespread resentment against the dynastic rule of the Abdullahs, and as voices demanding *Aazadii* started getting louder, insurgency gathered momentum in the valley. Popular discontent erupted in the streets against 'Indian rule'. Meanwhile, the end of Soviet occupation in Afghanistan in 1988 released a vast number of Mujahedin fighters, who were armed by Pakistan and USA. Supported and trained by the Pakistani army and government, they now joined the insurgency in Kashmir.

The pro-independence Jammu & Kashmir Liberation Front (JKLF) was formed in the early 1970s; it now gave a call for armed struggle against what many people saw as Indian occupation. The pro-Pakistan militant organization, Hijbul Mujahedin (HM) that came into existence in 1989, propped by Pakistan's Jamaat-e-Islam, started recruiting youths for armed insurrection and sending them across the LoC into training camps run by Pakistan's notorious Inter Services Intelligence (ISI). Hundreds of youth crossed the LoC into the Pakistan-Occupied Kashmir (POK) to receive arms and training before returning as militants to strike at the Indian military and paramilitary forces. The Indian state responded in a most ruthless and brutal manner, unbefitting of a mature democracy. Brutality inflicted by the militants was matched by even more brutality unleashed by the Indian State. Kashmir literally started weeping, bleeding, and convulsing with fear, death and anger.

After Farooq Abdullah resigned in 1990, Central rule was imposed upon Kashmir. Hundreds were arrested, tortured and killed. Indefinite curfews became the order of the day. Houses and families were destroyed, women raped and killed, villages burnt and extra-judicial arrests, torture and killings became commonplace. An estimated 4000 to 8000 people disappeared without a trace (Peer 2009, 128). Justice remained a far cry and human rights turned into jokes.

At Gawkadal Bridge near Srinagar's Lal Chowk, CRPF men fired upon unarmed protesters, killing about 100 of them. More massacres and atrocities followed, committed equally by both sides. Hundreds of innocent Kashmiri Pandits were brutally killed by the militants and their Pakistani sponsors and infiltrators. Under threat of persecution and massacres, most of the estimated 1.62 lakh Hindu families, including almost the entire Kashmiri Pandit community had to leave their homes in Kashmir by March, 1990, to live long years in misery and indignity of the refugee camps in Jammu and Delhi (Kak 2011: 291–3). By March, more than a million protesters had taken to the streets in Kashmir. To control the situation, the draconian Armed Forces (Special Powers) Act (AFSPA) 1958, was extended into the State in 1990. By the end of 2010, there were more than half a million army, paramilitary and police forces deployed in Kashmir, making it one of the most heavily militarized conflict zones in the world. Protests followed killings—even funeral processions by protesters were not spared, and killings brought more protests. Entire Kashmir was turned into a massive tornado of violence, hatred, and retribution. Security forces also paid a heavy price of war with their own lives, far away from their homes, in extremely inhospitable circumstances; they were also equally traumatized, though no amount of trauma would justify the human rights abuses that they inflicted on civilians, many of them students and teenagers.

Between 1990 and 2011, 43,460 people (Kak 2011: x) had been killed in the Kashmir insurgency, including 21,323 militants. 3,642 civilians were killed by the security forces who also lost 5369 people of their own, including 1500 Kashmiri policemen. But there was another slaughter that has gone largely unnoticed, slaughter of Kashmiris killed by militants. Of the 13,226 civilians killed by militants, 11,461 were shot and 1,765 died in grenade blasts and explosions. 'These deaths are the ugly truth that Kashmir has learnt to ignore. The civilians killed fall into a black hole that Kashmiri society never discusses, remembers or protests against….these deaths are forgotten the day after they occur…. These 13,226 Kashmiris just do not exist in the collective psyche.'[23]

But militancy was also exhausting itself, and by the mid-1990s, both JKLF and HM had become spent forces, and were ceding ground to fundamental Islamist outfits like Lashkar-e-Toiba and Jaish-e-Mahammed. After the NDA Government came to power in the centre, following Prime Minister Vajpayee's historic Lahore visit, there was a temporary thaw in the Indo–Pakistan relationship which ushered in a relatively peaceful period in Kashmir. The heavy military presence, effective surveillance at the border restricting infiltration of armed militants from POK and relentless chasing and persecution of militants by the army finally started showing results. Elections also became fairer. After 2003, security forces estimated a massive drop in the number of militants to only 2000 from around 30000 during early 1990s (Kak 2011: 33). Life slowly began returning to normal, and people started trying to come to terms with the trauma and losses suffered and to overcome the sense of hopelessness that characterized the 1990s. In 2009, Omar Abdullah became Chief Minister presiding over a coalition of NC and Congress. And then the Kashmir *Intifada* started.

It started with the cold-blooded murder of three innocent civilians at Machil in Kupwara district by the Indian Army in a fake encounter in April 2010. Widespread protests followed, led by the pro-independence alliance of All Parties Hurriyiat Conference. In June 2010, death of sixteen year old Tufail Ahmed Matoo after being hit by a tear gas shell finally ignited the fire. People defied curfews, burnt government buildings, and attacked security forces and vehicles with stones. It was this *Kani Jang*—war with stones—that marked that summer of discontent in Kashmir which saw the death of 112 protesters till September 2010, when the protests finally subsided. In October 2010, the centre appointed a group of interlocutors to design a political road map for Jammu & Kashmir, they submitted their report one year later. Occasional protests still erupt, but both sides are showing signs of restraint and security forces are displaying more sensitivity and discipline in handling these protests. In November 2014, five army officers were sentenced to life by the Court Martial for Machil killings.[24] The 2014 Assembly elections saw record voter turnout and peaceful elections. One can only hope that a new phase will shape the future of Kashmir now, with more candour and openness, and with forgiveness and hope.

Thus the origin of the present imbroglio in Kashmir can be traced to events following from independence, but events since then have been of no help either. Repeatedly rigged elections leading to loss of faith in the legitimacy of the electoral processes, repeated central interventions, and dismissals of governments on flimsy grounds, political manipulations, and replacement of one set of corrupt administrators by another who were equally corrupt and incompetent—all these have 'cast a deep and dark shadow over the State' and made Kashmir problem an intractable one. On top of all this, Pakistan has always maintained an elaborate terrorism architecture in POK for fomenting trouble in Kashmir. Thankfully, militancy is now clearly on the wane in this beautiful Valley. The Pakistan-sponsored terrorism has taken a sound beating and is clearly on the retreat. Kashmir today deserves and needs a clean, competent, and honest administration like never before, with reinforcement of sound democratic practices and transfer of real power to grassroots. The sooner this is achieved, the faster will the state be able to leave behind the painful memories of its last two decades and move on without carrying any baggage from the past.

Socio-Economic Scenario in Jammu & Kashmir

As observed earlier, J&K presents a rich mosaic of ethno-cultural diversity. Trade and religious links have brought people together here from Central Asia—Turkmenia, Tazakistan, Uzbekistan, Kazakhstan—from Georgia, Azerbaijan, Turkey, Iraq, Afghanistan, and China—who had intermingled and settled in the valley giving rise to its composite culture and varied socio-cultural milieu. The state comprises three main regions Jammu, Kashmir, and Ladakh. Nestled in the Karakoram range it is embraced by the Indus and its tributaries Jhelum, Ravi, Tawi, and Chenub. A series of stunningly beautiful lakes strewn across its breathtaking landscape attracts thousands of tourists every year.

As per the 1971 Census, Jammu & Kashmir had a population of 46 lakh, of which 81 per cent lived in rural areas. Like other special category states, it is also highly ruralized, with 73 per cent of its population still living in rural areas (2011). The state shares a 221 km international boundary with Pakistan in the Jammu region and 465 km with China in its Ladakh sector. The line of control (LoC), which divides the Indian state and POK, stretches along 1001kms.

The progress of socio-economic indicators of J&K has been shown in Annexure 2.5. Till the decade of 1960s, agriculture was the mainstay of its economy; in 1969–70, the share of primary sector to total state NSDP was 61 per cent, with agriculture contributing 56 per cent and forestry 5 per cent. In 1971, the primary sector employed more than 80 per cent of the total workers in the state and the secondary sector only about 6 per cent. The number of workers constituted less than 30 per cent of the total state population at that time. During the period 1980–81 to 2010–11, the share of the primary sector in NSDP had come down from 47 per cent to 25 per cent, while the share of secondary sector had increased from 13 per cent to 26 per cent. Share of the services sector improved from 40 per cent to 49 per cent. But primary sector was still the largest employer in the state, employing about half its working population (2001).

Grants under the special category status had helped the state to expand the network of government activities and public services. Through direct and indirect employment, it has been able to bring down poverty level, like in other special category states, to less than the national average. In 1973–74, J&K had a poverty ratio of 41 per cent compared to the national average of 55 per cent. In 1999–2000 the state had practically no poor people, the poverty ratio being only 3.48 per cent. However, poverty ratio had increased to 10 per cent in 2011–12. The NSDP at current prices grew at an average annual rate of 11per cent during the decade of the 1980s, but the rate of growth accelerated to 17 per cent during the decade of the nineties before falling again to 13 per cent during the next decade. The prevailing law and order situation and militant activities clearly affected the growth rates. But this higher growth of state income was not in response to the higher level of economic activities or an impact of the economic reforms of the nineties. The growth came more as a response to the increased government spending financed by higher central assistance which increased from 9 per cent of GSDP in 1980–81 to 25 per cent in 2010–11. As a result of higher growth, poverty had declined, not as much from generation of new employment or industrialization as from the tertiarization of the economy as a result of higher government spending in a state without any industrial infrastructure. The economy is heavily dependent on the scale of government activities; government's total expenditure in 2010–11 alone constituted about half its GSDP.

During the last three decades, as a consequence of higher plan assistance, there has been a huge expansion of educational infrastructure within the state, though only a moderate expansion in the network of public health. The state had moderately expanded its road network, with surfaced roads making up more than half the total roads in the state. But the road-density was extremely poor, and the 6 kms density of surfaced road in the state was way behind the national average of 71 kms in 2011.

Of the state's 6758 villages, more than 98 per cent were electrified and had drinking water supply by 2011. But the power scenario remains dismal in the state, with very little installed capacity. As the State Development Report says,

> The power sector in Jammu & Kashmir, however, is one of the most underdeveloped sectors in the state. It has not only been unable to keep pace with the growing demand but its supply to ultimate consumers has also been poor. In addition to large unexplored potential, inadequate transmission and distribution network, huge transmission and distribution (T&D) losses, low power tariff, power thefts as well as long gestation period of the power projects have contributed to the dismal situation of the sector.[25]

The instance of 390 MW Dulhasti Hydel Power Plant, set in the rugged mountain terrains without any infrastructure in Kishtwar district, has already become a case study in cost escalation and abnormal delay in project delivery. Conceived in 1985 at an estimated cost of Rs 160 crore, the project was finally completed in 2007, with final cost exceeding Rs 5000 crore.

As regards financial inclusion, in 1981 there were 470 bank branches in the state and the number had almost tripled during the next three decades, but the CD ratio had actually declined from 41 per cent to 37 per cent during the same period indicating reduced demand for credit. Industrial scenario in the state is characterized by predominantly small scale industries with large and medium industries conspicuous by their absence. The small scale sector did not expand since 2001, though the employment in it had almost doubled. In 1981 there were only 385 registered factories in the state employing 28000 workers. Due to the militancy related problems which brought economic activities to a standstill in the valley during the decade of the 1980s and early 1990s, the number of factories came down to 235 and employment fell by more than 50 per cent. But by 2011, there was a reversal of the situation and the number of registered factories had increased to 795 employing about 55000 people.

With a 46 per cent forest cover, its thick forests supply raw materials for several agro-based industries like poplar used by the match industry, poplar and willow for making cricket bats, walnut for the exquisitely carved pieces which are exported all over and of course plywood, hardboard, and chipboard and paper to manufacturing factories in both Jammu & Kashmir valleys. The handicrafts of Kashmir are famous all over the world; the lacquered woodwork, woodcarvings, Kashmiri hand-woven carpets and pashmina shawls generate significant export earnings. These industries existed even in the sixties and contributed significantly to the income from primary sector. The state is also rich in water resources and has a huge potential for generating hydro-electricity on a large scale, a potential that is yet to be tapped meaningfully.

Public Finance in Jammu & Kashmir

The structural weaknesses in its economy were reflected in its public finances as well. In 1969–70, when it had become a special category state, the state's own tax and non-tax revenues together amounted to 41 per cent of its total revenues. Fifty per cent of its revenues came from the central grants, only 9 per cent from its share of union taxes. The revenue receipts constituted 39 per cent of its total receipts into the Consolidated Fund, while capital receipts, i.e., borrowings, constituted the rest. The bulk of its borrowings amounting to 44 per cent of the total also came from the centre. Thus about two thirds of its total receipts then came from gross central transfers including loans. It was overwhelmingly dependent on the centre, like other special category states (Annexure 2.6).

Successive decades had, however, seen a progressive worsening of this dependence. While the share of central grants in total receipts increased to 66 per cent by 2010–11, share of its own revenue dwindled to only 21 per cent. The state's own revenue, as a result, could meet only a quarter of its revenue expenditure needs. 57 per cent of its aggregate disbursements were met from the total central transfers in 2010–11. The major sources of its tax and non-tax revenues were sales tax and receipts from the power sector respectively, contributing 70 per cent and 75 per cent to the respective totals.

A large part of the problem was due to the steep increase in non-developmental expenditure necessitated by the increased expenditure on law and order and on other administrative services for running the day to day administration. Its share went up from 27 per cent to 41 per cent of the total revenue expenditure during the period 1981–2011. Consequently developmental expenditure had to be curtailed, and the ratio of revenue expenditure on education and health to GSDP actually declined, limiting further expansion in these areas.

Jammu & Kashmir remains one of the most heavily indebted states in India. Debt burden was quite heavy even in 1969–70, and the Debt: GSDP ratio of 93 per cent of J&K was the highest in India even then. Interest payment claimed 30 per cent of revenue expenditure and total debt servicing charges including interest payments accounted for 50 per cent of total expenditure in that year. As a result of the special category status, after five years (1974–75), this share came down to 25 per cent but rose again to 50 per cent at the turn of the century. Real change came only after the 12th FC-driven measures were adopted by the state. The FRBMA was enacted in 2005-06, and the debt servicing charges gradually came down to 21 per cent of total expenditure in 2010–11; interest payments also reduced to 12 per cent of revenue expenditure. Debt: GSDP ratio had reached as much as 89 per cent in 1990–91; it had since come down to 46 per cent in 2010–11 which was still high. The net amount available after paying debt servicing charges was only about one tenth of the total amount borrowed. Capital outlay in the state had, however, increased substantially during 2001–11; and the ratio of capital outlay to GSDP had doubled during this period, but yet short of 13 per cent registered in 1969–70. The state now generates a substantial revenue surplus, but not enough to contain the ratio of its GFD to within 3 per cent of GSDP as demanded by the FRBMA. The ratio had in fact reached nearly 15 per cent in 1991 and it was creditable to bring it down to one third of that. But overall, it was not a comforting scenario that stared at the state at the turn of the century as far as public finances was concerned. The state is yet struggling to come out of it.

Planning in Jammu & Kashmir

Table 2.7 shows the plan expenditure in Jammu & Kashmir since it had become a special category state. As in the case of other special category states, the share of economic services in its plan expenditure declined gradually over successive plans—from 84 per cent in the fourth plan to 74 per cent in the eleventh plan, and the shares of social services have correspondingly increased from 16 per cent to 21 per cent during this period, while the share of general services increased from nil to 5 per cent. Among the economic services, energy had received the highest priority throughout, followed by transport and communication. The

Table 2.7 Plan Outlay/ Expenditure in Jammu & Kashmir: Fourth to Eleventh Plan (per cent)

Major Heads of Development	4th plan	5th plan	6th plan	7th plan	8th plan	9th plan	10th plan	11th plan
	1969–74	1974–79	1980–85	1985–90	1992–97	1997–02	2002–07	2007–12
Economic Services	**84**	**81**	**70**	**79**	**77**	**72**	**70**	**74**
Agriculture & Allied Activities	10	7	14	12	12	13	11	8
Rural Development	0	0	0	3	3	3	2	2
Special Areas Programme	1	0	2	6	4	5	5	3
Irrigation and Flood Control	13	16	14	17	12	11	10	7
Energy	34	32	14	27	29	19	18	32
Industry and Minerals	4	7	7	4	3	3	3	2
Transport and Communication	15	9	9	8	10	12	11	10
Other Economic Services	7	10	11	3	3	6	9	10
Social Services	**16**	**19**	**30**	**19**	**23**	**26**	**25**	**21**
Education	5	6	6	7	10	12	11	8
Medical and Public Health	2	4	8	5	5	7	7	5
Housing & Urban Development	2	3	5	5	6	5	3	4
Other Social Services	6	6	11	3	2	3	4	3
General Services	**0**	**0**	**0**	**2**	**1**	**2**	**5**	**5**
Total (Rs Crore)	**162**	**279**	**919**	**1656**	**4511**	**7542**	**13126**	**25833**

Source: Records of the Account General in Jammu & Kashmir.

other focus areas were agriculture and allied activities and irrigation and flood control. Among the social services, emphasis remained on education, public health, and housing and urban development.

Summing Up

Jammu & Kashmir has often been portrayed as a unique case in the history of Indian federalism, being the only state with a separate constitution in independent India. While discussing the structure of asymmetric federalism in J&K, some political analysts are tempted to look at Article 370 as a way of addressing religious cleavages, which, in view of the harmonious blend of Buddhism, Hinduism, and Islam in J&K, did not exist there. Actually the asymmetrical powers given to the state flowed not from any such cleavages but from the circumstances of its accession to India. The fault-lines that marred the political landscape of J&K since independence were not the same as those that existed in European countries, on the basis of religion, language, or crisis of identity.

However, after more than six decades since Article 370 was incorporated in the Indian Constitution, its relevance has almost been lost. Neither has it been so unique—special privileges have been conferred on other states by the Constitution of India like Article 371, the Fifth and Sixth Schedules. If Indian Parliament needs the State's concurrence to enact certain laws in respect of J&K, even other states like Nagaland and Mizoram have similar, if not identical, privileges in respect of indigenous customs and economic interests of tribals. If any difference did exist between J&K and other states in the northeast, it was only in the degree of internal autonomy; even this has since been so eroded as to render it almost inconsequential. What has become much more relevant to J&K is its special category status, which gives it access to liberal central funds. Abrogation of Article 370, if ever done, is unlikely to make any real difference to the state's development, but denying its special category status is sure to jeopardize growth prospects and imperil its survival.

All the three states—Assam, Nagaland, and J&K—were seriously beset with the problems of lack of capacity and infrastructure, which they had no economic resources to create or build with. Further impediments to development were created by political problems inherited by them from the past, which at times threatened the cohesiveness of the Indian federation. They were not equipped to deal with these problems on their own and needed outside help and resources. While debating the set of principles that should be evolved and adopted for allocation of central assistance to the states, the 24th NDC Meeting noted that 'there was a general feeling that States like Assam, Jammu & Kashmir, and Nagaland would, in any way, have to receive special treatment.' This would later translate into their special category status. As smaller states were carved out of bigger states, they were later added one by one to the special category and the facilities for additional central grants extended to them. Basically it was their need for external resources that guided the creation of the special category in the first place to help overcome their special development bottlenecks; what was not realized was that these bottlenecks could not be addressed just by injecting funds.

However, it was also true that without the additional central support that accrued to them by virtue of their special category status, they would possibly not have survived as states without adequate economic means. Being economically unviable, naturally they were heavily indebted, and ran high fiscal deficits. The fiscal space got further limited by their inability to generate future income through capital outlay. This support they received had indeed served to reduce poverty levels and created a reasonable network of social infrastructure that enhanced the quality of life of their people. But the arrangement of providing assistance had serious inherent flaws, as it did not address the structural weaknesses of their economies and only created an incapacitating all-out dependence on the centre. For the centre it was a political dependence for reasons of federal coherence; beyond that it took no responsibility for monitoring either the utilization of funds by these states or addressing the capacity and other constraints. The whole structure lacked accountability, in the absence of which such easy access to funds to the political class did

Annexure 2.1 Socio-Economic Parameters of Assam: 1970–71 to 2010–11[26]

Parameters	1970–71	1980–81	1990–91	2000–01	2010–11
A. State Income					
NSDP (Rs Crore)	774	2,298	9,498	33,760	1,00,627
Per Capita Income (Rs)	528	1,284	4,281	12,797	33,087
Share of Primary Sector (per cent)	50	48	44	36	27
Share of Secondary Sector (per cent)	19	12	11	17	24
Share of Tertiary Sector (per cent)	31	40	44	47	49
Per cent of people below poverty line	51.21 (1973–74)	40.47 (1983)	40.86 (1993–94)	36.09 (1999–2000)	32.0 (2011–12)
B. Demography					
Area (Sq. Km.)	87,438	78,523	78,523	78,438	78,438
Population (crore)	1.5	1.8	2.2	2.7	3.1
Per cent of Rural Population	91.2	NA[27]	88.9	87.1	86
Per cent of SC/ST Population	17.2	NA	19.3	19.3	NA
Density of Population per sq.km,	186	230	286	340	397
Literacy Rate (per cent)	33.9	NA	52.9	63.3	73.2
Females per 1000 Males	896	910	923	935	954
Per cent of Working Population	NA	NA	31.2	35.8	49
Per cent of Working Population engaged in the primary sector	65.8	76.0	63.0	52.7	NA
No. of Villages	NA	21,995	24,685	26,312	26,637

(Cont'd)

Annexure 2.1 (*Cont'd*)

Parameters	1970–71	1980–81	1990–91	2000–01	2010–11
C. Infrastructure					
i. Education					
No. of Junior Basic and Senior Basic Schools	20,337	28,938 (1983)	33,974	37,749 (2002)	45,335
No. of Secondary and Higher Secondary Schools	1,228	2,364 (1983)	3,432	4,507 (2002)	663
No. of Other Institutions of Higher Learning	141	209 (1983)	287 (1996)	379 (2002)	526
No. of Universities	2	3 (1983)	6 (1996)	7 (2002)	9
Per Capita Revenue Expenditure on Education (Rs)	NA	53	200	719	2,068
Per cent of Expenditure on Education to Total Budget (per cent)	NA	10	23	15	22
ii. Public Health					
No. of hospitals (only Govt. Allopathic hospitals are taken)	NA	111 (1984)	268	100 (2004)	153
No. of hospital beds	NA	9,645 (1984)	12,661	3,000 (2004)	7,622
No. of Primary Health Centres and Sub-Centres	117	1,507 (1984–85)	5,851 (1993–94)	5,720 (1998–99)	5,542
Per Capita Expenditure on Health (Rs)	NA	11	50	130	478
iii. Roads					
Total Road Length (km) (incl. municipality and panchayat roads)	17,030	59,579	68,913	79,796	2,41,789
Length of Surfaced Roads (Km)	3,683	8,166	10,841	10,252	37,816

(*Cont'd*)

Annexure 2.1 (*Cont'd*)

Parameters	1970–71	1980–81	1990–91	2000–01	2010–11
Length of National Highway (km)	1,365 (1974)	2,198	2,033	2,044	2,836
Surfaced Road per 100 sq. km	4.2	10.4	13.8	13.1	24.0
Total Road per 100 sq Km	19.5	75.9	87.9	101.7	308.3
Total Road per 1000 population	1.2	3.3	3.1	3.0	7.8
iv. Electricity					
Per Capita Power Consumption (kwh)	24	34	98	74 (2002–03)	205
Generation of electricity (million kwh)	518	465	1206	923 (1998–99)	1864
Installed Capacity (MW)	203 (1973–74)	202	514	574 (1998–99)[28]	470 (State)
Percentage of Villages electrified	7	26	54 (1985)	81	92.5
v. Post Offices and Banks					
Population served by a Post Office	4,311	6,011 (1983–84)	6,772 (1992–93)	5,698 (2001–02)	7,779
No. of Bank Offices	95 (1970)	507	1,095 (1989)	1,242 (1999)	1,563
Credit Deposit Ratio (per cent)	39.2 (1970)	46.9	55.4 (1989)	31.5 (1999)	36.5
D. Industry					
No. of Registered Small Scale Units	1,677 (1974)	4,153	4,430 (1988)	14,453	18,671 (2006–07)
No. of Persons Employed		NA	34,475 (1988)	64,623	1,57,058 (2006–07)

(*Cont'd*)

Annexure 2.1 (*Cont'd*)

Parameters	1970–71	1980–81	1990–91	2000–01	2010–11
No. of Registered Factories	1,592 (1970)	1,857 (1981–82)	1,548	1,435	2,795
Value of Output (Rs Crore)	146 (1970)	717 (1981–82)	2,887	8,741	42,367
Net Value Added (Rs Crore)	45 (1970)	140 (1981–82)	734	1,284	6,674
Profits (Rs Crore)	—	119 (1981–82)	654	1,019	3,993
Gross Fixed Capita Formation (Rs Crore)	—	46 (1981–82)	198	2,211	1,698
No. of persons employed in factories	69,000 (1970)	1,20,215 (1981–82)	1,13,769	1,12,542	1,66,657
State Government Employees	79,880	NA	NA	3,26,061	NA

Annexure 2.2 Public Finance in Assam: 1969–70 to 2010–11

A. Public Finance (Figures–Rs Crore)	1969–70	1980–81	1990–91	2000–01	2010–11	CAGR (per cent) 1969–2011
GSDP	685[29]	2516	10621	36814	112688	13.3
States Own Tax Revenue	28	66	312	1410	5930	14.0
Share of Central Taxes	20	98	596	1683	7969	15.7
Total Tax Revenue	48	164	908	3093	13899	14.8

(*Cont'd*)

Annexure 2.2 (*Cont'd*)

A. Public Finance (Figures–Rs Crore)	1969–70	1980–81	1990–91	2000–01	2010–11	CAGR (per cent) 1969–2011
Non-Tax Revenue	11	265	278	527	2373	14.0
State's Own Revenue (Tax + Non-Tax)	39	331	590	1937	8303	14.0
Grants from Centre	52	93	591	2018	6733	12.6
Total Revenue Receipts	111	522	1777	5638	23005	13.9
Capital Receipts, of which	161	341	2201	1501	2073	6.4
Central Loans	70	158	877	922	15	−3.7
Recovery of Loans and Advances	1	5	6	18	28	8.5
Total Receipts	272	863	3978	7139	25078	11.7
Receipt from Sales Tax	12	31	243	918	4319	15.4
Revenue Expenditure on General Services, of which	36	101	596	2548	7766	14.0
Interest Payment	15	30	263	865	1912	12.6
Revenue Expenditure on Social Services, of which	48	158	777	2815	10159	14.0
Expenditure on Education	24	95	439	1912	6431	14.6
Expenditure on Health	8	19	110	346	1480	13.6
Revenue Expenditure on Economic Services	40	95	535	1046	4669	12.3
Total Revenue Expenditure	125	357	1916	6418	22952	13.6

(*Cont'd*)

Annexure 2.2 (*Cont'd*)

A. Public Finance (Figures–Rs Crore)	1969–70	1980–81	1990–91	2000–01	2010–11	CAGR (per cent) 1969–2011
Grants in aid and Contributions	0	4	8	9	358	
Capital Outlay	18	76	247	561	2001	12.2
Loans and Advances, etc.	6	67	183	217	71	6.2
Capital Expenditure	143	571	2044	6333	2995	7.7
Total Expenditure	268	928	3960	12751	25947	11.8
Repayment of Public Debt	119	428	1614	5555	923	5.1
Debt Servicing (Principal + Interest)	134	458	1877	6420	2835	7.7
Net Public Debt Receipts on Consolidated Fund	21	–184	141	–5136	–833	
Gross Fiscal Deficit	37	–27	563	1540	1991	
Revenue Deficit	14	–165	139	780	–53	
Primary Deficit	22	–57	300	675	79	
Outstanding Debt	281	734	4309	10067	20144	11.0

B. Public Finance (Ratios)	1969–70	1980–81	1990–91	2000–01	2010–11
Own Revenue/ Total Revenues (per cent)	35.1	63.4[30]	33.2	34.4	36.1
Central Grants / Total Revenues (per cent)	46.8	17.8	33.3	35.8	29.3
Share of Central Taxes/ Total Revenues	18.0	18.8	33.5	29.9	34.6
Own Revenue/Revenue Expenditure (per cent)	31.2	92.7	30.8	30.2	36.2
Interest Payment/Revenue Expenditure (per cent)	12.0	8.4	13.7	13.5	8.3

(*Cont'd*)

Annexure 2.2 (*Cont'd*)

B. Public Finance (Ratios)	1969–70	1980–81	1990–91	2000–01	2010–11
Non-Developmental Rev Expenditure / Total Rev Expenditure (per cent)	28.8	28.3	31.1	39.7	33.8
Debt Servicing/Total Expenditure (per cent)	50.0	49.4	47.4	50.3	10.9
Capital Outlay/Capital Receipts (per cent)	11.2	22.3	11.2	37.4	96.5
Receipt from Sales Tax/ Own Taxes (per cent)	42.9	47.0	77.9	65.1	72.8
Central Transfers/Aggregate Disbursements (per cent)	53.0	37.6	52.1	36.3	56.7
State's Own Taxes/GSDP (per cent)	4.1	2.6	2.9	3.8	5.3
Outstanding Debt/GSDP (per cent)	41.0	29.2	40.6	27.3	17.9
Gross Fiscal Deficit/GSDP (per cent)	5.4	–1.1	5.3	4.2	1.8
Expenditure on Education/ GSDP (per cent)	3.5	3.8	4.1	5.2	5.7
Expenditure on Health/ GSDP (per cent)	1.2	0.8	1.0	0.9	1.3

Annexure 2.3 Socio Economic Parameters of Nagaland: 1980–81 to 2010–11[31]

Parameters (Area: 16579 sq km)	1980–81	1990–91	2000–01	2010–11
A. Income and Poverty				
NSDP (Rs Crore)	108	248	3160	10850
Per Capita Income (Rs)	1383	3464	16253	55582
Share of Primary Sector (per cent)	33	33	33	27
Share of Secondary Sector (per cent)	14	15	13	13
Share of Tertiary Sector (per cent)	53	52	54	60

(*Cont'd*)

Annexure 2.3 (*Cont'd*)

Parameters (Area: 16579 sq km)	1980–81	1990–91	2000–01	2010–11
Per cent of People Below Poverty Line	39 (1983)	38 (1993–94)	33 (1999–2000)	19 (2011–12)
B. Demography				
Population (crore)	0.08	0.12	0.20	0.20
Per cent of Rural Population	85	83	83	71
Per cent of SC/ST Population	84	88	89	NA
Density of Population per sq.km,	47	73	120	119
Literacy Rate (per cent)	48	62	67	80
Females per 1000 Males	863	886	909	931
Per cent of Working Population	48	43	43	56
Per cent of working population Engaged in the primary sector	80	83	68	NA
No. of Villages	960	1112	1317	1454
Net Irrigated Area to Net Cultivated Area (per cent)	NA	31	20 (2001–02)	24
C. Infrastructure				
i. Education				
No. of Junior Basic and Senior Basic Schools	1501 (1983)	1662 (1992–93)	1779 (2002–03)	2127
No. of Secondary and Higher Secondary Schools	113 (1983)	189 (1992–93)	255 (2002–03)	406
No. of Other Institutions of Higher Learning	19 (1983)	31 (1992–93)	54 (2002–03)	56
No. of Universities	—	—	1 (2002–03)	3
Per Capita Revenue Expenditure on Education (Rs)	150	375	870	3414

(*Cont'd*)

Annexure 2.3 (*Cont'd*)

Parameters (Area: 16579 sq km)	1980–81	1990–91	2000–01	2010–11
Per cent of Expenditure on Education to Total Budget (per cent)	6	8	9	10
ii. Public Health				
No. of hospitals (only Govt. Allopathic hospitals)	35 (1984)	31	48 (2004)	48
No. of hospital beds	1112 (1984)	1114	2060 (2004)	2150
No. of Primary Health Centres and Sub-Centres	154 (1984)	277	481 (2004)	522
Per Capita Expenditure on Health (Rs)	63	192	340	1197
iii. Roads				
Total Road Length (km)	6287 (1981–82)	8805 (1992–93)	20647 (2004)	34146
Length of Surfaced Roads (Km)	879 (1981–82)	6842 (1992–93)	6570 (2004)	15470
Length of National Highway (km)	105 (1981–82)	NA	NA	494
Surfaced Road per 100 sq. km	5.3 (1981–82)	41.3 (1992–93)	39.6	93.3
Total Road per 100 sq Km Area	38.0 (1981–82)	53.1 (1992–93)	124.5	206.0
Total Road per 1000 population (Km)	8.1 (1981–82)	7.2 (1992–93)	10.3	17.2
iv. Electricity				
Per capita power Consumption (kwh)	32	75	130	218
Generation of electricity (million kwh)	NA	95	NA	80
Installed Capacity (MW)	NA	6	NA	30

(*Cont'd*)

Annexure 2.3 (*Cont'd*)

Parameters (Area: 16579 sq km)	1980–81	1990–91	2000–01	2010–11
Percentage of Villages electrified	38	NA	64	63
v. Post Offices and Banks				
Population served by a Post Office	3087 (1983–84)	4082 (1992–93)	NA	6037
No. of Bank Offices	64 (1985)	66 (1994)	71	96
Credit Deposit Ratio (per cent)	35	18 (1997–98)	12	26
D. Industry				
No. of Registered Small Scale Units	345	509	568	1331
No. of Registered Factories	3 (1982–83)	50	129	84
Value of Output (Rs Crore)	0.20 (1982–83)	26	92	470
Net Value Added (Rs Crore)	0.03 (1982–83)	—	6.9	53.7
Profits (Rs Crore)	0.02 (1982–83)	−14.4	−2	39
Gross Fixed Capita Formation (Rs Crore)	—	—	3.9	0.74
No. of persons employed in factories	—	2513	3130	2208

Annexure 2.4 Management of Public Finances in Nagaland: 1974–75 to 2010–11

B. Public Finance (Figures – Rs Crore)	**1974–75**	**1980–81**	**1990–91**	**2000–01**	**2010–11**	**CAGR (per cent) 1974–2011**
GSDP	49[32]	119	655	3399	11759	16.4
States Own Tax Revenue	1.48	4	15	36	227	15.0
Share of Central Taxes	1.26	4	124	106	689	19.1
Total Tax Revenue	**2.74**	**8**	**139**	**142**	**916**	**17.5**
Non-Tax Revenue	2.02	51[33]	31	39	182	13.3
State's Own Revenue (Tax + Non-Tax)	**3.5**	**55**	**46**	**75**	**409**	**14.1**
Grants from Centre	35.04	84	241	1072	3900	14.0
Total Revenue Receipts	**39.8**	**143**	**411**	**1253**	**4998**	14.4
Capital Receipts, of which	7.77	39	150	673	466	12.0
Central Loans	1.41	13	57	50	0	
Recovery of Loans and Advances	0.37	1	8	6	2	4.8
Total Receipts	**47.57**	**182**	**561**	**1926**	**5464**	14.1
Receipt from taxes on Sales, Trade etc.	0.62	2	13	27	167	16.8
Revenue Expenditure on General Services, of which	13.54	33	144	623	1842	14.6
Interest Payment	1.5	3	31	177	394	16.7
Revenue Expenditure on Social Services, of which	11.49	30	120	351	1126	13.6
Expenditure on Education	4.34	12	45	174	659	15.0

(*Cont'd*)

Annexure 2.4 (*Cont'd*)

B. Public Finance (Figures – Rs Crore)	1974–75	1980–81	1990–91	2000–01	2010–11	CAGR (per cent) 1974–2011
Expenditure on Health	4.37	5	23	68	189	11.0
Revenue Expenditure on Economic Services	10.46	29	157	316	1219	14.1
Total Revenue Expenditure	**35.49**	**92**	**421**	**1290**	**4187**	14.2
Capital Outlay	**11.15**	26	87	224	**1123**	13.7
Repayment of Public Debt	0.15	68	74	383	261	23.0
Loans and Advances etc.	1.82	1	9	17	4	2.2
Capital Expenditure	**13.12**	**95**	**170**	**624**	**1388**	13.8
Total Expenditure	**48.61**	**187**	**591**	**1914**	**5575**	14.1
Debt Servicing (Principal + Interest)	1.65	71	105	560	655	18.1
Net Public Debt Receipts on Consolidated Fund	4.3	–33	36	96	–193	
Gross Fiscal Deficit	8.29	–25	98	272	314	10.6
Revenue Deficit	–4.31	–51	10	37	–811	15.7
Primary Deficit	6.79	–28	67	95	–80	
Outstanding Debt	38	66	459	1835	4914	14.5

B. Public Finance (Ratios)	1974–75	1980–81	1990–91	2000–01	2010–11
Own Revenue/ Total Revenues (per cent)	8.8	38.5	11.2	6.0	8.2
Central Grants / Total Revenues (per cent)	88.0	58.7	58.6	85.6	78.0

(*Cont'd*)

Annexure 2.4 (*Cont'd*)

B. Public Finance (Ratios)	1974–75	1980–81	1990–91	2000–01	2010–11
Share of Central Taxes/ Total Revenues	3.2	2.8	30.2	8.5	13.8
Own Revenue/Revenue Expenditure (per cent)	9.9	59.8	10.9	5.8	9.8
Interest Payment/ Revenue Expenditure (per cent)	4.2	3.3	7.4	13.7	9.4
Non-Developmental Rev Expenditure/Total Rev Expenditure (per cent)	38.2	35.9	34.2	48.3	44.0
Debt Servicing/Total Expenditure (per cent)	3.4	38.0	17.8	29.3	11.7
Capital Outlay/Capital Receipts (per cent)	143.5	66.7	58.0	33.3	241.0
Receipt from Sales Tax/Own Taxes (per cent)	41.9	50.0	86.7	75.0	73.6
Central Transfers/ Aggregate Disbursements (per cent)	77.6	54.0	71.4	64.2	82.3
State's Own Taxes/GSDP (per cent)	3.0	3.4	2.3	1.1	1.9
Outstanding Debt/GSDP (per cent)	77.6	55.5	70.1	54.0	41.8
Gross Fiscal Deficit/GSDP (per cent)	16.9	–21.0	15.0	8.0	2.7
Expenditure on Education/ GSDP (per cent)	8.9	10.1	6.9	5.1	5.6
Expenditure on Health/ GSDP (per cent)	8.9	4.2	3.5	2.0	1.6

Annexure 2.5 Socio-Economic Parameters of Jammu & Kashmir since 1980–81[34]

Parameters (Area: 2,22,236 sq km[35])	1980–81	1990–91	2000–01	2010–11
A. State Income				
NSDP (Rs Crore)	1050	2908	14328	46740
Per Capita Income (Rs)	1776	3816	14301	40089
Share of Primary Sector (per cent)	47	43	33	25
Share of Secondary Sector (per cent)	13	13	20	26
Share of Tertiary Sector (per cent)	40	44	47	49
Per cent of People Below Poverty Line	24 (1983)	25 (1993–94)	3 (1999–2000)	10 (2011–12)
B. Demography				
Population (crore)	0.60	0.77[36]	1.01	1.25
per cent of Rural Population	79	NA	75	73
Density of Population per sq.km,	27	34	100	124
Literacy Rate (per cent)	31	NA	56	69
Females per 1000 Males	892	896	892	883
Per cent of Working Population	NA	NA	37	40
Per cent of working population engaged in the primary sector	NA	NA	49	NA
No. of Villages	6503	NA	6652	6758
C. Infrastructure				
i. Education				
No. of Primary and Middle Schools	9092	11680	14464 (2002)	24323
No. of Secondary and Higher Secondary Schools	536	1396	1892 (2002)	3105
No. of Other Institutions of Higher Learning	34	47	125 (2002)	335
No. of Universities	2	3	5 (2002)	10
Per Capita Revenue Expenditure on Education(Rs)	68	242	789	2179

(*Cont'd*)

Annexure 2.5 (*Cont'd*)

Parameters (Area: 2,22,236 sq km)	1980–81	1990–91	2000–01	2010–11
per cent of Expenditure on Education to Total Budget (per cent)	6	8	6	9
ii. Public Health				
No. of Hospitals	40	72	76	92
No. of Hospital Beds	5422	NA	3295	3945
No. of Primary Health Centres and Sub-Centres	477	652	2213	2304
Per Capita Expenditure on Health (Rs)	28	99	356	806
iii. Roads				
Total Road Length (km)	8206	11838	21095 (2004)	26980
Length of Surfaced Roads (Km)[37]	5624	9379	8962 (2004)	14178
Surfaced Road per 100 sq. km	2.5	4.2	4.0	6
Total Road per 100 sq Km	3.7	5.3	9.5	12
Length of National Highway (km)	NA	NA	NA	1695
Total Road per 1000 population	1.4	1.4	2.1	2
iv. Electricity				
Per capita power Consumption (kwh)	NA	NA	255 (1998–99)	952
Generation of electricity (million kwh)	NA	NA	580	4275
Installed Capacity (MW)[38]	NA	NA	1161	1090
Per centage of Villages electrified	48	95	98 (2006–07)	96
v. Post Offices and Banks				
Population served by a Post Office	4481	4948	6019	7403 (2012)

(*Cont'd*)

Annexure 2.5 (*Cont'd*)

Parameters (Area: 2,22,236 sq km)	1980–81	1990–91	2000–01	2010–11
No. of Bank Offices	470	786	829	1302
Credit Deposit Ratio (per cent)	41	55	35	37
D. Industry				
No. of Registered Small Scale Units	4828	29963	14625	14534
No. of Persons Employed	42992	131164	50707	106122
No. of Registered Factories	327	235	356	795
Value of Output (Rs Crore)	109	452	1343	19024
Net Value Added (Rs Crore)	18	76	159	2779
Profits (Rs Crore)	0.3	43	7	1844
Gross Fixed Capita Formation (Rs Crore)	18	28	87	506
No. of Persons Employed in Factories	27859	13577	23216	55285

Annexure 2.6 Public Finances in Jammu & Kashmir: 1980–81 to 2010–11

A. Public Finance (Figures – Rs Crore)	1969–70	1980–81[39]	1990–91	2000–01	2010–11	CAGR (per cent) 1969–2011
GSDP	221[40]	1186	3614	16700	58073	14.6
States Own Tax Revenue	7	46	150	163	3483	16.5
Share of Central Taxes	6	31	376	675	3067	16.6
Total Tax Revenue	12	77	526	838	6550	16.5
Non-Tax Revenue	20	302	102	444	1093	10.3
State's Own Revenue (Tax + Non-Tax)	26	348	252	607	4576	13.4

(*Cont'd*)

Annexure 2.6 (*Cont'd*)

A. Public Finance (Figures – Rs Crore)	1969–70	1980–81	1990–91	2000–01	2010–11	CAGR (per cent) 1969–2011
Grants from Centre	33	112	907	3794	14591	16.1
Total Revenue Receipts	65	491	1535	5076	22234	15.3
Capital Receipts, of which	104	159	908	6685	7056	10.8
Central Loans	73	—	151	435	−1015	
Recovery of Loans and Advances	2	3	5	14	2	
Total Receipts	168	650	2443	11761	29290	13.4
Receipt from Taxes on Sales, Trade etc.	2	17	62	357	2425	18.6
Revenue Expenditure on General Services, of which	32	71	391	2448	7777	14.3
Interest Payment	22	33	180	769	2283	12.0
Revenue Expenditure on Social Services, of which	13	79	414	1649	5214	15.7
Expenditure on Education	8	41	186	797	2724	15.3
Expenditure on Health	4	17	76	360	1007	14.4

(*Cont'd*)

Annexure 2.6 (*Cont'd*)

A. Public Finance (Figures – Rs Crore)	1969–70	1980–81	1990–91	2000–01	2010–11	CAGR (per cent) 1969–2011
Revenue Expenditure on Economic Services	28	117	443	2523	5475	13.7
Grants in aid and Contributions	0	0	0	21	553	
Total Revenue Expenditure	**73**	**267**	**1248**	**6641**	**19019**	**14.5**
Capital Outlay	29	130	352	867	**6064**	**13.9**
Repayment of Public Debt	62	277	737	5991	3932	10.7
Loans and Advances etc.	3	8	30	59	72	8.1
Capital Expenditure	**94**	**415**	**1119**	**6917**	**10068**	**12.1**
Total Expenditure	**167**	**682**	**2367**	**13558**	**29087**	**13.4**
Debt Servicing (Principal + Interest)	84	310	917	6760	6215	11.1
Net Public Debt Receipts on Consolidated Fund	14	–159	–39	–134	769	
Gross Fiscal Deficit	39	–89	90	2477	2919	
Revenue Deficit	8	–224	–287	1565	–3215	
Primary Deficit	17	–122	–90	1708	636	
Outstanding Debt	**205**	**648**	**3227**	**8899**	**26516**	**14.5**

(*Cont'd*)

Annexure 2.6 (*Cont'd*)

B. Public Finance (Ratios)	1969–70	1980–81	1990–91	2000–01	2010–11
Own Revenue/Total Revenues (per cent)	40.8	70.9	16.4	12.0	20.6
Central Grants/Total Revenues (per cent)	50.3	22.8	59.1	74.7	65.6
Share of Central Taxes/ Total Revenues	8.8	6.3	24.5	13.3	13.8
Own Revenue/Revenue Expenditure (per cent)	36.2	130.3	20.2	9.1	24.1
Interest Payment/ Revenue Expenditure (per cent)	30.1	12.4	14.4	11.6	12.0
Non-Developmental Rev Expenditure/Total Rev Expenditure (per cent)	43.8	26.6	31.3	36.9	40.9
Debt Servicing/Total Expenditure (per cent)	50.3	45.5	38.7	49.9	21.4
Capital Outlay/Capital Receipts (per cent)	28.0	81.8	38.8	13.0	85.9
Receipt from Sales Tax/ Own Taxes (per cent)	32.8	37.0	41.3	219.0	69.6
Central Transfers/ Aggregate Disbursements (per cent)	67.0	—	60.6	36.2	57.2
State's Own Taxes/ GSDP (per cent)	3.1	3.9	4.2	1.0	6.0
Outstanding Debt/ GSDP (per cent)	92.8	54.6	89.3	53.3	45.7
Gross Fiscal Deficit/ GSDP (per cent)	17.6	–7.5	2.5	14.8	5.0
Expenditure on Education/GSDP (per cent)	3.6	3.5	5.1	4.8	4.7
Expenditure on Health / GSDP (per cent)	1.8	1.4	2.1	2.2	1.7

what it always does by corrupting institutions and distorting economic relationships—in short by disempowering the state even more.

Notes

1. Apart from the books mentioned in the references, the following also provided inputs for Assam: *Development Disparities in North East India, Economy of the North East: Policy, Present Conditions and Future Possibilities*, Gulshan Sachdeva, Centre for Policy Research, New Delhi, Konark Publishing, New Delhi, 2000; *Economic Planning and Development of North Eastern States*, ed. Amlesh Banerjee and Biman Kar, Kaniska Publishers & Distributors, New Delhi, 2007; and *Glimpses of Assam*, R S Arha and Latika Singh, ABD Publishers, Jaipur, 2008.

2. Available at http://indiaheritage.org/history/history_assam.htm; accessed on 2 May 2013.

3. Available at http://online.assam.gov.in/documents/10156/2beb50b9-f285-4ee8-a5c0-cff9ba939b5a; accessed on 2 May 2013.

4. *Assam Development Report*, Planning Commission, 2002, 22–3.

5. *Assam Human Development Report 2003*, Planning & Development Department, Government of Assam, p. i.

6. *Assam Human Development Report 2003*, Planning & Development Department, Government of Assam, p. 22.

7. Estimated figures since no census was conducted in Assam in 1981 due to the Assam agitation against foreign nationals.

8. Annual Report, Ministry of Road Transport and Highways, GoI, 2.

9. *Banking Statistics*, December, 1974, Reserve Bank of India quoted in Assam Development Report, Planning Commission, 2002, 534.

10. Economic Survey, Assam 1975–76, http://www.neportal.org/northeast-files/Assam/Economy/Report/ economic survey 75–76I.asp. Accessed 04 May 2013.

11. Economic Survey of Assam, 2012–13, 4.

12. Data for Tables 2.3, 2.6 and 2.7 have been obtained from records of the Accountant General (A&E) of respective states.

13. Statistical Tables 46–49, appended to the *Report of the Fifth Finance Commission*.

14. *Nagaland Human Development Report, 2004*, Planning Commission, 3.

15. 'Kashmir: History', *Imperial Gazetteer of India*, volume 15. 1908, 94–95.

16. Nehru's speech in All India Radio, Nov 02, 1947.

17. Sheikh Abdullah's speech on October 1, 1947.

18. Available at http://www.un.org/en/ga/search/view_doc.asp?symbol=S/RES/47percent281948percent29&referer=http://www.un.org/en/sc/documents/

resolutions/1948.shtml&Lang=E, Paras A, 1.(a) and 2.(a), Security Council Resolution No. 47.

19. In order to have better access to their trouble-torn province of Tibet Autonomous Region from Xinjiang in Western China, the Chinese army had entered the northeast portion of Ladakh and completed a military road through the Aksai Chin connecting Xinxiang and Western Tibet in the mid-1950s. India's belated discovery of this road led to border clashes between the two countries, culminating in the Sino–Indian war of October 1962.

20. Even within the Indian state also, about a quarter million Hindu Kashmiri Pandits have since been coerced by the militants to flee the Kashmir valley.

21. Constituent Assembly Debates.

22. Constituent Assembly Debates

23. *Times of India*, New Delhi, 20 June 2011; http://timesofindia.indiatimes.com/india/State-data-refutes-claim-of-1-lakh-killed-in-Kashmir/articleshow/8918214.cms, accessed 02/12/2014.

24. *Times of India*, 14 November 2014.

25. Jammu & Kashmir Development Report, Planning Commission Govt. of India, 116–7.

26. Common sources of data used in all Tables in Chapters 2 and 4 to 7 are: CSO data in respect of state incomes taken from the CSO website as on 1 March 2014 (data prior to 1975 taken from respective CSO reports); Census Reports of the Registrar General in respect of demographic data; Finance Accounts of the respective states for all public finance data used in this book; Economic Survey of the respective states for various years published by the Directorates of Economics and Statistics of the respective governments; Development Reports of different states published by the Planning Commission in different years; Basic Statistics of the North Eastern Region for various years published by the North Eastern Council in respect of north eastern states: Web portals of different governments and the Ministry of DoNER, Govt. of India; RBI Reports on Statistical Tables relating to Banks in India for different years in respect of banking statistics. *Assam Human Development Report 2003*, Government of Assam has also been used in this table.

27. Census in Assam could not be conducted in 1981 due to disturbed conditions in the State.

28. Including private and central agencies it was 971 MW.

29. For 1969–70, NSDP figures have been used.

30. The high figure is due to the fact that Rs 237 crore of debt was written off by the Centre in this year after recommendations of the 7th Finance Commission; this was treated as 'Misc. General Services'.

31. Please see Annexure 2.1 for data sources.

32. NSDP figure has been used.

33. In 1980–81, like Assam, Nagaland also received a loan waiver from the Central Government of Rs 46 crore, which inflated its revenue receipts artificially, resulting in abnormally high ratios involving revenue receipts.

34. Please see Annexure 2.1 for data sources.

35. Includes 78,114 sq. kms under POK, 37,555 sq. kms under illegal occupation of China in Ladakh and 5180 sq. kms illegally handed over by Pakistan to China.

36. Estimated population as no census was conducted in 1991 in Jammu & Kashmir due to disturbance.

37. Length of National Highway in 2010–11 was 832 kms.

38. From all sources.

39. Due to a huge amount of recovery in respect of pension and other retirement benefits made in 1980–81, the corresponding ratio of the State's own revenue to revenue expenditure was abnormally high in that year.

40. NSDP data for this year has been used.

3 Institutional Framework and Policies for Special Category States

As observed earlier, the special category status only implied a specific funding pattern to the states belonging to this category. No separate institutional arrangement was set up to cater to the specific capacity and resource requirements of this group of states as a whole. This was a major weakness in the entire scheme of channelling central funds to these states for development purposes, since these funds were accessible to the political class virtually free, without any accountability or performance requirements on their part. Without appropriate institutional framework to monitor the use of funds, these were vulnerable to misuse and waste. However, some institutions, agencies, and mechanisms evolved over time which achieved limited success, and only in the northeastern states. In this chapter, we shall first discuss the roles of these institutions, identify their constraints, and evaluate the policies and mechanisms having a bearing on their growth, like the centre's 'Look East Policy' and cross-border trade with neighbouring countries.

Benefits Available to Special Category States

As explained in the Introduction, 30 per cent of the centre's gross budgetary support for plan expenditure goes to the special category states on the basis of 90 per cent grants and 10 per cent loans. After the Twelfth Finance Commission recommendations, centre now gives only grants, and leaves it to all the states to raise loans from the market on market-determined rates of interest as per their requirements. For some special category states which are unable to raise such loans from the market on favourable terms on their own financial strength, centre still provides loans, but usually the 90 per cent grants plus 10 per cent loans formula for special-category states is now restricted only to the Centrally-Sponsored Schemes. As regards external aid, states cannot receive them directly except through the intermediary of the centre; such aids pertain usually to area-specific development projects. External aid is passed on to states in the exact mixture of loan and grants in which it is received by the centre.

Special category states also receive plan assistance under special central plan assistance and additional central assistance for different centrally sponsored projects, which include plan assistance for specific projects as discussed in the Introduction. In addition, assistance for various Externally Aided Projects is also available to them. Special Plan Assistance (SPA) is provided to these states for funding of projects that are not covered by any central scheme. Further untied Special Central Assistance (SCA) is also provided to meet their unmet developmental needs. For the eleventh plan, more than 70 per cent of total plan expenditure has come from central plan assistance for all special category states, and most of them have received more than 90 per cent of their total plan expenditure from the centre. Apart from plan grants, under recommendations of the Finance Commissions, they also receive non-plan grants for various purposes as well as for meeting state specific needs. Further, they are allowed to use up to 20 per cent of the central assistance for their non-plan expenditure.

Tax breaks are further provided to them in respect of excise duty for setting up of new industrial units within their territories as decided by the excise authorities for specific periods under various notifications issued by them. The special-category states get significant excise duty concessions, persuading industry to relocate/locate manufacturing within their territory, a sore point with neighbouring general-category states.[1]

The state-wise total devolution to the special category states under the Twelfth and Thirteenth Finance Commission recommendations have been shown in Table 3.1, from which it can be seen that the total devolutions have almost doubled during the periods covered by these two commissions. Their per-capita central plan assistance was several

Table 3.1 Total Transfers to Special Category State by Twelfth and Thirteenth Finance Commissions (FC)

	12th FC	13th FC
Arunachal Pradesh	3,526	9,104
Assam	24,329	57,833
Himachal Pradesh	14,450	21,692
Jammu & Kashmir	20,880	40,439
Manipur	6,870	13,567
Meghalaya	4,368	9,842
Mizoram	4,661	8,805
Nagaland	7,453	13,744
Sikkim	1,829	4,526
Tripura	8,417	13,128
Uttarakhand	12,194	20,308
Total	1,08,978	2,12,988

Source: Reports of the respective Finance Commissions.

times that of the general category states. Central transfers, in fact, drive the economy of many of these states.

Backward Region Grant Fund (BRGF)[2]

Special category states also receive funding under the Backward Region Grant Fund (BRGF), which is another means for accessing central funding to address state backwardness. The BRGF scheme, which subsumed the Rashtriya Sam Vikas Yojana, a scheme earlier administered by the Planning Commission was launched in 2007, as per Twelfth Finance Commission recommendations to redress regional imbalances in development. More specifically, its purpose is to bridge critical gaps in infrastructure and other development requirements that are not being adequately met through existing inflows, to strengthen and support the local level governance through Panchayats and Municipalities for capacity building and to facilitate participatory planning and decision-making, besides improving the performance and delivery of critical functions assigned to Panchayats and local bodies. Administered by the Union Ministry of Panchayati Raj, the scheme covered (March 2014) 272 districts in 27 states (except Goa). Of these, 254 districts are covered by the Panchayats and municipalities, and the remaining 18 districts are covered by other local government structures, such as Autonomous District and Regional Councils under the Sixth Schedule and state specific arrangements as in the case of Nagaland and the hill areas of Manipur.

Each district receives an amount depending upon its total population size and area. There are two funding windows—Development Grants are provided to address the critical gaps in integrated development while Capacity Building Funds (Rs 1 crore per district) are provided to build capacity of elected representatives and functionaries of Panchayati Raj Institutions. The allocation is untied, but is conditional to preparation of a District Development Plan indicating the development constraints affecting the district, for addressing the resource gaps after taking account of resources available through other schemes. During the Eleventh Plan Period (2007–12), total funds released under the BRGF amounted to Rs 21623 crore, and in 2012–13 Rs 3720 crore were released. Here again, monitoring and coordination between central and state agencies were lacking, affecting efficient delivery.

In fact, existence of plethora of schemes and mechanisms for accessing central funds for developmental purposes of backward regions has always posed problems of coordination and integration of all such schemes for better targeting and focussing on specific developmental activities to be undertaken and measurement of the impact thereof. Backwardness is not limited to the special category states alone, and since the Third Plan days, the criteria for backwardness had engaged the attention of policy makers. To identify the industrially backward areas, Planning Commission and National Development Council had appointed a plethora of Working Groups and Committees, like the Pande and Wanchoo Working Groups in 1968, Sukhmay Chakravorty Committee in 1972 and the National Committee on the Development of Backward Areas (NCDBA) in 1978. While the first three had suggested district as the unit of backwardness, the NCDBA recommended block to be the primary unit for identification of backward areas. But these exercises were at best peripheral; real change came only with the Constitution (Seventy Third) Amendment Act of 1992, which made the Panchayati Raj Institutions (PRIs) arbiters in the development process. But PRIs lacked both capacity and resources and BRGF was designed for filling this developmental gap. However, there was no mechanism for coordinating between BRGF and Plan Assistance for Special Category States to assimilate the developmental requirements into an integrated package covering districts, blocks, and villages within these states. Proper utilization of funds for special category assistance was never given any serious thought by the planners.

NEC and MDONER[3]

The agencies, apart from the Planning Commission, which were involved in the process directly or indirectly, were the North Eastern Council (NEC) and the Ministry of the Development of North East (MDONER) in respect of the eight northeastern states, all of which belonged to the special category. The NEC was created by an Act of Parliament in 1971, with its headquarters at Shillong, and all northeastern states as its members. The respective chief ministers and governors represent the states for achieving better integration with accelerated and balanced intra-regional growth and development. Besides their respective five year and annual plans, projects of inter-state nature in the region are funded by the NEC, which has a separate budget for this. Funding of the Council mainly comes from the central government, though a small part may be contributed by the individual members also. Sikkim was added to the NEC Act in 2002 when by an amendment to the NEC Act it was restructured into a regional planning body for the northeast. The council has to its credit a number of completed projects, mostly in power, infrastructure, and education sectors. It funds small power projects (producing up to 250 MW of electricity) and has taken up some major highway and bridge building projects, besides being instrumental for creating engineering and medical colleges in the region.

But despite its remarkable successes, the inherent structural weaknesses of the NEC render it partly ineffective. Though a member of the Planning Commission was also a member of NEC, the NEC was never directly involved in regional planning processes at all; that role was discharged by the Planning Commission. It was not invited to the meetings of the National Development Council. Planning Commission did the planning for the northeastern states instead of the NEC which is much more actively involved in their development. NEC remains only an advisory body.

The Department of Development of North Eastern Region was set up by the Government of India in September 2001 as a nodal department of the central government exclusively for dealing with socio-economic development of the northeast. Its basic role is to effect coordination between the central ministries/departments and the state governments of the northeastern region to remove infrastructure bottlenecks, provide basic minimum services, create a conducive environment for private investment, and remove impediments for lasting peace and security in the region, besides capacity building, international cooperation with neighbouring countries, advocacy and publicity, and overseeing the activities of the public sector enterprises of the member states. It was accorded the status of a full-fledged ministry (MDONER) on May 2004. The NEC was also brought under the administrative control of MDONER.

Non-Lapsable Central Pool of Resources (NLCPR)

In October 1996, the then Prime Minister had announced the 'New Initiatives for North Eastern Region' by earmarking at least 10 per cent of the budgets of the central ministries/departments. Next year, since the expenditure on the northeast by some union ministries fell short of the stipulated 10 per cent, the Planning Commission explored the possibility of creating a central pool of resources for the northeast out of the unspent amounts of stipulated 10 per cent of gross budgetary support for infrastructure development projects in the northeast. This pool was finally created through the budget of 1998–99; the then Finance Minister had said, when presenting the budget,

> Furthermore, it has been decided that a non-lapsable Central Resources Pool will be created for deposit of funds from all Ministries where the plan expenditure on the north eastern region is less than 10 per cent of the total plan allocation of the Ministry. The difference between 10 per cent of the allocation and the actual expenditure incurred on the north eastern region will be transferred to the Central Pool, which will be used for funding specific programmes for economic and social upliftment of the north eastern states.'(http://www.mdoner.gov.in/content/background-1)

To the extent of shortfall in the utilization of this provision by any ministry/department according to this norm, the amount would be transferred to a new Reserve Fund in the Public Account titled 'Central Resource Pool for Development of North Eastern Region'.

The broad objective of the NLCPR scheme is to ensure speedy development of infrastructure in the region by ensuring the continued flow of budgetary financing for new infrastructure projects/schemes. Both physical and social infrastructure sectors such as irrigation and flood control, power, roads and bridges, education, health, water supply, and sanitation—are considered for providing support under the Central Pool, with projects in physical infrastructure sector receiving priority.

It must be mentioned that like the Planning Commission itself, this machinery of NLCPR propagated by the Commission is also an extra-constitutional arrangement. Government finances follow the principle of lapsability of funds at the end of every financial year; fresh approval of the legislature is to be taken in the next financial year for continued expenditure. This ensures greater accountability of the executive and also avoids imposition of unnecessary burden upon the exchequer, since any expenditure is to be financed either out of taxes or borrowings, for both of which the taxpayer has to be charged. But the Planning Commission, lacking in accountability itself, never blinked an eye to create structures that defy the mechanism of accountability.

Even after creating the NLCPR, things have improved very little, the funds still lay unutilized for years, or get misspent and misused. It is more to do with creation of absorption capacity in the economy and institutional capacity in the state to guide in the effective use of the funds, both of which are, sadly, lacking in the extreme degree.

Autonomous District Councils

The Indian Constitution recognized the necessity for a separate political and administrative structure for the hill areas of the northeastern region to preserve the ethnic, linguistic, and cultural distinctiveness of its tribal communities, besides ensuring traditional autonomy in running their affairs. It was also important to protect the tribal people from possible exploitation by outsiders, from being marginalized and homogenized by the majority. Accordingly, Article 244 (2) of the Constitution added the Sixth Schedule to the Constitution for administration of the tribal areas in Assam (which included areas in the future states of Meghalaya, Tripura, and Mizoram) giving them significant autonomy. The Schedule identified Autonomous Districts in the hill areas of the composite state of Assam and provided for establishment of Autonomous District Councils (ADC) in these areas by conferring upon them substantial legislative, executive, judicial, and financial powers. Presently, there are 16 ADCs operating in the northeast (three in Assam, three in Meghalaya, six in Manipur, three in Mizoram, and one in Tripura).[4]

The ADCs are like miniature states having specific powers and responsibilities in respect of all the three arms of the government: legislature, executive, and judiciary. Out of 30 members in each district council, not more than four are nominated by the Governor and others are elected for a term of five years each, on the basis of adult suffrage. The finances of the councils are met by grants from the states under recommendations of the State Finance Commission to enable them to execute various development programmes. There is also a separate civil service for the council whose recruitment and control rest solely with the council. The Sixth Schedule further provides for an independent judiciary with powers to adjudicate both civil and economical cases at the village and district levels based on customary laws and practices as well as codified laws. The ADCs are provided with the powers to make laws for utilization of land, management of forests, regulating shifting cultivation, for establishment of village, and town communities, regulation of social customs including marriage and inheritance of property, etc. They have the powers to establish primary schools and dispensaries, roads, road transport and waterways, impose and collect land revenues and certain other taxes within their districts like taxes on professions, trade and calling, taxes for maintenance of roads, schools, etc, taxes on animals, vehicles and boats, and taxes on the entry of goods into a market. They are also empowered to control money lending and trading by the non-tribals. The Sixth Schedule thus provides for a comprehensive mechanism for self-governance in the tribal dominated areas, thereby helping people to safeguard their customs and practices and preserve their distinct cultural and ethnic identities. These identities have been forged by history, by strong bonds of kinship, community control of land, and of course by the traditional social institutions of tribal societies. However, the issue of identity has often been used as a bargaining chip to extract political and economic advantages.

But the institution of ADCs has also eroded and undermined the power and authority as well as the relevance of the traditional social institutions. These institutions could not adjust themselves to the new realities of the ADCs and adapt and transform themselves to the requirements of a constitutional set-up. The traditional hierarchical structure was not equipped to foster social change and transformation of the tribal ethos to the structure of a modern, democratic, and inclusive market economy. The simultaneous existence of these institutions along with the modern institution of governance has often led to situations of conflict and suspicion. Responsibilities and powers are not sharply defined between various institutions and authority is therefore often diffused between them, in which situation vested interests tend to get entrenched. This has become worse in the absence of a proper accountability structure and due to the lack of transparency. Coordination between the ADC and the state government is also missing, and ADCs do not play any significant role in the planning process at micro or macro level. Access to development funds has created entrenched nexus between the neo-rich middle class, traders, contractors, and bureaucrats who control the ADCs. This has given rise to the rent seeking politics, paving the way for unchecked corruption that is throttling all development in the region.

ADCs have not been successful in meeting the expectations of people due to the lack of adequate financial resources at their disposal and also due to structural weaknesses arising from a traditional, hierarchical set-up. In many District Council areas, ethnic minorities hardly find any representation in the councils. Political patronage, nepotism, and favouritism in the matter of recruitment are rampant, and vested interests dominate in matters of recruitment to various executive and non-executive posts. Mismanagement of public funds was widespread until 1969, when regular audit by the Comptroller & Auditor General of India was introduced (Prasad 2004).

One major reason for the sub-optimal performance of the ADCs is their almost total dependence on State Governments for their finances, though they have the power to levy and collect certain taxes stated earlier even within the jurisdiction of the Regional Council (which has no such power). But they can neither enforce the taxation for want of adequate powers, nor realize the amounts efficiently for want of administrative capacity. Income from their share of royalty from mining in an area within their jurisdiction is very meagre and the most important source of their income remains the grants-in-aid by state governments under Article 275(1) of the Constitution. States have the discretion of releasing these grants at a time of their choosing, rendering the ADCs vulnerable to the political pressures. Statutory provision is needed to make it obligatory for the state to release these grants to the ADCs in a timely manner so that ADCs are not left at mercy of the states for their finances (Prasad 2004).

According to Section 12 of the Sixth Schedule, no law passed by the Parliament or state legislature shall apply to matters within the purview of the ADCs without their concurrence. But in respect of Meghalaya, the section has been amended by inserting subsection 12A, giving overriding powers to the acts passed by the state legislatures and virtually taking away all powers conferred on the ADCs and making the purpose of Sixth Schedule and ADCs self-defeating. Emergence of PRIs through the Constitution (Seventy Third) Amendment Act of 1992 and the subsequent establishment of Gram Sabhas have given a new shift to the developmental process, seeking to transfer power to the grassroots at the village level, and rendering the ADCs that work mostly at the district level more irrelevant. There is an immediate need to integrate the ADCs as also the traditional tribal social institutions in the PRI-structure to achieve optimal synergy. However, as per Article 243 M of the constitution, the provisions relating to PRIs are not applicable to Meghalaya.

Roy Chaudhury (2005) had pointed out that the areas which the Sixth Schedule was supposed to protect had graduated from districts into full-fledged states such as Meghalaya and Mizoram. Therefore, 'the District Councils in these states are now an anachronism as they overlap the normal district administration and have tended to duplicate the former and become a rival focus of power and financial burden.' He further argues that the Sixth Schedule contributed to ethnic polarization and sub-nationalism and led to clash of interest between the non-tribal and tribal populations in their areas. It has rather promoted 'a de-facto regime of two-tiered citizenship' between the tribals and non-tribals, which could become a source of potential future conflicts. Similar issues have been discussed in Chapter 2 also. Thus, despite having a highly decentralized and democratic structure, the ADCs have not been able to perform optimally.

Look East Policy (LEP)

All special category states share international borders. Borders are the places for meeting of minds, they can also become flashpoints. The northeastern states share 5182 kms of international borders with neighbouring China (1395 km), Bangladesh (1596 km), Myanmar (1640 km), Bhutan (455 km), and Nepal (97 km), which together is more than 99 per cent of its total geographical boundary, leaving only a 22 km link to the Indian mainland through the 'chicken-neck' of Siliguri–Jalpaiguri corridor in North Bengal. More than 50 per cent of the total length of the Indo-Bangladesh border lies in this region. While this particular spatial setting has isolated it from mainland India, it has linked the fate of the region with its trans-border neighbours in a historical and geographical inevitability that cannot be ignored in any realistic policy framework. Trans-border movement and migration of peoples have taken place since ancient times, making the region a melting pot of cultures, religions, and ethnicity from different regions in east and southeast Asia. Vigorous cross-border trade was a vibrant economic activity in these states that provided a lifeline to the people in days prior to partition and remained so even after that, till it was stopped due to the geo-political compulsions and insurgency. The region provided transit route in trades between South-East Asian countries and the rest of India, as well as for export through ports in Bangladesh like Chittagong.

In the aftermath of the collapse of the Soviet Union, India's economic and strategic partner till then, India was forced to take a relook at its foreign policy. It also coincided with India's financial crisis of 1991, making it imperative to discard the earlier insularity and redefine economic policies and priorities. The Cold War having been a thing of the past, 'South Asia and Southeast Asia could no longer be treated as separate strategic theatres', and India took 'a conscious decision to plug into the dynamic Southeast Asian region'.[5] India's Look East Policy was born as a result, and was a paradigm shift in India's foreign economic policy. It was to end northeast India's long economic isolation imposed by its extended international borders, by re-establishing its lost connectivity with the southeast Asian nations. In 2003, focus of the policy was changed to forge closer partnerships with the ASEAN countries, which were correctly perceived as being 'integrally linked to the economic and security interests of the north-eastern region'.

The main drivers of the 'Look East Policy' were trade and economic benefits. In 1992 when this policy was launched, India's total trade with ASEAN countries was only US$ 2.5 billion and it was projected to cross US$ 45 billion by 2010–11.[6] This target was reached in 2008 itself and at the end of 2011–12, India's trade volume with ASEAN countries stood at US$ 79 billion. However, the benefits from this policy have so far not been very encouraging in terms of trade flowing through the northeastern states, as most of these volumes are accounted for non-neighbouring nations like Thailand, Singapore, and Malaysia with whom India always had strong economic relations. This necessitates 'a redefining of the Look East Policy to resolve outstanding issues of trade, transit and investment with the countries neighbouring the region. It also involves promoting Indian investment in infrastructure in partner countries, especially Myanmar, particularly in respect of ports such as Sittwe and international highways to connect the North Eastern Region to ASEAN.'[7]

One such highway was the Stilwell Road built by the Americans during the Second World War to facilitate movement of the army, connecting Arunachal Pradesh through Myanmar to Kunming city in the Yunnan province of China. This road is being reconstructed, and once it is open to trade and traffic, it is estimated to reduce the transportation costs for India–China trade by as much as 30 per cent. But India appears hesitant over reopening of the road for trade with China, weighing potential commercial benefits against national security concerns.[8] It is indeed important to reckon these problems related to border management given the problems of 'cross-border migration, terrorism, drugs and arms supply and other forms of non-conventional security threats for ensuring the rights and traditions of local ethnic groups comprehensively in the context of global forces of change'. But in the recent past, India has shown active interest to participate in developing cross-border road connectivity with Myanmar to facilitate trade and people to people movement. With the opening of Nathu-La pass in Sikkim, such links have also been established with China too, though the volume of such trade has so far been nominal. India is currently involved in the 1,400-km Trilateral Highway, linking India, Myanmar, and Thailand scheduled to be completed by 2016. Running from Moreh town in Manipur to Mae Sot in Thailand via Myanmar—this highway would open up India's landlocked northeast to economically vibrant Southeast Asia. It would also focus attention on road accessibility to the Dawei deep sea port in southern Myanmar that would provide a much shorter sea route to the Southeast Asian region and help boost trade further.[9]

As the document 'North Eastern Region Vision 2020' recognizes correctly,

> in explicit recognition of the need to break the fetters of the geo-political isolation of the Region, it is necessary to factor in .... 'new inputs' in foreign, defence, internal security and international trade policy. To this end, the immediate priority is to build the required infrastructure right up to the border areas, establishing connectivity and communication links to the cross-border points through which trade and economic exchanges with the countries neighbouring the North Eastern Region are proposed to be promoted under the Look East Policy.[10]

It also identifies the impediments to a more successful implementation of the policy and recommends removal of current restrictions on border trade via Moreh, Nathu La, and other entry points, unrestricted trade with neighbouring countries in certain commodities, providing a secure transport corridor for traders and promotion of people-to-people interaction through cultural and other exchanges across the borders.[11]

By and large, the LEP still remains restricted to rhetorics reiterated at the time of international events, rather than being translated into an energetic exchange of goods and ideas through increased trans-border people-to-people contacts. For the success of the policy, one needs to go much beyond the geographical contiguity of the region and aim at achieving much larger political and economic convergence by taking into account the changing landscape at the borders with all the difficulties of mediating competing interests and linkages. Closer coordination is needed between all agencies involved, on both sides of the borders. Actually, there are many identified and unidentified socio-economic and political factors that need to be handled deftly and an efficient administrative apparatus put in place before the policy starts yielding results. One must not forget that security plays a very vital role at these far-flung outposts, and LEP should be based on the core economic and security interests of India. Much of India's response to LEP has been, and will be, shaped by the dynamics of Sino-Indian relationships; Arunachal Pradesh still remains a sore point as are the activities of the Chinese in South Asian countries surrounding India, like Myanmar and Bangladesh, where China continues to be actively engaged. In fact, revival of historical linkage of trade and commerce with neighbouring countries was conceived partly as a way to counter the increasing Chinese influence in the region. The strategic location of the northeast with its external economic and cultural linkages with South East Asia gives it significance in India's foreign policy formulation, whose priorities can be aligned with the region's developmental needs (Brahma 2010: 30–2). With improved connectivity through better border road network, joint border management, institutional arrangement to encourage formal cross-border trade, equalization of tariff, the Northeast can be reintegrated into the economies South East Asia. Security will always remain a serious concern, especially in a region with porous borders, but the advantages of geography should not be allowed to fritter away by an obsession with security; in fact, people-to-people contact is an automatic safeguard against insecurity.

Cross-Border Trade

'Look East' Policy and Border Trade with Myanmar: Manipur, Mizoram, Arunachal Pradesh

As part of the LEP, border trading has started with all of India's neighbours. While border trading with Bhutan and Bangladesh are covered under South Asian Free Trade Area (SAFTA) which also includes other SAARC countries, trading with China and Myanmar takes place under Border Trade Agreements signed with those countries. Agreement was signed between the Governments of India and Myanmar in 1994 which became operational in 1995 in the Moreh-Tamu sector. Indo-Myanmar border trade takes place through three points: Moreh in Manipur, Zokhawthar (Champhai) in Mizoram, and Nampong in Arunachal Pradesh. It was initially based on barter trade for 22 items, mostly agricultural or primary commodities produced in the two trading countries, and subsequently expanded to include 40 items. Border trade has now been going on for last several years, but the volume of trade is quite limited (to less than US$ 1 million per year). The volume of trade in 2010–11 was only Rs 4.16 crore (Import – Rs 3.80 crore, Export – Rs 0.26 crore)[12] which is of course a small percentage in the total Indo-Myanmar trade of over Rs 6110 crore in that year (Rs 13182 crore in 2013–14).[13] The volume of informal trade is, however, estimated at around Rs. 2000 crore, excluding the smuggled items, drugs, and narcotics (B.P. Singh 2010: 239). Though the trade basket is diversified, the Indo-Myanmar border trade has so far only managed to give rise to a 'petty trading class' in Manipur instead of generating real employment.

Development of border trade was one area highlighted in the Mizoram Peace Accord of 1987. Mizoram shares international borders with Bangladesh and Myanmar and border trades, both legal and illegal, have been taking place between these countries and Mizoram. While legal trading with Myanmar are carried through the Land Customs Station (LCS) at Champhai, it is almost non-existent with Bangladesh, though there used to be an LCS at Thegmukh on the Bangladesh border prior to 1965 after which the LCS became defunct due to logistics problems and remoteness of the LCS from the nearest district headquarters at Rangamati in Bangladesh. As regards the illegal trade, a study conducted by the Indian Institute of Foreign Trade (IIFT) in 1995 estimated the value of illegal trade through Moreh in Manipur and Champai and Lungwa in Mizoram at Rs 2200 crore annually, of which Moreh's share was Rs 1600 crore, followed by Champai's share of Rs 500 crore, and Lungwa's only Rs 100 crore. It was also estimated that the volume of NER-Myanmar trade would be at least five times the volume of NER-Bangladesh trade (Kumar 2008: 154–5). Talks have been continuing between the governments of Bangladesh and India for identifying suitable locations for opening up of the border trade, which is also important in view of the fact that Mizoram has a Chakma Autonomous District Council since 1971 that is populated mainly by the Chakmas having their origin in the Chittagong Hill Tracts of Bangladesh (Pudaite 2010: 46).

Unfortunately, not much data are available on the border trade between Mizoram and the neighbouring countries. With the 'Look East Policy' opening up possibilities of economic growth through border trade, Mizoram can gain from the potential exports of its highly valued bamboo and bamboo products, metals and stone chips, fruits and horticultural products. Boosting bilateral ties with the neighbouring countries can ultimately lead to a borderless economic integration that has the potential of improving the living standards of people living on both sides of the borders. No data is available for border trade through Arunachal Pradesh also.

'Look East' Policy and Border Trade with China: Sikkim

The India China Border Trade started in 2006, between Tibet and India through the Nathu-la Pass in Sikkim, which was reopened after 44 years.

Initially, 29 commodities were identified for export from India and 15 commodities were identified for import from China. According to a report in the Peoples' Daily dated 12 December 2013, the volume of trade had increased in 2013 by more than 54 times since it was started in 2006 and reached US$ 14.3 million (Export from India : US$ 11.92 million; Import from China : US$ 2.38 million). It was still miniscule compared to the total volume of Indo-China trade (Rs 357914 Crore, or US$ 59.65 billion in 2013-14).[14]

'Look East' Policy and Border Trade with Bangladesh: Assam, Tripura, Meghalaya

Northeast India shares more than 50 per cent of the total length of the Indo-Bangladesh border, spread over four states. Part of its population in Cachar district of Assam and Tripura, especially those who had migrated after partition and after the 1971 war, also share close cultural and linguistic affinity with Bangladesh. The bilateral trade between northeast India and Bangladesh has increased from Rs. 179 crore in 1999–2000 to Rs. 916 crore in 2010–11 (Export: Rs 620 crore; Import: Rs 296 crore), as against total bilateral trade value of Rs 16784 crore in 2010–11. Assam, Meghalaya, and Tripura respectively accounted for 6 per cent, 55 per cent, and 39 per cent shares in the total volume of border trade with Bangladesh.

There is also a thriving informal trade which obstructs the free trade between these states and Bangladesh, the value of which through Tripura alone is estimated to be around US$ 500 million every year. The advantages of strategic location of Tripura in the international context are not yet fully tapped because of various constraints like lack of transport and communication facilities, inadequate infrastructure, poor road conditions, lack of cargo handling, and inadequate banking facilities, etc.

It is thus seen that the border trade through the NER is a miniscule fraction of total bilateral trade of India with these countries. Institutional and infrastructural weaknesses are responsible for this state of affairs, and these are also responsible for the thriving informal trade across the borders, often aided and abetted by the agents of state like border guards, etc. in exchange for illegal gratification. It is a collusive zone where the state agents and non-state illegal actors collaborate to mutual advantages. Army officers I have spoken to suggest that illegal trade is the lifeline that keeps the insurgency alive and the relationship between the two is often symbiotic. This indicates that economics of conflicts need not always spell disorder and anarchy, but can instead be a low-level equilibrium sustained by the collusive connivance of key institutional actors.

***

No specific institutional framework was set up as a whole for the special category states to coordinate and monitor the developmental activities undertaken through various centre and state-funded projects and schemes, neither was any system instituted to ensure proper and prudent utilization of central assistance. For the northeastern region, NEC, and later MDONER, having inadequate powers were equally ineffective in discharging their roles to plan and direct developmental efforts towards desired ends. Due to their inherent structural weaknesses as well as lack of capacity and other reasons, ADCs have made themselves rather irrelevant, and their structure was such that they could be easily corrupted. The purpose for which Sixth Schedule was incorporated in the Constitution thus remained unfulfilled in the absence of real autonomy percolating down to the grassroots level. The limited functional and fiscal autonomy of ADCs have again been severely constrained by parallel structures in the administrative hierarchy; there were no attempts to integrate and strike a synergy between the two. The result was a deepening of centralized control, increasing bureaucratization of administrative machinery that threatens to erode constitutional safeguards for local autonomy and instead of decreasing, rather increasing the role of the state. There was no recognition of the fact that without meaningful capacity augmentation at the local government level, real autonomy will always remain a chimera. The result was a top-down autonomy model, stumbling along all the way, and failing to deliver. Failure to factor diversity in the process of development led to loss of opportunity.

The Look East Policy needs to be looked through the 'eyes of the North Eastern Region' rather than through the prism of Delhi, making the North Eastern Region a 'dumping ground for Chinese goods' or a 'corridor for Indian products'. The people of Northeast have to be included as active planners, partners, and arbiters in any policy frame devised for their development. 'Looking East' implies looking towards sunrise, towards a new dawn. That dawn would continue to be elusive unless the actual stakeholders are included as players in shaping their own destiny.

Notes

1. Incentives provided to industrial units in special category states include capital investment subsidy, excise duty exemption and income tax exemption, besides subsidy under Transport Subsidy Scheme (modified as Freight Subsidy Scheme in 2013) for movement of goods. For NER and J&K, central interest subsidy and comprehensive insurance subsidy are additionally available. The NER states are also eligible for subsidy under North East India Industrial Investment and Promotion Policy of 2007.

2. Information obtained from http://www.panchayat.gov.in/brgf-background, accessed 6 July 2014.

3. Source of information for this and the next section is http://mdoner.gov.in/hi/node/142, accessed 11 July 2014.

4. A similar provision exists in the Sixth Schedule in respect of Autonomous Regions created by dividing an autonomous district with different tribal groups and establishment of Regional Council for their autonomous administration.

5. 'India's Look East Policy: A Critical Assessment', Interview with Amb. Rajiv Sikri, *Institute of Peace and Conflict Studies,* New Delhi, October, 2009.

6. *Editorial, Economic and Political Weekly*, Nov 27, 2010.

7. 'Vision Statement', *North Eastern Region Vision 2020*, North Eastern Council, 2008, vi–vii.

8. News Report, 'The Irrawady', Burma, 13 May 2013, http://www.irrawaddy.org/archives/tag/subir-bhaumik-the-irrawaddy.

9. Available at http://www.dnaindia.com/india/1873123/report-india-to-link-with-myanmar-port-to-boost-asean-connectivity; accessed 26 October 2013.

10. *North Eastern Region Vision 2020*, vi.

11. *North-Eastern Region Vision, 2020*: 285–6.

12. Available at http://mdoner.gov.in/content/border-trade, accessed 11 July 2014.

13. Available at http://commerce.nic.in/eidb/default.asp, accessed 11 July 2014.

14. Available at http://en.people.cn/business/8482387.html, accessed 14 January 2015.

4 Other Northeastern States

Meghalaya, Manipur, Tripura, Mizoram, and Arunachal Pradesh

After the special category status was accorded to Assam, Nagaland, and J&K in 1969, other northeastern states, as and when they were created, were also brought within this category. Meghalaya was carved out of Assam in 1972, and the union territories of Tripura and Manipur were accorded full statehood in the same year, followed by Mizoram and Arunachal Pradesh in 1987. These five states will be discussed in this chapter.

Meghalaya—An Overview

The word 'Meghalaya' means the abode of clouds. It is a hilly state bordering Bangladesh and covering a total area of 22,429 sq. kms spread over its seven districts in Khasi, Garo, and Jaintia hills. Shillong, the capital of the state, is a popular hill station famous for its scenic hills, lush green fields, and surrounding dense forests, but unplanned development, unchecked urbanization, and large-scale migration from outside, including Bangladesh, have given the once beautiful town an ugly face today. The state, like the other states in the northeastern region (NER) is endowed with rich natural beauty—it is a panorama of undulating hills, verdant valleys, singing waterfalls, meandering rivers, and exotic species of orchids, ferns, and other flora and fauna. Its forests are famous for their biodiversity and harbour a wide variety of mammals, birds, and plants. Meghalaya is one of the 'wettest' states in India with towns such as Cherrapunji and villages such as Mawsynram which are among the 'rainiest' places in the world. The forest cover in the state is about 42 per cent of its total geographical area (1991). The state is inhabited mostly by tribals and many of them still practise their own customs and religion. As per the 1971 census Meghalaya had a population of 10.12 lakh of which more than 85 per cent, i.e., 8.65 lakh, lived in rural areas. By 2011, the population had grown to 29.64 lakh, of which 23.69 lakh, i.e., 80 per cent, were still rural.

Meghalaya is predominantly inhabited by ethnic groups like Khasis, Pnars, Wars, and Bhois, in the Khasi and Jaintia Hills and the Garos in the Garo Hills. The splendid isolation in which the tribals lived induced them to invent their own distinctive and unique economic, political, and social systems; these still continue to exist along with modern social institutions. Though these tribes had lived in isolation in their mountainous lands, they were not immune to external influences, and there was considerable transformation of their social characteristics as a whole due to contacts with people belonging to the other hilly areas as well as from plains. The most remarkable social institution of the tribes is the matrilineal system where descent is traced from common female ancestors and goes down to the female line, with children bearing the title or surname of the mother. The predominance of women in many spheres of life and the respect and honour in which they are held are the hallmarks of their society.

The Khasis are divided into a number of exogamous clans like Kharkongor, Diengdoh, Sohkhlet, Marbaniang, and Syiemlieh, who trace their descent from their female line. Clans are bound together by strict ties of kinship, religion, ancestor veneration, and funeral rites. Even Christian converts adhere to the traditional rules of descent where ancestral property is passed down the female line. Marriage within the same clan is prohibited and considered a taboo. Similarly the Jaintias are also divided into a number of clans and have similar social, religious, and marriage systems.

Garos are mostly concentrated in the Garo Hills of Meghalaya, but their habitat also extends to the adjoining areas of the Khasi Hills district. They are divided into a number of dialectal and cultural groups. However, the basic social structure, customary laws, methods of agriculture, food habits, and value systems of all these groups are relatively uniform and all of them share a common tribal consciousness. Here

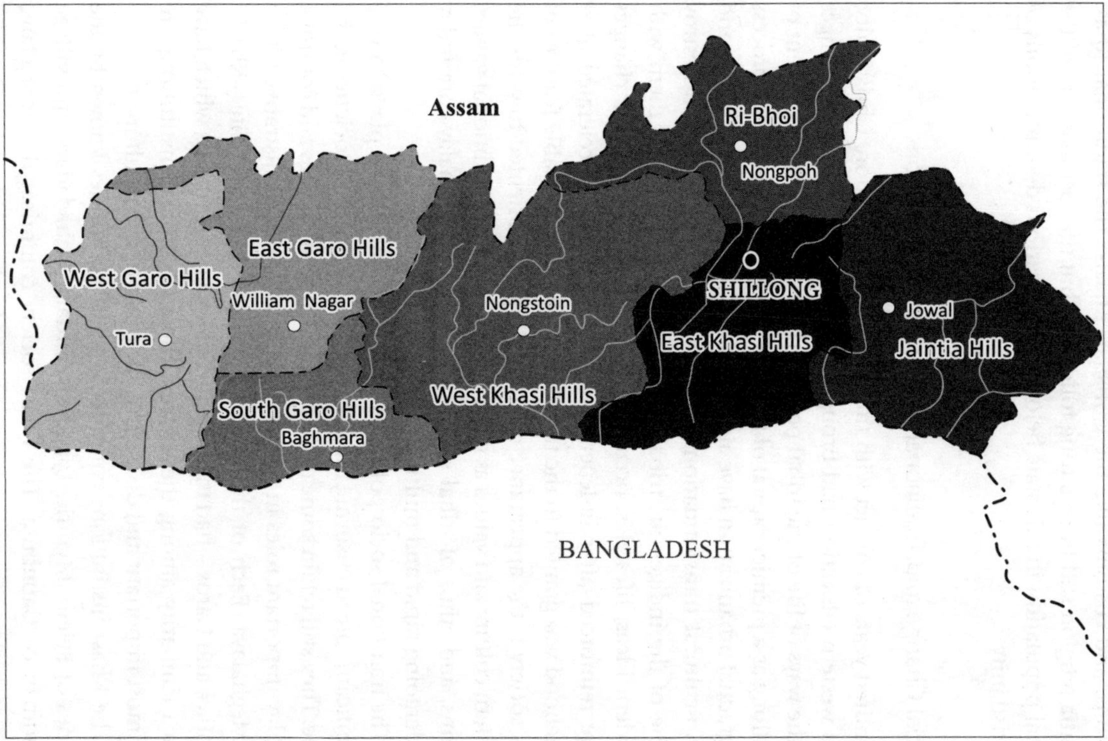

Map 4.1 Map of Meghalaya.

also Christianity has brought considerable changes in their lifestyles and culture. But the Christian Garos have retained the core features of the traditional system and social customs like clans, social organizations, and customs like the Christian Khasis. The traditional Khasi Jaintia religion still has a strong following, but the vast majority of the tribal population in this state belongs to the various denominations of Christianity.

Social Change and Traditional Socio-political Institutions

Hundred years of contact with the British administration, Christianity, and western education had brought about remarkable social changes in the ways of life of the tribal people. The growth and development of Shillong as a premier capital of the northeastern region and the process of gradual urbanization have also facilitated processes of economic and socio-cultural transformation. In some way, the changes did destroy some of the indigenous tribal characteristics by replacing them with modern ideas, lifestyles, occupations, and technology. These changes were reinforced after independence and their pace accelerated after statehood was granted to the tribals. One of the remarkable features of this society is the appearance of an intelligentsia oriented towards the western culture and values as distinguished from the traditional values, norms, and ethos of tribal society. The tribes of Meghalaya are today undergoing rapid and multi-dimensional transition.

The traditional socio-political institutions have always played a very significant role in ensuring the cohesiveness of the tribal societies in the state. They still retain some of their overarching influences and continue to play important roles in the socio-political and administrative set-up in Meghalaya. Each of the three tribes residing in the state—Khasis, Jaintias, and Garos—had their distinctive social institutions which have much similarity among themselves. These traditional institutions are the most important and distinctive attributes of tribal culture.

The Khasi institutions comprise a set of authorities known by the names of Syiem, Myntris, Lyngdohs, Sirdars, Wahadadars, and village headman or Gaonbura. The Khasi society comprises different clans, with each clan having its own respective Durbar or the Clan Council. Clan members reside in villages (Snings) and the village societies are governed by the Village Durbar (Village Council) headed by the village headmen (Gaonburahs, Sirdars, or Wahadadars) who preside over their meetings. The village headman is elected by the elders in the village and settles disputes and oversees the functioning of the village institutions, schools, roads, health centres, etc. He is also responsible for payment of taxes and tributes by the villagers to the Syiem, who is an equivalent of the local king. Apart from the village council, Raid Council is another important institution comprising a number of villages; affairs of this council are managed by the elected village headman, the Lyngdoh (village priest) and four other myntries. The Council looks after social welfare and administration of civil and criminal justice within the Raid, the largest political unit within a Khasi state. The State head, Syiem, is elected by an electoral college consisting of Lyngdohs, village headmen, and the members of a pre-ordained royal clan. Syiem, as head of the State Durbar, is responsible for the welfare of his subjects and for overall supervision and control of the affairs of the Khasi state, and is assisted by the Raid Durbar in carrying out these tasks. Syiems cannot interfere in the internal affairs of the villages or the Raids which are autonomous authorities. Syiem Durbar, known as Darbar Hima, has the powers to legislate and execute laws, impose and collect taxes, regulate the administration of the villages through Sanads (charters) that carry the Syeim's signature and is the supreme authority within the kingdom (Gopalakrishnan 1995: 115–29). Since a Durbar is elected by adult male members of society, it is like a bastion of patriarchy within a matrilineal social structure. It has a hierarchical structure—occupied by the Syiem on one end and the village headman on the other—at the lowest rung of the hierarchy; in between there are other functionaries—the Basans, the Lyngskars, the Myntries, the Dolois, etc. Doloi was one of the most important links in the chain, having the responsibility of administering an area *(Elaka)* administered according to popular will by the Elaka Durbar. Durbar is a sacrosanct institution in the Khasi state, and a decision taken by the Durbar becomes a law by itself.

It is to be noted that this traditional institutions of governance within a Khasi state was inherently participative, consultative, and democratic in structure. It ensured the participation of each village and clan within the Darbar Hima and constituted an efficient decentralized system of administration and justice within the Khasi states. Being apolitical, these institutions were also free from party politics. A very similar system existed in the Jaintia Hills, where the king ruled through the Darbar, members of which were drawn from different villages and units. Here the Dolois, known as Pattors, were directly elected by the people and exercised supervision over the village priests and the entire kingdom was divided among 23 Dollois. In the Garo Hills, clan chiefs were called Nokma, the succession to which is regulated by the customary laws. There are usually four Nokmas, of which the one called the Aking Nokma is responsible for maintenance of peace and governance within their jurisdiction (Gopalakrishnan 1995: 128–9).

When the Khasi, Jaintia, and Garo people from the hills were subjugated by the British and brought under their administration in Assam, this system of local administration in the hills was left more or less undisturbed by the British, with only minor changes but without unsettling their inherent autonomy. There were more than 20 Khasi states present at the time of their subjugation by the British, and these entities exist even today. In 1923, all the Durbar Himas together formed the Khasi National Durbar 'to safeguard the states from encroachment by foreigners who may disturb the peace of the Khasi states and to protect the rights of the Khasi people as well as age old customs, laws, usages of state properties such as forests, markets, rivers, etc'. (Gopalakrishnan 1995: 126). But subsequent developments have somewhat marginalized their role in modern Khasi society.

Lack of diversification in economic activities kept the people confined to their immediate neigbourhood to a community-based life. While it may have kept the Khasi society a close knit one, it also prevented the integration of this society with the mainstream of Indian society and the development of the sense of 'Indianness' among them.

Creation of Meghalaya

Under the Sixth Schedule, autonomy was granted to the hill districts in the erstwhile composite state of Assam. However, reluctance on the part of the Assamese leadership to share power with the emerging elites among the tribals had led to the formation of Eastern India Tribal Units (EITU) in 1954 to address issues of economic backwardness of hill areas and preservation of their distinctive linguistic and cultural identities. Meanwhile, the Government of Assam was considering the recognition of Assamese as the only official language of the state; this was strongly opposed by the EITU. The then Chief Minister of Assam, Shri

B P Chaliha, asked a member of his Cabinet and a leader of EITU from the Garo Hills, Captain Williamson A Sangma, to call for a conference of the hill leaders to 'ascertain their views regarding the official language of the state'. Accordingly, a conference was organized in Shillong in July 1960 calling the leaders of all political parties from the hills. This conference ultimately came to be known as All Party Hill Leaders' Conference (APHLC) which unanimously opposed the proposal to make Assamese, a language that was alien to the hills, the official language of the state (Bhagawati 2007: 27). In due course, APHLC would evolve into the most important political party of the hills.

The Assamese Language Bill, however, was passed by the Assam Assembly in October 1960, forcing the APHLC to raise its demand for a separate state for the tribal people. The Central government was initially reluctant for reasons of economic viability and suggested higher delegation of powers in 1961, which was rejected by the APHLC. A commission (Hill Areas Commission) appointed in 1964 recommended measures for economic advancement rather than political independence of the hills, prompting APHLC to go in for a non-violent movement. It was in the backdrop of this situation that the new Prime Minister Mrs. Indira Gandhi visited Shillong in December 1966 when she announced in a public meeting that 'Assam would be reorganized to give requisite status and dignity to the hill people'. In the general elections of 1967, APHLC had won all the seats from the Khasi-Jaintia Hills and the Garo Hills. In 1968 the Union Government decided to create a separate hill state within Assam with its own legislative assembly and council of legislators (Bhagawati 2007: 12).

By the 22nd Constitution Amendment Act, an autonomous state, short of a full-fledged state, was created within Assam by the Parliament, in accordance of which, the Assam Reorganisation (Meghalaya) Act 1969 was enacted along with the North Eastern Council Act that created the North Eastern Council (NEC) for integrated development of the northeastern region. When the autonomous state was finally created in pursuance of this in April 1970, Capt. Sangma was elected as the leader of the state. In the subsequent elections, APHLC emerged victorious with Capt. Sangma becoming the first Chief Minister of the autonomous state of Meghalaya. The North Eastern Areas (Reorganisation) Act was passed in Parliament in December 1971 creating three new full-fledged states in the region—Manipur, Meghalaya, and Tripura, besides two Union Territories: Mizoram and Arunachal Pradesh. Meghalaya was inaugurated as a full State by the Prime Minister on 21 January 1972 at Shillong. The creation of a tribal state in the region was an important milestone on the road to autonomy and empowerment of the local people; it was immediately given the 'special category' tag.

The new state promptly ensured that almost all jobs in the state were reserved for their indigenous tribal population and that tribal students get preference in admission in educational institutions in the state. The educational institutions in Shillong were famous for their quality; they were mostly manned by non-tribals, among them were Bengalis displaced from erstwhile East Pakistan, Assamese, Biharis, Marwaris, and Nepalis, who had settled in Shillong for generations. They now felt marginalized and started leaving the state slowly, having no job or economic prospects within the state. The state not only made no attempt to halt this slow exodus, but actually encouraged it actively by denying all opportunities to its non-tribal population, and in the process isolating itself further from mainstream India. At times, even the most urgent requirements of development—necessity to attract investments and capital to develop infrastructure and communication, even connectivity to improve accessibility within the state—were completely ignored in the pretext of preserving the unique cultural identity of the tribals, it was like withdrawing into a shell of exclusivity where only identity mattered, to the exclusion of development. A militant student organization called the Khasi Students' Union (KSU) took a lead in this regressive approach, strongly opposing the central government's proposals for bringing railway lines to the state that had none for fear of being 'swamped by outsiders'. The KSU turned out to be a rogue organization and its members, unrestrained by the state, went on bullying the non-tribals. In 1979, it engineered and orchestrated a violent communal riot directed against the Bengali community, engaging in a spree of arson, looting, and genocide that had left an indelible scar in the history of this state that had hitherto been an abode of peace and harmony. The scar is yet to be wiped out completely, even after so many years.

Riots have occurred in the state since then with astonishing regularity, engineered by the KSU and other outfits that were aiming at capturing political power in the state by any means (one leader of KSU later became a minister in the government). In 1987, KSU started an agitation against illegal immigrants—the agitation led to the closure of educational institutions in the state for prolonged periods, irreparably damaging the reputation of the educational institutions in Shillong that had refused to be cowed down by all earlier movements and agitations in the state. The academic sessions went awry and students, including tribals, started migrating outside the state, never to return. The KSU movements prevented capital from coming into their capital-starved state, and now the talent was also fleeing, putting its future growth into jeopardy. The following years—1988, 1989, and 1990—saw violence against the non-tribal residents, culminating in severe riots in 1992 against the minority non-tribals in the state, leading to genocide and brutalities committed against them at a scale hitherto unseen in this otherwise peaceful state (Borah, Tourangbam, and Meitei 2010: 96). Side by side, militant movements inspired by the ULFA (United Liberation Front of Assam) was also raising its ugly head in the state, led by an organization called HNLC (Hynniewtrep National Liberation Council). However, this organization subsequently broke up into several smaller outfits, and is now reduced to small-time criminal activities. Even the KSU has now matured and is trying for a make-over of its earlier rogue image. Militancy is no longer an issue in the state and by and large, public peace prevails, though instances of extortion, harassment, and violence against non-tribals occur from time to time, mostly on non-issues like the demand for an inner line permit as in recent times.

Socio-Economic Change

By far the most important occupation of the tribes like that of the other racial groups of northeast India is, of course, agriculture. Annexure 4.1 details the progress of social, economic, and financial indicators in Meghalaya over the three decades since 1981. With 80 per cent rural population, Meghalaya is a highly ruralized state (2011). The state economy is also largely agrarian rural, with 66 per cent of working population engaged in the primary sector—agriculture and animal husbandry—directly or indirectly, but this percentage is concentrated on less than 10 per cent of the geographical area of the state. The percentage of working population in the state has been around 40 per cent throughout.

Agricultural practices in the state were primitive, based on shifting cultivation, with very limited use of modern tools and techniques and hence characterized by low productivity and yield. Thus, even though agriculture was providing livelihood to most people, the share of agriculture in the state income was low—40 per cent in 1981 and only 17 per cent in 2011; as a result, the agriculture-dependent rural population could only eke out a subsistence type existence. Primitive though the agriculture is, Khasi Hills are, however, famous for their rich horticultural products. Besides having large forests, the state also produces timber and lac. Rudimentary arts and crafts, such as making of bamboo mats and plaiting of baskets, are carried on by Khasi women who play a very important role in the hill economy.

Services sector, contributor to half the state income, remains mostly concentrated in the urban areas, turning them into islands of affluence, in contrast with the impoverished rural areas. Manufacturing in the state remains confined mostly to the small scale cottage and family based industries. Poverty ratio in the state had remained practically the same till 2001, after which it declined sharply to 12 per cent (2011). This is a phenomenon we shall witness in all special category states; despite the absence of industries, poverty levels tend to be low. The reasons are increasing central assistance and tertiarization of economic activities instead of real growth in services. Government expenditure accounts for nearly one third of GSDP (2011); in 1980–81, it used to account for half the GSDP; a large part of government expenditure is spent on development projects that generate demands that cannot be fulfilled through indigenously manufactured goods in the absence of any industry, and leads to inevitable tertiarization.

The state also has some mineral resources, coal, limestone, uranium, and sillimanite being the most important ones. But lack of accessibility to these resources and dearth of investable capital are the two biggest constraints to their exploitation. The geographical isolation of the state is accentuated by the lack of transport infrastructure, absence of market, high transportation cost and dispersed nature of resources. Even four decades of being a special category state could do nothing to address these impediments to growth. But in a way it has certainly helped the state—through a massive expansion of social infrastructure of health and education, and especially the physical infrastructure of roads, which would not have been possible without the liberal central grants.

Between 15 per cent and 19 per cent of the state budget, equivalent to 5 per cent–7 per cent of GSDP, has been spent on education throughout.

The state income grew at an average annual rate of about 15 per cent during 1980–2011, but physical infrastructure, especially power, remained dismal. By 2011, electrification was done only in 73 per cent of its more than 6800 villages. But the most disappointing area of performance has been the absence of meaningful industrialization in the state. The reasons are many and often extremely convoluted. First the scheme of granting the special category status did not imply utilization of grants specifically for the purpose of creating industrial infrastructure and developing capacity and entrepreneurship within the state based on exploitation of locally available resources. Among the special category states, only Assam has some large public sector industries. Second, the paranoid mindset of identity propagated by the KSU and endorsed by politicians who lacked vision, imagination, and statesmanship, discouraged setting up of any large industry that would necessarily need and attract outside capital and skill, both of which were in short supply within the state. KSU had even successfully agitated against rail connectivity that the centre was willing to extend to the state for the same reason—it still does—and a government devoid of vision and imagination just looked away. It was a perverse kind of colonization being promoted, to deny people connectivity and hence opportunity for development so that a few of the mighty and powerful could rule and appropriate the spoils thereof. The result was a mélange of misdirected policies and initiatives that stymied the industrial growth in the state. Industries operate mostly in the small scale sector, relating to wooden furniture, motor repairing, bakery, rice and flour mills, tailoring, knitting, and cement which are the only major industries in the state. Financial inclusion cannot but be limited in such a scenario, and in the absence of demand for industrial credit, the Credit-Deposit Ratio also remained low—only 24 per cent in 2011. As we shall see, this story will be replicated in almost every special category state in the northeastern region.

Public Finance in Meghalaya

We have observed earlier that the special category status, by making the states perpetually dependent on centre, has turned out to be dysfunctional for their development and self-reliance. Just as in the case of Assam or Nagaland, in Meghalaya also, two-thirds of the state's total revenues came from central grants alone in 2000–01, and about 59 per cent in 2010–11. The extent of dependence worsened over the years; in 1980–81, the state's own resources yielded 39 per cent of its total revenues and paid for nearly 45 per cent of its revenue expenditure. Three decades later, in 2010–11, the state's own revenue yielded only one fifth of its total revenue and could meet just about as much of its revenue expenditure. The state's own tax: GSDP ratio has only increased marginally (from 2.4 per cent to 3.9 per cent) during this period.

The percentage of non-developmental expenditure on general services in its total revenue expenditure had increased from nearly 27 per cent to 37 per cent over this period, curtailing the availability of funds for development to that extent. Despite debt burden rising from 15 per cent to 23 per cent of GSDP during this period, the state had increased the capital outlay substantially over the years; from a paltry Rs 21 crore in 1980–81 to Rs 575 crore in 2010–11. The higher capital outlay was made possible through the generation of surpluses in its revenue account consistently throughout the period 1981–2011, courtesy the central grants. In 1980–81, the state used to generate a fiscal surplus, but as capital outlay was increased, the surplus turned into deficit and in 2000–01, the Gross Fiscal Deficit (GFD) had reached a dangerous level of more than 6 per cent of GSDP. Thanks to the Fiscal Responsibility and Budget Management Act (FRBMA) enacted in 2006–07, the GFD: GSDP ratio was brought back to 2.3 per cent in 2010–11.Consequently, the share of interest payment in total revenue expenditure came down from 10.5 per cent in 2000–01 to 6.4 per cent in 2010–11. The present debt level is not unsustainable; with further curtailment of primary deficit, the state should be able to manage it rather comfortably.

The face of Meghalaya has been changing slowly and irreversibly over the years and changes are quite visible. Dense forests are gradually disappearing due to increasing deforestation. Houses are increasingly seen dotting the urban landscape, often encroaching upon the surrounding greenery. Availability of faster means of communication has led to greater mobility and economic independence of the people. Towns and villages are coming closer together and villagers are being exposed to the articles of consumption in urban areas. The expansion of towns has created better marketing facilities for agricultural commodities produced in the surrounding villages. However, with diversification of sources of income, level of investment has not risen in the absence of proper avenues and the village economy still does not exhibit signs of accelerating growth. Tourism is a major source of income for the state but remains unexploited in the absence of quality tourism infrastructure.

Planning in Meghalaya

Table 4.1 shows the plan expenditure/outlay in Meghalaya from the fourth plan onwards, i.e., since the formation of the state. All special category states started their journey as states from very low economic bases, where infrastructure was almost totally absent. Hence, all these states show a pattern in their plan investments as we have observed earlier—initial priority being given to the creation of physical infrastructure—transport and communication, power, industry, and rural development, in that order. Thus, the initial focus of plan expenditure was on economic services. As physical infrastructure was slowly developed, the focus gradually shifted towards social infrastructure of education, health, water supply, housing, etc.—and social services started claiming increasing shares of plan expenditure. Further down the road, there was need to lift the standards of administration and hence general services also started claiming a share, albeit small, of the plan outlays. All special category states exhibit these features in their outlays through successive plans.

Meghalaya had spent 77 per cent of its fourth plan outlays on economic services alone; this share came down to less than 60 per cent during the Eleventh Plan. Side by side, the share of social services went up from less than 28 per cent to close to 38 per cent. Among the economic services again, priority attached to agriculture was diluted over the successive plans, and transport, communication, and power continued to enjoy high priorities throughout. Infrastructure took away most of the available resources and not much was left to develop industry and minerals.

Summing up, it can be said that the state was created to fulfil the aspirations of the hill people and to preserve their distinctive ethno-cultural identities—that end has been served, to the exclusion and marginalization of its non-tribal people. Economic viability of the state was always an issue, and given the scarcity of resources and the difficulty of

Table 4.1 Plan Outlay/Expenditure in Meghalaya: 4th to 11th Plan (per cent)[1]

Major Heads of Development	4th Plan	5th Plan	6th Plan	7th Plan	8th Plan[i]	9th Plan	10th Plan	11th Plan
	1969–74	1974–78	1980–85	1985–90	1992–97	1997–02	2002–07	2007–12
Economic Services	**77.3**	**76.3**	**67.6**	**62.9**	**66.4**	**62.0**	**63.4**	**59.3**
Agriculture and Allied Activities	20.7	22.1	20.7	18.5	14.5	11.6	10.0	8.0
Rural Development	6.4	2.4	2.0	1.2	3.7	5.4	6.9	8.7
Special Area Programmes					1.0	0.5	1.5	2.1
Irrigation and Flood Control	5.0	18.3	18.6	18.9		3.9	3.2	2.4
Energy[ii]					16.7	13.0	16.8	11.8
Industry and Minerals	6.6	6.1	4.8	4.4	4.1	4.1	4.8	3.2
Transport & Communications	38.7	21	21.2	18.2	20.1	19.2	18.0	17.7
Science and Technology					0.2	0.3	0.3	2.7
General Economic Services		6.4	0.3	1.7	6.0	4.0	2.0	2.8
Social Services	**17.7**	**17.1**	**29.1**	**27.9**	**26.1**	**33.8**	**34.4**	**37.9**
Education							12.2	14.5
Medical and Public Health							6.0	6.9
Water Supply and Sanitation							7.8	6.3
Housing							2.4	1.3
Urban Development							3.5	3.5
Others Social Services								5.3

General Services	5.0	2.4	3.2	6.5	6.9	4.2	2.2	2.8
Grand Total (Rs Crore)	36	72	259	440	1029	2501	3009	9185

Source: Meghalaya Statistical Handbook, Dept of Planning, Govt of Meghalaya for various years, Basic Statistics of North Eastern Region, North Eastern Council, Shillong for various years, http://megplanning.gov.in/handbook.htm, Planning Commission data for 10th and 11th plans. For 10th and 11th Plans, the figures refer to the approved outlays.

Notes: i. Data for agriculture and allied activities includes irrigation and flood control for the eighth plan.

ii. Data for energy up to the seventh plan is included in irrigation and flood control.

the terrains to access even the sparse resources, the state could not have been sustained without special central assistance—this was assured by according it the status of a special category state. But the status had not led to rapid inclusive growth and development of the state as a whole. Urban areas and the population living there have indeed benefited, but the benefits have not been evenly spread. Today, there is a huge intra-state disparity between the rural and urban areas in the still highly ruralized state. Most people still depend on agriculture for their livelihood using archaic methods, which only supports a subsistence-type living. The last decade brought some marginal gains, which were inadequate to address the basic structural weaknesses and fragile economic fundamentals of the state, a large part of which has to do with issues of good governance. Central assistance has reduced absolute poverty, but the special category status after serving a limited purpose seems to have created a dependency syndrome. This was perhaps inevitable in a situation where access to easy funds was given without a coherent and well-defined strategy for development.

Manipur—An Overview

Manipur with its capital at Imphal, lies at the northeastern boundary along India's border with Myanmar, covering an area of 22,327 sq km. The state has two major physiographic regions, the Manipur river valley and a large surrounding tract of mountainous territory (Hill). The main physical feature of the valley is the Loktak Lake, the largest freshwater lake in northeast India covering an area of 104 sq km, from which the Manipur river starts its meandering southwards journey into Myanmar, where it joins Myittha, a tributary of the Chindwin. There is another important river in the state, the Barak that originates in the northern hills and flows into Cachar district of Assam.

As per the 2011 census, Manipur has a total population of 27.22 lakh, of which 70 per cent live in the rural areas. About two-thirds of the people are the Meitei, who live in the Manipur valley and are largely Hindus, a majority of them Vaishnavites. Hindus constitute about 60 per cent of the population; there are also sizeable populations of Christians and Muslims. About a third of the population belong to the scheduled tribes, among who are the indigenous hill tribes like the Naga in the north and the Kuki in the south. But despite its

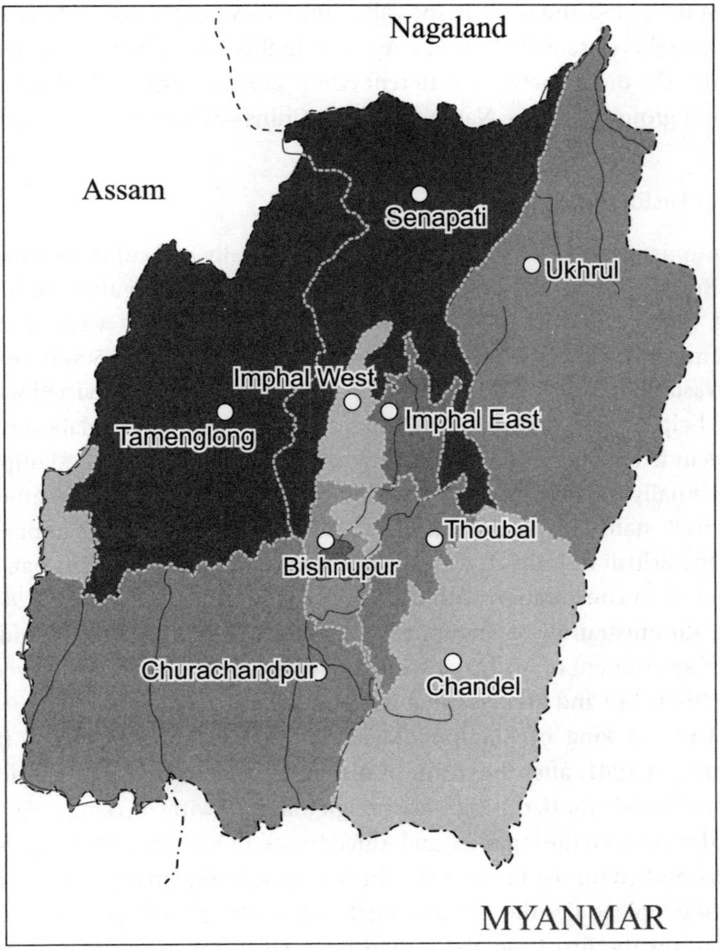

Map 4.2 Map of Manipur.

multi-ethnic and multi-ethnic character, Manipur is a deeply divided society. The valley and hill regions have many differences. The valley is a hill-girdled island covering just 10 per cent of the state area, but holds 60 per cent of the state's population spread amongst its four districts (Bishnupur, East and West Imphal, and Thoubal). The hill with its five sparsely populated districts (Churachandpur, Tamenglong, Senapati, Ukhrul, and Chandel) accounts for 90 per cent of the state's area but hosts only 40 per cent of the population. While the hill inhabitants can own their land and settle in the valley, the valley people do not have the same rights (Jasaal 2011: 20–1). Apart from this Hill-Valley divide, there is also the divide between different ethnic groups—especially the three major groups: Meiteis, Nagas, and Kuki-Chins—who inhabit the state.

Brief History of Statehood

Manipur, also known as Meitrabak, was ethnically and culturally closer to Burma (Myanmar) but started moving closer to India after embracing Vaishnavism in the eighteenth century. In 1919, it went under Burmese occupation, unleashing what is known as the 'Seven Years Devastation' from 1819 to 1826. The Burmese were finally evicted with the help of British East India Company, after Treaty of Yandaboo was concluded at the end of the first Anglo-Burmese War in 1826. Manipur was finally annexed to the British Empire in 1891 and thus became a princely state—it was the last of the independent states to be annexed by the British in India. It was ruled by the Maharaja and his Durbar, or Council in consultation with the British Political Agent.[2] In May 1907, the administration of Manipur's hill tribes was placed directly under the Government of Assam, sowing the seeds for future conflict between the hill tribes and Meiteis inhabiting the valleys.

The last king of Manipur, Meidingu Bodhchandra ascended the throne in 1941, after the death of his father Churachand, in the midst of the World War II, during whose reign Manipur witnessed many fierce battles between the Japanese and Allied forces. In February 1942, Imphal was bombed for the first time by the Japanese, killing many and forcing most people to flee the city, leaving the Manipur Valley largely deserted. Then, for the first time, the Indian national flag was raised in Indian soil by General Malik of the Indian National Army at Moirang on the southern part of the Manipur Valley on 14 April 1944. But the Japanese were beaten back before they could enter Imphal, in what was said to be a turning point of the War. But the colonial rule was on its way out, and with the impending demise of colonial rule, the old feudal world in Manipur too was fading away, ushering in democratic changes. Political awakening was taking place within the state against the colonial rule as much as against monarchy and in favour of democracy. The Maharaja had no choice but to respond to the demands of the people. He formed a committee to draft the constitution of Manipur in December 1946.

Under the new constitution, Manipur became a constitutional monarchy in July, 1947, with the responsibility of administration vested in the Maharaja-in-Council (Ray 1994: 252). Immediately afterwards, the interim Manipur State Council was formed by the Maharaja, appointing his brother, MK Priyobarta, as the first interim Chief Minister of Manipur. The first democratic election in Manipur was held in June 1948 under the Manipur State Constitution Act, 1947, and an elected coalition Government was formed which was, however, short lived. In 1949, Maharaja Bodhchandra was summoned to Shillong, the then capital of Assam, where after much persuasion (and with some coercion), he signed the Instrument of Accession merging his kingdom into India on 21 September 1949 (Singh 1998: 229–30). On 15 October 1949, the Manipur State Assembly and Council were dissolved and Manipur became a part of India. It was made a Part C State by virtue of the Part C State Act 1951, and then upgraded to a Union Territory in 1956 under the State Reorganisation Act 1956. Manipur acquired an elected legislature in 1963 and was conferred full statehood on January 21 1972 by the Manipur Statehood Act 1972. However, one year before the full statehood was granted, the Manipur (Hill Areas) District Council Act, 1971 introduced the Autonomous District Councils in Manipur, just as in Meghalaya (Ray 1994: 254). Manipur was accorded the special category status in 1972.

Insurgency in Manipur

The history of insurgency in Manipur can be traced to the Naga insurgency, but there were other factors like dissatisfaction with the attitude of the Indian Government, discontent among the educated Manipuris on the issue of merger with India and a nostalgia for the 'lost pride and glory of the political status of this state'. Economic factors like backwardness, lack of employment opportunities, poverty, and perceived neglect of the state by the central government also contributed to the growth of armed movements within the state (Singh 2005: 26–50). However, encouraged by the Nagas, in 1948, a section of Meitei youths had opposed the merger of Manipur with the Indian Union, but the movement failed to attract popular support and soon fizzled away. Militancy started springing their ugly heads in the valley during the 1960s, when a number of radical organizations were formed—United

National Liberation Front (UNLF) in 1964, Meitei State Committee (MSC) in 1967, People's Revolutionary Party of Kangleipak (PREPAK) in 1977, People's Liberation Army (PLA) in 1978, and Kangleipak Communist Party (KCP) in 1980. All of them demanded an independent Manipur, drawing inspiration from its past sovereignty and contesting its so-called 'forced merger' with India.[3] But actually Manipur had lost its sovereignty way back in 1891 when it was made a part of the British Empire in India, and for all practical purposes it was another princely state in India.[4]

Apart from these militant organizations vowing independence through armed struggle, there were many smaller outfits formed on ethnic lines. Ethnic clashes between the Nagas and Kukis in the early 1990s led to the formation of a number of Kuki outfits. Other tribal outfits also came up—even Islamist outfits like the People's United Liberation Front (PULF) for protecting the interests of the 'Pangals' or Manipuri Muslims. There are more than 30 militant outfits operating in Manipur today.[5] PLA, PREPAK, and UNLF have come together on a common platform called Manipur People's Liberation Front and remain the most active among all the groups (Upadhyay 2005b).

Militancy has seriously affected life and development in the state as a whole, especially in its five hill districts. Insurgency problem in Manipur has proved to be intractable due to a combination of several factors—ethnic composition of the state's population, spill-over effect from the insurgency in neighbouring Nagaland with their demand for the formation of a greater Nagalim including all Naga-inhabited areas in Manipur. The situation in Manipur is akin to a civil war; with the major ethnic groups in Manipur—Meiteis, Nagas, and Kuki-Chin-Mizo ethnic groups—being engaged in 'polarizing politics' with their separate objectives and agenda. It is the politicization of ethnicity and ethnicization of politics. While the Nagas want a 'Nagalim', the Kukis want a 'Kukiland' along with the Kukis of Myanmar. Meiteis of course want to free their pre-British territorial boundary from 'Indian occupation'.[6] All these three groups have different histories and memories, two factors that drive much of tribal aspirations in the northeast. The Manipuri society is deeply divided today—it is not only the hill-valley divide but also the Meitei-tribal divide, the divide being widened everyday due to the total absence of governance and development—in fact, the elected government had long abdicated its role.

The handling of militancy by the security forces has not helped either. The army and the paramilitary forces like Assam Rifles, empowered by the Armed Forces (Special Powers) Act (AFSPA) 1958, imposed after declaring the entire state as 'Disturbed Area' in 1980, had resorted to several strong arm tactics which almost completely alienated them from the people, as symbolized by the prolonged fast and force-feeding of Irom Sharmila. The alleged instances of human rights violations by the army and the paramilitary forces had galvanized the public to rally and protest against their atrocities, like the 'Mothers' nude protest' against the AFSPA in July 2004 on the discovery of the mutilated body of Thangjam Manorama, after she was picked up by the Assam Rifles and later found dead. It is not simply the security forces that have made life difficult for the people, the plethora of militant groups, known, little-known, or unknown, have equally contributed to the impossible imbroglio. People, serving in the government, educational institutions, business, professions and trades, and even religious establishments are daily being subjected to forced extortion by one such group or the other, and the writ of the Government does not run practically beyond the Secretariat. The Government is powerless to protect the life and property of its citizens who are terrorized by the militants on a daily basis. There are many permanent 'tax' collection points along National Highways 39 and 53 for the militants to extort tax from all civilians. They can strike and inflict damage almost everywhere within the state, with total impunity. As reported by the South Asia Terrorism Portal (SATP), from 2001 onwards till December 2011, altogether 2974 people were killed in Manipur, including 1832 militants, 318 members of security forces, and 824 civilians.[7] All these are affecting the state's economic growth, as the funds meant for development gets siphoned off to various militant groups. Bandhs and roadblocks are routine—often intended to create artificial scarcity of commodities to facilitate profiteering by traders affiliated to militant outfits. These outfits have marked their respective territorial jurisdictions for grabbing all government contracts pertaining to developmental schemes—with no encroachments tolerated. Norms of Government expenditure and GFR (General Financial Rules) are unheard of in these backyards of coercion and lawlessness. Only since 2010, thanks to the security forces being able to eliminate some top militant leaders, there has been a marked reduction in the incidents of militant-inflicted violence, but life within the state remains paralysed and growth stunted. The state remains sitting on a volcano that can erupt at any moment.

Corruption, drug smuggling, and trading are rampant among the militant groups and there is a close nexus between militants and politicians who are equally corrupt and self-serving. Ideology, having long taken a backseat among all militant groups, militancy is an alternative career now, with easy extortion money available to anybody wielding a gun. As Upadhyay (2005b) says, factional feuds among the various splinter groups and their alignment with other insurgent groups operating in the northeast with their foreign support link 'pushed the insurgency in a cross-current of strange socio-political whirlpool. Inter-ethnic clashes over control in drug trafficking added another dimension to insurgency. This also encouraged other smaller tribes like Paite, Vaiphei and Hmar in establishing their respective armed groups. Criminalization of insurgency, clandestine link of its leaders with various political parties, NGOs, government officials and their pressure on allotment of government contract works made the process of peace initiative more complicated.

Initially the Central Government treated the problem of insurgency as a pure law and order problem. After the 1971 Bangladesh War, arrest of a number of militant leaders, especially from the PLA, indeed led to a gradual decline in insurgency, but the militants recovered and regrouped during the late 1970s, when the state was declared a 'disturbed Area' and AFSPA subsequently imposed. As the number of militant organizations multiplied with their leaders being engaged in ethnic turf wars and the underground parallel economy boomed, powered by drug trafficking and extortion money collected without much effort or resistance, the entire insurgent movement shifted to a different pattern during the 1990s. Numerous vested interests, including politicians, contractors, and businessmen, militants and drug traffickers, and corrupt government officials connived together with other entrenched interests that harvested the benefits from this troubled state of affairs caring little for the enormous suffering and disruption in the daily life of ordinary people. The money extorted each year was estimated to be upwards of Rs 100 crore (Tarapot 2003: 54), which was enough to finance the lavish lifestyle of most leaders of the ever proliferating number of insurgent groups. These groups operated across the porous 350 km border with Myanmar, striking and taking shelter within Myanmar, sometimes fleeing to Bangladesh. Improvement in our relations with both these neighbours in recent times has cut this vital life support system of the insurgent groups, as reflected in the lesser number of strikes and casualty figures.

The central government also suffers from a lack of credibility within the state. First, it did very little to integrate the people of the state into mainstream India. Second, due to the ongoing militancy, no developmental activity could gather sufficient steam as to generate growth, income, and employment within the state, kindling some hope in the hearts of the people who continued to feel forsaken and neglected. Third, the high-handedness and sometimes illegal actions of security forces did not endear the centre to the people either. And lastly, the endemic corruption within the government has deprived the people from getting any meaningful benefit from the central poverty alleviation and other welfare schemes for which substantial funds were made available to the state (Upadhyay 2005b).

To be fair to the centre, it took a number of peace initiatives ever since the insurgency had begun troubling the state. Major militant outfits like the UNLF, the PLA, the PREPAK, and the KYKL are opposed to any negotiated settlement within the Indian Constitution, but more relevant may be the fact that in case of a settlement, they would stand to lose their secure sources of income. Civil society groups like the Meira Paibis (Women Torch Bearers), the Manipur Chanura Leishem Marup (Macha Leima), another leading women's organization, or the United Committee of Manipur (UCM) are active and vocal, but their concerns are focused mostly on AFSPA, civil liberties, and human rights issues—they are not so vocal against militancy itself.[8] The state government is offering substantial incentives of Rs 5 lakh as fixed deposit and a monthly stipend of Rs 5000 to the militants to surrender and lay down arms,[9] but so far the responses have not been very heart warming. Obviously the militants stand to benefit more by remaining outside the reach of law than by coming within it.

The power of the Indian State is too mighty for the militants ever to nurture any hope for an independent Manipur outside the Indian Constitution. Besides, the state is almost entirely dependent on central grants for its survival; it does not have enough resources to pay for even a small fraction of its own expenditure needs. In case militants are ready to negotiate without preconditions, some asymmetrical solutions might emerge. But the reality is that there are state and non-state actors who are stakeholders in the whole 'business' of militancy; they do not want a solution to the problem. 'The pretence on the part of both state and non-state actors, however, must continue so that they can hoodwink an already looted and tormented people; the militant says he is staging a 'revolution' for the masses whose cause he thinks his outfit must alone champion, while the powerful state actors say they are seriously engaged in the business of 'conflict resolution'. .... Both the militant and the politician involved in the industry of terrorism thus expediently exist for the sake of each other' (Jasaal 2011: 60–1).

Although there has been a drop in violent incidents in recent times, it is as yet far too less to be assuring. There has been some four dozen ceasefire agreements and 'multi-layered multi-channelled' contacts between New Delhi and Imphal so far, but peace has not returned to the state. Dialogue has taken place, but not the other essential 'D's: Development and Deterrence. Ghosts of history continue to haunt the state which is still poised precariously between a lingering hope and lurking despair. As the Report of SATP notes, 'The relief afforded by declining violence in Manipur continues to be tainted by the unresolved ethnic tensions in the state, and the Government's inability to effectively neutralize the polarized and violent militant formations claiming to 'represent' divergent ethnic interests' (Upadhyay 2005b).

Socio-Economic Change

The pre-colonial economy of Manipur was a peasant economy based on traditional jhoom-based agricultural production and inhibited by several barriers—structural, institutional as well as physical. The right to distribute the land was vested in the king. The primitive agrarian economy was, however, able to produce enough food-grains to feed more than 2 lakh which was the population of the entire state, and yet produced some surplus, though there was no market for this surplus to be traded. There was no manufacturing; the political stability needed for manufacture-based production was absent due to frequent wars with Burma and internecine conflicts between different tribal and ethnic groups. Hence the surplus from primary sector could not be absorbed by manufacturing and a small service sector gradually came into being.

Manipur came under colonial rule in 1891, and colonial rule ended the hitherto closed agrarian structure of the economy by opening it up to outsiders who started coming in from other parts of the country. To the existing agricultural and a much smaller service sector, now an export sector was added as a result of influx of outside traders, who exported the surplus produce to other states of India and to Burma (now Myanmar). With the demise of the old order, the Rayatwari system of land tenure came to be introduced in the Manipur valley, leading to 'monetization and marketisation of the economy and commercialization of agriculture'.[10] Exports, mainly of rice and rice products, boomed during the next few decades till the end of the nineteenth century and road links were established to Cachar, Dimapur, and Tamu on the border with Burma. But excessive reliance on exports had extracted its own price and by the end of the colonial rule, forest resources had become depleted and excessive export of rice resulted in soaring prices and scarcity for local consumption. This engendered the Nupi Lal (Women's Agitation) in 1939 against the export of rice clearly indicating the limits to export. However, feudal landlordism that was prevalent in many parts of mainland India was conspicuously absent in Manipur, thanks to the limit of acquisition of 10 hectares of land imposed by the Manipur State Darbar in 1925. But the transfer of a substantial part of the agrarian surplus through export led to economic retardation and pauperization of peasants; side by side 'there was a structural shift towards tertiarisation of the economy and occupations'(Patnaik 1999: 3). When the colonial rule ended, the structures of modern economic production, the monetized and marketed economy, absence of feudal relations, and open agrarianism with an expanded base were in place. It was on this expanded base that planned development of the state could have become a reality. Once exports were stopped and the surplus rice was internalized for consumption, the immediate impact was a huge jump in the population growth to 3.75 per cent and 3.26 per cent during the fifties and sixties compared to 2.5 per cent and 2.4 per cent for all India respectively. From a net exporter of huge rice surpluses during the colonial days, Manipur was fast turning into a net importer.[11]

By the time statehood was granted to Manipur, its economy was still agricultural, with a blossoming tertiary sector and a stagnant industrial sector. Agriculture in Manipur, like in the rest of northeast India, was and still remains primitive, beset with jhoom cultivation, limited irrigation, and continuous fragmentation of land. Manipur has quite a few deposits of considerable quantities of minerals like limestone, chromite, copper lignite, nickel, asbestos, and salt. But, since 1998–99, mining and production of minerals had virtually stopped due to insurgency. Once statehood was granted along with the special category status, large amounts of central government grants, both plan and non-plan, started pouring in. In 2000–01, the government expenditure itself accounted for 78 per cent of GSDP; in 2010–11, it was still 67 per cent; central grants in that year alone amounted to 43 per cent of the GSDP. These funds came with no strings and were open to appropriation by the unholy nexus of politicians, contractors, and bureaucrats, in the absence of any control and accountability structure. By the time of statehood, even the will to take corrective measures was itself missing.[12] A virtual withdrawal of entrepreneurial support systems killed whatever little scope for development still existed.

The structure of Manipur economy showed familiar trends of falling shares of primary sector and rising shares of the others, especially the tertiary sector, over the years. As with other special category states, despite the primary sector's falling contribution to the NSDP, its employment share was still 52 per cent in 2000–01. But there has been a role reversal of employment shares in the other two sectors of the economy; the secondary sector which employed 23 per cent of workforce in 1960–61 employed only 10 per cent of workforce in 1990–91. On the other hand, the tertiary sector which employed only 11 per cent of the work force in 1960–61, employed more than 20 per cent in 1990–91, indicating 'de-industrialization and tertiarization of the state's economy in the pre-reforms period'. By 2010–11, the share of primary sector in the NSDP had fallen to 25 per cent, and that of secondary sector had increased also to 25 per cent from 20 per cent a decade earlier, while the share of tertiary sector had changed only marginally from 49 per cent to 50 per cent during this decade. Unlike the rest of country where the growth of tertiary sector was led by trade, hotels, restaurants, banking, and insurance, in Manipur, the growth of this sector was driven mostly by government jobs.[13]

Bulk of the contribution from tertiary sector came from public administration (12.40 per cent in 1990 and 15.77 per cent in 2000). But economic liberalization worsened the structure of employment within the state. Between 1991 and 2001, the number of main workers reduced from 7.08 lakh to 6.59 lakh, while the number of marginal workers increased from 66,621 to 2.86 lakh. Most main workers were employed in agriculture, and they shifted out of it due to stagnating agricultural growth and lack of gainful employment. Thus liberalization brought more adversity than opportunity, leading to further 'pauperization' of the farmers.

The tribal polity in Manipur revolves around villages, termed as 'small republics' by colonial writers. The issues of ethnicity, identity, and land ownership are built into the psyche of the tribal people. The tribal concept of land extends much beyond their villages—it includes forests, territory, economy, and culture, also forms the basis of their social, cultural, and economic systems. The tribal land systems are based on the principle of common ownership of land by the community or the village, and authority for distribution of land is vested in the Village Council which also exercises agricultural control over jhoom cultivation. The land system is now undergoing the fundamental change due to the emergence of private property within the boundary of the tribal village, consequent upon the need felt for attracting outside investments to develop the pathetic village infrastructure (Ch. P. Singh 2010: 77–80). Physical infrastructure within the state is poor, though gradually improving in terms of surfaced roads, post offices, but continued availability of electricity is still a far cry, as installed capacity and generation are both extremely poor. Most of the state still lives in darkness for want of electricity. Both financial inclusion and Credit-Deposit Ratio, understandably, remained poor. But unlike the physical infrastructure, the development of social infrastructure has been at par with the national level, the literacy rate in the state was 69 per cent in 2001, nearly double of that in 1971 (Annexure 4.2).

Industrial scenario within the state remains dismal. The only industries in the state are handlooms and handicrafts in the small scale sector. With statehood, irrigation projects, and state-backed PSUs were established but they became sick in the prevailing disabling scenario. The manufacturing sector registered only a marginal increase (from 5.76 per cent to 8.18 per cent between 1990 and 2005), whereas the construction sector registered significant increase (from 7.99 per cent to 15.71 per cent during the same period). Even in the manufacturing sector, the growth share of registered manufacturing was negligible (0.08 per cent in 1990 and 0.21 per cent in 2005). It was primarily the contribution of unregistered manufacturing which increased from 5.68 per cent to 8.67 per cent during the same period. The 'informalisation of economy by cheap imported goods that flooded the local market' negatively impacted the growth of the registered manufacturing sector; the result was that the manufacturing sector became dependent on the self-employed workers or casual labours to run their units (Sharma 2010: 310–5). The opening up and decontrol of the economy that were radically transforming the economic landscape in the mainstream Indian states thus eluded Manipur and its trade and industrial scenario remained lopsided, the growth rate in trade and manufacturing between 1994 and 2005 being only 3.39 per cent (Th. P. Singh 2010: 263). All the districts within the state, according to the 2001 census, were categorized under 'No Industry District', like in many special category states.

Public Finance in Manipur

Reflection of this depressing scenario was seen in the state's public finances as well. State's total revenue receipts as a percentage of GSDP had fallen drastically during the nineties; only after militancy had shown signs of waning by 2010 had it picked up its growth again. From Annexure 4.2, it can be seen that till 1980–81, Manipur's was a story of growth and progress, it could pay for 47 per cent of its revenue expenditure from its own resources in 1980–81 when its own revenues constituted as much as 15 per cent of its GSDP and it became a fiscal surplus state. In stark contrast, in 2000–01 it could meet only 8 per cent of its revenue expenditure from its own revenues, tax and non-tax combined. About 88 per cent of its total revenues came from central grants alone in 1974–75, while state's own resources yielded only 4.5 per cent of its total revenues. This dependence has not reduced over the years and even in 2010–11, central grants constituted 72 per cent of its revenues, though the share of its own revenue had increased to nearly 10 per cent. But the overwhelming dependence on central grants has not reduced over the decades.

In 1980–81, the total government expenditure even exceeded the GSDP, again confirming that outside of the government, there was then very little economic activity. The state that year had a revenue surplus of nearly 19 per cent of its GSDP, another high level unprecedented in any mainstream Indian state, which also led to a fiscal surplus of 3 per cent of GSDP. But though the revenue account continued to generate surplus, the state had accumulated fiscal deficit exceeding 6 per cent of

GSDP in 2010–11. The outstanding debt was 69 per cent in 1974–75 and was brought down to 36 per cent in 1980–81; but in 2010–11, it rose again to more than 50 per cent of GSDP. A large part of the rising debt was owing to massive security expenditure, a major element of non-developmental expenditure. Non-developmental expenditure which constituted a quarter of total expenditure in 1974–75 had reduced to only 9 per cent in 1980–81, but then steeply rose to more than 30 per cent during the next three decades.

Manipur had faced and is still facing a very serious debt problem, with debt servicing including the payment of interest consuming 55 per cent of the total expenditure in 2000–01. Capital outlay used to constitute almost 92 per cent of its capital receipts in 1974–75 indicating that debt funds were used to create capital assets, while in 2000–01, it was only 10 per cent; 90 per cent of its capital receipts were used for repayment of its existing loans. However, by 2010–11 this trend was reversed, with capital outlay being more than six times the capital receipts and debt servicing being contained within 10 per cent of total expenditure.

Planning in Manipur

As we have seen in case of Meghalaya, Manipur also exhibits the same trends in respect of plan outlays. In the initial years after its emergence as a state, economic services claimed the lion's share of plan investments, and among the economic services also, transport and communications were given the maximum importance in terms of investments; they had claimed 40 per cent of total plan expenditure during the fourth plan, as shown in Table 4.2. The share of transport and communications in plan expenditure has since come down steeply over the successive plans, while the share of energy steadily increased. In the Eleventh Plan outlay, energy claimed the maximum share of 18 per cent among all economic services. Share of agriculture had declined over the plans, from nearly 12 per cent in the fourth plan to only 5 per cent during the eleventh plan. The overall share of economic services in plan investments had come down from nearly 74 per cent to 56 per cent between the fourth and eleventh plan periods, while that of social services increased from 25 per cent to 40 per cent. These trends were not limited to special category states alone other states also reflect these trends.

Table 4.2 Plan Outlay/ Expenditure in Manipur: Fourth to Eleventh Plan (%)

Major Heads of Development	4th Plan	5th Plan	6th Plan	7th Plan	8th Plan	9th Plan	10th Plan	11th Plan
	1969–74	1974–78	1980–85	1985–90	1992–97	1997–02	2002–07	2007–12
Economic Services	**73.7**	**78.3**	**66.7**	**67.9**	**67.6**	**64.2**	**59.8**	**55.9**
Agriculture and Allied Activities	11.9	16.1	18.7	12.6	9.2	5.1	4.1	5.4
Rural Development	1.5	1.3	0.8	3.1	3.7	4.4	4.3	3.3
Special Area Programmes						0.4	0.8	2.8
Irrigation and Flood Control	12.4	30.9	25.5	18.1	16.8	13.1	13.1	9.5
Energy[i]				9.9	15.1	19.4	8.2	18.4
Industry and Minerals	6.9	7.1	5.6	5.5	4.3	5.1	11.9	8.0
Transport & Communications	40.7	22.2	15.2	14.8	16.4	13.9	8.0	4.9
Science and Technology				0.4	0.4	0.3	0.6	1.6
General Economic Services	0.4	0.7	0.9	3.6	1.7	2.5	8.7	1.9
Social Services	**25.2**	**18.5**	**31.5**	**29.8**	**29.6**	**33.7**	**36.8**	**40.1**
Education							9.6	9.2
Medical and Public Health							2.9	1.3
Water Supply and Sanitation							11.5	13.9
Housing							2.9	3.8
Urban Development							4.8	2.9
Others Social Services							5.1	9.1

General Services	**1.0**	**3.3**	**1.8**	**2.3**	**2.8**	**2.2**	**3.4**	**4.0**
Total (Rs Crore)	**31**	**67**	**243**	**523**	**1225**	**1849**	**2804**	**8154**

Source: Statistical Abstract, Various Issues, Directorate of Economics and Statistics, Govt. of Manipur; For 4th–8th Plan data: http://manipuronline.com/business-economy/political-economy-of-manipur-transformation-within-the-mixed-economy-paradigm/2010/09/26; Basic Statistics of North Eastern Region, North Eastern Council, Shillong for various years, Planning Commission data for 10th and 11th plans (http://planningcommission.nic.in/plans/stateplan/index.php?state=b_outbody.htm). For 10th and 11th Plans, the figures refer to the approved outlays.
Note: i. Data for energy up to the sixth plan is included in irrigation and flood control.

Manipur today is saddled with many problems—stagnant agriculture, absence of industry, unemployment, inequality of income, poverty, migration of talent, non-availability of resources, and capital, endemic corruption, etc. and on top, a bloody and stubborn militancy that refuses to die down. At the time of getting statehood, it was beset with multitudes of problems which had since worsened due to the above factors, with no solution in sight. It remains a deeply divided society, and calls for some out-of-box asymmetrical solution. Granting the special category status could only address the state's financial vulnerability in a rather limited way without any coherent and consistent strategy, but without this financial support, the state would probably have fallen into an even bigger mess. The support, however, has corrupted the system and made it dysfunctional. The major problem remains the absence of the rule of law, in which situation the possibility of development becomes non-existent. The current situation points towards an improvement; one only hopes this will be permanent and not transitory as they have so far proved to be.

Tripura—An Overview

With an area of 10,491.69 sq km, Tripura is the third-smallest state of India with its capital at Agartala. It is flanked by Bangladesh on its three sides—west, south, and north—and is bounded by Mizoram on the east and Assam on the north-east. Inhabited by 36.71 lakh people (2011 census), it has five hill ranges running from north to south that harbour its four valleys: Agartala–Udaipur, Khowai–Teliamura, Kamalpur–Ambasa, Kailasahar–Manu, and Dharmanagar–Kanchanpur. Several rivers course their way through the state, the most important of these being the Gumti flowing into Bangladesh. The state is rich in mineral resources including natural gas and oil, much of which remains to be tapped. It is also immensely rich in biodiversity.

Tripura is a multi-cultural and multi-ethnic state with a composite culture that has evolved over a long period. Tribals, among which the Kokborok speaking Tripuris, constitute the majority (31 per cent) of population (2011 census). Non-tribal population mostly comprise Bengalis and Manipuris who have been living in the state since generations. Bengali culture coexists with rich tribal traditions, achieving assimilation in the composite culture of the state. It is one of the few

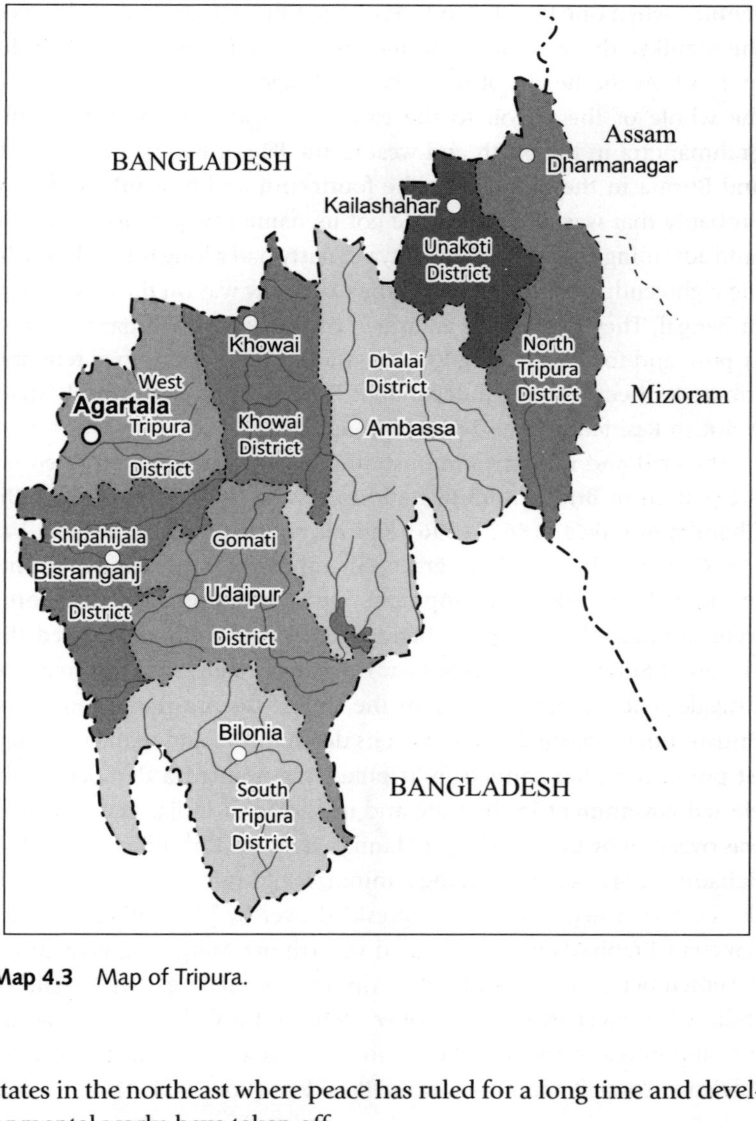

Map 4.3 Map of Tripura.

states in the northeast where peace has ruled for a long time and developmental works have taken off.

Brief History of Statehood

The origin of Tripura dates back to historical antiquity and is undocumented. The recorded history of Tripura begins in the thirteenth century, when one king Ratan Fa took the title of 'Manikya' and started the Manikya dynasty that continued till the state's merger with India in 1949. At the height of its glory, the Kingdom of Tripura included the whole of the region to the east of Bengal, extending from the Brahmaputra in the north and west to the Bay of Bengal in the south and Burma in the east during the fourteenth and fifteenth centuries. Probably that was when the state got its name (Twipra) meaning the land adjoining water.[14] The Manikya dynasty had a long line of kings. In the eighteenth century, the East India Company was on the ascendance in Bengal. They dispatched an armed contingent in February, 1761 to Tripura and forced the king Krishna Manikya to agree to pay rent and tribute to them, making independent Tripura virtually a princely state. A British Resident was also posted to Agartala.

The civil and military administration of Tripura were reformed on the pattern of British Administration in India during the reign of Bir Chandra Manikya (1862–1896) and his son Radha Kishore Manikya (1896-1909) who was also a great philanthropist. Far reaching reforms in agriculture, rural development, administration, and economy were introduced by King Bir Bikram (1927–47) who established the airport at Singerbed near Agartala. He actively supported the freedom struggle that was springing from the soil of this far flung outpost of British India. Colonial rule was on its death throes and many nationalist political parties formed in Tripura, who wanted a democratically elected government in the state and merger with India. The accession was overseen by the last king of Manikya dynasty, Kirti Bikram Manikya Bahadur (1947–49) who being a minor, could rule the state only with the help of a Regency Council presided over by his mother, Rajmata Kanchan Prabha Devi, who signed the Tripura Merger Agreement on 9 September 1949. Accordingly, Tripura was made a Part C state of India with effect from 15 October 1949 and a Chief Commissioner was appointed to rule the state with the assistance of a three member Advisory Council appointed by the President (Roy 2009: 41–4).

Following the recommendations of the States Reorganization Commission, Tripura became a Union Territory without legislature in November 1956. A constitutional amendment in 1963 gave it a 33 member Legislature and an elected Government was installed for the first time in July 1963.[15] Finally, under the North Eastern Areas (Reorganisation) Act 1971, passed by the Parliament, Tripura became a full-fledged state of the Indian Union on 21 January 1972. Immediately afterwards, it was accorded a Special Category Status.

Insurgency in Tripura

India shares 4097 km of its land border with Bangladesh, of which 2217 km lie in West Bengal alone. The northeastern states of Assam, Meghalaya, Tripura, and Mizoram share the rest. The entire stretch of this common border consists of riverine plains interspersed with hills and jungles. The area is also thickly populated, and 'cultivation is carried out till the last inch of the border at many stretches'.[16] All this makes the border extremely porous and easy for illegal migration and infiltration.

The entire northeast has been bearing the brunt of illegal immigration since independence. The Bangladesh Liberation War of 1971 saw large scale migration of Hindu Bengali people to India. But migration of Muslim population from across the border has been taking place through the large porous border at a steady rate ever since independence, upsetting and reversing the demographics in the northeastern states, and reducing the indigenous tribals into minorities in their native lands. The border districts are especially vulnerable to illegal immigration, turning most of these states into potential volcanoes that continued to erupt with regular frequency into violent ethnic conflagrations between the local tribes and non-tribal residents of these states, in which even the non-immigrant Bengali settlers of Tripura had often been the targets of tribal wrath. Ethnic strife has long been a part of life in the northeast, and Bengali-speaking Muslim community as also Bengalis from West Bengal, the Nepalese, Biharis, and other so-called 'outsiders' have often been subjected to ethnic cleansing ever since independence. Illegal migration has been a major issue behind many militant movements that sprang up in the region, like the prolonged AASU-led Assam agitation of the 1980s.

As in the other states in northeast, the density of population in Tripura has been going up by leaps and bounds at every successive census—from 62 in 1951 to 196 in 1981 to 350 at 2011. Such phenomenal increases cannot be explained simply by normal growth of population. By the 1970s, alteration in the demographic profile of the districts was clearly visible. The tribals were pushed to the hills, and the politics and administration in the state became dominated by the

Bengali speaking locals and migrants. Added to this was the strong sense of socio-economic deprivation and aspirations among the tribal youths for political power to counter the growing 'de-tribalization' of the state. The result was insurgency that had initially started as a protest movement against this phenomenon during the 1960s as a reaction to settling down of non-tribal refugees in the tribal reserve forest areas which was controlled by the government. Then in 1978, Bijoy Kumar Hrangkhawal, a young tribal leader of the 'Tripura Upajati Juba Samity' (TUJS), a regional tribal party, formed the Tripura National Volunteers (TNV) to carry on insurgent activities in collaboration with the Mizo National Front (MNF) of Mizoram. Widespread riots and killings took place within the state on ethnic lines leading to more than a thousand deaths. Hrangkhawal was arrested in June 1980 and released in December 1980. This outfit was dissolved initially, but continued with its activities till the signing of a tripartite agreement in 1988, paving the way for the surrender of the TNV cadres.[17]

Factionalism within TNV led to the formation of many militant groups: All Tripura People's Liberation Organization (ATPLO) and National Liberation Front of Tripura (NLFT) during the 1980s, All Tripura Tiger Force (ATTF) of 1990 and Borok National Council of Tripura (BNCT) in 2000. NLFT had established links with other militant outfits of the region like ULFA, NSCN (IM), National Democratic Front of Bodoland (NDFB), and operated mostly from Bangladesh, patronized by the Inter Services Intelligence (ISI) of Pakistan. They are now quiet. There are about two dozen splinter groups of militants—now mostly defunct—including Tripura National Liberation Front (TNLF).[18]

Militant insurgency had been contained in Tripura by 2005, though violence has not stopped altogether. The capital Agartala witnessed a series of blasts on October 1 2008, injuring 74 persons. No organization had claimed responsibility, but subsequent investigations revealed that apart from ATTF, HuJI (Harkat-ul-Jihad-al Islami), a Bangladeshi terror outfit, was also involved in the blasts. Between 1992 and 2010, at least 3479 insurgency related fatalities were recorded. But police and counter insurgency operations, especially since 2002, have been very effective. Between 2006 and 2008, as many as 871 militants belonging to the ATTF, NLFT, and BNCT had surrendered to the security forces.[19]

Camps in Bangladesh's Chittagong Hill Tracts (CHT) and Sylhet districts had been critical for the survival of militant outfits in Tripura.

But Government of India had successfully persuaded the Awami League Government of Bangladesh formed in December 2008 to ensure that the territory of Bangladesh was not allowed to be used for terrorist activities directed against India (Routray 2008). In 2003, the successful military assault on the ULFA and other north eastern rebels in the Bhutan forests led by the Bhutanese army had a tremendous demoralizing effect on the NLFT and the other northeastern insurgent groups. Now co-operation between Bangladesh and Indian Governments signalled a faster end to the insurgency in Tripura. In a big blow to the outfit, November 2009, NLFT supremo Biswamohan Debbarma was arrested by the Bangladesh Government from a posh area of Dhaka. Subsequent counter insurgency operations initiated by the Bangladesh Government against these outfits also weakened, frustrated, and demoralized them, leading to large-scale surrenders by its cadres.[20]

Several factors are responsible for the successful containment of the insurgency in Tripura. The militant groups survived on extortion, but Jamatiya Hoda, the Supreme Council of the Jamatiya tribe, the third largest tribal group in Tripura, in 2000, resolved not to pay any kind of 'tax' to the insurgent outfits operating in the state and later pledged support to the government in its fight against insurgency.[21] The effectiveness of the counter-insurgency strategy was another important factor that has left the militant groups in complete disarray.

The core of this strategy has been to establish control over most remote areas in the state, and to minimize the reaction time for counter-insurgent operations by establishing police and security force camps in the interior areas and creating a number of 'Special Police Pickets' in the strategic interior. Improved arms, communications, vehicles, etc. were provided to the security forces and intelligence network was beefed up. Finance, the lifeline of militant survival, was cut off by giving enhanced security cover to the traditional targets of extortion and abduction—traders, tea gardens, railway, and road construction managers—thereby choking off avenues of extortion (Sahni and Routray 2005). Simultaneously, the intelligence and support networks of militants were systematically destroyed. Tripura is one of the few Indian states that has successfully contained any major insurgency. Extremist groups today are struggling for their bare survival. 18 battalions of BSF are engaged in the state and close watch is kept on their movements across the border. As per report of Ministry of Home Affairs (MHA) in

June 2009, Tripura recorded the third lowest insurgency-related incidents in the northeastern region after Mizoram and Meghalaya.

But security operations alone can never ensure lasting peace, only the political and developmental processes can ensure that. To encourage the participation of more tribals in the political decision-making process and to assuage their sense of alienation and deprivation, Tripura Tribal Areas Autonomous District Council (TTAADC) legislation was enacted way back in 1979. TTAADC consists of about 527 village committees at the grass roots. Elections to TTAADC had always been violent, but 2005 and 2011 elections were peaceful, the latter recording a voter turnout of 85 per cent (Bhattacharjee 2012). Since 2005, public vehicles have been plying along NH44 without escorts. With dramatic improvements in law and order following the success of counter-insurgency activities, the state has also started to attract investors, encouraged by the overall socio-economic progress made by the state (Sahaya 2011).

Socio-Economic Change

The transition of the state's economy started in the late nineteenth century when the prerequisites of economic development were gradually introduced through administrative reforms and the process of socio-cultural transition in tribal society was sought to be aligned with the demands of a slowly emerging market economy. In nineteenth century Tripura, about one-third of the total population lived in the plains and two-thirds in the hills, which were inhabited by both tribals and non-tribals, as pointed out by Bhattacharjee (2009: 4–5), quoting from 'A Statistical Account of Bengal, Volume-VI, 1876' by W. W. Hunter. The state's economic structure was semi-feudal superimposed on a relatively simple and self-contained tribal economy. It was a subsistence economy without any production or accumulation of surplus, and as we know, economic surpluses alone can lead to investment and growth. The King or Maharaja had the power to distribute land and to collect taxes through local chieftains or Rajas who would pay to the king a tax (called Ghar-Chukti Kar) that had no uniform structure and differed from tribe to tribe and from place to place.

Rice was the only major crop grown. The rich forest resources generated revenues for the state but in the absence of any system of regulating or controlling forest produces, their exploitation led to wanton destruction of forests. This process was further pushed by the immigrant Muslim population from neigbouring Bengal who were invited to clear the forests and settle without having to pay any rent for a period. Besides causing unbalanced growth, this also helped create an affluent class of landed gentry, mostly dominated by non-tribals, dependant on the cheap immigrant labour for cultivation of their lands. This in turn generated social inequality between the tribals and non-tribals—and also created a third tier—an offshoot of the feudal social structure consisting of officials and tax collectors. By the turn of the century, the slow village-centric economy was changing as villages were transforming themselves into towns. Agartala, the present capital, was a village of only 875 persons in 1864, but started growing around its market places where goods were traded between Tripura and Bengal.

Surrounded by the socio-economic framework and infrastructure of British Bengal, Tripura became overwhelmingly dependent on Bengal's infrastructure of railways, road networks, waterways, seaports, and upon its postal and telecommunication links even for accessing parts of its own territory. With the partition, all these links were suddenly snapped irrevocably and Tripura found itself in complete isolation from the rest of the country. A massive refugee influx followed from the then East Pakistan, and their rehabilitation significantly impacted the economy of Tripura. The refugees contributed to the growth of agriculture, cottage industries, trade, and transport development as evidenced by the acceleration of agricultural growth after partition. As more land came under cultivation, the pattern and frequency of cropping also improved. The socio-economic integration between the two dominant groups also increased as did the level of education in them. All this was slowly changing the structure of its economy as well as its society.

In 1970–71, just before becoming a full-fledged state, Tripura had a population of 15.56 lakh, of which nearly 90 per cent lived in rural areas. But with 74 per cent rural population even in 2011, Tripura still remains a highly ruralized state. The abnormal increase in the density of population from 134 in 1970–71 to 350 in 2000–01 indicates massive influx of refugees as well as illegal immigrants after the Bangladesh war.

The four decades since the special category status in 1972 saw major improvements in the state's physical, social, and financial infrastructure as seen in Annexure 4.3 to this chapter. Massive expansion in schools and increases in educational expenditure helped the literacy rate jump from a pitiable 36 per cent in 1971 to 88 per cent in 2011. Health infrastructure has not registered such progress, but the gains in physical infrastructure like roads, power, and also in the financial sector have been quite remarkable—credit deposit ratio improved from 3 per cent in 1968 to 35 per cent in 2011, which in itself was not much, but remarkable in comparison to 1968. But for the liberal grants brought by its special category status, such gains could not have accrued to the state that was economically backward and starved of resources, especially during the initial years of its statehood.

Like the other states in the northeast, Tripura is also an agrarian state whose agriculture is beset with many handicaps. Only 27 per cent of the total land is available for cultivation, the rest lying either in the hilly terrains or under thick forests. Though at the turn of the century half its population derived their livelihood from agriculture, it contributed only 24 per cent to the state income (20 per cent in 2011) and there was no surplus from agriculture which retained its subsistence character. Cropping pattern is also skewed, with rice alone claiming 91 per cent of the total cropped area. Though Tripura is the second largest producer of natural rubber in India after Kerala, there is no rubber processing industry in the state and the entire produce in more than 49000 hectares of area is to be exported out for processing and value addition.[22] Agriculture is still dependent on primitive methods like shifting cultivation and characterized by the absence of modern methods and irrigation facilities. Even in 2010–11, only 22 per cent of the net cultivated area had access to irrigation. The primary sector thus became a drag unto itself in the absence of any surplus.

The NSDP at current prices grew at a moderate annual rate of 12.7 per cent during the last four decades. And while the share of the primary sector declined significantly from 70 per cent to 24 per cent, the secondary sector stagnated till 1991, after which its share improved to 20 per cent by 2010–11. But the share of tertiary sector improved from 23 per cent in 1971 to 56 per cent in 2010–11. Thus, in the absence of any growth in manufacturing, the decrease in the share of primary sector could not be absorbed by the secondary sector, and obviously led to the tertiarization of its economy, as in Manipur and many other states in the northeast. After agriculture, the maximum number of workers were engaged in retail trade (28.21 per cent of total non-agricultural workforce), followed by manufacturing (18.60 per cent), public administration (14.54 per cent), and education (14.40 per cent).[23] Absence of the manufacturing sector also impacted the economy in other ways; the import sector grew in the absence of adequate internal production, which inhibited industrialization and rapid growth of Tripura's economy.

Stagnation of the secondary sector after 2001 and the resulting tertiarization of the economy led to lopsided growth. In the absence of industry, government or government-backed services were the only avenues for employment. Even village industries, especially its well-known handicrafts and hand-woven cotton fabrics, wood carvings, and bamboo products could not generate adequate subsidiary occupation in the rural sector because of their lack of scalability. The economy scenario was dismal at the time of creation of the state; even after four decades since then, it retains many of its earlier limitations and disabilities.

Industrial Scenario

A study referred to by Bhattacharjee (2009: 109–10) and conducted by the National Council of Applied Economic Research in 1961 had noted: 'It is difficult to attract capital to this isolated area inhabited by people with a low standard of life. Generally speaking, Tripura lacks conditions for any major growth of big or medium industries. ' These remarks apply to Tripura even today by and large.

The first all India census of registered small scale industrial units in the country conducted for 1971–72 had identified altogether 246 registered small scale industrial (SSI) units in Tripura, employing 1698 people, mostly engaged in food, mineral, and metal products. The second survey for 1987–88 found 812 registered units employing 10069 people, including 190 units registered under the Factories Act, of which 17 were engaged in the export sector. However, only about 50 per cent (438) units were engaged in manufacturing and 45 per cent of the units (365) were located in the rural areas, implying that traditional village industries dominated the industrial scenario. However, with 603 closed units, the survey also highlighted significant sickness in the industrial scenario. According to the results of the Third All India Census for Small Scale Industries in the year 2001–02, Tripura had 959 working registered SSI units and 1077 closed units (Sinha and Chakravarty 2010: 132).

Under the Fifth Five Year Plan, Tripura established a jute mill, a sugar mill and a paper mill, the first two in the public sector. In fact, development of medium and large scale industries has been attempted only through the public sector in Tripura, but they again failed to generate adequate surplus. Performance of major public sector undertakings is poor, many are sick also. Heavy industries are conspicuous by their absence within the state.

Discovery of large quantities of natural gas in the state has raised hope of an industrial revival. As estimated by Oil and Natural Gas Corporation (ONGC), the state has a reserve of 400 billion cubic metres of natural gas, out of which 16 billion cubic metres are recoverable. ONGC had produced 480 million cubic meter natural gas in the state in 2006–07 (Sinha and Chakravarty 2010: 135).The state has been trying to woo large industrial houses to set up industries in Tripura, but is yet to attract them despite various incentives offered by the government. For any meaningful industrialization to take place, modernization and diversification of the state's primary sector is a pre-requisite, which has not happened so far. The cottage and village industries and co-operativization have been success stories, but these successes are not enough to overcome the physical impediments like geographical isolation, lack of capital, under-developed infrastructure, poor base of raw materials, and absence of industrial climate, all of which inhibit the growth of productive economic organization.

Public Finance in Tripura

The state of public finance in Tripura was a replication of the situation prevailing in other special category states, being characterized by heavy dependence on central resources and inadequacy of its own resources. In 1970–71, central grants constituted more than 91 per cent of the state's total revenues. State's own revenues could not even meet one tenth of its revenue expenditure. Central grants amounted to 12 per cent of GSDP then and the total government expenditure accounted for 16 per cent of GSDP. Four decades later in 2010–11, the situation has only improved marginally; central grants still constituted 64 per cent of its total revenues, but accounted for 18 per cent of its GSDP, much higher than in 1970–71. But the share of total government expenditure in GSDP had almost doubled to 31.5 per cent over this period, indicating the increasing dependence of economy on government activities.

However, the contribution of state's own revenues in total revenues has marginally improved to 15 per cent in 2010–11 compared to 9 per cent in 1970–71. Gross fiscal deficit that was a manageable 2.6 per cent of its GSDP had increased to more than 8 per cent during the decades of eighties and nineties, indicating increasing indebtedness of the state. In fact, debt servicing in 2000–01 accounted for 15 per cent of its total expenditure compared to only 7 per cent in 1970–71 and interest payments had also increased from 5 per cent to 13 per cent of revenue expenditure over the same period. The level of outstanding debt had increased from 18 per cent of its GSDP in 1970–71 to 40 per cent in 2000–01. However, the situation has seen much improvement since then, thanks to the Twelfth Finance Commission's recommendations and enactment of FRBMA in 2006-07. In 2010–11 debt: GSDP ratio had declined to 32 per cent and fiscal deficit was only 1.3 per cent of its GSDP. Because of consistent surpluses generated in the revenue account, the state could increase its capital outlay significantly from Rs three crore to 1058 crore between 1970–71 and 2010–11. But the unproductive non-developmental expenditure on running the administration that used to be only 18 per cent of total expenditure had increased to 37 per cent over the same period.

Planning in Tripura

Table 4.3 shows the plan expenditure/outlay of Tripura since the Fourth Five Year Plan, when Tripura emerged as a full-fledged state. Keeping with the general trend of plan outlay in other special category states discussed so far, in the initial years of Tripura's statehood, economic services claimed the lion's share of plan investments as well. Among the economic services, irrigation, and flood control, transport and communications and development of agriculture were given priority; together they claimed 71 per cent of total plan expenditure during the fourth plan. After the seventh plan, their shares declined. Side by side, from the seventh plan onwards, the share of social services in plan expenditure increased over the successive plans. Investments on industry was too inadequate to make a difference in the industrial scenario of the state; in any case, development of industry does not only depend on investments alone but on many other factors like availability of power, infrastructure, market, skill, entrepreneurship, etc. which were, and by and large still are, absent within the state.

Table 4.3 Plan Outlay/ Expenditure in Tripura: Fourth to Eleventh Plan (per cent)

Major Heads of Development	4th Plan	5th Plan	6th Plan	7th Plan	8th Plan	9th Plan	10th Plan	11th Plan
	1969–74	1974–78	1980–85	1985–90	1992–97	1997–02	2002–07	2007–12
	74.8	**77.6**	**68.6**	**61.5**	**67.6**	**51.7**	**58.0**	**54.9**
Agriculture and Allied Activities	18.2	24.1	24.9	22.2	24.7	8.0	10.0	7.8
Rural Development	1.4	1.6	2.0	1.4	6.5	11.9	12.0	10.2
Special Area Programmes					8.0	6.1	7.0	5.6
Irrigation and Flood Control	28.9	30.5	24.7	21.8		6.0	8.0	5.9
Energy#					10.7	4.9	5.0	7.2
Industry and Minerals	1.8	7.0	4.1	3.7	5.7	3.7	3.0	3.1
Transport & Communications	24.4	14.2	12.7	11.8	9.3	10.6	11.2	11.6
Science and Technology					0.2	0.1	0.3	0.5
General Economic Services	0.1	0.2	0.2	0.6	2.4	0.4	1.5	2.9
Social Services	**24.7**	**22.3**	**30.3**	**36.9**	**31.0**	**47.2**	**40.5**	**43.2**
Education							12.7	12.1
Medical and Public Health							5.6	7.2
Water Supply and Sanitation							5.1	5.4
Housing							8.5	5.5
Urban Development							1.7	2.7
Others Social Services							7.0	10.3

General Services	0.5	0.2	1.1	1.6	1.4	1.1	1.5	1.9
Total Rs Crore	35	50	293	440	1130	2255	4500	8852

Note: Data for Energy up to the seventh plan are included in Irrigation and Flood Control.

Source: Statistical Abstract of Tripura, various years, Directorate of Economics & Statistics, Planning (Statistics) Department, Government of Tripura; Planning Commission data for Tenth and Eleventh plans (For 10th and 11th Plans, the figures refer to the approved outlays). (http://planningcommission.nic.in/plans/stateplan/index.php?state=b_outbody.htm), accessed 26/10/13.

Summing up, it is seen that economic backwardness was only one of the problems faced by Tripura when it became a full-fledged state of the Indian Union and acquired the special category status. It had to cope with multiple handicaps like lack of connectivity and accessibility, illegal immigration, ethnic conflicts, and violent militancy. With its limited capability and resources, the state would not have been able to survive as a functioning state without additional financial support that its special category status had provided. The status had indeed helped the state to expand its social infrastructure and road networks, and take education and public services to its remotest corners. The state had successfully fought and subdued a stubborn militancy that otherwise would have rendered impossible whatever little development it has achieved, which is not small. It had brought peace, stability, and law and order back into the lives of its people. At the same time, without the support of a coherent strategy or enabling institutions, the constraints that jeopardized its development could not be addressed by mere financial support from the centre. The fundamental structural weaknesses that had plagued the state and prevented it from embarking on a path of rapid industrialization still continue to afflict it. Unless these structural constraints are addressed, faster growth and self-reliance will remain a chimera.

Mizoram—An Overview

Mizoram, the Land of Mizos, was formerly a district of Assam called the Lushai Hills District, which was rechristened as Mizo district with effect from 29 April 1954. It was made into a Union Territory on 21 January 1972 by virtue of the North Eastern Areas (Reorganisation) Act of 1971. Full-fledged statehood and special category status were finally awarded to the state on 20 February 1987. Mizoram has a total geographical area of 21,087 sq. kms and shares 404 kms of border with Myanmar and 318 kms of border with Bangladesh, but it shares more than mere borders with these countries. People of the same stock live in both these countries—Mizos in Myanmar and Chakmas in Bangladesh, the common root going back to centuries in the past (Kumar 2012: 20).

Mizo means inhabitants of the hills and Ram means land; the state comprises mostly mountainous terrains interspersed by rivers that flow both north and south cutting across steep hills and creating deep gorges,

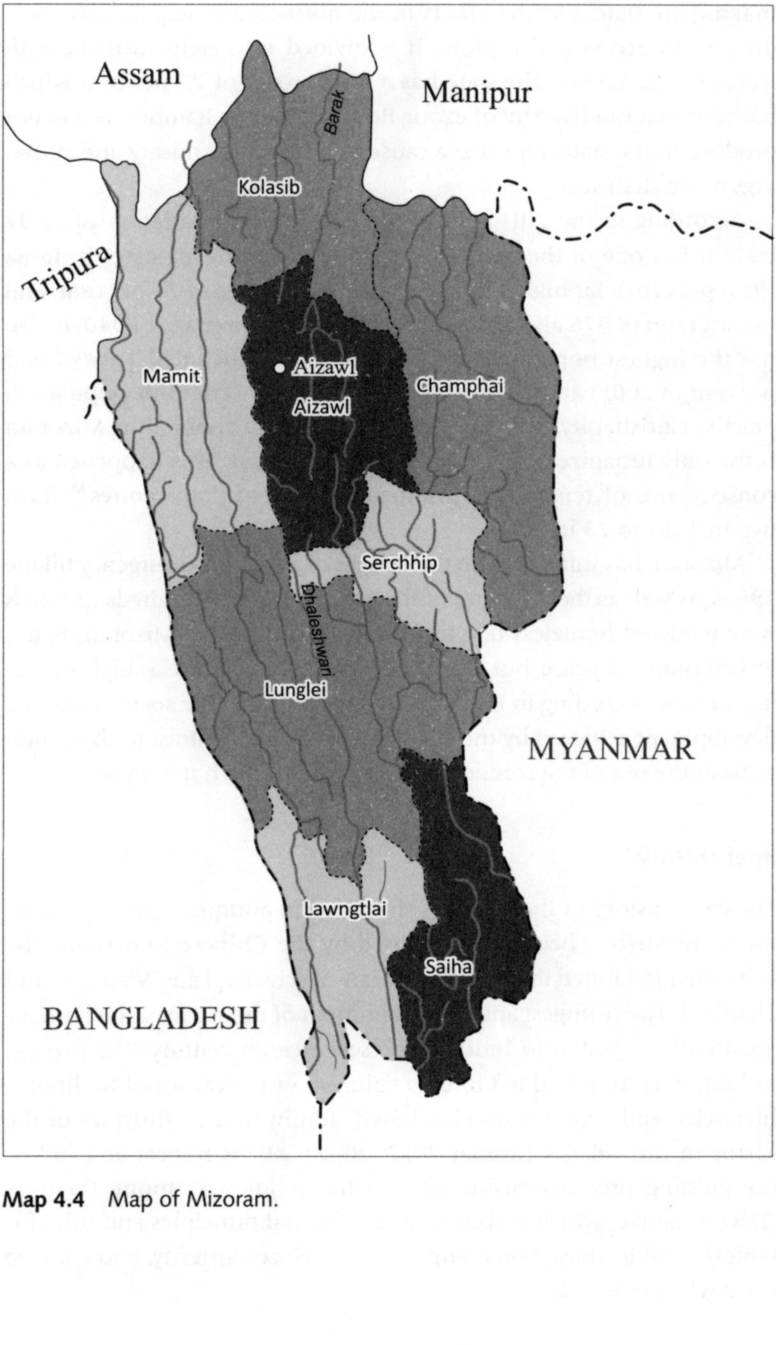

Map 4.4 Map of Mizoram.

making the state, like the others in the northeastern region, extremely difficult to access and explore. It is divided into eight districts, with its capital at Aizawl. The state has a forest cover of 79 per cent which harbour rich biodiversity of exotic flora and fauna. Bamboo is a major produce in the state, and also a cause of much of its misery and sufferings as we shall see.

According to the 2011 census, the state has a population of 10.97 lakh; it has one of the highest literacy rates among all states in India (91.6 per cent), far higher than the national average of 74 per cent, and the sex ratio of 976 also higher than the national average of 940. It also has the highest population percentage of the Scheduled Tribes (94.5 per cent in 2001) among all states. About 88 per cent of its population practise Christianity. With only 48.5 per cent rural population, Mizoram is the only urbanized state in the entire northeast. This happened as a consequence of remarkable proliferation of its urban centres[24] from two in 1981 to 23 in 2011.

Mizoram has suffered from the ravages of a nagging insurgency till the 1980s, as well as the atrocities of the security forces. Hundreds of Mizos were rendered homeless due to insurgency, but today, Mizoram is not just an island of peace, but also a state that does not have a single homeless person, according to the 2011 census reports.[25] The socio-economic development achieved by the state stands in stark contrast to the conditions in the rest of the conflict ridden region of which it is a part.

Brief History

The early history of the Mizos is shrouded in antiquity and mystery—the word Mizo is believed to be used by the Chinese to describe the tribes that inhabited the hills of Yunnan, Szechwan, Laos, Vietnam, and Thailand. The strongest and most dominant of these tribes, the Lushais, apparently migrated to India in the seventeenth century. The process of long migration had led to the evolution of typical social traditions, hierarchy, and 'closely-knit clan-based' administrative structure of the Mizos in the villages (Kumar 2012: 20–2). Mizos respect and follow the guiding precepts enshrined in what is known among them as 'Tlawmngihna', which embodies a set of moral principles and rules for ethical conduct, based on compassion, sacrifice, austerity, and courage (Lianzela 1994: 6–11).

Among the traditional social institutions of the Mizos, Chieftainship was the most important—a Chief or 'Lal' was the guardian of the people, a leader and defender 'in times of attack by the enemy and above all, giver of food in times of scarcity'. The Chief was assisted by a council called 'Upa', its members being chosen from among the influential persons in the village (Lianzela 1994: 12). Land belongs to the community in the village; only now the impact of market economy has started altering the scenario rather radically.

The Lushai Hills were annexed to British India by 1898. There were 259 chiefs in the Lushai Hills till the end of British rule—most of them belonged to the Sailo clan that had emerged as the ruling class among the early Lushai settlers (Patnaik and Lalthakima 2008: 9). As British administration along with Christianity and the British systems of justice and taxation made inroads into the Mizo society, it began to be perceived as eroding the autonomy and democracy that were inherent in the indigenous customs and social organization of Lushais. This led to feelings of resentment and opposition to the British rule. The Government of India Act 1935 further isolated the Mizos by declaring the Lushai Hills district as an 'Excluded Area' which kept the Mizos outside the mainstream Indian polity. Thus the political consciousness that was galvanizing the rest of the country into a spontaneous and powerful movement against the colonial rule could not reach Lushai Hills. Further, since the provincial Government of Assam had the authority over budget allocation for the Excluded Areas in respect of which it had no power of administration, it adversely affected the economic activities in the Lushai Hills district, as hardly any resources were made available. This led to widespread resentment among the people, but in the absence of any political party or political representation of the Mizos in federal or provincial legislatures, these feelings could not be consolidated into a sustained and orchestrated movement against British rule.

The first political party was born in Lushai Hills in April 1946; it was called Mizo Common Peoples' Union, the name was later changed to Mizo Union (MU). At that time, the British were negotiating for a 'policy of isolated independence for the Lushai Hills working through the Chiefs'. The political party was formed in response to this, demanding the abolition of Chieftainship and institution of elected village councils, which was granted later, under the Assam Lushai Hills District

(Acquisition of Chiefs' Rights) Act 1954; these rights were subsequently transferred to the Mizo District Council in 1958.

As Independence drew near, differences emerged among Mizos on their future. While the Mizo Union favoured staying within India with substantial political and financial autonomy, a secessionist group called United Mizo Freedom Organisation (UMFO) was formed by disgruntled members of MU, patronized by the Chiefs. Meanwhile, under the Sixth Schedule of the Indian Constitution, six Autonomous District Councils (ADC) were formed in Assam, one of these being in the Lushai Hills. The MU swept the elections to the newly formed ADC in Lushai Hills in April 1952, capturing 17 of the 18 elected seats (the remaining 6 seats being nominated). After abolition of the chieftainship, the MU again won elections to all the 259 village councils held in April 1954 (Ray 1993: 151–5). In the same year, the Lushai Hills were also rechristened as Mizo Hills, fulfilling another long standing demand of the MU.

Meanwhile, a strong movement was growing within Assam for formation of a separate hill state to cater to the rising aspirations of hill people within Assam and for the preservation of their distinctive ethnocultural characteristics. A new political party called the Eastern India Tribal Union (EITU) was formed under the leadership of Captain W A Sangma in response to these demands. UMFO joined EITA in 1957, having already lost its appeal with Mizo voters and chiefs after abolition of chieftainship and having no coherent economic or political agenda. EITU would ultimately be transformed into the All Party Hill Leaders' Conference (APHLC) in the 1960, a development that has been traced earlier in this book.

Insurgency in Mizoram and Statehood

In 1959, Mizo Hills suffered a dreadful famine—the worst in living memory—triggered by a phenomenon known as 'flowering of bamboos'. Bamboo is one of the most important produces of Mizo Hills, it is also extremely important for its economy whose full ecological and economic potentials remain vastly underutilized. Mizoram has an abundant reserve of bamboo forests covering an area of 12,54,400 hectares with three million metric tonnes of yield a year, equivalent to 14 per cent of the all India bamboo stock.[26]

Bamboo shoots serve as food for humans and bamboo stems and leaves serve as food for livestock. Bamboo plants generally flower only once in their life cycle, usually in 40 to 50 years. Once the bamboo plant flowers, it dies. But the flowering of bamboo plants almost invariably leads to an abnormal increase in the rodent population, apparently due to an increase in their fertility rates. As the seeds of the flowers fall upon the ground, before they can sprout, they are devoured by the hungry rats which mature and proliferate with astonishing speed. Having finished the bamboo flowers and seeds, the fast multiplying rat population then turn their hunger onto the standing crops in the fields devouring these in no time and bringing what is known as the 'Mautam famine', the word Mautam meaning death of the bamboo. Once the bamboo plants start flowering, there is hardly anything anyone can do to prevent the destruction of crops and the inevitable famine that follows in its wake.

The last Mautam famine in Mizoram had occurred in 1911–12. In 1958, bamboos started flowering all over the Mizo Hills, turning the hills into a blaze of colours that brought the inevitable destruction of crops in its wake in 1959. Relief was inadequate and far short of what was needed to prevent the disaster; even that inadequate relief could not be reached to the people in time. The whole episode was perceived by the affected people as gross mismanagement and callousness on the part of the Assam Government (Patnaik and Lalthakima 2008: 14–5). The inaccessibility and lack of roads made the situation worse as it took weeks to take relief to affected people in the remote areas. The Mizo Union provided some succour and was later rewarded for this in the Village Council elections in 1960, when it won 280 seats, against only 83 secured by EITU.

To mobilize assistance and relief for the distressed, a relief organization called the Mizo National Famine Front (MNFF) was formed in 1960, under leadership of a man known as Pu Laldenga, an ex-clerk of the District Council and an ex-Seviceman, 'suspended for misappropriation of funds' (Pudaite 2010: 17). The Mizo people only saw Laldenga and his men carrying relief materials to the remote parts of the district; within a year the MNFF had established such a credibility that Laldenga found it opportune to drop the word 'Famine' from its name and to make it into a political party called the Mizo National Front (MNF) in October 1961, declaring the achievement of 'sovereign independence for greater Mizoram' as its goal. It would dominate the state polity for the next quarter of a century and determinedly chart out its future course. Laldenga urged the Mizo people, who were 'Mongolians' and 'not Indians' to rise against 'Indian colonialism and achieve complete independence.' In February 1966, the MNF declared an open armed revolt against the Indian state, demanding their sovereign independent Mizo nation. On 28 February, raids were launched by more than 1000 armed MNF volunteers against security posts of Assam Rifles all over the Mizo Hills, many were killed and injured, and some were taken hostage. The Government Treasury at Aizawl was looted and the road to Aizawl from Silchar in Cachar district of Assam—the lifeline to Mizoram—was cut off at Vairengte, the first village in the Mizo Hills. Large scale violence and disturbances were unleashed by the MNF cadres that continued unabated for days. The MNF captured a few towns including Aizawl and Lunglei, the two most important towns of Mizoram. On 1 March 1966, the MNF in a statement signed by Mr. Laldenga and 60 others, declared independence for Mizoram. In retaliation, the next day, the Government of Assam declared the entire district as 'Disturbed Area' and moved in the Army by helicopter.

On 5 March 1966, for the first and the only time in the history of independent India, IAF jets strafed the MNF positions in Aizawl which was by then a deserted city; it continued bombing of the city before it could be secured from the rebels on 6 March. Other cities captured by the rebels were secured by April 1966. The MNF cadres, unable to withstand the onslaught from the Indian army, had by 1969, fled across the border to take shelter in the Chittagong Hill Tracts area of the then East Pakistan and Chin and Arakan Hills of the then Burma, where they set up training camps and from where they continued to carry out their sporadic guerrilla attacks on the Indian security forces (Ray 1993: 162). Subsequently, the government banned the MNF under the Unlawful Activities (Prevention) Act 1967 and moved the security forces in greater strength into Mizoram. Some excesses committed by the army using its enhanced powers under the Act led to widespread resentment among the people and added to their already high sense of alienation. The state was set for a protracted and nagging confrontation that would take nearly two decades to resolve.

From 1969, Laldenga, then settled in East Pakistan and patronized by the ISI of Pakistan, was trying to contact the Indian Government to find a way out of the impasse and restore normalcy in Mizoram

(Pudaite 2010: 18–9). The success of the security forces in containing the insurgency had made it clear that there was no hope for an independent Mizoram to be achieved through armed struggle against the Indian State. Meanwhile, the success of Indian forces in the Bangladesh War completely demoralized the MNF cadres located in Bangladesh, prompting Zoramthanga, then private secretary of Mr. Laldenga and later the Chief Minister of Mizoram, to propose 'surrendering to the advancing Indian forces at Subalong'on 16th December 1971. After the creation of independent Bangladesh, Laldenga was forced to settle down in Islamabad from where, in 1975, in a letter to the Indian Prime Minister Mrs. Indira Gandhi, he proposed a solution to the Mizo problem within the framework of Indian Constitution, thereby finally abjuring his fond dream of an 'independent sovereign Mizoram' (Pudaite 2010: 17). Meanwhile, under the North Eastern Areas (Reorganisation) Act 1971, Mizo Hills district was made a Union Territory in January 1972 with a legislature of 33 seats (30 elected and three nominated), with Lieutenant Governor as the administrative head; simultaneously full statehood was also granted to Meghalaya, Manipur, and Tripura.

The first election to the Legislative Assembly was held in April 1972, in which MU came to power with a thumping majority. In 1974, the MU was merged with the Congress Party in Mizoram headed by Mr. Lalthanwala. In April 1975, a new political party opposed to the MNF and known as the Peoples' Conference was floated under the leadership of a retired Brigadier of Indian Army named Thenphunga Sailo. The party rapidly started gaining popularity as people wanted to put their hopes on Mr. Sailo after the exit of Pu Laldenga to Pakistan. Mr. Sailo became the Chief Minister in 1979 and again in 1982, but lost in 1984 to Congress (I), when Mr. Lalthanwala became the Chief Minister.

From time to time, Peoples' Conference had been raising demands for full statehood for Mizoram without any success. It was only after a Congress Ministry was installed in Aizawl that the prospect for lasting peace in Mizoram became a distinct possibility. Meanwhile in Delhi, Mr. Rajiv Gandhi became the prime Minister after the assassination of Mrs. Indira Gandhi in October 1984. Mr. Lalthanwala offered to vacate the post of Chief Minister in favour of Mr. Laldenga without which the MNF would never agree to lay down arms. A Memorandum of Settlement was signed on 30 June 1986, between the Union Home Secretary, the Chief Secretary of Mizoram, and Mr. Laldenga. This settlement, known as the Mizoram Peace Accord, provided for granting of full statehood to Mizoram, cessation of all underground activities by MNF, laying down of all arms and ammunitions by them, and rehabilitation of their cadres. Upon signing the agreement, Mizoram was granted full statehood vide the Constitution (53rd Amendment) Bill and the State of Mizoram Bill 1986, with the creation of a 40-member Legislature, three Autonomous District Councils and 30 Village Councils. Special category status was accorded immediately to the newly-created state. Mr. Laldenga was installed as the first elected Chief Minister after his party had won the first elections in 1987in the state of Mizoram. Mizoram today is an abode of peace and development—an oasis of hope in a region otherwise marred by conflict and violence for a long time.

Socio-Economic Change

The economy of Mizoram is almost wholly dependent on agriculture and agro-based occupations like sericulture, horticulture, fishing, and animal husbandry. Though agriculture contributes to a relatively small proportion of the total state income (21 per cent in 2011), it provides livelihood to about 60 per cent of the state's working population. Most of the state's subsidiary industries are also agro-based. Agriculture in Mizoram is based on low yielding Jhoom cultivation method, like in other northeastern states. Its craggy hills and rugged terrains are not conducive to cultivation of many crops, and paddy is the most important crop followed by sugarcane, cotton, tapioca, oilseeds, etc. The adverse physical conditions do not facilitate irrigation, and in 2011 only 10 per cent of the net cultivated area was under irrigation. Progress of the socio-economic indicators of Mizoram has been shown in Annexure 4.4 at the end of this chapter.

Unable to produce the goods and commodities it needs, its economy thus became an import economy, as a consequence of which tertiarization of economy took place, as in many other northeastern states. Trading activities flourished, giving rise to a service sector that was largely driven by plains people from outside. The contribution of service sector to state income was as much as 63 per cent in 2011, but actually it was the government sector that was driving the economy, with government expenditure constituting 65 per cent of GSDP in 2011. The government sector

(Government Departments and PSUs) alone employed about 50,000 people, or about 6 per cent of state population in 2001. Central transfers to the State (excluding loans) was more than the State GDSP in 1990–91 and 40 per cent of GSDP in 2001. The state's economy is sustained by central funds, like in the other special category northeastern states.

The secondary sector's share in state income was 16 per cent in 2011, out of which construction alone accounted for 13 per cent. No major industries could develop due to various inhibiting factors common to the other northeastern states. In the 1970s and 80s, the entire state was a Notified Backward Area, categorized under 'No Industry District'. The development of infrastructure could gather some momentum only after attainment of statehood in 1987, but the process of industrialization was tardy and ineffective. The only industries that could develop, deriving sustenance from its rich bamboo forests and its agricultural, horticultural, and sericultural products, were cottage industries, handloom and handicrafts, and some food processing industries. All of these were small scale industries, of which there were about 1746 registered units in March 2006.[27]

The state income grew at an average annual rate of 16 per cent. The poverty level in the state was much lower than the national level or even the levels prevalent in other northeastern states. Poverty level came down from 50 per cent in 1970–71 to only 19 per cent in 2001 and then increased marginally to 21 per cent in 2011. Elimination of insurgency and the consequent thrust on economic activities were major driving factors behind this significant reduction in poverty as was the investment in infrastructure. Infrastructure of educational and health was expanded significantly during the decades since statehood. In 2001, Mizoram spent 18 per cent of its revenue expenditure on education, which was among the highest in the country; in 2011 this came down to 14 per cent.

Physical infrastructure of roads also registered significant expansion as did rural electrification; but the capacity augmentation in electricity generation would still need enormous efforts. The banking scenario in the state has shown healthy signs of improving of late. In 2001, there were only 36 bank offices in the state that has 22 towns and 817 villages and the Credit-Deposit Ratio was a pitiable 26 per cent. In 2011, the number of branches had increased significantly to 102 and the Credit-Deposit Ratio also improved to 43 per cent.

Despite the significant development of infrastructure, the inherent debilitating factors—resource constraints, remoteness, poor market linkages, difficult topography, and limited flat terrains, inadequate power supply, etc. are hindering industrialization and rapid growth of economy. Tourism that has great potential could not develop because of the lack of quality tourism infrastructure.

The New Industrial Policy of 2000 had identified Electronics and Information Technology, bamboo and timber based products, food and fruit processing, textiles, handloom and handicrafts as thrust areas. The government also set up Industrial Growth Centre (IGC) at Aizawl, Export Promotion Industrial Park (EPIP) at Lengte, Integrated Infrastructural Development Centre (IIDC) at Lunglei and a Food Park at Chhingchhip, besides upgrading the existing industrial estates. Setting up of Export Oriented Units (EOUs) was also encouraged in certain sectors like apparel and gems.[28] But the liberal infusion of funds to develop industry has been sub-optimal due to administrative inefficiency and lack of managerial talent within the state; besides, there have been too many leakages of funds due to injudicious non-developmental expenditure and overheads that did not actually contribute to broadening of the industrial base and had little impact on the output (Kumar 2012: 174). The small scale sector remained confined to the urban centres and could not penetrate into the rural areas. No major industry has come up in the state so far that could make a difference to the economic growth of the state. While the social sector has been developed with the help of central assistance, the industrial sector still remains undeveloped.

Public Finance in Mizoram

As already observed, the state, after attainment of its statehood and special category status in 1987, was overwhelmingly dependent on central transfers. In 1990–91, four years after becoming a special category state, the total amount of central transfers was about 20 per cent higher than GSDP. The abnormally high level of the state's non-tax revenue in 1991 was due to the writing off of outstanding loan of Rs 110.49 crore from the Government of India as per recommendations of the Ninth Finance Commission; this was accounted for as non-tax revenue. Because of this, the state's own revenue could account for 45 per cent of its revenue expenditure in that year. The ratio of state's own revenue to revenue expenditure reverted to 5.4 per cent in 2000–01 and 8.5 per cent in 2010–11.

Indebtedness remains a serious problem in Mizoram, like other special category states. Its outstanding debt was 55 per cent of GSDP in 1990–91 which increased to 77 per cent in 2001, a dangerous level of indebtedness not uncommon among the special category states. Interest payments in 1991 as well in 2001 consumed about 10 per cent of its revenue expenditure. The enactment of the FRBM Act in 2006–07 did little to ease the debt problem, as the state could not generate any surplus in its revenue account. However, the Debt: GSDP ratio improved to 58 per cent in 2010–11, but the state needs to do more to bring the ratio further down.

In 2001, central grants constituted about 40 per cent of its GSDP and 83 per cent of its total revenues. Along with the share of central taxes, central transfers accounted for about 93 per cent of the state's total revenue receipts and 76 per cent of its revenue expenditure; state's own revenues, tax, and non-tax combined, could barely meet 6 per cent of its revenue expenditure. In 2010–11 also, central transfers amounted to 90 per cent of total revenue and 79 per cent of the revenue expenditure of the state.

The Gross Fiscal Deficit (GFD) was nearly 22 per cent of its GSDP in 2000–01, the highest in India, and a level unsustainable by any standards but for the central assistance. It reduced to 16 per cent in 2010–11, which again was abnormally high, caused by heavy deficits in the revenue account. However, despite revenue deficit increasing to Rs 401 crore from Rs 193 crore in 2000-01, the state had invested Rs 600 crore in 2010–11 on capital assets, which was why the fiscal deficit had shot up. But given the scarce resource position of the state, there was no other alternative left but to create capital assets for future development. Investments take time to translate into income generation and the process cannot be short circuited.

Planning in Mizoram

The plan investments in Mizoram are shown in Table 4.4. The pattern seen earlier in the case of other northeastern states in this chapter are replicated in case of Mizoram too, the gradual shift of focus from economic services towards social services and the dominance of infrastructure

Table 4.4 Plan Outlay/ Expenditure in Mizoram: Fifth to Eleventh Plan (per cent)

Major Heads of Development	5th Plan 1974–78	6th Plan 1980–85	7th Plan 1985–90	8th Plan 1992–97*	9th Plan 1997–02	10th Plan 2002–07	11th Plan 2007–12
	75.3	**67.5**	**64.5**	**65.3**	**65.5**	**54.6**	**56.6**
Agriculture and Allied Activities	34.4	23.0	17.8	10.9	9.5	7.0	8.5
Rural Development				17.1	14.5	6.8	3.6
Special Area Programmes					0.0	1.8	1.0
Irrigation and Flood Control	8.6	16.4	15.6	13.6	1.1	1.2	3.6
Energy#					13.9	8.5	12.5
Industry and Minerals	6.8	3.5	5.1	5.8	4.3	2.6	3.6
Transport & Communications	25.5	24.6	26.0	13.5	16.8	21.0	16.0
Science and Technology				0.3	0.2	0.2	1.6
General Economic Services				4.1	5.2	5.5	6.3
Social Services	**22.9**	**28.2**	**32.5**	**27.8**	**32.7**	**41.6**	**41.7**
Education					9.4	12.7	13.7
Medical and Public Health					6.9	5.4	9.0
Water Supply and Sanitation					8.9	5.4	8.7
Housing					2.4	9.9	5.8
Urban Development					3.5	5.9	2.4
Others Social Services					1.6	2.3	2.2
General Services	**1.8**	**4.3**	**3.0**	**6.9**	**1.8**	**3.8**	**1.7**
Total (Rs Crore)	**46**	**131**	**260**	**763**	**1,619**	**2,300**	**5,534**

(Cont'd)

Table 4.4 (*Cont'd*)

Notes: *Data for Agriculture and Allied Activities includes Rural Development up to the seventh plan.
Data for Energy up to the eighth plan are included in Irrigation and Flood Control.
Source: Statistical Handbook, various years, Directorate of Economics & Statistics, Planning (Statistics) Department, Government of Mizoram; Basic Statistics of North Eastern Region, North Eastern Council, Shillong for various years; Planning Commission data for 10th and 11th plans. For Tenth and Eleventh Plans, the figures refer to the approved outlays.

sector—especially road transport and power—among the plan outlays in economic services. During the Fifth Plan, the agriculture sector had claimed more than a third of the total plan outlays, but during the Eleventh Plan, its share had reduced to merely 8.5 per cent of the total investments. Shares of rural development, irrigation, and flood control in plan outlays also reduced over time. But investments in transport, communications, and energy remained significant throughout.

Among the social services, like in all other special or even general category states, education, health, and housing were priority areas; another priority area was water supply in the water-starved hilly state.

Summing up, it was truly remarkable that after recovering from a protracted and bloody insurgency that crippled the state for more than two decades, Mizoram could still register remarkable achievements in education and social development within a relatively short time. Without political stability and lasting peace this would have been impossible. It has remarkably expanded its social infrastructure, reduced poverty, and established a fully functional state, unlike some of its neighbours. It could not have achieved all this without the help of liberal central assistance it got by virtue of its special category status. However, the economic fundamentals remain as weak as ever, and the state is unable to generate much internal resources due to which it is absolutely dependant on the central grants and transfers for its survival. Government activities by and large sustain its economy which in turn is supported by central transfers. The special category status has not been able to address the structural weaknesses in its economy and public finances.

Arunachal Pradesh—An Overview

Arunachal Pradesh, a magical and mystical land tucked away in the northeastern tip of India and known as the 'Land of First Sunrise' in India, became a full-fledged state in 1987. Before that it was a union territory known as NEFA or the North Eastern Front Agency. With its capital at Itanagar, the state is located most strategically, sharing long strategic international borders with three countries: 1030 kms with China, 440 kms with Myanmar and 160 kms with Bhutan. Home to more than 100 tribes and sub-tribes including 25 major tribes belonging to the Tibeto-Burman family of the Mongoloid race, Arunachal Pradesh presents a most interesting study in ethnic diversity (Bora 2008: 1–2). These tribal groups had migrated to Arunachal Pradesh in different groups and at different times through the tunnel of time. Through adaptation to a difficult terrain in the magnificent isolation imposed by geography, they have evolved their unique customs, social organization, traditions, and their unique and delightful culture. Located in the remotest corner of the country and having been geographically inaccessible, the state had remained a 'hidden land' for centuries.

India had fought a war with China in October–November 1962 when Chinese troops overran the entire territory of Arunachal Pradesh, then known as NEFA, and withdrew unilaterally before entering the plains of Assam to their pre-war positions. The roots of this conflict go back to the days of colonial imperialism, but it had brought the area into focus and after centuries of isolation and economic stagnation, it was given some attention. Getting full statehood 25 years after the conflict, the state had started its march in the path of socio-economic development, but still has a long way to go. Today it has a population of 13.82 lakh (2011 census) spread across an area of 83,743 sq. kms.

Predominantly a craggy and hazardous mountainous terrain, its jagged hills rise to a height of 6500 metres. With little accessibility to roads and other means of transport and communication, it's a *terra incognita*—unknown terrain to most of India. A permanent snow lining marks the McMahon Line that divides the Indo-China border. A part of the eastern Himalayas, the state is richly endowed with biodiversity of its exotic flora and fauna. A thick forest cover with variegated vegetation, picturesque mountain peaks, beautiful plateaus, swift rivers fed by snows from the Himalayas and countless rivulets, verdant valleys,

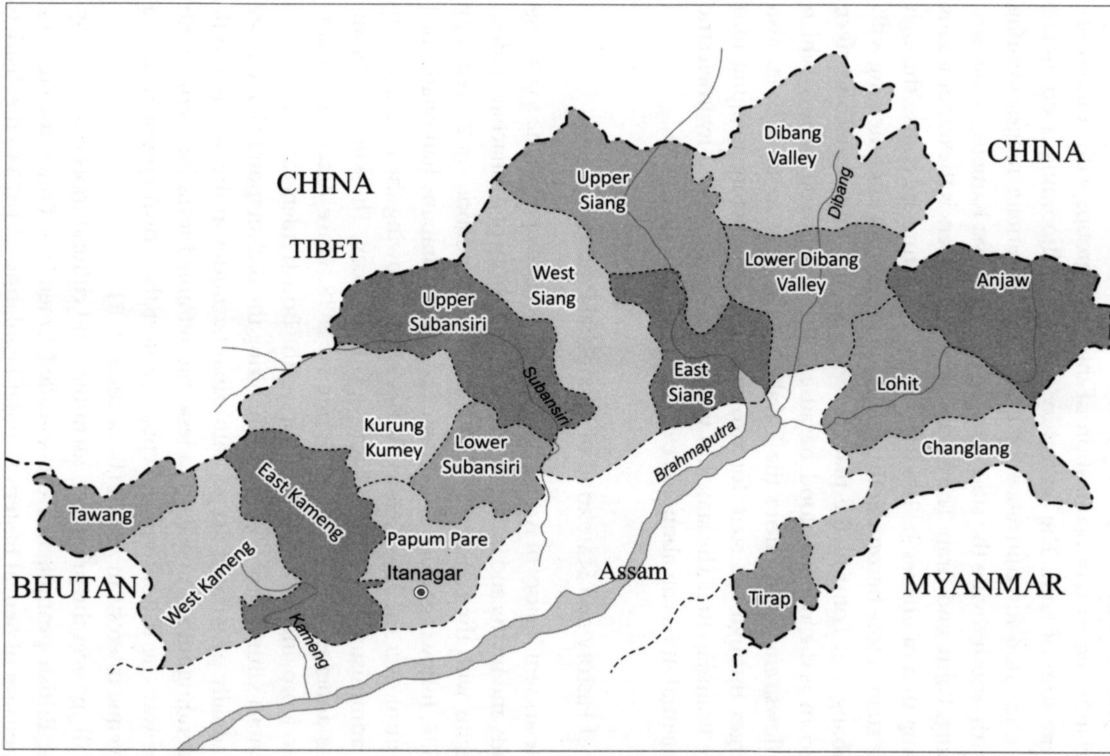

Map 4.5 Map of Arunachal Pradesh.

and gorges crisscrossing the state make it a paradise of scenic beauty. Nature, though, has not been as liberal with her resources—besides some coal, petroleum, and limestone, there are no other economically viable mineral deposits in the state. The social structure involves a clan-based social organization of the tribal groups with community ownership of land. The unhealthy practice of jhooming is dominant as a method for cultivation of crops. The mountain ranges running north–south divide the state into five river valleys: Kameng, Subansiri, Siang, Lohit, and Tirap. The mightiest of these rivers is the tempestuous Siang that originates in Tibet as Tsangpo and runs its course through the state before becoming the mighty Brahmaputra after merging with Dibang and Lohit in the plains of Assam. The turbulent Lohit river, known as the 'river of blood' because of the lateritic soil through which it flows, emanating from the Zayal Chu range in eastern Tibet, also surges through the state for two hundred kms before merging into the Brahmaputra. The state has vast and as yet untapped hydroelectric potential. It has an abundance of cane and bamboo forests.

Brief History and Statehood of Arunachal Pradesh

The ancient history of Arunachal Pradesh is enveloped in the fog of legends and myths and is unwritten. Modern history of Arunachal Pradesh begins with the conclusion of the Treaty of Yandaboo on 24 February 1826, following which the British East India Company had established control over the lower Assam Valley while allowing the Ahom royalty to administer the Ahom territory in Upper Assam. The whole of Assam was annexed to the British Empire in 1838. Once Assam was made into a province of the British Empire, the British rulers came into direct contact with the tribal groups inhabiting the Brahmaputra Valley. They gradually penetrated deeper into tribal territories in the northern hills extending into Arunachal Pradesh, but refrained from interfering with the way the tribes lived, except to protect their own commercial and revenue interests in Assam (Bora 2008: 2–8).

To protect the privileges, identities, and cultural traits of the tribals, the British promulgated the so-called Inner Line Policy through the extension of Bengal Eastern Frontier Regulation of 1873 to the districts of Lakhimpur and Darrang of the Assam Province by laying down a line in these districts beyond which one could not move without appropriate authorization. The Inner Line[29] laid down the rules regarding trade, possession of land beyond the line, and other related matters. In 1874 it was extended to the areas that today constitute Arunachal Pradesh. A chain of enactments followed with the objective of separating the administration of the frontier hills from the plains of Assam. In 1914 the Government of India extended the Assam Frontier Tracts Regulation of 1880 to the hills inhabited by the tribal groups which were separated from the Darrang and Lakhimpur districts of Assam and constituted into a separate North-East Frontier Tracts; these tracts subsequently became the North East Frontier Agency, which is now Arunachal Pradesh. The 885 km long northern boundary of the tract (northern boundary of Arunachal Pradesh today) determined at that time became known as the McMahon Line; it has been a bone of contention between India and China ever since.

This boundary between Tibet, an independent country at that time, China, and British India, takes its name from Sir Arthur Henry McMahon, the then Secretary to the Government of India. The spiritual and temporal leader of Tibet was then the Thirteenth Dalai Lama who, taking advantage of the declining Qing Dynasty in China, had expelled all the Chinese troops from Tibet in 1912, proclaiming the independence of Tibet from Chinese occupation and seeking international recognition for this independence. A conference was therefore held in 1914 in Simla (now Shimla) between Tibet, India, and China to settle the frontier and other matters relating to Tibet (French 2004: 233–4). While India was represented by Sir McMahon, Mr. Ivan Chen represented China, and Lonchen Ga-den Shatra Pal-jor Dorje represented His Holiness the Thirteenth Dalai Lama. The accord signed on 3 July 1914, known as the Simla Convention, created a distinction between inner and outer Tibet: 'The Governments of Great Britain and China, recognizing that Tibet is under the suzerainty of China, and recognizing also the autonomy of Outer Tibet, engage to respect the territorial integrity of the country, and to abstain from interference in the administration of Outer Tibet (including the selection and installation of the Dalai Lama), which shall remain in the hands of the Tibetan Government at Lhasa.' The Convention further agreed that, 'The Government of China engages not to convert Tibet into a Chinese province. The Government of Great Britain engages not to annex Tibet or any portion of it.'[30] Though the Convention recognized the nominal suzerainty of China over Tibet, a new border was drawn ceding the Tibetan region of Tawang, the birthplace of the Sixth Dalai Lama, to India. This border following the crest of the high Himalayas was drawn by Sir McMohan and has since become known as the McMohan Line that today separates China from India. Delegates from India, China, and Tibet agreed on this frontier, but the talks broke down on the issue of the boundary between inner and outer Tibet. Two days later, the Chinese government disavowed its delegate and refused to sign the Convention.[31]

However, the Tibetan and Indian (British) representatives went ahead with the Simla Agreement and declared, 'We, the Plenipotentiaries of Great Britain and Tibet, hereby record the following declaration to the effect that we acknowledge the annexed convention as initialled to be binding on the Governments of Great Britain and Tibet, and we agree that so long as the Government of China withholds signature to the aforesaid convention she will be debarred from the enjoyment of all privileges accruing therefrom' (Sinha 1966). China refused to sign the Convention and 'stated formally, emphatically and repeatedly at the time that she would not recognize any bilateral agreement between Tibet and Britain' (French 2004: 254, quoting Neville Maxwell). The Chinese position was that Tibet was not independent from China, so Tibet could not have independently signed treaties, and as per the Anglo-Chinese (1906) and Anglo-Russian (1907) conventions, any such agreement was invalid without Chinese assent. But Chinese rule on Tibet had effectively ceased by then and China was too weak to challenge the might of the British Empire in India; hence, no one challenged the authority of Tibet to sign the agreement. At the instance of civil service officer Olaf Caroe, the Survey of India finally published a map showing the McMahon Line as the official boundary in 1938. As Patrick French (2004: 255) writes, 'The Simla Convention, having no validity in international law, was not included in British India's diplomatic bible, Aitchinson's 'Collection of Engagements, Treaties and Sanads. In an act of astonishing duplicity, Caroe rectified this by arranging for a new edition of the relevant volume to be printed, with the missing text included, and for the new book to be surreptitiously substituted for the original in London's House of Commons Library and elsewhere. India and China were to fight a Himalayan war in 1962, and their long border remains under dispute…'[32,33] The McMohan Line boundary extends from Bhutan border to the tri-junction of India, Tibet, and Burma.

The Assam Government Act 1915 and its amendments in 1919 gave legal status to the North-East Frontier Tracts and made the Governor of Assam responsible for administration and social welfare of these backward tracts. The Government of India (Excluded and Partially Excluded Areas) Order of 1936 declared the North-East Frontier Tract 'politically a part of Assam' and vested the Governor of Assam with legal and administrative authority in respect of this region. In the late 1930's, reports of Tibetan incursions and forcible tax collection by Tibetan officials led to further revision of British frontier policy, extending the administrative reach deeper into the wild terrain up to the McMahon Line. Subsequently, Government of India established outposts at Karko and Riga in 1940 and their 'Control Area' was extended till the McMahon Line in 1941. A military outpost was also set up at Sela in 1943 (Bora 2008:4–5).

At independence the North-East Frontier Tracts consisted of three frontier tracts at Balipara, Sadiya, and Tirap, besides the Naga Tribal Area that lay beyond the administrative jurisdiction of Assam. Tuensang Frontier Division was finally separated from NEFA and amalgamated into the Naga Hills Area to form the Naga Hills District in Assam in 1957, NEFA being reduced to the remaining five Divisions which became districts in 1966. The North-East Areas (Regulation) Act of 1971 changed the name of NEFA to Arunachal Pradesh. On 21 January 1972, under Section 7 of the North Eastern Areas (Reorganisation) Act, 1971, Arunachal Pradesh became a Union Territory. The process of political evolution was completed when full statehood was conferred on Arunachal Pradesh on 20 January 1987, making it the 25th State of the Indian Union. Special category status followed immediately thereafter.

Unlike the other states in northeast India, Arunachal Pradesh did not have to face the problem of insurgency. But occasionally there had been threats from certain insurgent groups including the National Socialist Council of Nagaland (NSCN), who are believed to have base camps in the districts of Changlang and Tirap. There are also reports of these groups harassing local people for extortion of money.

Society and Socio-Economic Change

Many tribal groups live in Arunachal Pradesh within their somewhat distinct cultural spaces organized into groups on the basis of tribal identity, language, religion, and culture. The most populous Adi group constitutes about 20 per cent of the population, comprised of several tribes. Nishis constitute the next most populous group with 16 per cent of the population, followed by Monpas and Noctes, each constituting about 5 per cent of the population. Most practice Buddhism, but a large number also follow shamanistic-animistic religious traditions such as Donyi-Polo and Rangfrah, besides Christianity.

Isolation has engendered strong kinship and community feelings among the tribes and given rise to their unique social institutions and practices that increased the interdependence among members of the community. Such community-based institutions also provide security to the people, security that otherwise ought to be provided by the government and the administrative machinery. An institution of this kind in Arunachal was the 'Mutual Insurance' or 'Reciprocity', which evolved to provide security against fluctuations in agricultural production based on mutual reciprocity. If a family was facing starvation due to crop failure, other families would automatically come to its aid. The mutual insurance and other community institutions prevented the growth of large scale inequalities in the distribution of economic resources, a feature present in almost all tribal societies.[34]

Tribal people of Arunachal Pradesh also used to enjoy a fair measure of autonomy in their villages and localities; villages or confederations of adjacent villages acted like small republics. In some communities, village councils acted as the centre of administration and were responsible for the arbitration of all disputes arising in the village. In other communities, chieftainship prevailed. But this localized administration rarely had any communication with the regular government administration located outside these isolated and remote hamlets.[35]

Till Independence, barter was the usual form of exchange and trade between people—monetization of trade would still take a few more decades. Cash economy was unknown to most people till the last decade of the twentieth century, it was a barter-trade economy. Different tribal groups not only used barter for their inter-group trade but also for trading with tribes living in Tibet and Assam. They traded forest and agricultural products such as animal hides and rice for items such as salt, copper, woollen garments and semi-precious stones from Tibet, and salt and endi (a type of silk) from Assam. The people of Tirap and Changlang traded with Burma across the Patkai Range.

In 1947, there were only three jeepable roads for 170 kms, two lower primary schools and 13 rudimentary health units in Arunachal Pradesh, then NEFA, and till 1954 there were only six post offices in the state. In 1967, a survey conducted by the National Council of Applied Economic Research (NCAER), New Delhi, reported that 'statistics can hardly convey the story of the suffering, ignorance and despair of the NEFA hill men and of the limited opportunities due to the surrounding mountains'. The people were not only cut from the rest of India, they even lacked means of basic communication between themselves. Their knowledge of the world was limited to their immediate neighbourhoods. While there were some trading and social interactions between tribal villages located at the central regions either with the southern plains of Assam or with Tibetan tribes in the north depending on the location of the villages, practically there was no east-west communication. Thus the tribes in Lohit or Tirap were complete strangers to Monpas in Kameng or Apatanis and Nishings in Subansiri districts. The barriers of languages and geographical isolation reinforced each other and kept the region from getting the benefits of civilization and development. The development of NEFA actually began only after the 1962 Indo-Chinese war in which the Chinese troops overran the entire state and advanced to the plains of Assam without practically any resistance, before withdrawing unilaterally, perhaps because of the fear of getting cut off from their supply lines in the incoming winter. A similar kind of situation used to cut off NEFA from the rest of India due to the almost complete absence of communication and transport facilities and lack of motorable roads, a vital reason behind the defeat of Indian forces. It was only after this that some attention was given to development of infrastructure in the state (Datta 1991: 32–6).

The NCAER study emphasized that the existing tribal institutions were to be harnessed as far as possible for development of local resources and that indigenous talent should be used to the maximum. It stressed that the immediate focus should be on meeting the basic needs of food, water, clothing, and medical support of the population along with improving education. Economic activities including trading should be carried out within the socio-political organizational setting in a particularly backward region like NEFA. Given the demand, resource availability, and potential in adjoining areas, it suggested setting up of local industries like integrated paper and pulp factory, wood based industries along with development of hydro power which could set the stage ready for rapid economic development. The development of resources like land, forests, and livestock was also emphasized. The study observed that the 'normal yardstick of costs and benefits will be inappropriate in charting a programme of development of NEFA. Because of the shortage of manpower and inaccessible terrain, the cost of practically every scheme is bound to be higher compared to that of a similar scheme in rest of India. The justification of a scheme will have to be sought not in the direct monetary benefits which it will lead to, but in terms of the social and economic costs of the alternatives.' In accordance with this, it can be seen that during the entire process of planned development, per capita outlay of Arunachal Pradesh has been almost double the Indian average and the highest among north-eastern states. This was because Arunachal was a late starter in planned development and it had much more pronounced backwardness in every sphere of economic activity requiring much larger investment in infrastructure than anywhere else within the region. Its reserves of coal and petroleum and its vast hydroelectric potential remain untapped because of inaccessibility of its terrains and absence of transport linkages. The major transportation networks serving the state are located in Assam, including the nearest airport at Lilabari.

Annexure 4.5 shows the socio-economic indicators of Arunachal Pradesh since 1970–71. In 1971, 96 per cent of the state's population used to live in rural areas and there were only four towns in the state. Its density of population was only six per sq km. Seventy-nine per cent of its population were tribals and it had a pathetic literacy rate of only 13 per cent. Eighty per cent of its working population were engaged in the primary sector. In 1990–91, soon after attaining full statehood and becoming a special category state, its population had nearly doubled, but still 87 per cent of the population lived in rural areas and density of population had increased to just 10 per sq. km. The last two decades saw improvement in the literacy rate to 67 per cent (2011), but 77 per cent of its population were still rural and average density of its population improved to just above 16 per sq. km, the lowest in the country. Majority of working population still earned their livelihood from the agricultural sector, but agriculture again was based upon the slash-and-burn jhoom method, leading to low productivity and low yield. Agriculture was also limited to the production of paddy, the staple food of the people, and the other livelihood activities were those of hunter gatherers: hunting, fishing, and the collection of forest produce. 'Directly or indirectly, all people depended on agriculture. Except for a few pockets where individual property rights—more accurately family property rights in land were well-established—agricultural land was communally held.'[36] Due to low productivity of agriculture, and the virtual non-existence of any form of industry, it was a subsistence economy, with hardly any marketable surplus or capital formation which prevented the emergence of monetized economy.

The induction of money through the various development programmes of the central and state governments brought far-reaching changes, and the insular barter economy began to integrate with the national economy. 'The cash economy brought with it its own dynamics; disturbing the way of life that many communities had followed for generations. The biggest changes came into the institution of ownership, especially the ownership of land... With the shift in ownership from the community to individuals, community-level institutions such as mutual insurance and social mobilisation of labour became weak and tended to be replaced by market-based institutions. Relations based on contract began to replace clan relations.'[37]

Between 1980–81 and 2010–11, the NSDP (at current price) of Arunachal Pradesh had grown at an average annual rate of 16 per cent. Primary sector's share to total state income had decreased from 47 per cent in 1981 to 42 per cent in 2011, while the share of secondary sector increased from 22 per cent to 27 per cent over this period. The share of the tertiary sector had increased from 21 per cent to 31 per cent, indicating increasing tertiarization of the economy driven by the trades, but the primary sector still was the largest contributor to state income. The number of people living below the poverty line decreased consistently from 41 per cent to 35 per cent. The social infrastructure of education and health expanded moderately along with improvement of road networks and power generation. Credit deposit ratio was stagnating below 25 per cent in 2004 in the absence of credit absorption capacity which was impossible without improvement in infrastructure, power, market linkages, extraction of natural resources, and greater financial inclusion.

In particular, the industrial scenario of the state remained bleak throughout. Except a few home-based small-scale industries like basketry, weaving, carpets, and other handicrafts, and some factory based small scale units like rice and oil mills, fruit processing units, and manufacture of forest-based products or sericulture (raw silk production), no major industry could take any root in Arunachal Pradesh. Despite government policies encouraging industrial expansion and establishment of industrial estates in Itanagar, Naharlagun, Pasighat, and Deomali, industrial activity in the state is yet to take off. Out of about 20,400 micro, small, and medium enterprises (MSME) that existed in the state in 2006–07, more than 18,000 units were engaged in trading only. Manufacture was limited to furniture, bakery, cutlery, jewellery, apparel, and grain products—and less than 1800 units were engaged in all these activities.[38]

Summing up, as the Arunachal Pradesh Human Development Report rightly notes, statehood had only provided the administrative mechanism for development, but the task of establishing the necessary institutional infrastructure in a hilly and sparsely populated land is a monumental task, made even more daunting due to the difficulties in terrain and differences in culture, language, and institutions among the different tribal communities. Given the priorities of the administration and politicians that development must be in consonance with the cultural ideology and aspirations of the people, industrialization will be a slow process in this far-flung outpost of India.

Public Finance in Arunachal Pradesh

Even before Arunachal Pradesh became a full-fledged state with special category status in 1987, it was overwhelmingly dependent on central grants. In 1983–84, central grants constituted about 40 per cent of its GSDP and 84 per cent of its own revenues when it was still a union territory; its own revenues constituted barely 16 per cent of the total revenues of the union territory at that time and could meet about 18 per cent of its revenue expenditure. Though it had a small revenue surplus in 1983-84, the borrowings made for capital purposes led to a high fiscal deficit of 15 per cent of the GSDP. Such high levels of fiscal deficit would naturally make it highly indebted, and in 1983–84, its Debt:GSDP ratio was as high as 95 per cent, and interest payments amounted to 10 per cent of revenue expenditure.

In 1987–88, its outstanding debt had even exceeded its GSDP. In 1990–91, the situation improved as Rs 20,349 crore of loans were written off under recommendations of the Ninth Finance Commission, making for a huge fiscal surplus in that year, and reducing the outstanding debt stock to only 32 per cent of the GSDP. The outstanding debt would shoot up again and soar to 52 per cent in 2001, when the fiscal deficit at 16 per cent of GSDP would breach the levels seen in 1983–84. The ratio of Debt: GSDP stood at 43 per cent in 2010–11.

In 1987–88, after it became a full-fledged state, it had started to get its own share from the central pool of divisible taxes. The revenue receipts now jumped to 31 per cent of GSDP from 8 per cent in 1983–84, though the share of the state's own revenues in it improved only marginally to 8 per cent. Central grants now constituted 66 per cent of the state's total revenues, but along with the state's share of divisible pool, it amounted to about 89 per cent of the total revenues of the state, the rest being the state's own contribution. In 2010–11, central grants constituted 73 per cent of its revenue and including the share of divisible pool, central transfers constituted 84 per cent of the total revenues and 82 per cent of total expenditure.

Thus, the state had remained as dependent on the centre as it was before it became a full-fledged state that was awarded the special category status. Statehood did little to change its almost complete dependence on central transfers for own sustenance. Without the special category status, it would not have made the progress that it has been able to make.

Planning in Arunachal Pradesh

The plan outlays/expenditure in Arunachal Pradesh since the Fifth Five Year plan are shown in Table 4.5. Here we find that Arunachal Pradesh had defied the general trend observed in all other special category states of a gradual shift of plan expenditure from economic to social services. Instead, the proportion of plan investments made on economic services had remained more or constant throughout the period from fifth to eleventh plans. In fact, the plan outlay on social services had declined marginally during the last two plans. While among the economic services, the outlay on agriculture had been reduced significantly from 25 per cent to less than 10 per cent of the total plan outlay over the period, the share of plan outlay had increased in multipurpose power projects covering power and irrigation. Though the share of transport had been reduced from one third of total plan expenditure during the fifth plan, the transport sector still claimed one fifth of total plan investments during the Eleventh plan. Share of industry was only around

Table 4.5 Plan Outlay in Arunachal Pradesh: Fifth to Eleventh Plan (per cent)

Major Heads of Development	5th Plan	6th Plan	7th Plan	8th Plan	9th Plan	10th Plan	11th Plan
	1974–78	1980–85	1985–90	1992–97	1997–02	2002–07	2007–12
Economic Services	**69.16**	**71.9**	**73.4**	**68.1**	**64.7**	**65.9**	**69.7**
Agriculture and Allied Activities	25.03	18.3	21.6	11.3	13.2	13.3	9.5
Rural Development	1.74	1.7	1.4	0	0	4.1	3.3
Special Area Programmes						1.7	5.4
Irrigation and Flood Control	6.87	17.9	15.7	20.6	20.9	4.7	6.5
Energy						12.8	16.2
Industry and Minerals	2.05	2.1	2.4	2.8	1.3	2.0	2.5
Transport & Communications	33.03	31.6	31.8	32.1	26.0	21.2	20.1
Science and Technology						0.1	0.6
General Economic Services	0.44	0.3	0.5	1.3	3.3	6.0	5.6
Social Services	**30.84**	**27.6**	**26.2**	**28.8**	**33.0**	**31.9**	**28.3**
Education						13.4	14.3
Medical and Public Health						5.9	3.6
Water Supply and Sanitation						4.8	3.5
Housing						3.2	2.4
Urban Development						2.7	2.9

(*Cont'd*)

Table 4.5 (*Cont'd*)

Major Heads of Development	5th Plan	6th Plan	7th Plan	8th Plan	9th Plan	10th Plan	11th Plan
	1974–78	1980–85	1985–90	1992–97	1997–02	2002–07	2007–12
Others Social Services						1.9	1.5
General Services	0	0.5	0.3	3.1	2.3	2.3	2.0
Total (Rs Crore)	63	212	400	1,155	2,593	3,888	7,901

Source: Basic Statistics of North Eastern Region, North Eastern Council, Shillong, for various years; Planning Commission data for 10th and 11th plans. (For 10th and 11th Plans, the figures refer to the approved outlays). Also, Joshi, HG, Arunachal Pradesh: Past and Present, 2005, Mittal Publications, New Delhi, 81.

2 per cent of total plan investments throughout, hardly an incentive for real industrial growth.

In case of all northeastern states, it was evident that central support was not only an essential element in their survival, but was also most vital for their subsequent socio-economic growth and development. Heavy spending on health and education in all these states was a key factor for improvement of the socio-economic indicators and reduction of poverty. None of these states would have survived, let alone prosper, without their special category status that gave them access to liberal central grants.

All these states share certain common traits. 'But while socio-economic indicators have improved significantly in all these states, there has been little or no industrialization in any.' Except Mizoram, all these states remain ruralized and still dependent on low-productivity, subsistence type agriculture based largely on archaic forms of cultivation. All continue to suffer from the inherent structural economic weaknesses they had inherited from their isolation of centuries shaped by history and geography. Special category status was devised especially to address these innate weaknesses that had made these states outliers in the story of development and progress of the nation, but in the absence of coherent objectives and strategy backed by enabling institutions, the development potential could not be realized optimally. Infusion of huge funds in a region that has neither institutional capacity nor managerial skill rather distorted the economic relations, giving way to endemic corruption and growth of an unscrupulous, rent-seeking class in the absence of any monitoring mechanism and accountability structure.

Most states again bled from protracted insurgency that crippled public life and stymied their economic growth. The Indian state responded in most cases with force, often without adequate understanding of the problem and displayed an awful rigidity to address the inherent asymmetry in this region. This asymmetry arose from the evolution of the tribes in their specific environment with their unique set of customs, traditions, ethos, and mores shaped again by their history and environment. A better appreciation of these traits accompanied by little more openness towards accommodation would probably have led to quicker integration, lesser bloodshed, and tangible economic growth. 'While all states within the region still remain overwhelmingly dependent on central funds for their survival and sustenance, they continue to nurture feelings of mistrust and alienation towards the rest of India, though not as strongly as before.'

Annexure 4.1 Socio-Economic and Public Finance Parameters of Meghalaya: 1980–81 to 2010–11

Parameters	1980–81	1990–91	2000–01	2010–11
A. State Income				
NSDP (Rs crore)	200	890	3593	12852
Per Capita Income (Rs)	1361	4375	15657	49261
Share of Primary Sector (%)	40	29	27	17
Share of Secondary Sector (%)	17	22	23	29
Share of Tertiary Sector (%)	43	49	50	54
Per cent of people below poverty line[39]	38.81 (1983)	37.92 (93–94)	33.87 (99–00)	12
B. Demography				
Population (lakh)	13.36	17.75	23.18	29.67
Per cent of Rural Population	82	81	80	80
Per cent of SC/ST Population	81	86	86	NA
Literacy Rate (%)	34	49	63	76
Females per '000 Males	954	955	972	986
Per cent of Working Population	43	40	42	NA

(*Cont'd*)

Annexure 4.1 (*Cont'd*)

Parameters	1980–81	1990–91	2000–01	2010–11
Per cent of working population engaged in the primary sector	73	70	66	NA
Net Irrigated Area to Net Cultivated Area (%)	26 (81–82)	23	26	25 (2007–08)
C. Infrastructure				
i. Education				
No. of Primary Schools	4130 (1983)	4170 (1992)	5807 (2003)	8886
No. of Middle and Secondary Schools	790 (1983)	1019 (1992)	1636 (2003)	801
No. of Other Institutions of Higher Learning	29 (1983)	40 (1992)	103 (2003)	88
No. of Universities	1	1	1	6
Per Capita Revenue Expenditure on Education (Rs)	109	317	1016	2527
Per cent of Expenditure on Education to Total Budget (%)	15 (83–84)	19 (89–90)	18 (02–03)	16
ii. Public Health				
No. of Govt. Hospitals	11 (1984)	8	9	39
No. of hospital beds	2005 (1984)	1635	NA	2837
No. of Primary Health Centres and Sub-Centres	178 (1984)	421 (1883)	496	514
Doctor: Population ratio	1: 6363 (1984)	NA	1:5411 (1998)	NA
Per Capita Expenditure on Health (Rs)	120	277 (89–90)	370	923
iii. Roads				
Total Road Length (km)	5211 (81–82)	7832 (91–92)	7728 (02–03)	11884
Per cent of Surfaced Road to Total Road Length	53 (81–82)	37 (91–92)	NA	60

(*Cont'd*)

Annexure 4.1 *(Cont'd)*

Parameters	**1980–81**	**1990–91**	**2000–01**	**2010–11**
Road per 100 sq. km	23 (81–82)	35 (91–92)	41 (01–02)	53
Length of National Highway (km)	462 (81–82)	NA	717 (02–03)	1171
iv. Electricity				
Per capita power Consumption (kwh)	69 (83–84)	108 (89–90)	354	675
Generation of electricity (million kwh)	368 (81–82)	339	NA	528
Installed Capacity (MW)	134 (1984)	134	329[40]	190
No. of Villages electrified	700	2271	NA	5008 (73%)
v. Post Offices and banks				
Population served by a Post Office	3018 (1984)	3830 (92–93)	NA	6122
No. of Bank Offices	122 (1985)	128 (1994)	180 (2004)	223
Average Population per bank Office	10900 (1985)	13800 (1994)	13000 (2004)	13300
Credit Deposit Ratio (%)	25 (12/84)	20	17	24
D. Industry				
No of Registered Small Scale Units	233	587 (1988)	1939 (2002)	4511 (2007)
No. of Registered Factories	55	55	NA	94
No. of persons employed	3095	3075	NA	7671
Employment in organized Sectors	48260	68801	82000	NA
Per cent Employed in Public Sector	91.06	93.42	89.02	NA
E. **Public Finance (Ratios)**	**1980–81**	**1990–91**	**2000–01**	**2010–11**
State's Own Taxes/GSDP (%)	2.4	6.1	3.0	3.9
Grants from Centre/GSDP (%)	28.0	24.3	19.3	17.1

(Cont'd)

Annexure 4.1 *(Cont'd)*

Parameters	1980–81	1990–91	2000–01	2010–11
State's Share of Central Taxes/ GSDP (%)	3.6	9.3	4.1	6.1
State's Own Revenue/Revenue Expenditure (%)	44.8	23.6	19.0	21.8
Central Grants/State's Total Revenues (%)	62.2	61.2	67.4	58.5
State's Own Revenue/ Total Revenues (%)	39.4	20.8	18.1	20.5
Gross Fiscal Deficit/ GSDP (%)	−3.7	4.6	6.3	2.3
Debt/ GSDP (%)	15.1	23.3	26.5	23.0
Interest Payment/ Revenue Expenditure (%)	2.4	5.8	10.5	6.4
Non-Developmental Expenditure/Total Revenue Expenditure (%)	26.8	28.0	37.2	30.9
Debt Servicing/Total Expenditure (%)	20.1	6.3	10.1	8.3
Expenditure on Education/ GSDP (%)	4.7	6.8	5.9	5.2
Expenditure on Health/GSDP (%)	3.7	2.3	1.8	1.9
Capital Outlay/Capital Receipts (%)	314.5	257.4	160.5	149.7
Public Finance (Figures in Rs Crore)	**1980–81**	**1990–91**	**2000–01**	**2010–11**
GSDP	**200**	**890**	**3961**	**14583**
Total Tax + Non Tax Revenue Receipts	**34**	**137**	**369**	**1770**
State's Own Revenue	27	73	205	873
Total Tax Revenue	12	118	283	1468
Non-Tax Revenue	22	19	87	302
State's Own Taxes	5	55	119	571
Grants from Centre	**56**	**216**	**763**	**2491**
State's Share of Central Taxes	7	82	164	896

(Cont'd)

Annexure 4.1 (*Cont'd*)

Parameters	1980–81	1990–91	2000–01	2010–11
Total Revenue	**90**	**353**	**1132**	**4260**
Capital Receipts	7	29	154	384
Total Receipts	**97**	**382**	**1286**	**4616**
Gross Fiscal Deficit	–7	41	250	341
Revenue Deficit	–30	–42	–53	–248
Capital Outlay	21	75	226	575
Primary Deficit	–9	23	136	84
Outstanding Debt[41]	30	208	1050	3359
Non-Developmental Revenue Expenditure	16	87	401	1317
Interest Payment	1	18	114	257
Revenue Expenditure on Social Services	20	114	410	1376
Revenue Expenditure on Economic Services	24	109	268	1320
Expenditure on Education	9	61	236	758
Expenditure on Health	7	21	71	277
Revenue Expenditure	**60**	**311**	**1079**	**4013**
Capital Expenditure	**42**	**95**	**344**	**757**
Total Expenditure	**102**	**406**	**1424**	**4770**
Capital Outlay	21	75	226	575
Debt Servicing (Principal Amount)	19	8	29	141
Loans and Advances, etc.	2	12	89	42
Discharge of Debt Obligations (Principal + Interest)	21	26	143	398
Net Debt Receipts	–16	–9	–91	32
Recovery of Loans and Advances	1	4	13	27

Source: Please see endnote 26 in Chapter 2 for data sources of all tables in this chapter.

Annexure 4.2 Socio-Economic and Public Finance Parameters of Manipur: 1974–75 to 2010–11

Parameters	1974–75	1980–81	1990–91	2000–01	2010–11
A. State Income					
NSDP (Rs Crore)	86	200	723	2814	8020
Per Capita Income (Rs)	739	1419	3976	12369	28931
Share of Primary Sector (%)	61	49	40	31	25
Share of Secondary Sector (%)	13	8	11	20	25
Share of Tertiary Sector (%)	26	43	49	49	50
Per cent of people below Poverty Line	49.96 (1973–74)	37.02 (1983)	33.78 (1993–94)	28.54 (1999–2000)	37
B. Demography					
Population (Crore)	10.73 (1971)	14.21	18.37	22.94	25.70
% of Rural Population	87 (1971)	74	72	75	70
% of SC/ST Population	33 (1971)	29	36	37	NA
Literacy Rate (%)	38 (1971)	47	60	69	80
Females per '000 Males	980	971	958	978	987
% of Working Population	NA	40	39	44	52
% of Working Population engaged in the Primary Sector	71	69	70	52	NA
No. of Villages	1949	2035	2182	2391	2639
Net Irrigated Area to Net Cultivated Area (%)	NA	46	NA	46 (2001–02)	NA

(Cont'd)

Annexure 4.2 (*Cont'd*)

Parameters	1974–75	1980–81	1990–91	2000–01	2010–11
C. Infrastructure					
i. Education					
No. of Primary Schools	2856 (1971)	3286	3877	3356	3167
No. of Middle and Secondary Schools	123 (1971)	290	430	614	884
No. of Institutions of Higher Learning	26	65	62	71	92
No. of Universities	0	1 (1983)	1 (1992)	2 (2003)	2
Per Capita Revenue Expenditure on Education (Rs)	NA	131	452	1168	2107
% of Expenditure on Education to Total Budget (%)	16	8	14	11	9
ii. Public Health					
No. of hospitals		21 (1984)	25 (1992)	103	225
No. of hospital beds		1266 (1984)	1460 (1992)	2286	1385
No. of Primary Health Centres and Sub-Centres		274 (1984)	490 (1993)	440	500
Doctor: Population ratio		1:2884 (1984)	NA	1:2427 (2003-03)	NA
Per Capita Expenditure on Health (Rs)		25	102	289	774
iii. Roads					
Total Road Length (km)		5321 (1982)	6765 (1992)	7172	19133
Per cent of Surfaced Road to Total Road Length		37 (1982)	41 (1992)	62	43

(*Cont'd*)

Annexure 4.2 (*Cont'd*)

Parameters	**1974–75**	**1980–81**	**1990–91**	**2000–01**	**2010–11**
Road per 100 sq. km		23.8 (1982)	30.3 (1992)	NA	86
Length of National Highway (km)		431 (1982)	NA	957	1317
iv. Electricity					
Per capita power Consumption (kwh)	5	6	80 (1989–90)	184	240 (2009–10)
Generation of electricity (million kwh)		NA	1.53	0.83	16
Installed Capacity (MW)		23 (1984)	12	11.8	50
No. of Villages electrified		602 (30%) (1985)	1487 (68%)	2001 (92%)	2058 (78%)
v. Post Offices and Banks					
Population served by a Post Office		2587 (1984)	2727	3342	3868
No. of Bank Offices		57 (1985)	56 (1994)	80	85
Credit Deposit Ratio (%)		48 (1982)	NA	39	33
D. Industry					
No of Registered Small Scale Units		3422	2892 (1988)	9635	NA
No. of Employees in Organised Sector			78600 (1995–96)	82800	NA
E. **Public Finance (Ratios)**	**1974–75**	**1980–81**	**1990–91**	**2000–01**	**2010–11**
Grants from Centre/ GSDP (%)	29.9	32.3	29.8	25.4	42.8

(*Cont'd*)

Annexure 4.2 (*Cont'd*)

Parameters	**1974–75**	**1980–81**	**1990–91**	**2000–01**	**2010–11**
Share of Central Taxes/ GSDP (%)	2.7	3.4	13.8	5.3	10.8
Own Revenue/Revenue Expenditure (%)	5.1	47.1	9.6	8.1	12.9
Central Grants/Total Revenues (%)	87.6	63.6	62.7	75.7	72.0
State's Own Revenue/ Total Revenues (%)	4.5	29.7	8.2	8.7	9.7
Gross Fiscal Deficit/ GSDP (%)	9.7	-2.8	9.3	7.3	6.2
Outstanding Debt/ GSDP (%)	68.8	36.4	48.9	61.9	50.1
Interest Payment/ Revenue Expenditure (%)	8.1	7.2	9.6	15.8	9.0
Non-Developmental Revenue Expenditure/ Total Revenue Expenditure (%)	25.3	8.7	17.7	21.2	30.3
Debt Servicing/Total Expenditure (%)	9.4	55.7	26.3	54.9	7.8
Expenditure on Education/ GSDP (%)	7.5	8.5	10.1	8.6	6.2
Expenditure on Health/ GSDP (%)	0.5	1.6	2.3	2.1	2.3
Capital Outlay/ Capital Receipts (%)	91.6	29.3	68.2	10.0	639.3
Public Finance (Figures in Rs Crore)	**1974–75**	**1980–81**	**1990–91**	**2000–01**	**2010–11**
GSDP	**86**[42]	**218**	**821**	**3112**	**9137**
Total Tax + Non-Tax Revenues	**4**	**40**	**145**	**254**	**1518**

(*Cont'd*)

Annexure 4.2 (*Cont'd*)

Parameters	1974–75	1980–81	1990–91	2000–01	2010–11
Tax Revenue	2	10	126	213	1258
Non-Tax Revenue	2	30	20	42	260
State's Own Revenue Receipts	1	33	32	91	527
Grants from Centre	**26**	**71**	**245**	**790**	**3912**
State's Share of Central Taxes	2	8	113	164	991
Total Revenue	**30**	**111**	**390**	**1045**	**5430**
Capital Receipts	**12**	**115**	**187**	**1471**	**300**
Total Receipts	**42**	**226**	**577**	**2516**	**5730**
Gross Fiscal Deficit	8	–6	76	227	569
Revenue Deficit	–3	–41	–54	79	–1352
Capital Outlay	11	34	128	148	1918
Primary Deficit	6	–11	44	49	204
Outstanding Debt	59	79	401	1927	4581
Non-Developmental Revenue Expenditure	10	19	103	515	1643
Interest Payment	2	5	32	177	365
Revenue Expenditure on Social Services	10	30	129	398	1238
Revenue Expenditure on Economic Services	7	21	104	211	1084
Expenditure on Education	6	19	83	268	569
Expenditure on Health	0	4	19	66	209
Revenue Expenditure	**27**	**70**	**336**	**1123**	**4078**
Capital Expenditure	**13**	**152**	**249**	**1303**	**2037**
Total Expenditure	**39**	**222**	**585**	**2426**	**6115**
Capital Outlay	11	34	128	148	1918
Debt Servicing (Principal Amount)	2	119	121	1155	115

(*Cont'd*)

Annexure 4.2 (*Cont'd*)

Parameters	1974–75	1980–81	1990–91	2000–01	2010–11
Loans and Advances etc.	0	2	4	1	4
Discharge of Debt Obligations (Principal + Interest)	4	124	154	1333	480
Net Debt Receipts	9	–9	34	138	–98
Recovery of Loans and Advances	0	0	1	1	1

Annexure 4.3 Socio-Economic and Public Finance Indicators of Tripura: 1970–71 to 2010–11

Parameters	1970–71	1980–81	1990–91	2000–01	2010–11
A. State Income					
NSDP (Rs crore)	138	264	917	5114	16573
Per Capita Income (Rs)	888	1307	3370	15983	46050
Share of Primary Sector (%)*	70	60	43	24	24
Share of Secondary Sector (%)	7	9	7	26	20
Share of Tertiary Sector (%)	23	31	50	50	56
Per cent of People below Poverty Line	51.0 (1973–74)	40.0 (1983)	39.0 (1993–94)	34.4 (1999–2000)	14
B. Demography					
Population (lakh)	15.56	20.53	27.57	31.99	36.74
Per cent of Rural Population	89.6	89	84.7	83	74
Per cent of SC/ST Population	41.4	43.5	47.3	48.4	
Density (persons/sq km)	134	196	263	304	350
Literacy Rate (%)	36	48	60	73	88

(*Cont'd*)

Annexure 4.3 (*Cont'd*)

Parameters	**1970–71**	**1980–81**	**1990–91**	**2000–01**	**2010–11**
Females per '000 Males	943	946	945	948	961
Per cent of Working Population	27.8	32.3	31.3	36.2	50
Per cent of working population engaged in the primary sector	74.4	61.8	57.3	50.9	NA
No. of Villages	NA	856	855	870	901
Net Irrigated Area to Net Cultivated Area (%)		11.8 (1981–82)		13.2 (2001–02)	22
C. Infrastructure					
i. Education					
No. of Primary Schools	1384	1643	2029	2081	3553
No. of Middle and Secondary Schools	309	734	734	830	840
No. of Other Institutions of Higher Learning	NA	11	16 (1992)	17	37
No. of Universities	NA	0	1 (1992)	1	3
Per Capita Revenue Expenditure on Education (Rs)	35	78	381	1263	2311
Per cent of Expenditure on Education to Total Budget (%)	NA	NA	9	5	15
ii. Public Health					
No. of Hospitals	11	12	21	17	32
No. of hospital beds	NA	1457	1830	2385	3032
No. of Primary Health Centres and Sub-Centres	101	133	521	538	711
Doctor: Population ratio	1:9099	1:4908 (1984)	NA	1:3087	NA
Per Capita Expenditure on Health (Rs)	9	20	101	259	549

(*Cont'd*)

Annexure 4.3 (*Cont'd*)

Parameters	1970–71	1980–81	1990–91	2000–01	2010–11
iii. Roads					
Total Road Length (km)		4303	5675	15177	33772
Per cent of Surfaced Road to Total Road Length		16.2	34.2	NA	42.1
Road per 100 sq. km		76	124	145	322
Length of National Highway (km)		198 (1982)	NA	333	400
iv. Electricity					
Per Capita Power Consumption (kwh)	5	13	47	96 (1999–00)	336 (2009–10)
Generation of Electricity (million kwh)		51 (1981–82)	58	NA	714
Installed Capacity (MW)	5	16	45	85	170
Percentage of Villages electrified		40	49 (1988)	84 (1998)	91
v. Post Offices and Banks					
Population served by a Post Office	4485	4097	3842	4468	4520
No. of Bank Offices	5 (1968)	104 (1985)	181 (1994)	179 (2004)	249
Credit Deposit Ratio (%)	2.9 (1968)	73.9 (12/1984)	43.0 (1994)	23.0	35
D. Industry					
No. of Large and Medium Industries	NA	NA	1 (1993)	2 (1999)	NA
No. of Registered Small Scale Units	246 (1972)	NA	809 (1988)	959	1253
No. of persons employed in SSI	1698	NA	10069	NA	26794

(*Cont'd*)

Annexure 4.3 (*Cont'd*)

Parameters	**1970–71**	**1980–81**	**1990–91**	**2000–01**	**2010–11**
No. of Registered Factories	NA	218	242	239	472
E. **Public Finance (Ratios)**	**1970–71**	**1980–81**	**1990–91**	**2000–01**	**2010–11**
Grants from Centre/GSDP (%)	11.5	26.4	28.6	21.5	18.4
Share of Central Taxes/ GSDP (%)	0.0	4.2	15.1	3.3	6.3
Own Revenue/Revenue Expenditure (%)	9.2	41.3	8.9	15.9	17.3
Central Grants/State's Total Revenues (%)	90.8	61.2	59.5	72.1	63.7
Own Revenue/ Total Revenues (%)	9.2	29.2	9.0	16.8	14.6
Gross Fiscal Deficit/ GSDP (%)	2.6	-3.3	8.3	8.1	1.3
Outstanding Debt/GSDP (%)	18.1	19.6	46.8	40.3	32.3
Interest Payment/ Revenue Expenditure (%)	4.8	3.6	7.7	13.0	10.3
Non-Developmental Expenditure/Total Expenditure (%)	17.6	13.5	20.4	29.7	37.0
Debt Servicing/Total Expenditure (%)	6.8	24.7	16.0	14.7	11.6
Expenditure on Education/ GSDP (%)	4.0	5.6	10.2	7.4	4.8
Expenditure on Health/ GSDP (%)	1.0	1.4	2.7	1.5	1.1
Capital Outlay/Capital Receipts (%)	60.3	133.1	63.9	164.6	189.3
Public Finance (Rs Crore)	**1970–71**	**1980–81**	**1990–91**	**2000–01**	**2010–11**
GSDP	138	286	1031	5499	17868

(*Cont'd*)

Annexure 4.3 (*Cont'd*)

Parameters	1970–71	1980–81	1990–91	2000–01	2010–11
Revenue Receipts	2	48	200	456	1876
Tax Revenue	1	16	182	362	1744
Non-Tax Revenue	1	32	18	95	132
State's Own Revenue Receipts	2	36	44	275	622
Grants from Centre	16	75	295	1182	3292
State's Share of Central Taxes	0	12	156	181	1122
Total Revenue	17	123	495	1638	5168
Capital Receipts	6	20	138	211	559
Total Receipts	23	143	633	1849	5727
Gross Fiscal Deficit	4	–9	86	445	228
Revenue Deficit	0	–36	2	96	-828
Capital Outlay	3	26	88	347	1058
Primary Deficit	3	–12	47	219	–219
Outstanding Debt	25	56	483	2217	5769
Non-Developmental Revenue Expenditure	4	20	134	646	1912
Interest Payment	1	3	38	226	447
Revenue Expenditure on Social Services	8	41	212	664	1667
Revenue Expenditure on Economic Services	6	26	151	424	679
Expenditure on Education	6	16	105	404	855
Expenditure on Health	1	4	28	83	203
Revenue Expenditure	17	87	497	1734	4359
Capital Expenditure	4	62	157	444	1265
Total Expenditure	22	149	654	2178	5624
Capital Outlay	3	26	88	347	1058
Debt Servicing (Principal Amount)	1	34	67	93	206

(*Cont'd*)

Annexure 4.3 (*Cont'd*)

Parameters	1970–71	1980–81	1990–91	2000–01	2010–11
Loans and Advances etc.	0	2	2	4	1
Discharge of Debt Obligations (Principal + Interest)	1	37	105	319	653
Net Debt Receipts	4	−17	33	−109	135
Recovery of Loans and Advances	0	1	7	2	3

Annexure 4.4: Socio-Economic Indicators of Mizoram: 1970-71 to 2010-11

Parameters	1970–71	1980–81	1990–91	2000–01	2010–11
A. State Income					
NSDP (Rs Crore)		62	306	1567	5772
Per Capita Income (Rs)		1289	4474	17826	50956
Share of Primary Sector (%)		29	30	21	21
Share of Secondary Sector (%)		17	20	14	16
Share of Tertiary Sector (%)		54	50	65	63
Per cent of People below Poverty Line	50.32 (1973–74)	36.0 (1983)	25.66 (1993–94)	19.47 (1999–2000)	21
B. Demography					
Population (lakh)	3.32	4.94	6.90	8.89	10.97
Per cent of Rural Population	88.6	75.3	53.8	51.4	48.5
Per cent of SC/ST Population		93.6	94.8	94.5	NA
Literacy Rate (%)	52	59.9	81	88.8	92

(*Cont'd*)

Annexure 4.4 (*Cont'd*)

Parameters	1970–71	1980–81	1990–91	2000–01	2010–11
Females per '000 Males	945	919	924	938	976
Per cent of Working Population		41.7	48.9	52.6	60
Per cent of Working Population Engaged in the Primary Sector		73.1	65.8	59.8	NA
No. of Villages		721	785	817	853
Net Irrigated Area to Net Cultivated Area (%)		12.3 (1981–82)	NA	13.6 (2001–02)	10
C. Infrastructure					
i. Education					
No. of Primary Schools		840 (1983)	1066 (1992)	1253 (2002–03)	3174
No. of Middle and Secondary Schools		522 (1983)	826 (1992)	1187 (2002–03)	636
No. of Other Institutions of Higher Learning		16 (1983)	20 (1992)	55 (2002)	48
No. of Universities		1	1	1	2
Per Capita Revenue Expenditure on Education (Rs)		NA	652	2079	5355
Per cent of Expenditure on Education to Total Revenue Budget (%)		NA	15	18	14
ii. Public Health					
No. of hospitals (Including Community Health Centres)		12 (1984)	14 (1992)	16	27

(*Cont'd*)

Annexure 4.4 (*Cont'd*)

Parameters	1970–71	1980–81	1990–91	2000–01	2010–11
No. of hospital beds		853 (1984)	1128 (1992)	1684	1430
No. of Primary Health Centres and Sub-Centres		182 (1984–85)	282 (1993)	496	427
Doctor: Population ratio		1:4981 (1984)	1:5000	NA	NA
Per Capita Expenditure on Health (Rs)		NA	216	606	1582
iii. Roads					
Total Road Length (km)		2508 (1982)	3708	5075 (2002)	9810
Per cent of Surfaced Road to Total Road Length		45 (1982)	34	59 (2006)	71
Road per 100 sq. km		11.9 (1982)	17.6	23	47
Length of National Highway (km)		240 (1982)	NA	927 (2007–08)	1027
iv. Electricity					
Per capita power Consumption (kwh)		25 (1983–84)	57 (1989–90)	91 (2001–02)	377
Generation of Electricity (million kwh)		2.98	18.17 (1996–97)	12.45 (2001–02)	102
Installed Capacity (MW)		5.67 (1984)	30.63 (1996–97)	34.35 (2001–02)	90
Percentage of Villages Electrified		45 (1985)	85 (1996–97)	87 (2001–02)	80

(*Cont'd*)

Annexure 4.4 (*Cont'd*)

Parameters	1970–71	1980–81	1990–91	2000–01	2010–11
v. Post Offices and Banks					
Population served by a Post Office		1760 (1983–84)	1934 (1992–93)	NA	2828
No. of Bank Offices		17 (1985)	26 (1994)	36 (03/2004)	102
Credit Deposit Ratio (%)		23.1 (03/1982)	26.0 (12/91)	25.5	43
D. Industry					
No of Registered Small Scale Units			917	1742 (2005–06)	3714
E. Public Finance (Ratios)			**1990–91**	**2000–01**	**2010–11**
Grants from Centre/ GSDP (%)			67.6	39.5	33.3
Share of Central Taxes/ GSDP (%)			34.7	5.0	7.0
Own Revenue/ Revenue Expenditure (%)			44.9	5.4	8.5
Central Grants/Total Revenues (%)			47.5	82.8	74.5
Own Revenue/ Total Revenues (%)			28.2	6.6	9.7
Gross Fiscal Deficit/ GSDP (%)			–34.7	21.6	16.0
Outstanding Debt/ GSDP (%)			55.0	76.6	58.0
Interest Payment/ Revenue Expenditure (%)			10.7	10.1	3.3

(*Cont'd*)

Annexure 4.4 (*Cont'd*)

Parameters	**1970–71**	**1980–81**	**1990–91**	**2000–01**	**2010–11**
Non-Developmental Revenue Expenditure/ Total Revenue Expenditure (%)			20.85	23.19	20.9
Debt Servicing/Total Expenditure (%)			19.55	19.6	23.0
Expenditure on Education/ GSDP (%)			13.2	10.6	9.2
Expenditure on Health/GSDP (%)			4.4	3.1	2.7
Capital Outlay/ Capital Receipts (%)			–86.9	41.0	205.0
Public Finance (Figures in Rs Crore)			**1990–91**	**2000–01**	**2010–11**
GSDP			**341**	**1737**	**6388**
Total Tax + Non-Tax Revenue Receipts			**255**	**142**	**729**
Total Tax Revenue			122	102	582
Non-Tax Revenue			133	40	147
State's Own Revenue Receipts			137	55	130
Grants from Centre			**230**	**686**	**2127**
State's Share of Central Taxes			118	87	452
Total Revenue			**485**	**828**	**2856**
Capital Receipts			**–67**	**399**	**300**
Total Receipts			**418**	**1227**	**3156**
Gross Fiscal Deficit			–118	375	1019
Revenue Deficit			–181	193	401
Capital Outlay			58	164	615
Primary Deficit			–151	272	913
Outstanding Debt			187	1330	3704

(*Cont'd*)

Annexure 4.4 (*Cont'd*)

Parameters	1970–71	1980–81	1990–91	2000–01	2010–11
Non-Developmental Revenue Expenditure			87	335	1011
Interest Payment			32	103	106
Revenue Expenditure on Social Services			97	371	1237
Revenue Expenditure on Economic Services			120	316	1008
Expenditure on Education			45	185	589
Expenditure on Health			15	54	174
Revenue Expenditure			**304**	**1022**	**3256**
Capital Expenditure			**115**	**422**	**917**
Total Expenditure			**419**	**1444**	**4173**
Capital Outlay			58	164	615
Debt Servicing (Principal Amount)			49	228	273
Loans and Advances etc.			7	31	30
Discharge of Debt Obligations (Principal + Interest)			82	331	379
Net Debt Receipts			–149	68	430
Recovery of Loans and Advances			3	12	26

Annexure 4.5 Socio-Economic Indicators of Arunachal Pradesh: 1970–71 to 2010–11

Parameters	1970–71	1980–81	1990–91	2000–01	2010–11
A. State Income					
NSDP (Rs Crore)	21	98	460	1665	8347
Per Capita Income (Rs)	463	1571	5398	15260	60896
Share of Primary Sector (%)	59	47	46	35	42
Share of Secondary Sector (%)	20	22	22	24	27
Share of Tertiary Sector (%)	21	31	32	42	31
% of People below Poverty Line	51.93 (1973–74)	40.88 (1983)	39.35 (1993–94)	33.47 (1999–2000)	35
B. Demography					
Population (lakh)	4.68	6.32	8.65	10.98	13.84
% of Rural Population	96.2	93.3	87.2	79.6	77
% of SC/ST Population	78.8	69.8	64.1	64.7	NA
Density of Population per sq. km.	6	8	10	13	17
Literacy Rate (%)	13.3	25.6	41.6	54.7	67
Females per '000 Males	861	862	859	893	920
Per cent of Working Population	57.6	52.7	46.2	44	54
Per cent of Working Population Engaged in the Primary Sector	80	69	64	62	NA
No. of Villages		NA	3649	3863	5589
Net Irrigated Area to Net Cultivated Area (%)		21	NA	26	26
C. Infrastructure					
i. Education					
No. of Primary Schools		965	1371	1417	2861
No. of Middle and Secondary Schools		164	368	517	309

(Cont'd)

Annexure 4.5 (*Cont'd*)

Parameters	1970–71	1980–81	1990–91	2000–01	2010–11
No. of Other Institutions of Higher Learning		4	8	12	25
No. of Universities		0	1	1	2
Per Capita Revenue Expenditure on Education (Rs)	NA	437	1261	6500	
Per cent of Expenditure on Education to Total Budget (%)	NA	15	14	16	
ii. Public Health					
No. of Hospitals		NA	18 (1992)	14	161
No. of Hospital Beds	1189	1473	NA	2229	NA
No. of Primary Health Centres and Sub-Centres		121 (1985)	239 (1992)	454	383
Doctor: Population Ratio	1:3030	1:2439	NA	1:2352 (2002–03)	NA
Per Capita Expenditure on Health (Rs)		NA	197	520	2900
iii. Roads					
Total Road Length (km)		NA	7520 (1992)	15297	21555
Per cent of Surfaced Road to Total Road Length		16 (1982)	33 (1992)	49	67
Road per 100 sq. km		NA	9 (1989)	18	26
Length of National Highway (km)		330 (1982)	NA	392	2027
iv. Electricity					
Per Capita Power consumption (kwh)		4 (1983–840	37.2 (1992–93)	56.6 (2002)	470

(*Cont'd*)

Annexure 4.5 (*Cont'd*)

Parameters	**1970–71**	**1980–81**	**1990–91**	**2000–01**	**2010–11**
Generation of Electricity (million kwh)		16.6 (1981–82)	NA	153.8	223
Installed capacity (MW)		10.7 (1984)	NA	70.5	90
Percentage of Villages electrified		28 (1986)	54 (1993)	60	52
v. Post Offices and Banks					
Population served by a Post Office		NA	2974 (1992–93)	3601	4682
No. of Bank Offices		46 (1985)	49 (1994)	49 (2004)	88
Credit Deposit Ratio (%)		17.6 (1982)	17.0 (1991)	25.4 (2004)	23
D. Industry					
No. of Registered Small Scale Units		189	NA	NA	451
E. Public Finance (Ratios)	**1983–84**	**1987–88**	**1990–91**	**2000–01**	**2010–11**
Grants from Centre/ GSDP (%)	39.6	58.9	45.7	42.6	43.9
Share of Central Taxes/ GSDP (%)	0.0	22.7	13.5	6.5	8.0
Own Revenue/Revenue Expenditure (%)	17.7	11.0	103.6	–4.1	18.8
Central Grants/Total Revenues (%)	84.1	65.5	40.9	79.2	73.0
Own Revenue/ Total Revenues (%)	15.9	9.2	47.1	–4.2	13.7

(*Cont'd*)

Annexure 4.5 (*Cont'd*)

Parameters	**1970–71**	**1980–81**	**1990–91**	**2000–01**	**2010–11**
Gross Fiscal Deficit/ GSDP (%)	15.1	11.9	–36.3	15.9	–0.3
Outstanding Debt/ GSDP (%)	94.5	100.9	32.2	51.8	42.6
Interest Payment/ Revenue Expenditure (%)	9.6	13.5	6.3	12.3	10.1
Non-Developmental Expenditure/Total Expenditure (%)	12.5	29.2	18.0	25.9	72.9
Debt Servicing/Total Expenditure (%)	10.4	13.9	15.6	12.1	8.5
Expenditure on Education/ GSDP (%)	5.8	9.5	7.4	7.8	5.4
Expenditure on Health/ GSDP (%)	2.4	3.8	3.4	3.2	2.3
Capital Outlay/Capital Receipts (%)	92.3	523.8	–79.9	201.6	1319.2
Public Finance (Figures in Rs lakh)		**1987–88**	**1990–91**	**2000–01**	**2010–11**
GSDP		330	508	1787	9013
Revenue Receipts		**102**	**336**	**200**	**1465**
Tax Revenue		77	71	12[43]	935
Non-Tax Revenue		25	265	64	530
State's Own Revenue Receipts		27	268	–40	215
Grants from Centre		**194**	**232**	**761**	**3957**
State's Share of Central Taxes		75	69	116	720
Total Revenue		**297**	**568**	**961**	**5422**
Capital Receipts		**16**	**-156[44]**	**131**	**125**
Total Receipts		**313**	**413**	**1093**	**5547**
Gross Fiscal Deficit		39	–184	284	–26

(*Cont'd*)

Annexure 4.5 (*Cont'd*)

Parameters	1970–71	1980–81	1990–91	2000–01	2010–11
Revenue Deficit		–48	–310	18	–1619
Capital Outlay		86	125	264	1649
Primary Deficit		6	–201	163	–426
Outstanding Debt		333	164	926	3843
Non-Developmental Revenue Expenditure		103	79	332	1265
Interest Payment		34	16	121	400
Revenue Expenditure on Social Services		67	77	299	994
Revenue Expenditure on Economic Services		79	103	349	1485
Expenditure on Education		31	38	139	489
Expenditure on Health		12	17	57	207
Revenue Expenditure		**249**	**258**	**980**	**3953**
Capital Expenditure		**102**	**178**	**301**	**1738**
Total Expenditure		**351**	**436**	**1281**	**5691**
Capital Outlay		86	125	264	1649
Debt Servicing (Principal Amount)		15	52	34	86
Loans and Advances etc.		2	2	3	2
Discharge of Debt Obligations (Principal + Interest)	49	68	155	486	
Net Debt Receipts		–33	–224	–24	–178
Recovery of Loans and Advances		0	1	2	2

Notes

1. Sources of planning data in Tables 4.1 4.5, 5.1, 6.1, and 7.2 are: Statistical Handbook/ Diary of the Dept of Planning/ Statistics of respective Governments, Basic Statistics of North Eastern Region published by the North Eastern Council for North Eastern States, Economic Survey and Planning Dept portal of the

respective governments, and Planning Commission data for 10th and 11th plans. For 10th and 11th Plans, the figures refer to the approved outlays in all tables.

2. *Encyclopaedia of India*, Vol III, CD Edition, Encyclopaedia Britannica Publication, 2012.

3. 'Overview: Insurgency & Peace Efforts in Manipur', Centre for Development and Peace Studies, Guwahati, Assam, 26 January 2011 (http://cdpsindia.org/manipur_insurgency.asp).

4. Another bone of contention was said to be the gifting away of Kabaw Valley in 1953 to Myanmar then Burma) by Prime Minister Nehru. But it was just formalizing an arrangement that had existed since 1834 as a consequence of the Anglo-Burmese War.

5. Names of the outfits can be found in Sharma, S.C., 'Insurgency or Ethnic Conflict' Magnum, 2000, 217–18.

6. Sharma, 'Insurgency of Ethnic Conflict', 2000.

7. Available at http://www.satp.org/satporgtp/countries/india/states/manipur/index.html

8. 'Overview: Insurgency & Peace Efforts in Manipur', Centre for Development and Peace Studies, Guwahati, Assam, 26 January 2011 (http://cdpsindia.org/manipur_insurgency.asp).

9. 'Overview: Insurgency & Peace Efforts in Manipur', Centre for Development and Peace Studies, Guwahati, Assam, HTTP://CDPSINDIA.ORG/MANIPUR_INSURGENCY.ASP).

10. 'Dealing with the Issues: Manipur's Economy Historical Roots and Structural Evolution', Editor, http://manipuronline.com/research-papers, 2010.

11. Dealing with the Issues: Manipur's Economy Historical Roots and Structural Evolution', Editor, http://manipuronline.com/research-papers, 2010.

12. Dealing with the Issues: Manipur's Economy Historical Roots and Structural Evolution', Editor, http://manipuronline.com/research-papers, 2010.

13. Dealing with the Issues: Manipur's Economy Historical Roots and Structural Evolution', Editor, http://manipuronline.com/research-papers, 2010.

14. Another version is that Tripura got its name from the Temple of Tripureshwari or Tripura Sundari.

15. 'The State of Human Development', Tripura Human Development Report 2007, Government of Tripura (http://hdr.undp.org/en/nhdr/support/other/national/Tripura_india_hdr_2007.pdf).

16. Ministry of Home Affairs, GoI, http://mha.nic.in/pdfs/BM_MAN-IN-BANG(E).pdf.

17. 'Overview: Insurgency & Peace Efforts in Tripura', Centre for Development and Peace Studies, Guwahati (http://cdpsindia.org/tripura_insurgency.asp). Accessed on 12 October 2012.

18. Overview: Insurgency & Peace Efforts in Tripura', Centre for Development and Peace Studies, Guwahati (http://cdpsindia.org/tripura_insurgency.asp). Accessed on 12 October 2012.

19. Overview: Insurgency & Peace Efforts in Tripura', Centre for Development and Peace Studies, Guwahati (http://cdpsindia.org/tripura_insurgency.asp). Accessed on 12 October 2012.

20. 'Overview: Insurgency & Peace Efforts in Tripura'.

21. 'Overview: Insurgency & Peace Efforts in Tripura'.

22. 'Economic review of Tripura 2009–2010', Directorate of Economics and Statistics, Planning (Statistics) Department, Government of Tripura (http://destripura.nic.in/review2009_10.pdf). Accessed on 12 October 2012.

23. Economic Census 2005 report quoted in *Economic Review of Tripura 2010–11*, Directorate of Economics and Statistics, Planning (Statistics) Department, Government of Tripura http://www.destripura.nic.in/review2010_11.pdf, accessed 12 October 2012.

24. Urban area is defined as a place with: (i) a minimum population of 5,000; (ii) at least 75 per cent of male working population engaged in non-agricultural pursuits; and (iii) a density of population of at least 400 per km^2, as per Census 2011.

25. *Indian Express*, New Delhi, 17 April 2012, http://www.indianexpress.com/news/census-report-says-mizoram-only-state-without-homeless/937604/

26. Available at http://mizoram.gov.in/downloads/bamboopolicy.pdf

27. Statistical handbook of Mizoram, 2006, Tables 9.1 and 9.2. Directorate of Economics & Statistics of the Governments of Mizoram.

28. Available at http://india.gov.in/knowindia/state_uts.php?id=19 accessed on 26 October 2013.

29. The Inner Line Act continues to be operational even today and people who do not belong to Arunachal need an Inner Line Permit to enter the State. They cannot own any land nor any fixed assets in this State.

30. Article 2, Simla Convention, McKay, Alex. *The History of Tibet*, Routledge, 2003, 95–8.

31. In 1938, the Simla Convention was published by the British for the first time; in the same year, Survey of India also published a map showing Tawang as part of North Eastern Frontier Tracts. In 1944 Britain established administrations in the area. Peoples' Republic of China, which never recognized the McMahon Line, came into existence in 1949 under the leadership of Mao Zedong and with it Tibet's future looked uncertain. India declared the McMahon Line as its boundary in November 1950. The positions of India and China have since remain unchanged. The Chinese position was that Tibet was not independent and hence had no authority to sign the Simla Convention with a foreign power. His Holiness the 14th Dalai Lama, who had ruled over Tibet from 1950 till he left Tibet in 1959, had stated that Tawang was 'actually part of the Tibetan administration' before the Simla Convention. He clarified his position in 2008, saying that as far as Tibet was concerned 'Tawang is part of India' (*Times of India*, New Delhi, 4 June 2008).

32. 'The Simla Convention and its appended Indo-Tibetan agreement did not appear in Aitchison's Treaties (the official GoI record), including the final 1929 edition, since the unratified Simla Convention was not a valid international treaty and the Indo-Tibetan agreement was secret. The 1929 edition was withdrawn by a British Indian official, Olaf Caroe, in 1938, and a new edition was issued that included the Simla Convention and the McMahon-Shartra notes (but not the Anglo-Tibetan agreement or the McMahon Line map).' (Smith, Warren, *Tibetan Nation: A History of Tibetan Nationalism and Sino-tibetan Relations*, Westview Press, 1997, p201, n163.)

33. 'Whereas the Simla Convention itself after being initiated by the Chinese Plenipotentiary was not signed or ratified by the Chinese Government, it was accepted as binding by the two other parties as between themselves.'— Aitchison, C.U., *A Collection of Treaties and Sanads*, Vol XIV, Calcutta 1929, 21 & 38.

34. *Arunachal Pradesh Human Development Report, 2005*, 11, Govt. of Arunachal Pradesh (quoting Arun Roy, N. C. and P. K. Kuri, *Land Reform in Arunachal Pradesh*, Classical Publishing House, New Delhi, 2002).

35. Ibid, 9, quoting Talukdar, A. C, 'Land Tenures and Land Use Pattern in Arunachal Pradesh: A Review,' in M. C. Behera and N. C. Roy, (Eds.), *Trends in Agrarian Structure in the Hills of North- East India*, New Delhi: Commonwealth Publishers, 1997.

36. *Arunachal Pradesh Human Development Report, 2005*, 11.

37. *Arunachal Pradesh Human Development Report, 2005*, 11.

38. Ministry of MSME, GoI, 2006–07, www.indiastat.com . Accessed on 10 January2013.

39. The poverty ratio was 50.20% in 1973–74 and 55.19% in 1977–78.

40. Out of this, installed capacity of NEEPCO, a Central Govt Undertaking was 70 MW. Of the state's installed capacity, hydel capacity alone was 231 MW.

41. In all tables related to public finances of states, outstanding debt and net debt included small savings and provident fund components.

42. GSDP figures not available for 1974–75, in the absence of which NSDP figures have been used for this year.

43. Recovery of excess taxes paid by Centre in 2000-01.

44. Loans written off Rs 20,349 crore as per recommendations of the 9th Finance Commission in 1990–91.

5 Sikkim

Overview

With an area of 7096 square kms and a population of only 6.11 lakh (2011), Sikkim is the smallest state in India, in terms of both area and population. It is a landlocked state nestled in the Himalayas to the south of Tibet, surrounded by West Bengal, Nepal, and Bhutan on its south, west and east respectively. It was earlier a protectorate of India and merged with India in 1975. Though the problems that had plagued the development in other northeastern states were also present in Sikkim, yet it has been able to make rapid strides in development and has almost caught up with the rest of India. The special category status of course has helped the state to achieve rapid economic growth and development, but there were other factors at work as well.

Like other northeastern states, Sikkim is also a panorama of natural beauty and rich biodiversity. It is a land of unparalleled beauty and ethereal charm, enveloped in mysticism in the midst of lofty mountains, a land dotted by countless Buddhist monasteries. The name of Sikkim is probably derived from the word 'Su khyim' which means a 'new palace'—it is a palace for peace today, one of the few states in the region where insurgency and terrorism could not raise their ugly heads so far. Lepchas, the original inhabitants of Sikkim, call it 'Nye-mae-el' or paradise. Bhutias, later settlers, call it 'Bay-mul Deng Jong' meaning 'The hidden valley of rice'. Lepchas used to produce rice in the valleys of

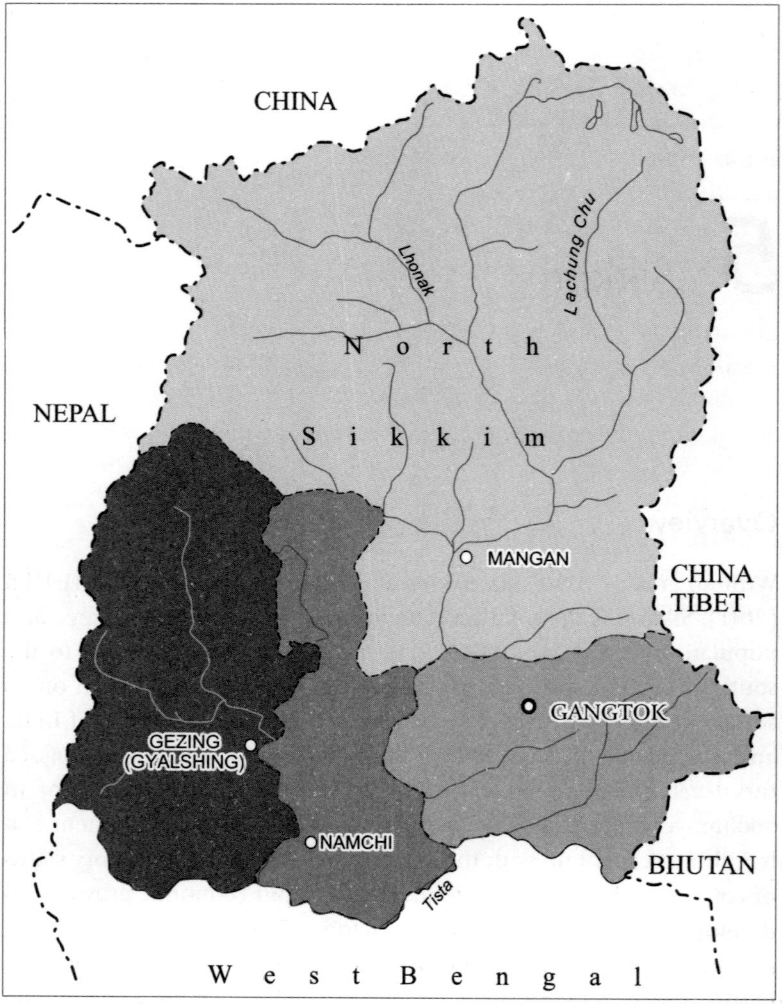

Map 5.1 Map of Sikkim.

Tista and other rivers, and in the fourteenth century, when the Bhutias started migrating from Tibet, they found rice hidden in the valleys between the mountains (Debnath 2009: 4).

Sikkim has a population composed of mainly three racial groups—Lepchas, Bhutias, and Nepalis. Lepchas and Bhutias are more or less equal in number and together constitute about 30 per cent of the total population of Sikkim; Nepalis constitute the rest. Bhutias started immigrating into the state from Tibet from the fourteenth century. Large scale Nepali migration took place in Sikkim during the nineteenth and twentieth centuries—today Sikkim is the only state in India with a majority of Nepali population.

Ethnic rivalries between culturally and linguistically diverse groups have often jeopardized inter-group dynamics and resulted in internecine conflicts between Lepchas and Bhutias in the past. Lepchas were the original inhabitants of Sikkim. They had probably migrated from Assam-Myanmar (then Burma) border and had ruled Sikkim till the middle of seventeenth century, when Bhutias migrating from Tibet overpowered them. Driven first by the Bhutias and then by the Nepalis, they moved south into the forests and lower valleys from their original habitats, deriving livelihood from the forests and resorting to shifting cultivation along with their shifting habitats. The Nepalis undertook massive deforestation of their land for paddy cultivation, thereby shrinking the living space of the Lepchas and depriving them of their hunting and gathering grounds. But political rights were denied to the Nepalis for a long time till the twentieth century due to opposition from the Bhutias; in the first place, they were settled by the British to counter the Tibetan influence on Bhutia monarchy (Debnath 2009: 16). However, even though conflicts among the different groups have now diminished, cleavages still remain and social and political cohesiveness are yet to be achieved among them in full measure.

Brief History

Like many other special category states, the early history of Sikkim is shrouded in mystery and obscurity, and sometimes intertwined with folklore and legends. There are few authentic sources from which the past socio-cultural mosaic of the state can be reconstructed. The modern history of Sikkim was reconstructed by the British and Indian historians who had travelled extensively among the inhospitable terrains to prepare the first volume of the *Imperial Gazetteer of India*. They reported that the Lepchas, who were primarily hunter gatherers, lived a close knit community life centred around their villages and followed polyandrous marriage practices, perhaps arising from the economic necessity of preserving and protecting their scarce cultivable landholdings in rough and rugged mountainous areas from being subdivided and fragmented.

In 1642, the Bhutia king Phuntsog Namgyal started ruling over Sikkim, establishing a dynasty that would rule Sikkim until its merger with India in 1975. He was consecrated as the first temporal and spiritual ruler, the Chogyal, of Sikkim, and ruled from his capital at Yuksom over a vast territory, the borders of which extended far beyond the present boundary of Sikkim into Tibet, Bhutan, and Nepal and to the borders of Bihar and Bengal. Much of his vast territory would, however, be ceded to the Bhutanese and the Gurkhas from Nepal later by his successors. The capital would also be shifted to the present capital Gangtok in 1894.[1]

Sikkim was subjected to repeated incursions by the Nepali army who was fighting with the British East India Company during the early nineteenth century, which brought the British into Sikkim. In 1835, the British East India Company forced Sikkim to cede the Darjeeling district, which formed the southern part of Sikkim, to them in exchange for an annual subsidy. In 1861, Darjeeling district along with Morang tract of Sikkim were annexed by the British into their Indian empire. Side by side, Sikkim's relations with neighbouring Tibet also worsened, being trapped between two, or rather three powers that controlled its fate: the British Empire in India, China, and Tibet (Raizada 2012: 24–30).

Acquiring Darjeeling gave British a firm foothold in Sikkim and offered it access to Tibet, but it also deteriorated Sikkim's relationship with the British. After some skirmishes, peace was finally established by a treaty signed on 28 March 1861 at Tunglong, by which Sikkim effectively became a protectorate of the British Empire in India. By this treaty, Sikkim was not allowed to cede or lease any part of its territory to any other state without the permission of the British and its military was obliged to help the British troops deployed in the hills. It was not to allow armed forces of any other country to pass through Sikkim without permission of the British and to impose no import or export duties on British goods. Further, by this treaty, British Government acquired the rights to unrestricted movement and trade in Sikkim and to construct roads in the state. This treaty would become the cornerstone of future Indo-Sikkimese relations.

This status of Sikkim as a British Protectorate was recognized by the Chinese in the Anglo-Chinese convention signed between Great Britain and China in March 1890. Clause 2 of the convention stated:

> It is admitted that the British Government, whose protectorate over Sikkim is hereby recognised, has direct and exclusive control over the internal administration and foreign relations of that State, and except through and with the permission of the British Government, neither the Ruler of the State nor any of its Officers shall have official relations of any kind, formal or informal, with any other country.

This relationship remained unaltered de facto till the British left India in 1947 and even after that till the merger of Sikkim in India in 1975 (Debnath 2009: 23).

The 1890 convention had demarcated the border between Sikkim and Tibet, settled the status of Sikkim effectively as a part of the British Empire in India and also gave the British almost exclusive rights to travel freely within and to conduct trade in Tibet (Raizada 2012: 69–77). The British continued to increase their interference in the internal affairs of Sikkim. In 1904, as the British were getting worried by the growing Russian influence in Tibet, Francis Younghusband, a British military officer, had led an expedition to Tibet via Sikkim. The expedition was resisted by the Tibetan army but Younghusband defeated them and forced a treaty on Tibet, securing monopoly trading rights in Tibet for the British through Sikkim.

The Second World War broke out during the reign of Maharaja Tashi Namgyal (1914–1963), an enlightened ruler who had introduced a number of socio-economic and administrative reforms in the state during his long rule lasting nearly five decades. Sikkim took part in it as a British ally, and the demands of war left its economy shattered. In May 1946, Lord Wavell, the then Viceroy of India, declared on behalf of the British Government that Britain would cease to exercise the powers of paramountcy in relation to the Indian states. Sikkim, as an Indian state under the Government of India Act of 1935, came within the scope of the above declaration. In 1947 when India became independent, the Maharaja managed to obtain a special status for Sikkim. He wanted a treaty relationship with independent India, but until that was concluded, agreed to maintain the former relationship. Accordingly, a Standstill Agreement was signed on 27 February 1948 between the Sikkim Durbar (Royal Court) and the Government of India 'according to which all agreements, relations and administrative arrangements as to matters of common concern existing between the British Crown and the Sikkim state on August

14, 1947 were deemed to continue pending the conclusion of a new treaty' (Debnath 2009: 25).

Merger with India

Democratic movements could not make much headway in Sikkim during the British rule. The feudal relations in an economically backward state were exploitative, and the Indian national freedom movement ignited the hope of liberation from feudal exploitation in the minds of the people of Sikkim. But in the absence of any democratic institution like a political party, these resentments could not be converted into a sustained movement for freedom and democracy. After Indian Independence, however, the situation started changing gradually. The experiment with democracy in India and the liberties guaranteed to the Indian people by the Indian constitution helped to inspire the people of Sikkim, especially of the Sikkimese peasantry 'which had been groaning under the jack-boots of Bhutia land ownership for more than 300 years' to rise against the oppressive monarchy and its feudal overlords (Raizada 2012: 131–2). However, India preferred a gradual transformation of Sikkim in the process of democratization, partly due to geopolitical considerations in the region arising from Chinese advancements and aggression in Tibet. It desisted from actively interfering in the internal affairs of Sikkim, an economically backward country wedged between two larger powers. To maintain the status quo, the Maharaja was forced to seek India's help and cooperation.

Demand for democracy led to the formation of Sikkim State Congress in December 1947 which gave a call for the abolition of Zamindari system, landlordism, and institution of a popular government. It also favoured a full-scale merger with India. To contain the rising resentments and Satyagraha movement led by the Sikkim State Congress that was gathering huge momentum in the state, on the advice of the Political Officer of India, the Maharaja formed the first popular government of Sikkim in May 1949 with Tashi Tshering, leader of the Sikkim State Congress, and a democrat at heart who stood for the unity of the Lepchas, Bhutias, and the Nepalis, as the Chief Minister. To counter the influence of the Congress, another political party, the Sikkim National Party was formed that opposed merger with India, but favoured a treaty relationship.

The popular government, however, had a turbulent relationship with the Maharaja from the beginning because of its insistence on merger and was dismissed by the latter soon afterwards. The Indian Government under Prime Minister Nehru turned a blind eye to it, which was a sad betrayal to the people of Sikkim. The Government of India, instead appointed J. S. Lall, a Civil Service Officer, as Dewan to the Maharaja, who started organizing the administration along modern lines and replaced the Standstill Agreement of 1948 with the Indo-Sikkim Agreement signed on 5 December 1950, which confirmed the status of Sikkim as an Indian Protectorate by making India responsible for its defence, external affairs, communication, and custom.[2] With this agreement, a new chapter on mutual cooperation was opened in the history of Indo-Sikkimese relationship. After the visit of Jawahar Lal Nehru, the first Prime Minister, in 1952, Sikkim started showing interest in planned economic development and initiated various reforms and development projects. Encouraged by their results, in 1953–54, the Maharaja enforced the Indian Penal Code and the Civil Code along with the Indian Marriage Act in Sikkim.

In 1953, a legislative body called the Sikkim State Council was created with limited powers, with 12 members to be elected, six each from Bhutia-Lepcha and Nepali communities and five members to be nominated by the Maharaja. Elections were held for the first time in the State, in which the Sikkim State Congress won all the six Nepali seats and the National Party won all the six Bhutia-Lepcha seats. The body politic of the state was thus completely polarized along communal lines from the beginning, while the real power remained vested in the Dewan. A second election held five years later could not alter the character of the Council (Raizada 2012: 139–44). In 1961, dissidents from these two parties and some other political parties joined hands and formed the Sikkim National Congress with Kazi Lhendup Dorji, a former Head Lama of the famous Rumtek Monastery, as President. Political unity was however unattainable due to polarization along communal lines, and the parties enjoyed ethnicity-based support. To resolve this, Sikkim Subjects Regulation was promulgated in 1961 providing citizenship to the three distinct groups of people: Lepchas, Bhutias, and Tsongs that included Nepalis and others. But the legislative process came to an abrupt halt as Sino-Indian War broke out in October 1962, and the Council was dissolved in 1963. Sikkim's border with Tibet, already under Chinese occupation, was also sealed off.

Maharaja Tashi Namgyal passed away on 2 December 1963 and was succeeded by his son Palden Thondup Namgyal. Instead of the Indian title of Maharaja for the ruler, he assumed the Tibetan title of 'Chogyal.'[3] Soon afterwards, the Chogyal started to assert his independence, being inspired by his American wife, Gyalmo Hope Cooke Namgyal, who found the overbearing presence of Indian officials in most important positions a clear sign of Indian hegemony. She wanted Sikkim to chart a course of her own, forgetting the historical and ground realities. In 1966, a supra-political group called Study Circle was formed in Sikkim. Encouraged and patronized by the Chogyal and the Gyalmo, the group advocated for revision of the Indo-Sikkimese Agreement of 1950 and soon raised demands for Sikkim's independence. The Chogyal took up the issue of revision of the 1950 Treaty with the Indian Government in 1967 on the ground that Sikkim had progressed much since the time the treaty was signed. In a statement to the Press, he articulated this position clearly, 'We want India to look after our defence and leave the rest to us.' *Sikkim Herald*, the bulletin of the Government of Sikkim commented, 'Sikkim had its geographical dimensions, entity, history and culture. It has its own existence and expects to survive. Above all it aspired to breathe independently' (Raizada 2012: 149–55). Under active encouragement from the Chogyal and the Gyalmo, a virulent anti-Indian tirade was launched in the state by the local media that propagated the idea that India constituted the biggest danger to Sikkim's culture, nationality, and identity. The Chogyal was trying gradually to dissociate Sikkim from Indian policy and to make it completely independent, like its neighbours Bhutan and Nepal, demanding separate representation in UN bodies. He was also inciting the people to rise up in revolt against India. But the extent of people's support for an independent Sikkim under the Chogyal was grossly overestimated, and when people finally revolted, they revolted against the Chogyal.

The Chogyal himself had proved to be extremely unpopular with his people who were increasingly demanding an end to his autocratic rule and the exploitation of peasantry by erstwhile landlords even though landlordism was abolished. People hated the rampant corruption and crony capitalism through which massive development funds from India were being siphoned off to the coterie of Chogyal. The Chogyal himself maintained as many as 15 private estates, besides owning a number of buildings in the capital. By the beginning of 1970s, the rumbling in the ranks and file was becoming louder, with people demanding an end to monarchy. In this scenario, general elections were held in Sikkim in April 1970, which were contested by the four major political parties, the Sikkim State Congress, the National Congress and the Janata Party, all of which were anti-monarchy and pro-democracy, besides the National Party, which became known as the Chogyal's Party, and which had made the revision of the 1950 Indo-Sikkim Treaty into a major election plank. Taking advantage of the communal representation in the electoral system, the National Party won seven seats compared to only two in the previous elections in 1967. The Chogyal now started filling the top posts in administration with his loyal and anti-Indian followers. On 1 June 1972, he assumed all executive powers which were hitherto being exercised by the Dewan. On 26 March 1973, Dorzi Dahdul, a former Chief Secretary to Sikkim Government, was appointed as the President of the State Council, a post that was held by the Dewan since 1953.

In February 1973, the fifth general elections were held in Sikkim. The National Party whose election manifesto promised UN membership for Sikkim along with exclusive rights for Bhutias and Lepchas won 11 of 18 seats in elections which were rigged on a massive scale. This led to widespread protests and demonstrations in Gangtok. On 27 March 1973, the Chogyal responded by arresting the leader of the Janata Congress, a party that was formed by merger of Janata Party and Sikkim State Congress. This event precipitated a crisis and ignited the anger of the people against the Chogyal administration, culminating in widespread agitation against the Chogyal and complete collapse of the administration. Demonstrators and protesters overran several police posts and thousands marched to lay seize upon Chogyal's palace. The Chogyal frantically appealed to the Government of India for military help, and so did the leaders of opposition who demanded that the Government of India should take over the administration completely as the stage of negotiation was over. The Indian Government helped restore order in the state by sending military help to rescue the Chogyal and then mediated an agreement signed by the Chogyal, leaders of the political parties in Sikkim and the Indian Foreign Secretary on 8 May 1973, by which it was agreed to establish a fully responsible democratic government under supervision of a Chief Executive to be nominated by the Government of India. The agreement provided for a Legislative Assembly elected on the basis of universal adult franchise and an Executive Council responsible to the Assembly (Raizada 2012: 213–21). In effect, it provided for a constitutional monarchy in Sikkim under the Chogyal.

The two major political parties in the state, the Janata Congress and the National Congress merged together to form the Sikkim Congress that won 31 of 32 seats in the Assembly elections held in April 1974, the last election before merger, and Kazi Lhendup Dorji was elected the Leader of the House. The provisions in the May 8 Agreement were legalized by the Government of Sikkim Bill passed by the Sikkim Assembly on 3 July 1974 and by the 35th Constitution Amendment to the Indian Constitution passed by the Indian Parliament in September 1974, making Sikkim an 'associated' state of India and making India solely responsible for Sikkim's defence, territorial integrity, and regulation of its external relations. Though Assembly elections were held in April 1974, Government could be formed only after the Government of Sikkim Act was promulgated in July, 1974, with Kazi Lhendup Dorji as Chief Minister.

Unable to get reconciled to his new status as a mere constitutional head of the state, the Chogyal still refused to give in to the will of the people. Instead, he continued to harbour his ambitions for a separate identity and tried to manipulate and sabotage the process of democracy. Finally, the Sikkim Assembly passed a resolution on 10 April 1975, stating that 'The institution of the Chogyal is abolished and Sikkim shall henceforth be a constituent state of India' (Raizada 2012: 250). On 14 April 1975, a referendum was held on the issue of merger with India in which 63 per cent of all registered voters participated and 97.6 per cent voted in favour of merger. On 26 April 1975, the Indian Parliament passed the Constitution (Thirty-Sixth) Amendment Bill, making Sikkim the 22nd state of India. The special category status was granted immediately.

Social Transformation in Sikkim

Sikkimese society was basically feudal in character, with the king being the sole proprietor of the land. Control over land constitutes the primary determinant of a feudal society and Sikkim was no exception to this. But the other features of feudalism—like the peasant being tied to his master and to a particular land—were absent, primarily because of the practice of shifting cultivation that forced the labourers to shift their cultivation and also due to the meagre quantity of cultivable land. The economy was based on hunter-gatherer type subsistence, with primitive agricultural practices and barter modes of transaction.

Once Sikkim came under the British rule, the revenue collection system was streamlined and modernized. As more revenues were available, public works were undertaken for the expediency of British rule and for facilitating trade with Tibet. This facilitated the transformation of the economy by monetizing and expanding it through trade, which in turn produced a new economic class as traders came from outside as officials to handle the increasingly complex task of an administration that required various skills. Introduction of money also started altering the traditional nature of relationships in society. The influx of people from neighbouring Nepal in search of jobs and opportunities marginalized the indigenous people—Lepchas and Bhutias. Ultimately the Nepalis came to control most of the agricultural land and brought in the concept of individual ownership of land. With the abolition of forced labour, labour became a commodity that commanded a price. The feudal society thus slowly started acquiring the characteristics of a capitalist society (Debnath 2009: 47–51).

Sikkim was primarily an agricultural state that was highly ruralized, with 89 per cent of its population living in rural areas. Rural indebtedness arising from the low productivity and infertility of the soil had always remained a bane of the agricultural sector and a major reason for its underdevelopment. It placed the rural masses under the mercy of moneylenders, mostly people from the Indian mainland, especially the Marwaris. Measures taken by the government to save the peasants from the vicious debt trap, like the Sikkim Durbar Law of 1910 limiting the interest rate to 12.5 per cent, were unsuccessful because of poor implementation. Thus, there was never any surplus generated by agriculture that could create an industrial demand for goods and services and the industrial entrepreneurship was totally missing. Power and transport were practically non-existent till Sikkim embraced planned development following the introduction of economic planning in independent India (Debnath 2009: 52–8).

After merger, the migrant Bhutias who had hitherto constituted the ruling class under monarchy also became gradually reconciled to the dominance of the majority Nepali community. While farming was dominated by the mostly Hindu Nepali people, pastoralism and border trades were dominated by the predominantly Buddhist Bhutias. The once-animist Lepchas had by then embraced Christianity; they depended on the forest and cultivation for their livelihood (Chakravarti 2009: 4–12). The 8 May 1973 Agreement had brought about ethnic parity and equilibrium among the three communities. It facilitated a peaceful post-merger transition of the state and its integration into India without much ethno-social cleavages and conflicts. Democracy has helped resolution of those conflicts without the kind of violence seen elsewhere within the northeast, making Sikkim a multi-ethnic state where tradition has blended seamlessly into modernity. Today it is one of the fastest growing states of India.

Socio-Economic Change

Sikkim's history since merger has not been tarnished by insurgency, terrorism or violence. Political stability and rule of law have marked the transition of this backward state to a forward looking one, and ushered in economic development and prosperity. Annexure 5.1 at the end of this chapter captures this transition in terms of socio-economic and public finance indicators of Sikkim from the time of its merger through 2010–11.

Peace is a necessary precondition to development, and the peaceful nature of post-merger transition of the state has enabled it to reach the fruits of development to the poorest in terms of basic public services—education, healthcare, electricity, drinking water, etc. The inclusive nature of development helped it bring down poverty level from 51 per cent in 1973–74 to only 13 per cent in 2010–11; this in itself is a remarkable achievement for a state that was a feudal monarchy only until four decades ago.

Sikkim's economy, like that of other special category states, was dependent on agriculture, animal husbandry, and forestry. Given the harsh natural conditions and difficult terrain without irrigation facilities, agricultural activities were necessarily in the nature of subsistence. However, though jhoom cultivation was widely prevalent, Sikkim increased its agricultural productivity by substituting mono-cropping by double or triple croppings which increased the variety as well as yield. It also resorted to cultivation of a wide variety of crops by taking advantage of the widely varying geographical and climatic conditions. But even then, only 15 per cent of its total land area is fit for cultivation, and that places a limit on the self-sufficiency the state can achieve in food-grain production (Bhattacharya 2009: 56–7). About 40 per cent of the total land areas of Sikkim are under perpetual snow and about 45 per cent are under forests. Only 18 per cent of the total cultivable land was irrigated till 2000–01. After 1975, some land reforms measures were implemented including abolition of intermediaries, provision of land rights to landless tillers and passing of the Agricultural Land Ceiling Act 1977. In 1996, a land bank was created by the government for redistribution of the surplus land among the landless.

Effect of all these showed in the increase in food-grain production from nearly 31,000 MT in 1975–76 to 76,900 MT in 2001–02; side by side, agricultural productivity had also shoot up from 669 kg per hectare to 1235 kg per hectare during the same period, due to increasing coverage by high yielding varieties. The growth in agriculture during the period has been about 6 per cent, higher than the national average. The agricultural sector employed 85 per cent of the total workforce at the time of merger and 70 per cent at the turn of the century, when it used to contribute 22 per cent to NSDP; this share declined to only 8 per cent by 2010–11. Besides physical constraints imposed by harshness of the terrain, the major factors hindering the growth of agricultural sector were the increasing demographic pressure on cultivable land, lack of adequate infrastructure, and the total absence of marketable surplus in agriculture. Government's expenditure on agricultural sector has also been insignificant—agriculture accounted for less than 1 per cent of total budgetary allocations in 1980–81 and 1.22 per cent in 1999–2000 (Debnath 2009: 22–4).

Sikkim's economy started getting transformed during the first decade of the new millennium; the state income grew at a CAGR of 22.7 per cent during this decade (2001–11) compared to only 14.9 per cent during the previous decade. Industry in Sikkim was at a nascent stage till the turn of the century, but its share in the NSDP increased appreciably during the last decade, from 23 per cent in 2001 to as much as 62 per cent in 2011, during which period the share of the services sector declined from 55 per cent to 30 per cent. Unlike in the other special category states where construction dominates the industrial scenario, in Sikkim, it is manufacturing (41 per cent share of NSDP) that drives industrialization and not construction, whose share in NSDP was only 10 per cent in 2010–11. Sikkim, in fact, is the only state among all special (and many general) category states where the secondary sector is the most important contributor to the state income.

In the 1950s, when the Nehruvian model of economic planning was introduced in India, Sikkim also adopted the same model. In 1955, the first development plan was introduced in Sikkim with emphasis on development of infrastructure, commercial farming, and cottage industries. Industrial expansion was made the priority during the third Five Year Plan in 1966. The industries which came up before the merger included fruit preservation, distillery, and horticulture based industries, apart from traditional craft-based industries like carpet weaving and woodworks. One major industry that came up in the state taking advantage of its dust-free environment was the watch-industry. In 1977, the Sikkim Time Corporation (SITCO) was established in Gangtok under technical collaboration with HMT Limited. Most prerequisites for growth of industry like, political stability, stable law and order, almost zero crime rate and absence of militant trade unionism, were present in Sikkim, though there were hindrances also—absence of technical and managerial skills, poor infrastructure, poor connectivity, absence of marketing networks, and lack of adequate institutional credit support, etc.— which still continue to plague the industrial growth in the state. Among the state public sector, SITCO whose employee strength had grown from 25 to 350 is a success story. The industrial scenario in Sikkim is dominated by industries in the small scale, mainly in sectors like pharmaceutical, eco-tourism, diary and food-processing, breweries, paper, cosmetics, plastics, etc. As of 2010–11, Sikkim had 64 registered factories employing 6,844 workers that generated a total profit of Rs 2437 crore from total output of Rs 4460 crore.

The state has vast water resources with tremendous potentials for electricity; this potential remains largely untapped, though there are a number of power projects in the state at various stages of development and completion. The estimated potential for electricity within the state is 3000 MW firm power and 8000 MW of seasonal power (Lama 1994: 125). Tourism, another vital sector having tremendous potential of the state, has also remained much untapped due to the absence of quality tourism infrastructure. The number of domestic tourists visiting Sikkim had increased from 19,115 in 1981 to 3,02,300 in 2006, while the number of foreign tourists had increased from 2739 to 20,005 during the same period. Sikkim had declared tourism as an industry in the Tenth Plan only, but the tourism infrastructure is yet to come of age. Also transport and communication, trade, hotels and restaurants, banking and insurance which are essential for attracting more tourists into the state together constituted only 9 per cent of GSDP in 2010–11, as in 1980–81. Bulk of the contribution of the tertiary sector comes from government expenditure on public administration and other services. Of late, Sikkim is emerging as a hub for education industry. Air connectivity which can boost its economy is also missing. Government sector plays a vital though diminished role in its economy and government expenditure constituted 46 per cent of the GSDP in 2010–11, compared to 70 per cent at the time of merger.

Public Finance

Between 1975 and 2011, the state's own revenue receipts increased phenomenally, especially after 1991. Their share in GSDP also increased from 7 per cent in 1975–76 to 12 per cent in 2000–01, but in the next decade the GSDP grew faster than the revenues and hence the share of revenues in GSDP declined to 4 per cent. Central transfers (grants plus share of taxes) constituted only 22 per cent of GSDP in 2010–11, as against 42 per cent in 1975–76. Share of these transfers in total revenues of the state had also come down remarkably from 70 per cent to 54 per cent during this period, indicating the lesser dependence and increased self-reliance of the state, a welcome trend that defies the dependency syndrome seen in all other northeastern states. In 2010–11, the state's own revenues could meet 49 per cent of its revenue expenditure, up from 34 per cent in 1975–76.Non-tax revenues were always important in the revenue system of Sikkim and a major source of non-tax revenue was the revenue from the state lotteries. Yield from non-tax revenues, in fact, has always been several times higher than tax proceeds.

Sikkim was one of the two states which did not enact the FRBMA until 2010, (the other one being the highly indebted West Bengal), due to a reduction of grants for meeting the non-plan revenue deficits by the

Twelfth Finance Commission. It was a Hobson's choice before the government— without enacting the FRBMA, the state was not eligible for the substantial debt relief allowed by the Twelfth Finance Commission, even though it satisfied the other condition of having a consistent revenue surplus. But with the FRBMA, it had to limit its fiscal deficit, and hence would not be in a position to make investments in capital assets to the required level for building infrastructure, for which borrowings were imperative. But the heavy capital outlay also led to high indebtedness, and Sikkim's Debt: GSDP ratio in 2000–01 climbed to 72 per cent. Its Gross Fiscal Deficit (GFD) had soared to nearly 8.7 per cent of GSDP in 1990–91 and stood at 5 per cent in 2000–01. Due to the heavy debt burden, interest payments rose and the non-developmental expenditure also increased from only 10 per cent to as much 52 per cent of total revenue expenditure between 1975–76 and 2010–11, imposing constraints upon the state's ability to spend on developmental activities. FRBMA was finally enacted in September 2010, after which Debt: GSDP ratio declined to 31 per cent and GFD came down to 4.3 per cent of GSDP in 2010–11.

Expenditure on health could not be increased much beyond 3 per cent of GSDP during 1975–2001, but expenditure on education was raised substantially from 4 per cent to 11 per cent of GSDP by 2000–01, before the ratio came down to 7.5 per cent 2010–11 due to 22 per cent average growth rate of GSDP during the 2000–2011 decade. The result was the increase in literacy from 20 per cent to 82 per cent during the period 1975–2011. The consistently high capital outlay maintained by it was a major contributor to its visible economic progress, and also an important factor responsible for the return of its ruling party to power four times in a row.

Planning

Planning scenario in Sikkim reflected the priorities in respect of socio-economic growth and development. As shown in Table 5.1, initially the priority was to develop the basic infrastructure and hence economic services claimed the major share of plan funds. Among the economic services also, predictably, the bulk of the funds went towards developing the transport and communications infrastructure to overcome the basic handicaps of remoteness and inaccessibility. Other areas that

Table 5.1 Plan Allocation under Major Sectors: 1954–2002 (per cent)

	1st Plan	2nd Plan	3rd Plan	4th Plan	5th Plan	6th Plan	7th Plan	8th Plan	9th Plan	10th Plan	11th Plan
	1954–61	1961–66	1966–71	1971–75	1974–79	1980–85	1985–90	1992–97	1998–2002	2002–07	2007–12
Economic Services	**83.0**	**76.2**	**76.5**	**66.3**	**61.7**	**66.8**	**52.1**	**59.1**	**58.7**	**56.3**	**54.5**
Agriculture and Allied Activities	21.5	20.0	15.0	14.2	15.9	26.0	21.1	13.6	12.8	10.6	5.8
Rural Development	—	—	—	—	—	—	—	—	3.4	4.5	10.8
Special Area Programmes	—	—	—	—	—	—	—	—	—	1.8	2.2
Power	9.2	8.3	7.3	8.8	10.0	9.4	17.4	24.9	21.4	14.7	10.8
Irrigation and Flood Control									2.6	1.9	1.8
Industries	4.3	0.5	6.7	3.5	6.6	4.2	4.0	3.9	4.4	3.7	5.0
Transport and Communication	48.0	47.4	47.5	39.8	29.2	27.2	9.6	16.7	10.8	16	11.6
General Economic Services	—	—	—	—	—	—	—	—	3.4	2.4	3.4
Social Services	**17.0**	**23.8**	**23.5**	**33.7**	**38.3**	**33.2**	**47.9**	**40.9**	**38.5**	**40.2**	**39.9**
Education	7.4	12.4	7.9	8.8	7.4	7.0	12.2	10.7	12.5	13.2	16.9
Health	7.1	7.2	9.4	4.1	4.5	3.5	2.5	1.1	3.1	4.8	7.8
Others[4]	2.5	4.2	6.2	20.8	26.4	22.7	33.2	29.1	22.9	22.2	15.2

(Cont'd)

Table 5.1 *(Cont'd)*

	1st Plan	2nd Plan	3rd Plan	4th Plan	5th Plan	6th Plan	7th Plan	8th Plan	9th Plan	10th Plan	11th Plan
	1954–61	1961–66	1966–71	1971–75	1974–79	1980–85	1985–90	1992–97	1998–2002	2002–07	2007–12
General Services	—	—	—	—	—	—	—	—	2.8	3.5	5.6
Total (per cent)	100.0	100.0	100.0	100.0	100.0	100.0	100.0	100.0	100.0	100.0	100.0
Total Outlay (Rs Crore)	3.24	6.37	9.71	20.36	40.10	147.80	282.40	724.50	1602.80	1655.74	4720.00

Sources: 10th and 11th Plan Documents, and Sikkim Human Development Report, 2001, Planning Commission, Govt of India, available at http://www.planningcommission.gov.in/plans/stateplan/sdr_pdf/shdr_sikkim01.pdf

Others include rural development, irrigation and flood control, communication and other social, economic and general services for the data in respect of 1st to 8th plans (Source: Sikkim Human Development Report, 2001, 18).

reflected the priorities in plan expenditure were power and agriculture, though the investment on the latter gradually declined. From the Seventh Plan onwards, i.e., only a decade after becoming a full-fledged state of the Union of India, Sikkim started devoting adequate attention towards developing its social infrastructure, and outlays for education and health were progressively increased. Their respective shares in the plan expenditure also went on increasing with successive plans. Such expenditure played no mean role in the subsequent socio-economic development of the state.

Sikkim's remarkable achievements would not have been possible without the central grants that increased from Rs 7 crore in 1975–76 to Rs 1105 crore in 2010–01, at an annual average rate of 15.6 per cent, during which period the State GSDP grew at a higher rate of 18.6 per cent. As we shall see later, Sikkim's socio-economic parameters at the end of the first decade of the new millennium were comparable to those of advanced Indian states, and this would not have been possible without its special category status that allowed substantial grants to be passed to this state. It goes to the immense credit of the state government that it had used the grants judiciously, and thereby successfully addressed the problems most states could not circumvent. There are lessons to be learnt from the Sikkim experience by other special category states about what transformation can be ushered through peace and stability combined with good governance, and what it can achieve. Despite enormous physical constraints and having to carry the baggage of a feudal past riddled with socio-ethnic cleavages, by judicious use of public funds and good governance with an inclusive agenda, Sikkim today has risen almost from the ashes to secure its place among the forward states of India.

Annexure 5.1 Socio-Economic and Public Finance Indicators of Sikkim: 1975–76 to 2010–11[5]

Parameters (Area: 7096 sq km)	1975–76	1980–81	1990–91	2000–01	2010–11
A. State Income					
NSDP (Rs Crore)	17	49	213	855	6636
Per Capita Income (Rs)	820[6]	1571	5302	16077	108972
Share of Primary Sector (per cent)		52	46	22	8
Share of Secondary Sector (per cent)		18	13	23	62
Share of Tertiary Sector (per cent)		30	41	55	30
Per cent of People below Poverty Line	50.86 (1973–74)	39.71 (1983)	41.43 (1993–94)	36.55 (1999–2000)	13
B. Demography	**1971**	**1981**	**1991**	**2001**	**2011**
Population (lakh)	2.1	3.16	4.06	5.41	6.11
Per cent of Rural Population	90	84	91	89	74
Per cent of SC/ST Population	NA	29	28	26	NA
Density of Population per sq.km,	29	45	57	76	86
Literacy Rate (per cent)	20	40	57	69	82
Females per '000 Males	863	835	878	875	889
Per cent of Working Population	53	47	40	39	58
Per cent of working population engaged in Primary sector	85	63	68	70	NA
No. of Villages	NA	NA	447	454	460
Net Irrigated Area to Net Cultivated Area (per cent)	NA	NA	NA	18	NA

(Cont'd)

Annexure 5.1 (*Cont'd*)

Parameters (Area: 7096 sq km)	1975–76	1980–81	1990–91	2000–01	2010–11
C. Infrastructure	**1975-76**	**1980-81**	**1990-91**	**2000-01**	**2010-11**
i. Education					
No. of Primary Schools				497 (2002–03)	993
No. of Middle and Secondary Schools				223 (2002–03)	185
No. of Other Institutions of Higher Learning				13 (2002–03)	8
No. of Universities				1 (2002–03)	5
Per Capita Revenue Expenditure on Education (Rs)				2077	9233
per cent of Expenditure on Education to Total Budget (per cent)				13	16
ii. Public Health					
No. of Hospitals				5	33
No. of Hospital Beds			730	920	1560
No. of Primary Health Centres and Sub-Centres				171	170
Per Capita Expenditure on Health (Rs)				587	1983
iii. Roads					
Total Road Length (km)				2431	4630
Per cent of Surfaced Road to Total Road Length				73	89
Road per 100 sq. km			25.8 (1996–97)		65
Length of National Highway (km)				41	149

(*Cont'd*)

Annexure 5.1 (*Cont'd*)

Parameters (Area: 7096 sq km)	1975–76	1980–81	1990–91	2000–01	2010–11
iv. Electricity					
Per Capita Power Consumption (kwh)				192 (1999–2000)	218
Generation of Electricity (million kwh)			160	43	80
Installed Capacity (MW)		3 (1979)	21	39	30
No. of Villages electrified					63
v. Post Offices and Banks					
Population Served by a Post Office				2647	2908
No. of Bank Offices			42 (03/1996)	47	85
Credit Deposit Ratio (per cent)			21.1	14.4	38
D. Industry					
No. of Registered Small Scale Units	10	13	115	338	124
No. of Registered Factories					64
E. Public Finance (Ratios)	**1975–76**	**1980–81**	**1990–91**	**2000–01**	**2010–11**
Own Taxes/GSDP (per cent)	6.6	5.1	4.8	11.7	3.7
Grants from Centre/GSDP (per cent)	41.2	62.1	41.2	43.0	14.9
Share of Central Taxes/GSDP (per cent)	0.7	0.7	10.8	1.9	7.1
Own Revenue/Revenue Expenditure (per cent)	34.0	26.6	29.7	53.4	48.6
Central Grants/Total Revenues (per cent)	68.7	79.2	60.4	50.5	36.3
Own Revenue/Total Revenues (per cent)	30.1	20.0	23.8	47.2	46.4

(*Cont'd*)

Annexure 5.1 (*Cont'd*)

Parameters (Area: 7096 sq km)	**1975–76**	**1980–81**	**1990–91**	**2000–01**	**2010–11**
Gross Fiscal Deficit/GSDP (per cent)	7.9	4.3	8.7	5.0	4.3
Outstanding Debt/GSDP (per cent)	7.6	20.3	60.0	71.9	31.4
Interest Payment/Revenue Expenditure (per cent)	0.0	1.2	8.2	11.0	6.4
Non-Developmental Revenue Expenditure/ Total Revenue Expenditure (per cent)	9.7	19.6	23.1	53.2	52.0
Debt Servicing/Total Expenditure (per cent)	0.0	2.5	7.5	12.3	7.6
Expenditure on Education/GSDP (per cent)	4.2	6.2	9.8	11.1	7.5
Expenditure on Health/ GSDP (per cent)	2.2	2.1	3.4	3.1	1.6
Capital Outlay/Capital Receipts (per cent)	1176.2	528.1	179.3	213.8	1960.9
Public Finance (Figures in Rs Crore)	**1975–76**	**1980–81**	**1990–91**	**2000–01**	**2010–11**
GSDP	17	52	234	1014	7412
Total Tax + Non- Tax Revenues	3	9	63	427	1937
Total Tax Revenue	1	3	37	138	799
Non-Tax Revenue	2	6	27	289	1138
State's Own Revenues	3	8	38	407	1413
State's Own Taxes	1	3	11	118	275
Grants from Centre	7	32	96	436	1105
State's Share of Central Taxes	0	0	25	19	524

(*Cont'd*)

Annexure 5.1 (*Cont'd*)

Parameters (Area: 7096 sq km)	1975–76	1980–81	1990–91	2000–01	2010–11
Total Revenue	10	41	160	863	3042
Capital Receipts	0	2	28	71	23
Total Receipts	11	43	188	933	3065
Gross Fiscal Deficit	1	2	20	51	316
Revenue Deficit	–1	–10	–31	–99	–140
Capital Outlay	2	12	50	151	451
Primary Deficit	1	2	10	–34	129
Outstanding Debt	1	11	140	729	2324
Non-Developmental Revenue Expenditure	1	6	30	406	1581
Interest Payment	0	0	10	84	187
Revenue Expenditure on Social Services	2	6	43	192	816
Revenue Expenditure on Economic Services	6	18	56	165	498
Expenditure on Education	1	3	23	112	554
Expenditure on Health	0	1	8	32	119
Revenue Expenditure	9	31	128	763	2908
Capital Expenditure	3	13	55	184	531
Total Expenditure	12	44	183	947	3439
Capital Outlay	2	12	50	151	452
Debt Servicing (Principal Amount)	0	1	3	33	73
Loans and Advances etc.	0	1	1	0	6
Discharge of Debt Obligations (Principal + Interest)	0	1	14	117	260
Net Debt Receipts	0	1	14	–46	–44
Recovery of Loans and Advances	0	0	0	1	1

(*Cont'd*)

Annexure 5.1 *(Cont'd)*

Sources: Apart from data sources mentioned in endnote 26 in Chapter 2, *Sikkim Human Development Report*, 2001, Planning Commission, Govt. of India have also been used.
Data in respect of many indicators are not available prior to 1990–91.
Per capita NDSP figure for Sikkim for the year 1975–76 has been adopted from the Fifth Finance Commission Report, Annexure VII.3, 88. In the absence of any other estimate, figure for Nagaland was adopted for Sikkim for the three years 1973–74 to 1975–76. The NSDP figure has been calculated on this basis and the same figure has been used for the GSDP as well in this table.

Notes

1. Available at sikkim.nic.in/sws/sikk_his.htm (Accessed on 14 September 2013).
2. The main provisions of the Treaty were:

   i. Sikkim shall continue to be protectorate of India and, subject to the provisions of this Treaty, shall enjoy autonomy in regard to its internal Affairs'. [Article 2]
   ii. The Government of India will be responsible for the defence and territorial integrity of Sikkim. It shall have the right to take such measures as it considers necessary for the defence of Sikkim or the security of India whether preparatory or otherwise, and whether within or outside Sikkim. In particular, the Government of India shall have the right to station troops anywhere within Sikkim.' [Article 3(I)]
   iii. The external relations of Sikkim, whether political, economic or financial, shall be conducted and regulated solely by the Government of India, and the Government of Sikkim shall have no dealings with any foreign power.' [Article 4(I)]
   iv. If any dispute arises in the interpretation of the provisions of this Treaty which cannot be resolved by mutual consultation, the dispute shall be referred to the Chief Justice of India whose decision thereon shall be final.' [Article 12][Vide Appendix II]

3. Before 1965, the Chogyal was known by the Indian title 'Maharaja'. Palden Thondup changed the title to the Tibetan 'Chogyal' meaning the Defender of Faith (Cho = Religion and Gyalpo = Ruler or King) possibly to assert the independent status of Sikkim. His American wife Hope Cooke became the Gyalmo (Queen). Govt. of India also accepted this change in title. The title of the 'Dewan' was also changed to the Tibetan 'Sidlon'.

4. Others include rural development, irrigation and flood control, communication, and other social, economic, and general services for the data in respect of first to eighth plans.

5. Data in respect of many indicators are not available prior to 1990–91.

6. Per capita NDSP figure for Sikkim for the year 1975–76 has been adopted from the Fifth Finance Commission Report, Annexure VII.3, 88. In the absence of any other estimate, figure for Nagaland was adopted for Sikkim for the three years 1973-74 to 1975-76. The NSDP figure has been calculated on this basis and the same figure has been used for the GSDP as well in this table.

6 Himachal Pradesh

Overview

The mighty Himalayas span seven nations and more than a dozen languages and cultures, besides hundreds of dialects and tribes across a length of 3,000 kilometres. Stretching from Nanga Parbat in Pakistan to Namcha Barwa massif in Arunachal Pradesh, which lies just inside the Great Bend of the mighty Yarlung Tsangpo as it enters India and becomes the mighty Brahmaputra, the Himalayas have stood as a sentinel to the Indian subcontinent since ancient times. The entire range of the Himalayas is divided into three distinct geographical regions: the Western Himalayas covering Jammu & Kashmir and Himachal Pradesh, the Central Himalayas covering Uttar Pradesh, and the Eastern Himalayas covering Sikkim and Arunachal Pradesh. Himachal which literally means the 'Land of Snow' is ensconced in the lap of the Western Himalayas. With its eternally snow-capped and lofty mountain peaks, lush green valleys and meadows, meandering streams and enchanting lakes, and biodiversity-rich thick forests, Himachal Pradesh has a bewitching variety of landscapes, rivers, and mountains that is rarely seen elsewhere. In the ancient scriptures, the region was referred to as Dev Bhumi, or Abode of Gods.

Bounded by five states—Punjab, Haryana, Uttar Pradesh, Uttarakhand, and Jammu & Kashmir—and Tibet, Himachal Pradesh is a mountainous province of India with an area of 55,673 sq. kms divided into 12 districts.

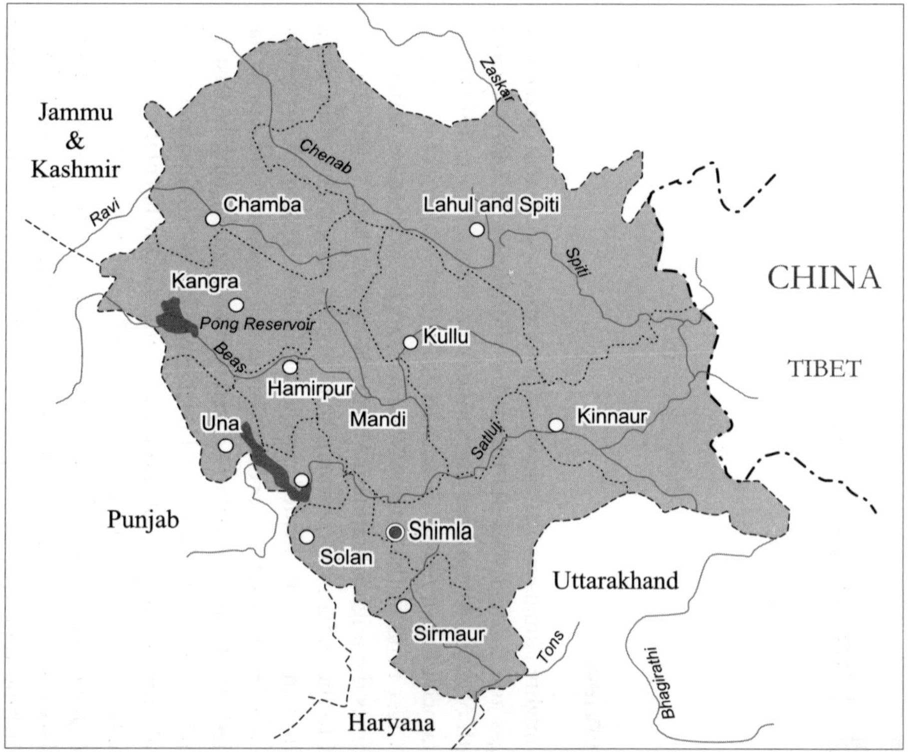

Map 6.1 Map of Himachal Pradesh.

The Dhauladhar range of the Himalayas rises majestically over Kangra valley on the western part of the state, while the Pir Panjal range stands guard over Chamba, Kullu, and Kinnaur districts. The Great Himalayas tower over the Lahaul Spiti district on the northernmost region of the state bordering Tibet beyond the Pir Panjal range, rising in a gradual elevation into lofty peaks covered by eternal snow. The Zanskar range separates Spiti and Kinnaur from Tibet. The Shiwalik separates the plains of Himachal and Punjab. Five perennial rivers wash the land—Sutlej, Chenab, Ravi, Beas, and Yamuna. The five rivers flowing through the state have created ample scope for development of hydal power, though the hilly terrain undermines their utility for irrigation purposes.

According to the 2011 census, the state has a population of 68.57 lakh, of which 72 per cent live in the rural areas. Though handicapped in various ways and sharing the same problems of weak infrastructure, economic backwardness, remoteness, and difficulties of terrain with all the other special category states, the state has been able to overcome many of its handicaps and today it is one of the most dynamic hill states of India. It has made significant achievements during the past decades in agriculture and horticulture, road construction, power generation, and promotion of tourism as well as in building up a decent network of institutions for providing basic public services like education, health, supply of drinking water, and sanitation in its rural hinterland.

During the last few decades, Himachal Pradesh has achieved remarkable social, administrative, and political transformation. At independence it was a conglomeration of 30 princely states, which were joined together to constitute a Chief Commissioner's Province in 1948. From these princely states, it had inherited a feudal economic structure with grossly inadequate infrastructure and primitive institutional framework. To transform these princely states into a coherent, integrated administrative unit was the first priority for any development. But a consistent emphasis on building roads and schools from the very beginning in a systematically planned manner, undertaken in all sincerity, had helped the state to almost eliminate poverty and ensure delivery of better public services in most respects.

Of course, it had some inherent advantages, like a homogeneous and peace-loving population speaking the same language—Hindi, and practicing the same religion—more than 95 per cent of the population are Hindus. The homogeneity of the population and the responsiveness of the state to popular aspirations have contributed in no small measure to the absence of any conflict or insurgency in a state that bordered Jammu & Kashmir, where a protracted and bloody insurgency has taken a heavy toll on development and normal life of the people. Political stability and absence of conflicts have allowed the state to develop from the scratch and emerge as one of the most enterprising states of India.

Among the major tribes of Himachal are the Gaddis, the Gujjars, and the Pangwalas who live mostly in Chamba district, the Kinners who live mostly in Kinnaur district and the Lahaulas that mostly inhabit the Lahaul-Spiti district. There are some other minor tribes also, who until recently were leading a nomadic existence. Many of these tribes, like the Gaddis and the Gujjars, still live a semi-nomadic, semi-pastoral existence sustained by agriculture and rearing of livestock (Ahluwalia 1998: 806).

The harsh terrain and permanence of its eternal snow clad mountains have imparted some solidity to the character of its people. The quiet splendour of its mountains, tranquillity of its lakes, and meadows, the fury of its monsoon and the harshness of its long winter months have made its people a strange blend of toughness and humility. The rich ancient heritage of the state is preserved in its temples and their architecture, in their woodcarvings, stone sculpture, and paintings.

Brief History

The ancient history of Himachal Pradesh takes us back to the paleolithic age, as testified by the discovery of stone tools and flakes in the Shiwalik foothills and in the river valleys of Beas and Sutlej. Evidence also suggests that between 3000 and 1750 BC, Indus Valley Civilization had penetrated Himachal areas. From the prehistoric days, various groups of people had migrated and settled in Himachal at different periods, last of these being the Khasas who had organized themselves into small, independent tribal republics in the region. These independent republics had continued till the rise of the Gupta Empire in Central and North India (Ahluwalia 1998: 20–2).

The republics came under the control of the imperial Guptas and after the fall of the Gupta Empire broke up into a number of independent principalities which were constantly at loggerheads with each other. They were brought under the central political authority of Harsha Vardhan (606–647 AD), during whose reign the Chinese traveller and pilgrim Xuang Xang (or Hiuen-Tsang) had visited India. Xuang xang also came to Himachal Pradesh around 629 AD and left a rich account of the region which indicates prosperity and peace prevailing therein. After the death of Harsha Vardhan, the region again disintegrated into a number of small units controlled by local chieftains who were notoriously feuding amongst themselves. Finally, the Mughals established their domination over most of these principalities, but taking advantage of the inhospitable nature of terrains, they continued to enjoy some degree of autonomy even under the Mughals. After the death of Aurangzeb in 1707 AD, the Mughal power declined rapidly. Gradually Sikhs, Gurkhas, and finally the British established their supremacy over most of these hill states. At the end of second Anglo-Sikh war in 1849, by defeating the Sikhs, the British consolidated their rule over Himachali territories lying between the Sutlej and the Beas (Verma 1995: 30–5). In March 1849, Lord Dalhousie annexed Punjab to the British Empire by a proclamation, pushing the frontiers to 'the natural limits of India'—to the base of the mountains of Afghanistan. The policy of annexation and British expansion into the hills continued unabated during the next few years till 1857 (Majumdar, Raychaudhury, and Dutta 1978: 740).

The twentieth century ushered in the ideas of political independence and democracy in the national consciousness and people started rising up in protest against the British rule all over the country. These ideas also penetrated the hills and the hill people, oppressed as they were by the feudal exploitation of the local rulers, also started demanding justice, end of autocratic rule by their rulers, and their rightful share in governance. The widespread resentment against the rulers led to the formation in 1939, of the Himalayan Riyasti Praja Mandal (HRPM), an umbrella organization that spearheaded the protest movements of hill people. The objective of the Praja Mandal was social reforms and democratization of administration and initially their focus was not so much against the British rule as it was against the high-handedness and disguised slavery under the autocratic rule of the chiefs of hill states. But it engendered political awareness among the hill people which ultimately transformed into movement against colonial rule, led by the Himalayan Riyasti Praja Mandal which gathered strength during the 1930s and 1940s.

As the Second World War ended, the princely states realized that the end of the British rule in India was imminent and with that also the end of their 'divine' right to rule and enjoy the attendant privileges. Some of them were forced to introduce reform measures, albeit half-heartedly. At Independence there were 30 princely states in Himachal Pradesh. In a conference organized by the Government of India in Delhi in March 1948, the rulers of these states were persuaded to merge their states into the Union of India. They signed an agreement to that effect on 8 March 1948, merging their states into a new province to be called Himachal Pradesh which was created as a separate centrally administered unit under article 239 of the Indian Constitution, with Chief Commissioner as the executive head. The new entity that had thus come into being was organized into four districts—Chamba, Mandi, Mahasu, and Sirmaur—with a total area of 27,018 sq kms and population of 9.35 lakh. An Advisory Council was set up in September 1948 to assist the Chief Commissioner, comprising two erstwhile princes (Rajas of Mandi and Baghat) and six representatives of people (including Dr. Y. S. Parmar) all nominated by the Central Government in consultation with the Chief Commissioner (Majumdar, Raychaudhury, and Dutta 1978: 596–7: Verma 1995: 134).

Struggle for Statehood

But, the new administrative arrangement failed to meet the aspirations of the people—it was, for all purposes, a centrally ruled state without any popular government. As the Constitution of India took effect on 26 January 1950, Himachal Pradesh, like other Chief Commissioners' provinces, became a 'Part C' state but little else changed. In September 1951, a 36 member Vidhan Sabha was created and the Congress party led by Dr Y. S. Parmar won 24 seats in the elections held in November 1951, becoming the first elected Chief Minister of Himachal Pradesh. Still it was far from a fully democratic set-up. The office of Chief Commissioner was now replaced by the office of Lieutenant Governor who presided over the Cabinet meetings, undermining the authority of the Chief Minister.

Himachal Pradesh also had other problems to deal with, mostly connected with the erstwhile Patiala and East Punjab States Union (PEPSU). Some areas of Punjab like the Kangra district separated Chamba from the rest of Himachal. The geographical boundaries of

Himachal were disrupted by Patiala and East Punjab State Union. Even the capital Shimla was in Punjab. The political and geographical set-up was so riddled with problems that Prime Minister Nehru proposed the merger of Himachal with Punjab, following the logic that weaker and non-viable entities should be merged with the neighbouring provinces (Ahluwalia 1998: 34). In 1955, the States' Reorganisation Commission was appointed to reorganize the states on linguistic basis. While two members of the Commission supported the idea of merger of Himachal Pradesh with the neighbouring states of Punjab, the Chairman, Mr. Fajal Ali, gave a dissenting note to the majority decision, mindful of the volatile communal situation, and law and order condition in Punjab, as also its language problem, none of which existed in Himachal. The draft State Reorganisation Bill 1956, however, mentioned that 'The Government of India has also taken note of the sentiment in Himachal Pradesh in favour of its continuation as a separate administrative unit for the time being... While ultimately Himachal Pradesh has to form a part of Punjab, it may for the present be continued as a centrally administered unit' (Verma 1995: 35–8).

The Himachal Pradesh Vidhan Sabha hotly debated the Bill and passed a resolution that, 'Himachal Pradesh be retained as a State and not be merged with Punjab; Secondly, that the enclaves of the Pradesh be integrated; and lastly, that the hilly areas contiguous to the Pradesh be merged therein at the will and option of the people of these merged areas'(Verma 1995:189–90).Nevertheless, in January 1956, Government of India accepted the recommendation of the Commission. This came as a rude shock to the people of Himachal Pradesh who considered it as a 'step backwards', an undoing of all their struggles for freedom and democracy. As per the States Reorganisation Act 1956, Himachal Pradesh thus became a centrally administered Union Territory from 1 November 1956—downgraded from being a Part C State—to be governed through a Territorial Council. The legislature and council of ministers ceased to exist and the Territorial Council only had the power to make by-laws that also needed the approval of the Central Government, with all real powers being vested in the Centre. *De-facto* it became a centrally ruled state, with no real democratic rights of the people. It was a 'queer Constitutional experiment' and the state remained in that 'suspended animation' for the next one decade (Ahluwalia 1998: 37). In 1963, a legislature was granted to the

Union Territory and the Congress Party headed by Dr Y. S. Parmar again formed the Government in July 1963 after the elections.

Meanwhile, the *Punjabi Suba* movement of the 1950s that demanded a cultural and linguistic state for the Punjabis in Punjab had fizzled out during the 1960s; it was again revived by Sant Fateh Singh, leader of the Akali Dal. After the Indo-Pak War of 1965 in which Sikh soldiers had played a heroic role, the Government of India finally conceded their demands for a unilingual state for the Punjabis. With the subsequent reorganization of Punjab on a linguistic basis in November 1966 and its Hindi speaking areas forming the state of Haryana, the hill areas in Punjab—Shimla, Kangra, Kullu, Lahaul, and Spiti districts—were transferred to Himachal Pradesh. The problem of enclaves was thus finally settled, fulfilling the long cherished dream of the Himachali people. In the elections held in 1967, the Congress Party headed by Dr Parmar won and he was sworn again as the Chief Minister. With the merger of hill areas into Himachal Pradesh, 'all doubts regarding its separate identity were permanently set aside. Himachal now became larger in size than some other ' "A" class states like Punjab, Haryana, Nagaland, and Kerala' (Ahluwalia 1998: 39–40). All parties unanimously supported full statehood for Himachal Pradesh and in July 1967, the Vidhan Sabha too adopted a unanimous resolution to that effect. In deference to all their wishes, on 18 December 1970, the Parliament passed the State of Himachal Pradesh Act and on 25 January 1971, Himachal Pradesh finally emerged as a full-fledged state of the Indian Union. Immediately afterwards, it was granted the special category status.

Socio-Economic Changes

In the pre-statehood period, Himachal was largely a conglomeration of human settlements in its many hamlets and villages scattered across its fertile valleys. It was a farm economy sustained by cultivation and livestock. These isolated settlements gradually developed into towns and revenue villages. Urbanization was limited and even at the turn of the present century, 90 per cent of the population lived in its 17,495 villages. Manufacturing activities were limited to weaving. There were quite a few tourist centres like the British-developed hill stations of Shimla, Dharamsala, Dalhousie, Kasauli, etc. The British had also introduced tea plantation in the Palampur area in 1849, and the tea industry was attracting immigrant labour from neighbouring provinces. There were also a few cantonment towns. On the whole, it was a ruralized agrarian state, with weak economy, undeveloped physical, financial, and social infrastructure and low level of catalytic skill available within the state. The constraints faced by the state were many—geographical remoteness, inaccessibility, harsh climate, low agricultural productivity, and formidable bottlenecks in communication and transport. In 1955–56, at the time of reorganization of the states, only three states and union territories in the country (Bihar, Odisha, and Manipur) had a per capita income lower than that of Himachal Pradesh. But in less than three decades since its formation as a special category state, its economy had undergone a miraculous transformation, catapulting the state among the advanced states in the country—a state that has been able to provide a dignified living standard for most of its people. In 1997–98, it had moved to the eighth rank in the country in terms of per capita income. Side by side, its socio-economic indicators as shown in Annexure 6.1 at the end of this chapter also progressed by leaps and bounds.

The state NSDP (at current price) had increased at an annual rate of 14 per cent between 1971 and 2011 but growth had picked up after 1985. Between 1991 and 2001, NSDP grew at a rate of 19 per cent annually, higher than the national average. The structure of economy also invariably changed with growth. In 1970–71, the primary sector contributed 59 per cent to the state income and employed 78 per cent of the main workforce. By 2010–11, the economy had undergone a complete transformation, from a farm-based economy, it had evolved into a service driven economy, with services sector commanding 42 per cent of the state income, and the primary sector contributing only 20 per cent. The manufacturing sector that used to contribute only 17 per cent to NSDP in 1970–71, had increased its share to 38 per cent. As a result of the growth, there had been significant reduction in poverty level, from 26 per cent to 8 per cent between 1973–74 and 2010–11.[1] Himachal Pradesh, today, is among the states with the lowest poverty ratios in the country.

The problems today are intra-state disparities and uneven development across its districts. The districts lying in the low hills and plains in its south—like Bilaspur, Hamirpur, Kangra, Solan, and Una had achieved a high level of development while the districts in the high mountains—Chamba, Lahaul & Spiti, Kinnaur, Shimla, Sirmaur, Kullu, and Mandi, had lagged behind due to reasons of geography, with higher incidence of rural poverty compared to the districts in the southern plains and low hills.[2] Though economic growth achieved by the state as a whole during the past decades has been fairly impressive, its performance has still been sub-optimal in comparison with its more prosperous neighbours, Punjab and Haryana.

The resources of the state are forest, water and minerals. It has abundant reserves of water in its rivers fed by glaciers in the upper reaches of its mountains, in its many lakes and reservoirs at Sunder Nagar, Gobind Sagar, Pandoh, and Pong, but despite the wide availability, due to the difficulties imposed by the state's physiography, only one fifth of the total cultivable land is irrigated. The estimated hydel potential of about 20000 MW is also yet to be tapped due to the huge capital requirements, high ecological, and rehabilitation costs involved.[3] Himachal has a forest cover of 64 per cent and is rich in biodiversity—its western Himalayan ecosystem nurtures a rich variety exotic plants and animals.

Despite the falling contribution of the primary sector to the state income during the last four decades, the rural base of its economy has not changed. As in 1971, more than 90 per cent of its population still lived in villages even in 2010–11, and more than two thirds of the main working population were still employed in agriculture. But with less than 20 per cent of its cultivated area having access to irrigation in 2000–01, agriculture was still dependence on rains. Though there are perennial rivers flowing through the state, their steep gradients limit the scope of flow irrigation. Agricultural productivity also remains low due to the high input and transportation costs and 'the intrinsic character of marginality of land resource in the mountain regions at large'. There is abundant rainfall in the state, but due to the hilly nature of the terrains, crops are cultivated on the slopes of mountains—often in terraces—and the cultivable fields are thus exposed to large scale erosion of the fertile topsoil. Access to market is another factor impeding the growth of agriculture within the state in the absence of all-weather roads in most of its villages, leading to their economic isolation during the long and hard winter months. Agriculture in the state is yet to come of age, with only 10 per cent of the total geographical area being under cultivation of some sorts, 31 per cent being under forests and 32 per cent under permanent pastures and other grazing lands. The state produces a wide variety of agricultural and horticultural produces depending on the altitude and climate of the areas. Horticulture is a major strength of the state that employs about 5 lakh farming families and generates a turnover of more than Rs 600 crore annually.[4]

The mountainous terrains, rugged topography, and challenging climate make the creation and maintenance of infrastructure in a hilly state like Himachal Pradesh much more difficult and costlier than in the plains. Natural calamities like frequent landslides and consequent road blockages further add to the time and cost overruns of infrastructure projects. Yet the state has progressed remarkably in terms of creation of social and physical infrastructure. The number of primary schools increased more than four folds during the four decades from 1971 to 2011, lifting literacy rate from 32 per cent to 84 per cent during the period. Number of institutions of higher learning also multiplied from a paltry 15 in 1971 to 401 in 2010–11. Rural and urban infrastructure of public health services had expanded significantly, with the result that Himachal today fares better than the national averages in respect of all health related parameters—birth and death rates, infant mortality rate, and life expectancy at birth. Infant mortality rate was brought down from 118 per thousand in 1971 to 38 in 2011 (national average 44). Life expectancy for males and females went up from 58 and 55 years respectively to 66 and 67 years during this period.

Accessibility, power availability, and existence of communication networks—these are the three vital links to development in a mountainous region. The road network in Himachal Pradesh had increased by four and half times during the four decades since its statehood, but still many of its villages have no road connectivity though among the hill states of India, Himachal Pradesh has the highest road density. Though its vast hydel potential still remains largely untapped, each of its villages has access to electricity. The installed capacity, mostly hydel-based, had increased from 51 MW to 1160 MW between 1971 and 2011, and the generation of electricity had increased many-folds. Himachal Pradesh is today among the states with higher tele-density (i.e. the number of telephones per 1,000 people) than the national average (8.4 compared to 5). Communications infrastructure in the state was quite developed even in the late nineties. Today, all telephone exchanges in the state are digitized and are interconnected to each other by optical fibre cables. Financial infrastructure in the state has been improving of late, with credit-deposit ratio rising to 40 per cent in 2011, compared to only 22 per cent in 2001, reflecting low credit-demand due to an under-developed industrial sector.

The state also has rich reserves of minerals like limestone, dolomite, pyrites, gypsum, quartzite, magnesite, barytes, rock salts, slate, and uranium. At the time statehood, there was hardly any industry in Himachal Pradesh, but a number of public sector companies were established soon. Several industrial estates were created in the districts and a few 'Industrial Areas' were set up to provide basic industrial infrastructure and fiscal incentives to units setting up industries therein. Over time, these ushered an industrial climate in the state in which further development could take place. As of 31 March 2002, there were 41 industrial areas and 15 industrial estates in the state, most of which were located in the industrially backward districts. The increase in the share of secondary sector in the total state income as noted earlier had come gradually as a result of all these interventions. Between 1979 and 2012, the number of large and medium industries in the state had increased from a meagre 22 to 487. The sectors in which these industries were set up included electronics, steel, chemicals, textiles, food products, paper, engineering, plastic, beverages, cement, leather, and ceramic. The registered factories also multiplied in number, from 174 in 1971 to 2210 in 2011. The number of small scale industries proliferated to more than 39000 units, and total employment in all industries (including in medium and large industries) was 2.75 lakh workers, as of March 2013.

Despite sickness of more than 40 per cent of the SSI units, all these figures tell the tale of a state on the move—to fast industrialization.[5] But there are still some impediments to overcome, including the absence of sizeable markets within the state for the products. The state still has to rely upon markets elsewhere, in bordering Punjab and Haryana, for meeting its requirements of raw materials and also for selling its products.

Public Finance

On attaining statehood in 1971, Himachal Pradesh had total revenue of Rs 24 crore from tax and non-tax sources, of which its own revenues were Rs 23 crore. Including the share of central taxes and grants, its total revenue receipts was only Rs 57 crore, which constituted about a quarter of its GSDP at that time. The special category status entitled it to liberal central grants, and the revenue receipts of the state rose consequently. During the period from 1970–71 to 2010–11, while the GSDP grew at an annual rate of 15 per cent (at current prices), state's own tax revenues grew at an even higher rate of nearly 17 per cent, with central grants growing at a rate of 14 per cent. But during this period, non-tax revenue of the state grew at the rate of 12 per cent only, partly because of less realization from its forest products because of environmental concerns, and also because the regeneration of higher altitudes forests has a lower success rate.

But while the revenues increased almost at par with the GSDP, the committed expenditure of the state also increased steeply, on account of the huge number of government employees. In 1990–91, there were 1.14 lakh government employees in the state, which increased to 1.40 lakh by 2000–01. Consequently, in 2000–01, salary expenditure of the government was Rs 1683 crore and the annual pension and retirement liabilities amounted to Rs 391 crore. These two elements consumed 68 per cent—more than two thirds of the state's total revenues, forcing a huge deficit of Rs 1283 crore in the revenue account of the government. Even 10 years later, the deficit has practically remained the same, despite continuous increases in revenue. To meet this deficit, and also finance its capital expenditure for building the much needed road and other infrastructure, it had to borrow heavily. Successive borrowings had increased its inherited a debt burden of Rs 106 crore at an average rate of 15 per cent annually till 2010–11, almost at the same rate of growth of GSDP, making such debt levels dangerous. The interest liability that was only Rs 4 crore in 1970–71 rose to Rs 1950 crore by 2010–11, equivalent to 14 per cent of revenue expenditure of the state. The gross fiscal deficit stood at a high level of 5.5 per cent of GSDP in 2010–11, but still much lower than 11.8 per cent seen in 2000–01, which was among the highest in the country.

Himachal Pradesh would continue to remain amongst the most heavily indebted states. In 2010–11, its debt: GSFP ratio of 43 per cent was somewhat lower than 50 per cent registered in 2000–01. Debt servicing charges constituted 17 per cent of its total expenditure in 2010–11, up from only 7 per cent in 1970–71. In the primary account, the state had a deficit of more than Rs 1000 crore since 2000–01, and this, together with the fact that outstanding debt has been growing as fast as the GSDP, would make such debt levels clearly unsustainable, leaving very little fiscal space to the state for making any structural adjustments. The same was the situation, as we have seen, with most special category states.

Because of this high indebtedness, over time, the state's dependence on centre has not decreased appreciably. Share of its revenues, tax and non-tax combined, in total revenue expenditure was nearly 40 per cent in 1970–71; in 2010–11, this ratio increased to only 42 per cent. Central transfers, including grants and state's share of central taxes constituted 56 per cent of revenue expenditure in 1970–71; in 2010–11, it was at 53 per cent. Total government expenditure constituted only about 29 per cent of the GSDP in 2010–11.

One major weakness in the public finance of the state is its inability to generate reasonable surplus in its revenue account. A large part of its borrowings had to be utilized for financing the revenue deficit and augmenting its ability to invest on capital assets was limited to that extent. In 1970–71, it used to spend more than 8 per cent of its GSDP on education and health and this ratio had declined to just above 6 per cent in 2010–11. Unless the committed expenditure on account of interest, salary, and pension is brought down, its perilous debt situation will not improve, and this will continue to impose severe restrictions on its ability to take social development and economic growth to a higher level.

Planning

Table 6.1 shows the plan allocations in Himachal Pradesh from the Fourth Plan when it became a special category state through the Eleventh Five Year Plan. Towards the initial phase of planning, especially during the first five plans, the emphasis was on economic services and about 80 per cent of the total plan expenditure was made on these services. Among the economic services, transport and communication and power were given the maximum allocations for building infrastructure that was largely absent in the state. But once the minimum road and power infrastructure were built, the emphasis was then shifted to social services, and from sixth plan onwards, we see a marked increase in expenditure on social services. By the end of the tenth plan, allocations for economic services had declined to 51 per cent and those for social services had increased to 48 per cent. The planning process entailed

Table 6.1 Plan Outlay/Expenditure in Himachal Pradesh: Fourth to Eleventh Plan (per cent)

	4th Plan	5th Plan	6th Plan	7th Plan	8th Plan	9th Plan	10th Plan	11th Plan
Major Heads of Development	1969–74	1974–78	1980–85	1985–90	1992–97	1997–02	2002–07	2007–12
Economic Services	**82.0**	**81.1**	**74.4**	**75.2**	**62.9**	**57.4**	**51.5**	**52.9**
Agriculture and Allied Industries	24.1	26.0	15.8	19.6	13.9	11.6	11.7	10.7
Rural Development	3.2	1.1	4.7	3.7	3.3	3.9	4.3	2.6
Irrigation and Flood Control	0.1	1.6	5.8	5.4	4.2	4.0	4.4	8.9
Power	21.6	25.0	27.0	26.6	18.9	16.0	12.0	8.1
Industry and Minerals	3.7	3.3	3.1	3.2	2.5	1.5	1.0	1.3
Transport & Communication	29.1	24.0	17.8	14.8	12.6	14.1	15.9	15.6
Science, Technology & Environment	0.0	0.0	0.0	0.1	0.1	0.1	0.1	1.0
General Economic Services	0.3	0.1	0.1	1.8	7.4	6.2	2.2	4.8
Social Services	**18.0**	**16.7**	**22.5**	**22.7**	**34.7**	**40.7**	**47.5**	**44.0**
Education	6.5	4.8	4.8	7.4	13.0	19.5	26.5	12.2
Medical and Public Health	3.0	2.6	3.4	3.3	4.7	6.6	7.7	10.5
Water Supply and Sanitation, Housing	6.0	6.9	11.9	9.3	14.9	10.7	6.3	15.4
Others Social Services	2.5	2.5	2.4	2.7	2.1	4.0	7.1	5.9
General Services	**0.0**	**2.2**	**3.2**	**2.1**	**2.4**	**1.6**	**0.8**	**3.0**

(Cont'd)

Table 6.1 *(Cont'd)*

Major Heads of Development	4th Plan 1969–74	5th Plan 1974–78	6th Plan 1980–85	7th Plan 1985–90	8th Plan 1992–97	9th Plan 1997–02	10th Plan 2002–07	11th Plan 2007–12
Special Area Programs	0.0	0.0	0.0	0.0	0.0	0.3	0.2	0.2
Expenditure/ Outlay (Rs Crore)	**113**	**162**	**665**	**1325**	**3499**	**7897**	**10300**	**14000**
Per Capita Annual Investment (Rs)	**61**	**101**	**288**	**765**	**1354**	**2205**	**NA**	**NA**
Growth rate of HP	3.0	4.6	3.0	8.8	6.3	6.4	7.6	8.1
Growth rate of India	3.4	5.2	5.3	6.0	6.2	5.6	7.8	7.9

Sources: *Himachal Pradesh Development Report*, 2002, *Himachal Pradesh Economic Survey*, 2011, 16 and The Wonderland of Himachal Pradesh, Op.cit, 1024-1063. For the 10th and 11th Plans, projected outlays are shown. The growth rates at the end of the table are as reported in the Himachal Pradesh Economic Survey, 2011, 16.

Annexure 6.1 Socio-Economic and Public Finance Indicators of Himachal Pradesh: 1970–71 to 2010–11

Parameters (Area: 55673 sq km)	1970–71	1980–81	1990–91	2000–01	2010–11
A. State Income					
NSDP (Rs Crore)	232	642	2521	13852	46216
Per Capita Income (Rs)	678	1704	4910	22795	68297
Share of Primary Sector (%)	59	47	40	26	20
Share of Secondary Sector (%)	17	20	22	32	38
Share of Tertiary Sector (%)	24	33	38	42	42
% of people below poverty line	26.39 (1973–74)	16.40 (1983)	28.44 (1993–94)	7.63 (1999–00)	8
B. Demography	**1971**	**1981**	**1991**	**2001**	**2011**
Population (lakh)	34.6	42.81	51.7	60.78	68.57
% of Rural Population	93	92	91	90	90
% of SC/ST Population	26	29	30	29	NA
Density of Population per sq. km	62	77	93	109	123
Literacy Rate (%)	32	49	64	77	84
Female: Male Ratio (%)	958	973	976	970	974
% of Working Population	NA	34	34	32	NA
% of Working Population Engaged in the Primary Sector	77.58	78.08	74.8	68.65	NA

(*Cont'd*)

Annexure 6.1 (*Cont'd*)

Parameters (Area: 55673 sq km)	1970–71	1980–81	1990–91	2000–01	2010–11
No. of Villages (inhabited)	NA	16807	16997	17495	20690
Net Irrigated Area to Net Cultivated Area (%)	17	16	18 (1989–90)	19 (2001–02)	19
C. Infrastructure					
i. Education					
No of Primary Schools	3768	6093	7471	10633 (2001–02)	16460
No of Middle and Secondary Schools	1177	1697	2191	3722 (2001–02)	3193
No of Other Institutions of Higher Learning	15	52 (1982–83)	78 (1993–94)	132 (2004–05)	401
No of Universities	1	2	3	3	14
Per Capita Revenue Expenditure on Education (Rs)	4	10	35	143	3897
% of Expenditure on Education to Total Revenue Budget (%)	24	23	20	20	16
ii. Public Health					
No. of Hospitals (all types)	692 –1975	831 –1983	1031 –1992	1770 (2003–04)	150

No. of hospital beds	5224 –1975	5974 (1983)	7958 –1992	10811 (2003–04)	8479
No. of Primary Health Centres and Sub-Centres	328 –1975	1444 –1985	2182 –1995	2913 –2004	2520
No. of Doctors	731 –1975	NA	2623 –1996	3526 (2003–04)	NA
Per Capita Revenue Expenditure on Health (Rs)	1	3	14	43	1106
iii. Roads					
Total Road Length (km)	10617	17433	22445	27737 –2002	47963
% of Surfaced Road to Total Road Length	NA	26	31	48	69
Road per 100 sq. km	5	31	42	54 –1995	60
Length of National Highway (km)	239	NA	733 –1995	1239 (2002)	1506
iv. Electricity					
Per Capita Power Consumption (kwh)	NA	66.4	191.9 (1989–90)	339 (1999–00)	1380
Generation of Electricity (million kwh)	528	2451	12624	13060 (1997–98)	4821
Installed Capacity (MW)	51	128	272	301 (1997–98)	1160

(*Cont'd*)

Annexure 6.1 *(Cont'd)*

Parameters (Area: 55673 sq km)	1970–71	1980–81	1990–91	2000–01	2010–11
Of which Hydel Capacity	49	126	272	299	
% of Villages Electrified	77 (1992–93)	NA	99.73 (1995)	100	85 –2013
v. Post Offices and Banks					
Population served by a Post Office	2058	1812	1982	2208	2468
No. of Bank Offices	NA	NA	756 (1994)	782	1103
Credit Deposit Ratio (%)	NA	NA	27 (1994)	22	40
D. Industry					
No. of Large and Medium Industries		22 (1979–80)	110	188	487 (03/2012)
No. of Registered Small Scale Units		6969 (1979–80)	20545	28731	39018 (03/2013)
No. of workers in SSI, Large and Medium Industries		NA	101352	151792	275455
Investment in SSI, Medium and Large Industries (Rs Crore)		NA	351.38	2954.03	17155.54
No. of Registered Factories	174	549	1308	2097 (2002–03)	2210
No. of Persons Employed in Factories	11214	15700	34568	80114	156396

E. Public Finance (Ratios)	**1970–71**	**1980–81**	**1990–91**	**2000–01**	**2010–11**
Own Taxes/GSDP (%)	3	4.3	5.7	4.7	6.3
Grants from Centre/GSDP (%)	14.5	17.1	14.2	11.6	9.8
Share of Central Taxes/GSDP (%)	0.4	2.7	6.7	2.1	3
Own Revenue /Revenue Expenditure (%)	36.4	71.9	24.4	20.9	38.3
Central Grants /Total Revenues (%)	58.8	46.4	49.4	59.4	44.5
Own Revenue/Total Revenues (%)	39.5	46.2	27.3	29.7	42
Gross Fiscal Deficit/GSDP (%)	7.1	-4.5	9.9	11.8	5.5
Outstanding Debt/GSDP (%)	45.4	22.7	46	51.1	42.5
Interest Payment/Revenue Expenditure (%)	5.4	5.4	12.3	18.4	14
Non- Developmental Revenue Expenditure /Total Revenue Expenditure (%)	17.4	23	30.9	37.3	41.5
Debt Servicing /Total Expenditure (%)	7.2	26.5	55	40.4	16.8
Expenditure on Education/GSDP(%)	6.5	5.5	6.5	5.6	4.7
Expenditure on Health /GSDP (%)	1.7	1.6	2.5	1.7	1.3
Capital Outlay/Capital Receipts (%)	67.4	198.7	11.3	17.4	72
Public Finance (Figures in Rs Crore)	**1970–71**	**1980–81**	**1990–91**	**2000–01**	**2010–11**
GSDP (Rs Crore)	233	794	2815	15661	56355
Total Revenue	24	157	408	1236	7053
Own Revenue	23	135	220	905	5338

(Cont'd)

Annexure 6.1 *(Cont'd)*

Public Finance (Figures in Rs Crore)	1970–71	1980–81	1990–91	2000–01	2010–11
Total Tax Revenue	8	56	349	1059	5358
Non-Tax Revenue	16	101	59	177	1695
State's Own Taxes	7	34	161	728	3643
Grants from Centre	34	136	398	1810	5658
Share of Central Taxes	1	22	188	330	1715
Total Revenue Receipts	57	292	807	3046	12711
Capital Receipts	17	26	1324	3162	2484
Total Receipts	74	319	2131	6207	15195
Gross Fiscal Deficit	17	–35	279	1845	3178
Revenue Deficit	5	–105	95	1283	1235
Capital Outlay	11	53	149	549	1789
Primary Deficit	13	–46	168	1047	1228
Outstanding Debt	106	180	1294	8006	24439
Non- Developmental Revenue Expenditure	11	43	278	1614	5279
Interest Payment	3	10	110	798	1950
Revenue Expenditure on Social Services	28	84	356	1561	4979
Revenue Expenditure on Economic Services	23	60	265	1134	3682
Expenditure on Education	15	44	183	870	2689

Expenditure on Health	4	13	71	263	763
Revenue Expenditure	62	188	901	4329	13946
Capital Expenditure	14	150	1277	2580	2886
Total Expenditure	77	338	2178	6909	16832
Debt Servicing (Principal Amount)	2	79	1088	1991	870
Loans and Advances etc.	1	18	40	40	227
Discharge of Debt (Principal + Interest)	6	90	1198	2789	2820
Net Debt Receipts	11	-63	126	372	396

Source: Apart from data sources mentioned in endnote 26 in Chapter 2, *Himachal Pradesh Human Development Report* 2002 has also been used.

development of the most basic physical and social infrastructure on which future economic growth and development would take place, and by the 1990s, when large scale economic reforms were introduced in the country, these basic infrastructure, in rural as well as in urban areas, were already more or less in place. Till the seventh plan onwards, the state's growth was lagging behind the national average, but from then on, the state started growing at a faster rate and its growth rate either exceeded or was maintained at the national level.

From a Chief Commissioner's Province in 1948 to a Part 'C' state in 1951, then a Union Territory in 1956, with territorial consolidation in 1966 giving physical contiguity and compactness, and finally to a full-fledged state of the Union of India in 1971, Himachal Pradesh has made a long and interesting journey, unique in many ways. Inheriting the legacy of feudal political structure of the princely states, with grossly inadequate economic opportunities and an infrastructure that could hardly address the barest needs of inaccessible locations and harsh mountainous terrains of a hill state, Himachal, perhaps would have taken ages to come up to the present stage of development and achieve the kind of socio-economic progress without the special assistance that came by virtue of its status as a special category state. But with proper planning, correct prioritization, and pragmatic policies implemented through a good governance model, it has been able to create a structure of socio-economic development that has significantly impacted and improved the living standards of people of this hill state. Over 40 years since its statehood, it has progressively transformed its subsistence economy into a modern market-based economy by sustained development of its horticulture, power, tourism, and information technology without causing damage to its environment and ecology. It has remarkably improved the delivery system in respect of public services. Its administration, irrespective of the party in power, has by and large been responsive; it has also been efficient in handling the natural disasters that regularly visit the state. The state has been known for its relative political stability, absence of terrorism, militancy or insurgency, minimal class or caste conflicts, and almost total absence of law and order problems. Special category status and the social, religious, and linguistic homogeneity had helped in achieving all this, and the state has also been able to overcome the absolute dependence on centre for its own needs, something most other special category states have not been able to achieve as yet.

Notes

1. The figure of 28 per cent in 1993–94 is attributed to imperfect measurement by the Planning Commission—even an expert group appointed by the Commission had questioned its methodology.

2. *Himachal Pradesh Human Development Report, 2002*, Planning Commission, Govt. of India, 21–2.

3. *Himachal Pradesh Development Report, 2002*, Planning Commission, Govt. of India, 32.

4. *Himachal Pradesh Development Report, 2002*, Planning Commission, Govt. of India, 220–1.

5. *Himachal Pradesh Development Report, 2002*, Planning Commission, Govt. of India, 272–74.

7 Uttarakhand

Overview

Land of snow-clad peaks and glaciers in the mighty Himalayas that gave birth to two of the holiest rivers of India, the Ganga and the Yamuna, of verdant valleys and luxuriant meadows harbouring myriads of lakes and countless streams, a land that has always been a bastion of unmatched beauty and attracted people from all over, Uttarakhand (earlier Uttaranchal) entered the political map of India as its 27th state on 9 November 2000. In September 2001, it was accorded the special category status. Surrounded by Himachal and UP, Uttarakhand comprises essentially of two regions of the erstwhile UP, Garhwal and Kumaon, which now form the two administrative divisions (Mandal) of the state. The western part of this region, referred to as Garhwal Mandal, comprises seven districts: Rudra Prayag, Tehri Garhwal, Chamoli, Pauri Garhwal, Uttarkashi, Haridwar, and Dehradun, while the eastern region known as the Kumaon Mandal comprises the six districts of Almora, Nainital, Udham Singh Nagar, Champawat, Bageshwar, and Pithoragarh. People inhabiting these regions had existed for a long time as two different hill communities speaking their distinct Pahari dialects—Garhwali and Kumaoni—but there are also over 10 other distinct tribal languages spoken in the state (Kumar 2000: 21). Almost 85 per cent of its population are Hindus, and about half of the state's Muslim population lives in the religious town of Haridwar sacred to the Hindus.

Map 7.1 Map of Uttarakhand.

The state of Uttarakhand is spread over the Middle Himalayan Range. The northern part of the state is covered by perpetual snowline, high peaks and vast glaciers two of which, the Gangotri and the Yamunotri, are the sources of the Ganga and the Yamuna respectively. Garhwal has some of the highest peaks in the Himalayas including, Nanda Devi (7,818 meters), Chaukhamba (7,412 meters,) and Bandarpoonch (7,168 meters). Kumaon region has Trishul (7,120 metres), Nanda Kot (6,663 meters), Maiktoli (6,803 meters), and Tharkot (6,099 meters). The lower regions of the state are under thick forest covers.

The state has always been a major centre of pilgrimage for the Hindus and Sikhs. Some of the holiest shrines and pilgrimage centres of these two religions are located in this state, including the many prayags or confluence of rivers where bathing is considered to be holy. In the past, the region was deeply anchored in the mainstream Hinduism and its four *Dhams* (abodes of Gods)—Kedarnath and Badrinath in Chamoli and Gangotri and Yamunotri in Uttarkashi—still attract millions of devotees belonging to the Hindu and Sikh faiths every year. Religious tourism is, in fact, a major source of employment in the hills of Uttarakhand. It was a famous centre of sanskritization and learning of scriptures—the eighth century scholar and religious reformer Adi Shankaracharya had established Joshimath (Jyotirmath) as a centre of learning and restored some of the most sacred shrines, including those at Badrinath and Kedarnath. Since ancient times, people here have kept alive their tradition of deep spirituality, religiousness, and ecclesiastical learning, a tradition that continues till today.

Uttarakhand has an area of 53,483 sq. kms with population of 101 lakhs, of which 70 per cent live in the rural areas as per the 2011 census. The human development indicators of the state compare well with some of the developed general category Indian states. Like all other special category states, the major source of livelihood for the people of Uttarakhand is agriculture, which, by and large, remains low yield and high cost—largely due to the difficulties of its hilly terrain. Industrialization in the state has been low and development uneven, and the incidence of poverty is also higher compared to the neighbouring states. To be fair, the achievements of the state that was created only about a decade ago has been quite remarkable, which may be partly attributed to its special category status. It has great potential for tourism and hydel power, both of which remain untapped due to constraints arising from an underdeveloped infrastructure and difficulties of terrain.

Brief History

The ancient history of this region goes back to the Vedic times. Later, Uttaranchal formed part of Maurya, Gupta and Vardhana empires in the fourth century BC and fourth and fifth century AD respectively (Sati and Kumar 2004: 15–17). After the demise of the Vardhana Empire, it disintegrated into a number of small principalities ruled by local chieftains. The two constituent divisions of the state, the Garhwal and the Kumaon Mandals have existed for most part of their history as independent and hostile entities; their separate histories often intersected but merged together only in the nineteenth century.

The chronological history of Garhwal begins only in the eighth century AD, when Raja Kanak Pal started the famous 'Panwar' dynasty that would rule until the twentieth century. The word 'Garhwal' means the land of many 'garhs' or forts. This region was made up of many small forts ruled by local chieftains. In the fifteenth century, King Ajai Pal had unified the 52 separate principalities, each with its own garh, and merged them in his single kingdom. For the next 300 years, Garhwal remained as one kingdom, with its capital initially at Srinagar (on the left bank of Alaknanda river) which was shifted to Tehri early in the nineteenth century. Even during the reign of the mighty Mughals, Garhwal retained its independence, one of the few kingdoms in north India to have done so. But Garhwal and Kumaon had been fighting among themselves since late seventeenth century—these two kingdoms fought 35 wars between themselves, and both sides suffered immense losses without any conclusive victory for either (Bahadur 1916: 140–4).

The Panwars, or Shahs as they were called later, ruled Garhwal till their defeat by the invading Gurkhas from Nepal in 1803. Gurkhas ruled over the land till 1815, who subjected the indigenous population to brutality, enslavement, and misery—many were forced to flee outside Garhwal. Kumaon also came under the Gurkhas during this period (1790–1815); in fact, most of Uttaranchal and even parts of Himachal came under their ruthless domination. Under the onslaught of the Gurkhas, the Panwar rulers had fled to the lower plains of Rishikesh, Haridwar, Kankhal, and Dehradun, from where they took the help of the British to reclaim their kingdom after the conclusive defeat of the Gurkhas by the British forces at Nalapani in 1814. But the trade-off proved costly; under the Treaty of Sigauli (December: 1815), they had to concede half of their kingdom including Pauri, Dehradun, and even the capital Srinagar to the British who merged it with the Kumaon hills, which also came under their domination at about this time (Kumar 2000: 50). The Shahs ruled over the truncated kingdom, known as the Tehri Garhwal kingdom, from 1815 to 1949.

People of Garhwal, who were oppressed and exploited under the British rule, took active part in India's freedom struggle and rose in revolt several times, the prominent among these being the forest uprising in Chandrabadni (1906), peasant revolts of Rawain (1930) and Saklana (1947) (Guha 1990: 84). Led by Praja Mandal, a popular movement that started growing in the late 1930s, they fought against both the British and the king who supported them. After independence, Praja Mandal continued its movement demanding democracy and end of the dynastic rule. Finally, in 1949, the 60th and the last Panwar ruler Manvendra Shah accepted the sovereignty of Indian Government and acceded to India and Tehri Riyasat was merged into the state of Uttar Pradesh as a district.

Kumaon followed a different trajectory. From the seventh to eleventh century AD, it was ruled by the Katyuri dynasty who had vastly expanded their empire. The eleventh century saw the decline of the Katyuri dynasty after which the once mighty kingdom gradually disintegrated into many small principalities ruled by local chieftains. During the twelfth century, Chand kings of Pithoragarh brought these principalities under a single kingdom. Their dynasty ruled for a long time, and like every dynasty, it was weakened by the internecine fights among clan members. Finally, they yielded to the Gurkhas who invaded and conquered the territory in 1790 (Kumar 2000: 74–5). The brutal reign of the Gurkhas brought unspeakable misery to the people of Kumaon, like the Garhwalis. Both were rescued from this misery by the British, as already narrated. There being no heir to the Kumaoni throne, the entire kingdom was made a part of the British Empire in India. Part of Garhwal that the British gained from them was also merged with Kumaon. Later in 1839, this territory was divided into two districts, Kumaon and Garhwal. Headquarters of the Kumaon division was shifted to Nainital, which was 'discovered' by the British in 1842. Later Kumaon district was split into Almora and Nainital districts.

Like the Garhwalis, Kumaonis also took active part in India's freedom struggle. The Kumaon Parishad was set up in 1916 by leaders like

Govind Ballabh Pant, Badri Dutt Pande, Har Govind Pant, and others, not only to oppose the British but also to fight against social evils like prostitution and tradition of 'Devadasis'. This focus on social and cultural issues was a hallmark of the emerging political consciousness in the hills of Kumaon and Garhwal from the late nineteenth century onwards. Like the Kumaon Parishad in Kumaon, Garhwal Sabha had emerged in Garhwal in 1914. 'Shilpkar Sabha' which came up in Kumaon around this time had contributed significantly to this social and political awakening. These organizations spearheaded the social reforms and inculcated pride in indigenous culture and language, leading to a kind of 'Renaissance' in the hills of Uttaranchal. Initially these efforts were within the established political framework and not overtly political, but ultimately they gave rise to nationalistic fervour, leading to resistance against colonial rule by the hill people. Kumaon Parishad eventually merged with the Congress in 1926 (Kumar 2000: 55–60). The Civil Disobedience Movement of 1930–34 sparked spontaneous response from hundreds of Kumaonis in Nainital and Almora. The Quit India Movement also evoked strong and sometimes violent responses from urban and rural areas alike.

Movement for Statehood

In 1856, British East India Company under Lord Dalhousie had formally annexed the state of Avadh from its ruling monarch Wazid Ali Shah. In 1801, the Doab—the fertile and rich 60,000-square-km territory between the Ganga and the Yamuna extending from Siwalik to Allahabad—was occupied by the East India Company under the Subsidiary Alliance of Lord Wellesley Avadh was made into a province in 1856. In 1901, Avadh was joined with Agra, which was a part of the Doab, to form the United Province of Agra and Avadh, the name of which was changed to United Provinces in 1935. In 1950, United Provinces was renamed as Uttar Pradesh and Uttaranchal remained a part of Uttar Pradesh until November 2000 when it became the 27th state of India.

The Uttaranchal region languished in backwardness and underdevelopment with a pathetic lack of infrastructure long after independence. Even in 1991, only 18 per cent of its 15,117 villages were connected by *Pucca* roads. It lagged way behind its neighbour Himachal Pradesh, which had very similar demographic and topographic features and was neglected by successive Uttar Pradesh (UP) Governments—so much so that in the psyche of the people of the region, the 'identity of the hill dwellers has been linked with their economic and social neglect for over forty years of independence. The lack of an autonomous political authority in the region has led to continuous economic degradation. The vast mineral, water, and forest resources of the hills have either remained unexploited or have been exploited by outsiders for the benefit of outsiders, thereby resulting in further 'development of under-development' in the region' (Kumar 2000: 80–1). It was perceived to be internal colonization by the UP Government, leading to the migration of youth away from the hills in search of education, economic opportunities, and employment.

The idea of a separate hill state for the region had been raised from time to time since the 1930s. The hill economy depended on the forest produces—timber, resin, fuel—that were used by the locals conventionally. But under the UP administration, these rights were transferred to the State Forest Department whereby contractors came to exercise complete control over these resources.[1] This contractor dominance bled the region economically, draining away the resources of the hills to outside, and in the process turning the region into a 'hinterland of the country's affluent classes and regions'. The raw materials from the forests and other natural resources like limestone and minerals were systematically being transported to factories located outside the hills, accentuating the process of 'development of under-development' and migration of its youth and labour force. The difficulties of terrain made agriculture sector unviable and without the state's support as in neighbouring Himachal Pradesh, neither could the horticulture sector create additional employment for the youth of the industry-starved region (Kumar 2000: 82–3). Thus, the region was turning into a money-order economy, subsisting on the remittance sent monthly by its migrant workers.

The first agitation for the hill state was organized in 1957, but the demand remained confined to the intellectual and political circles. It started to become a popular movement with the establishment of the Uttarakhand Rajya Parishad in 1973 that provided a platform for struggle for a separate state. The movement produced a political party called Uttarakhand Kranti Dal (UKD) in July 1979. In June 1987, a pledge was taken for formation of separate Uttarakhand state in an all-party meeting, but with only 19 MLAs in a house of 425 and with only four MPs from the region in a total of 85 from UP, its voice was audible neither in Lucknow nor in Delhi. It would be only in the 1990s that the movement would gather momentum.

1990s was the period when identity politics was making its foray in North India—most notably in UP and Bihar. With the dominance of the Congress Party coming to an end by 1989 in UP as well as in the national politics, identity-based regional parties started consolidating their strength. While the emergence of Bahujan Samaj Party (BSP) in the political firmament of UP signalled the consolidation of Dalits—Scheduled Castes and Scheduled Tribes, the OBCs like Yadavs, Kurmis, Koeries as well as the Muslims who broke away from the Congress vote bank rallied around the Samajwadi Party of Mulayam Singh Yadav. This caste and communal fragmentation and consequent polarization also saw the rise of BJP, which garnered the high caste voters, buttressed by its Hindutva politics, and deriving significant political mileage from the Babri Masjid—Ram Temple agitation in Ayodhya. These three parties emerged as dominant forces in UP politics in the 1990s.

In the mid-term elections of 1991, the BJP which had promised for resolution of the statehood issue of Uttarakhand in their election manifesto had formed the Government in UP after winning 199 seats.[2] In accordance with its electoral promise, the ruling BJP Government under Chief Minister Mr Kalyan Singh adopted a resolution for the creation of an 'Uttaranchal' state; it was not approved by the Government of India (Agarwal and Agarwal 1995: 110). The BJP Government lasted only for two years in UP and in 1993, UP faced another election, in which, despite winning 166 out of 393 Assembly seats, BJP could not form the Government. The SP and BSP with a combined strength of 165 seats but with the support of Congress and Janata Dal formed the government with Mr Mulayam Singh Yadav as the Chief Minister. Even this government would last for only two years. 1990s was indeed the era of polarization, bizarre coalitions, and deadlocks in UP politics. UP faced assembly elections four times during the period 1989–96—in 1989, 1991, 1993, and 1996.

Mulayam was not against the formation of a hill state in UP as he had nothing to lose by agreeing to it. SP had practically no base there, having elected only one MLA; besides, formation of a separate

Uttarakhand would mean dilution of strengths of both BJP and Congress in the post-Uttaranchal UP Assembly. Soon after coming to power, in 1994 he set up two committees, the Vinod Barthwal Committee and the Ramashankar Kaushik Committee,[3] for evaluating the demands for Uttarakhand. In June 1994, the Kaushik Committee submitted its report supporting the formation of a hill state in UP covering nine districts—eight in Uttarakhand hills and the Haridwar district—with the village known as Gairsain as the proposed capital of the new state (Sati and Kumar 2004: 20). The UP Assembly adopted a resolution on 24 August 1994 for the formation of a new state and again sent it to the centre. But meanwhile, a decision taken by the UP Government would make the hills erupt in anger.

Earlier, the V P Singh Government (1989–90) at the centre had retrieved the Report of the Mandal Commission (1978–80) out of cold storage into which the previous Congress Governments had put it and accepted its recommendations in August 1990 to reserve 27 per cent of all government jobs as well as seats in government-funded educational institutions, plunging the entire country and especially Uttar Pradesh into political and social turmoil, with rallies and riots between pro and anti-reservationists breaking out spontaneously all over the country. The Mandalization of UP politics greatly benefited the SP and helped it to come to power in December 1993 (Verma 2003: 255–8). One of the first decisions of this government was to pass the Uttar Pradesh Public Services (Reservation for Scheduled Castes, Scheduled Tribes, and Other Backward Castes) Act on 22 March 1994, providing 21 per cent reservation for Scheduled Castes, 2 per cent for Scheduled Tribes, and 27 per cent for Other Backward Castes. In June 1994, the Uttar Pradesh Panchayat Act 1947, was also amended, extending the same reservations to Panchayat Raj institutions (Ayres and Oldenburg 2004: 140). Thus, the policy of UP was being imposed on the proposed new state of Uttarakhand without consulting their people. This was the spark needed to ignite the hills.

These announcements galvanized the till-then marginalized Uttarakhand agitation and transformed it into a powerful mass movement for formation of the new state. The reservation issue, in fact, became the turning point in the history of the movement. As *India Today* observed in its 13 September 1994 issue: 'What angers the hill residents is that the 27 per cent quota is being enforced in the hills although the OBCs constitute less than 2 per cent of the population here...but Mulayam remained strangely unmoved. He has variously dismissed it as a 'BJP conspiracy' and even tried to play off the hill folk against the people in the plains. At a recent press conference, he said the stir could boomerang if the people in the plains decided to target the hill folk working there.' The Uttarakhand movement was actually forging a different identity for the hill people, quite distinct from the identity that sprang from caste-based politics in the plains of UP, 'a united Uttarakhandi identity among Garhwalis and Kumaonis who had historically coexisted in a relationship of sometimes confrontational, and at other times, cordial hostility. That the independent cultural identity of the Garhwali or Kumaoni could be willingly subsumed in the new identity of the Uttarakhandi became possible precisely because this new identity invoked not some primordial cultural affiliation, but an essentially secular shared attribute, viz, the specificity of belonging to the mountains, and the distinctiveness of mountain society' in short a 'Pahari' identity as opposed to those belonging to the 'Maidan' (Jayal 2000).

Demonstrations broke out everywhere in the region against this unjust policy. The most vociferous responses were predictably from students and young people who feared that the hills would now be swamped with 'outsiders' from the plains, who would monopolize the very few educational and employment opportunities available there. On 2 August 1994, a major demonstration broke out in Pauri, followed by another on 8 August in which police had to resort to lathi charge and firing, injuring several agitators. In the days following, several demonstrations were held at Pauri, Joshimath, Uttarkashi, and other places. On a demonstration at Khatima near Nainital, on 1 September 1994, police again opened fire, killing several persons and injuring many more. Curfew was imposed in Haldwani and Khatima. The following day, police again opened fire on the protestors in Mussoorie, killing seven. Mass protests broke out all over following these killings, and on 8 and 9 September 1994, all markets in the hill region remained closed. What followed these demonstrations was complete mayhem and repression in a scale not witnessed very often in independent, democratic India.

On 14 September 1994, police forces had unleashed terror on demonstrators by resorting to indiscriminate lathi charges and firing at Pauri, Ukhimath, Khatima, and Mussourie. On 2 October, on the birthday of Mahatma Gandhi, the prophet of non-violence, Mulayam Singh's forces fired at a rally in Muzaffarnagar, killing at least ten and injuring over a hundred people; even women protesters were not spared from police brutalities. On 3 October, three more fell victim to police firing in Nainital, Rishikesh, and Dehradun. Despite curfew, destruction of government property and accompanying violence by both sides continued unabated. The UP Congress Party which was supporting the Mulayam Singh Government as well as BJP demanded dismissal of the UP Government. On 7 October 1994, one more woman was killed in police firing and the Allahabad High Court ordered a CBI probe into the violence and police firing. On 13 October, another person was killed in Dehradun during curfew (Agarwal and Agarwal 1995: 454–8). This was a mass upsurge and the hills were erupting with anger. As reported by the *Indian Express* (New Delhi) on 22 September 1994, 'Never before have the hills of western UP reverberated in such union with peoples' voices as they are now. From the picturesque vales of Dehradun to the inhospitable upper reaches of Garhwal hills, the cry for fulfillment of just aspirations has taken the form of a demand for a separate state. It is a virtual mass movement on a scale perhaps unparalleled in the recent past... What initially began as a student stir against the reservation policy has now turned into a full-fledged movement for a separate state of Uttarakhand ...'

But the Centre was not willing to concede to the demands for creation of a new state as yet. 'The Prime Minister P V Narasimha Rao told an Opposition delegation on 3 October that granting full statehood for UP hill regions would open the Pandora's Box and lead to similar demands elsewhere in the country.'[4] He was in favour of an autonomous status for the hill region. But the anger in the hills was enormous. As the local poet Chary Chand Chanola wrote, *Pahar ka swabhav hai chup rehna/ jis din lagegi unke swabhiman par chot/ pani mein paida hogi aag/ pahhar-pathar ban jayega bom* (The mountains are inherently tranquil and the rivers flow quietly; the day their inherent nature is hurt, there will be fire in the rivers and the Himalayas will burst like a bomb.)[5] As the *Independent* (Bombay) reported angrily on 6 October, 1994, 'Pseudo-socialist rhetoric coupled with pro-rich policies must not be allowed to masquerade as social justice .... The message must be unequivocal: Uttarakhand is not for burning.' The categorical refusal of Prime

Minister Rao and his Home Minister S B Chavan further fuelled the agitation. In a poignant story, *Hindustan Times* (New Delhi: 1994) described the situation in the hills, 'Blood stains mark the route to the hill districts of Uttar Pradesh – the curfew bound 'abode of the Gods'.... It is almost as if a primordial manthan (churning of the oceans) has taken place in the normally placid mountain sides. Nobody shouts slogans anymore...only the eyes reflect the dark abyss of determined fury....In Uttarakhand there is no debate any longer. Uttarakhand IS.'

The situation was turning extremely volatile and was almost getting out of hand; hills were, in fact, resounding with calls to arms for independence from 'the raj of Mulayam Singh'.[6] Meanwhile other events in UP politics would temporarily shift the focus away from the agitation as political uncertainty was again enveloping Uttar Pradesh, after BSP suddenly withdrew support to the Government in UP on June 2 1995, in a sort of a coup, prompting Mulayam to launch a vicious physical attack by his supporters on the BSP leader Mayawati in the State Guest House where she was staying, in a dastardly act of political brinkmanship. Mayawati survived the attack, but the two would forever be archrivals from that point. The next day, backed by the BJP from outside, she became the Chief Minister of UP, but her government lasted only four months. It went to polls again in September 1996. But in a deft move, to take the momentum away from the Uttarakhand movement, on 15 August 1996, Prime Minister H D Deve Gowda, announced the centre's intention of forming the Uttarakhand State and asked for the opinion of the State Assembly on it, though there was no Assembly at that time. But the agitators felt their objective has been achieved and there was a lull in the agitation (Sati and Kumar 2004: 22).

The 1996 assembly elections returned a hung Assembly. BJP having secured 174 seats in a House of 424 seats emerged as the largest party. But Governor Ramesh Bhandari placed the state under the President's rule without even inviting it to form the government. Finally BJP and BSP together formed the government in March 1997, on the basis of a novel agreement on the rotation of chief ministership. Mayawati became Chief Minister for the first six months, after which she refused to hand over power and broke the alliance, forcing the BJP leader Kalyan Singh to engineer 'splits' and large scale defections from Congress and BSP both. Thus a government headed by Kalyan Singh took over the reins of administration in September 1997. On 24 April 1997, UP State assembly passed a motion urging the centre again for creation of the hill state. Meanwhile at the centre, the NDA Government had come to power after the mid-term Lok Sabha elections in 1998, with Atal Behari Vajpayee as the Prime Minister. The Uttar Pradesh Reorganisation Bill 2000 creating the new State called Uttaranchal was passed in the Parliament in August 2000. On 9 November 2000, Uttaranchal state was inaugurated as the 27th state of the Indian Union with Dehradun as the capital, thus fulfilling the aspirations of the hill people after a long-drawn and bitter struggle and after the avoidable sacrifices of so many lives. In August 2006, Union Cabinet conceded the four-year-old demand of the Uttaranchal Assembly to rename the state as Uttarakhand.

In the 49th Meeting of the National Development Council held on 1st September, 2001 and presided over by Prime Minister Vajpayee, special category status was accorded to the newly created state of Uttaranchal. All states welcomed its inclusion in the list of special category states; however, some states expressed the view that there were other areas that needed special attention and such areas should also be considered for special category status instead of including states as a whole in the special category. Some states also expressed the view that inclusion of a fresh member should be accompanied by overall higher plan allocation to the special category states as a whole, as otherwise the existing states belonging to this category would stand to lose in terms of plan allocations. This was necessary especially in the view of the fact that the externally aided projects and other special requirements were taking more and more of the plan funds, leaving less and less for meeting the needs of others including the existing special category states.[7]

Socio-Economic Changes

Before statehood, Uttarakhand was a backward region of Uttar Pradesh incapacitated by various factors, but after becoming a state, it has made great strides in development. But development has somehow been confined to the plains and foothill areas of the state, due obviously to their better accessibility and better economic fundamentals. The hill districts have been left behind in the process of development, where primarily, it still remains a remittance economy, characterized by low productivity, shortage of inputs, and lack of marketing facilities forcing villagers to produce only for self-consumption. Distribution of its population is also uneven, with almost half the population being concentrated in just three districts, Haridwar, Dehradun, and Udham Singh Nagar. The three districts of Champawat, Rudra Prayag, and Bageshwar together account for only 8 per cent of state population. The process of urbanization in the state has been slow, with 69 per cent of the population still living in rural areas in 2011 compared to 74 per cent in 2001. Even then, Uttarakhand at the time of its creation was more urbanized than most of the other special category states, and its 26 per cent urban population was comparable with the national figure of 28 per cent in 2001.

Annexure 7.1 shows the progress of socio-economic parameters of Uttarakhand since its formation. At the time of its creation, economic activities in Uttarakhand were limited mainly within the primary sector with conspicuous absence of secondary and tertiary sectors. People migrated to the plains and other states in search of livelihood. There were some small and medium scale industries in the Terai region; agriculture, horticulture, and subsistence farming were the major occupations and sources of sustenance of the people. In 1993–94, agriculture employed 80 per cent of the state population but generated hardly any savings and the capital formation consequently was extremely low (Krishna 2002: 1843).

Soon after attainment of statehood, however, the picture began to change. The per capita income in 2001–02 was Rs 13,924 at current prices, compared to the national average of Rs 18,450. In 2006–07, it rose to Rs 29,373 and was catching up with the national average of Rs 31,206. By 2010–11, the per capita income of the state (Rs 73,819) was way ahead of the national average of Rs 54,021. The structure of state income also underwent some changes. The contribution of primary sector to the state NSDP in 2010–11 came down to only 14 per cent, from 29 per cent a decade ago. The predominantly agrarian character of the state was changing into a state driven now by tertiary (54 per cent share in NSDP in 2011) and secondary sectors (31 per cent share in NSDP in 2011) just after one decade of its existence as a separate state.

During the period 2000–05, Uttarakhand had witnessed an impressive real growth rate of 11.6 per cent per annum, largely due to growth of secondary and tertiary sectors. The growth of Uttarakhand stands out in stark contrast to the growth scenario in its neighbouring states during the same period (Himachal: 8.6 per cent, UP: 7.8 per cent, J&K: 5.8 per cent). The inevitable conclusion was that being a part of Uttar Pradesh had stymied its growth and hindered its development. Growth in its secondary sector was truly impressive, at nearly 14 per cent per annum. Registered organized manufacturing provided a boost to its economy, and the annual growth in services sector almost doubled to 19 per cent during this period. Table 7.1 shows the difference in growth rates before and after separation of the state from Uttar Pradesh.[8] The change as reflected in this table was visible and the growth was palpable to any tourist who had visited the state immediately after its formation like this author who had witnessed the massive pace of developmental works and construction of roads and bridges in 2003.

But despite significant growth in income, in 2004–05, nearly 40 per cent of the state's population lived below the poverty line, compared to the national average of 27.5 per cent. The incidence of poverty in Uttarakhand was in fact higher than in Uttar Pradesh (32.8 per cent)

Table 7.1 Growth Rates of Uttarakhand before and after Formation of the State

	CAGR		
	1993–94 prices		2004–05 prices
Industry	**1993–94 to 1999–00**	**1999–00 to 2004–05**	**2004–05 to 2010–11**
Agriculture & allied activities	2.33	1.81	1.49
Mining & quarrying	3.75	29.18	–0.51
Manufacturing	–4.52	13.99	26.90
Electricity, gas & water supply	8.46	19.23	13.41
Construction	2.00	20.42	5.19
Trade, Hotels & restaurants	1.19	10.39	22.39
Transport, storage & communication	5.39	16.28	16.46
Banking & insurance	6.92	7.87	19.14
Community and social services	6.01	12.81	4.89
All	**3.17**	**10.03**	**13.63**

Source: Mamgain (2008) and www.mospi.gov.in.

which had lower per capita income, and Himachal Pradesh (10 per cent) which had about 40 per cent higher per capita income than Uttarakhand. In 2004–05, the per capita incomes at 1993–94 prices in the three states were respectively Rs 21278, Rs 11599, and Rs 29630. Per capita income seemed to have little relationship to poverty across the states.[9] For Uttarakhand, a combination of high per capita income and high poverty was indicative of high inequality and inequitable distribution of income, with higher levels of disparity compared to the other states. However, the Gini Coefficient of Uttarakhand as per NSSO 61st Round data (2004–05) was 0.31 (Rural: 0.29 and Urban 0.33), which was not very high. The high poverty ratio of Uttarakhand seems to be a bit paradoxical. A BPL survey carried out in the rural areas in 2002 identified only 31.48 per cent of rural families eligible for the BPL benefits under the various plan schemes for poverty alleviation, which also does not point to the high poverty estimates following the Planning Commission methodology.[10] In 2011–12, however, following the Tendulkar Methodology, poverty in Uttarakhand was estimated at only 11.3 per cent, which appear to be closer to reality.

There were, however, wide variations in poverty ratios across the districts and between rural and urban areas, as in every state in India. In Uttarakhand, according to Planning Commission, estimates for 2004–05, urban and rural poverty ratios were respectively 36.5 per cent and 40.8 per cent, compared to all India figures of 25.7 per cent and 28.3 per cent respectively. While the neighbouring state of Himachal Pradesh had poverty ratio of 3.4 per cent and 10.7 per cent for urban and rural areas respectively, the comparative figures in UP were 30.6 per cent and 33.6 per cent respectively.[11]

The Green Revolution of UP had almost passed the state by, except irrigated valleys, where the HYV-seeds programme had been successful. The low hills (between 600 to 1000 metres) are more suitable for tropical fruits than crop production. However, the infrastructure support like soil and water conservation measures, irrigation facilities, access to bank credit, and marketing infrastructure were largely missing when the state was created. The agricultural yields in Uttarakhand had historically been low due to the above factors as well as the fragmentation of holdings and near total dependence on rainfall. Farm mechanization was also largely absent and irrigation costly and uneconomical (Krishna 2002: 1843–44). One decade of existence as a separate state has not changed this scenario in agriculture. The state is still unable to tap its stupendous biodiversity in medicinal and aromatic plants, or to increase the farm income through livestock and dairy development.[12] Investment in agriculture is also low.

The state is not very rich in natural resources, apart from its thick forests, it has few mineral resources like dolomite, limestone, magnesite, steatite, etc. In 2000–01, the total value of mineral production was only Rs 6 crore, of which magnesite alone accounted for more than 50 per cent. Uttarakhand is a major producer of magnesite in India; its magnesite reserves in Almora and Pithoragarh districts account for about 66 per cent of total recoverable reserves in the country. But industries based on magnesite are yet to come up in the state. Among the secondary sector, manufacturing accounted for 22 per cent share of NSDP in 2010–11, up from 12 per cent a decade ago. There were 15,285 registered small scale units in the state in 2001–02, employing 50,541 employees. By 2010–11, the number of units had grown to 37,928, while employment had grown by more than three times to 1.62 lakh. There were 29 identified industrial clusters in the state having more than 100 units in each, the largest among them being in Udham Singh Nagar and Uttarkashi. Most of the industrialization in Uttarakhand had taken place in Udham Singh Nagar, Haridwar, Dehradun, and Nainital districts. Uttarkashi, Rudraprayag, Pithoragarh, and Chamoli did not have any registered factory at all.[13]

Tourism is perhaps the most important contributor to Uttarakhand's economy. It can also be the biggest source of employment as well, besides facilitating linkages for local area development. It has been estimated (2009) that every rupee of tourist expenditure generates an output of Rs 0.65 in the tourism sector and Rs 2.17 in the whole economy. Similarly it has been estimated that every rupee of tourism expenditure generates an income of Rs 0.736 in the economy taking into account the direct and indirect effects, and that every Rs 1 lakh spent on tourism creates 1.126 jobs. Given this potential, tourism can be the biggest source of employment in Uttarakhand, besides creating linkages for local area development.

Uttarakhand has 178 important tourist places covering places of pilgrimage, cultural tourism, nature tourism, adventure tourism, wildlife tourism, eco-tourism, and amusement and leisure tourism. Tourist arrival to Uttarakhand increased from 9.6 million during 2001 to 19.45 million in 2006, or from 3.97 per cent to 4.12 per cent of all tourists visiting India during these years respectively.[14] Uttarakhand is the first state in the country to have created a Tourism Development Board by legislation. The Board has already adopted the Uttarakhand Tourism Development Master Plan for 2007–22 in coordination with the Government of India, United Nations Development Programme, and World Tourism Organization. But the tourism infrastructure is still far short of meeting the needs of world class tourism infrastructure like hotels and roads.

The physical infrastructure of the state was indeed very poor at the time of its formation and remains so even after a decade of its existence as a separate state. Being a hill state with altitudes varying between 100 metres and 7800 metres, and with minimal rail network confined mainly to the plains and the foothills, connectivity is rather poor. The length of National Highways had increased significantly during the first five years after creation of the state (1328 kms from 526 kms). 40 per cent of the state's 15,761 villages lacked access roads even in 2009.[15] However, by 2010–11, the state had achieved almost universal electrification (99 per cent) of its villages.

As regards power, the state had installed generating capacity of 1337 MW in 2001-02, of which 1019 MW was owned by the state. Of the total installed capacity 1050 MW (79 per cent) was due to hydro-electricity alone. In 2010–11, the total installed capacity increased to 1800 MW, the increase being only on account of hydro and steam generated electricity. The per capita consumption of electricity in Uttarakhand (717 kwh in 2010–11) was always higher than the national average. Uttarakhand has a huge potential for hydel electricity generation estimated at more than 18000 MW, not even 10 per cent of which is being currently exploited.[16] As regards financial infrastructure, the credit deposit ratio (CDR) of the banking sector was low till 2006–07; even in 2010–11, the CDR was only 40 per cent compared to the national average of more than 75 per cent.

The state has made significant progress in improving its social infrastructure. The per capita expenditure on education as well as health had increased nearly three folds during the decade 2001–11. The educational and health infrastructure expanded significantly as a result. The teacher: pupil ratio and gross enrolment ratio of the state are both comparable with the national averages. The state has expanded its infrastructure in respect of higher education also, having increased the number of institutions of higher learning by almost twice during the last decade. The number of universities also went up from six to 16 during this period. It is fast emerging as an educational hub in respect of technical education in India.

Health infrastructure in Uttarakhand comprises a network of rural and urban healthcare institutions. Apart from district and sub-divisional hospitals, there is a three-tier arrangement of community health care centres, primary health centre, and sub-centres at the district, block, and village levels respectively in the rural areas, as in other states. For the urban areas, there is a network of hospitals and dispensaries managed by municipalities, apart from state hospitals. During the last decade, the state had significantly expanded the number of healthcare institutions under each category.

Public Finance

On its creation in November 2000, Uttarakhand Government had inherited a liability of Rs 3186 crore on account of internal debt (Rs 1114 crore), loans and advances from the Central Government (Rs 1619 crore) and Provident Fund and Small Savings, etc. (Rs 432 crore). In 2000–01, it ended up with a gross fiscal deficit (GFD) of Rs 3630 crore. The special category status was awarded to the state soon afterwards, and the liberal central grants that came along with it did address its fiscal and financial problems to a large extent, and in the next year, 2001–02, the GFD came down to only Rs 643 crore (4.1 per cent of GSDP). Capital outlay was increased continuously, from Rs 208 crore in 2001–02 to Rs 1855 crore in 2010–11, for building up the infrastructure of roads and transportation that was grossly neglected earlier by the UP Government. But despite increases in borrowing to finance the increased capital outlay, FRBM Act legislated in 2006 ensured that the state GFD remained within the FRBMA limit of 3 per cent. In 2010–11, the GFD was Rs 1844 crore (2.2 per cent of GSDP).

The state's revenue increased by more than four times during the period 2001–11, but the revenue account went into a surplus of Rs 898 crore in 2006–07 from a deficit of Rs 331 crore in 2001–02, though the surplus could not be maintained at that level. In 2010–11, the revenue account had a nominal surplus of only Rs 14 crore. While the yield from non-tax revenue stagnated after 2006–07, state's own tax revenues increased more than four times during this period, from 809 crore to Rs 3727 crore, while the total revenue receipts including central grants and state's share of central taxes increased more than six times. The share of state's own revenue in the total revenues has practically remained the same (about 38 per cent) during the decade and the state's own revenue could barely meet 40 per cent of its revenue expenditure in 2010–11. Central transfers constituted about 56 per cent of the state's total revenues throughout the decade, but these funds financed as much as 43 per cent of its total expenditure of the state in 2010–11, compared to only 24 per cent in 2001–02, further deepening the state's dependence on central funds despite substantial increases in its own revenue. Government expenditure constituted 29 per cent of the state GSDP in 2001–02; in 2010–11, it came down to only 18 per cent, indicating increasing economic activities outside the public sector.

The state has created some fiscal space by reducing its debt servicing charges. In 2000–01, debt servicing used to constitute almost 40 per cent of total expenditure; in 2010–11, it came down to only 14 per cent. Outstanding debt as a percentage of GSDP also reduced from 27 per cent to 24 per cent during 2001–2011. However, the borrowings were not yet being fully utilized for creation of capital assets, as shown by the 59 per cent ratio between capital outlay and capital receipts in 2010–11. However, the debt position appears to be within manageable limits. The special category status had served the state well to effect improvement in its fiscal and financial scenario by increasing capital outlay and utilizing the plan assistance productively for developmental purposes.

Planning: Linkage between Investment and Growth

Table 7.2 shows the sectoral plan outlay in the Uttaranchal areas and Uttarakhand state since the Seventh Plan (1985–90). Given the initial historical backwardness of the state, significant investments had to be made in agriculture and rural development, social services, transport, and communication as well as energy. During the seventh eighth, and ninth Plans, agriculture and rural development and transport claimed half of the total plan outlay. Social services like education and health were given high priority throughout; during the eleventh Plan, 39 per cent of the total plan funds were allocated to social services with education alone claiming 10 per cent of total plan allocations. Higher plan

Table 7.2 Plan Outlay/Expenditure in Uttaranchal Area and Uttarakhand: Seventh Plan to Eleventh Plan (per cent)

Major Heads of Development	7th Plan	8th Plan	9th Plan	10th Plan	11th Plan
	Percentage share in total outlay (per cent)				
Economic Services	68	71	65	61	59
Agriculture and Rural Development	34	37	28	19	16
Special Area Programmes				0	0
Irrigation and Flood Control				5	6
Energy	13	13	9	13	12
Industry and Minerals	4	3	1	5	1
Transport & Communication	16	14	24	15	20
Science, Technology, Environment and General Economic Services	2	4	2	4	5
Social Services	28	23	30	35	39
Education				11	10
Medical and Public Health				4	5
Water Supply and Sanitation				6	6
Housing				0	1
Urban Development				6	8
Others Social Services				7	8
General Services	4	6	5	4	2
Grand Total (Rs Crore)	1,075	2,104	4,430	11,776	42,798

Source: Statistical Diary, Uttarakhand Division, 1995, State Planning Institute, Govt of Uttar Pradesh, and Ninth Five Year Plan, Uttaranchal Sub-Plan, Govt of UP.

allocations had been a major factor in the expansion of educational infrastructure within the state. Since the Tenth Plan, irrigation and flood control were also accorded due importance. During the Tenth Plan (2002–07), the newly formed state had significantly increased the allocations for forestry, rural development, irrigation and flood control, industry, welfare of SCs/STs and urban development. Road transportation was given the highest priority with 14 per cent of allocations going into it.[17]

Created with a legacy of backwardness and without much economic opportunities, Uttarakhand did not initially have the kind of infrastructure that could address the problems of its inaccessible and harsh geographic terrains. The state would have taken ages to come up to the present stage of development and to achieve the kind of socio-economic progress it has achieved without the special assistance which accompanied its special category status. Even with that, there were problems that could not be addressed during the last ten years, like modernization of agriculture, diversification of sources of livelihood for the hill people, exploiting the huge potential for developing hydel power or creation of world-class tourism infrastructure. But it is undeniable that the state has achieved remarkable progress in the few years since its formation and significantly accelerated economic growth, though this growth and development has been uneven and somewhat lopsided. The special category status had indeed helped the state to achieve this level of development, but it has also, in turn, increased the state's dependence on centre rather than making it more self-reliant. Whatever it had achieved was facilitated by the absence of irreconcilable asymmetry within the state, a peaceful environment and some sincerity on the part of administration. But the fragility of the ecosystem and the effect of unplanned growth had been made apparent by the devastating calamities that visited the state during the peak of the tourist season in 2013, and it will take the state a long time to recover from it.

Annexure 7.1 Socio-Economic and Public Finance Indicators of Uttarakhand: 2000–01 to 2010–11

Parameters (Area: 53,483 sq km)	2000–01	2010–11
A. State Income		
NSDP (Rs Crore)	12,879	72,970
Per Capita Income (Rs)	15,482	73,819
Share of Primary Sector (%)	29	14
Share of Secondary Sector (%)	22	31
Share of Tertiary Sector (%)	49	54
% of People Below Poverty Line[i]	39.6 (2003–04)	11.3 (2011–12)

(Cont'd)

Annexure 7.1 (*Cont'd*)

Parameters (Area: 53,483 sq km)	2000–01	2010–11
B. Demography	**2001**	**2011**
Population (lakh)	84.89	101.17
Per cent of Rural Population	74	69
Per cent of SC/ST Population	21	18
Density of Population per sq.km,	159	189
Literacy Rate (%)	72	80
Females per 1000 Males	962	963
Per cent of Working Population	37	NA
Per cent of Working Population Engaged in the primary sector	58	NA
No. of Villages	15,761	15,761
Net Irrigated Area to Net Cultivated Area (%)	43.75	45.67 (2009–10)
C. Infrastructure	**2001–02**	**2010–11**
i. Education		
No. of Junior Basic and Senior Basic Schools	17,373	20,025
No. of Secondary and Higher Secondary Schools	1,827	2,776
No. of Other Institutions of Higher Learning	79	426
No. of Universities	7	16
Per Capita Revenue Expenditure on Education (Rs)	1,146	3,485
per cent of Expenditure on Education to Total Budget	15	21
ii. Public Health		
No. of hospitals (only Govt. Allopathic hospitals are taken)	325 (2003–04)	695
No. of hospital beds	1,080 (2003–04)	7,965
No. of Primary Health Centres and Sub-Centres	217 (2002–03)	257
No. of Health Sub-Centres	1,480 (2002–03)	2,004

(*Cont'd*)

Annexure 7.1 (*Cont'd*)

Parameters (Area: 53,483 sq km)	2000–01	2010–11
No of Community Health Centres	34 (2002–03)	55
Per Capita Expenditure on Health (Rs)	165	680
iii. Roads	**March 2000**	**March 2011**
Total Road Length (km)	18,946	35,950
Length of Surfaced Roads (Km)	7,559	NA
Length of National Highway (km)	526	1,376
Surfaced Road per 100 sq. Km	17	NA
Total Road per 100 sq Km	35	67
Total Road per 1000 population	2.23	3.55
iv. Electricity		
Per capita Power Consumption (kwh)	263	717
Generation of Electricity (million kwh)	2,229	4,906
Installed Capacity (MW)	1,337	1,800
Percentage of Villages Electrified	82 per cent	99 per cent
v. Post Offices and Banks		
Population served by a Post Office	NA	5,021
No. of Towns (population> 1 lakh)	4	6
No. of Bank Offices	857	1,514
Credit Deposit Ratio (%)	22	35
D. Industry	**2001–02**	**2009–10**
No. of Registered Small Scale Units	15,285	37,928
No. of persons employed	50,541	1,62,453
No. of Registered Factories	698	2344
Value of Output (Rs Crore)	5,214	79,322
Net Value Added (Rs Crore)	825	17,719
Profits (Rs Crore)	24	12,850
Gross Fixed Capita Formation (Rs Crore)	220	10,412
No. of Persons Employed in Factories	4,08,80	2,38,795

(*Cont'd*)

Annexure 7.1 *(Cont'd)*

Parameters (Area: 53,483 sq km)	2000–01	2010–11
E. Public Finance (Ratios)	**2001–02**	**2010–11**
Revenue Receipts		
Grants from Centre/ GSDP (%)	8.4	4.8
Share of Central Taxes/ GSDP (%)	1.0	2.9
Own Revenue/Revenue Expenditure (%)	33.0	37.9
Central Grants/Total Revenues (%)	50.8	35.0
Own Revenue/ Total Revenues (%)	37.2	38.0
Gross Fiscal Deficit/GSDP (%)	4.1	2.2
Outstanding Debt/GSDP (%)	26.6	23.6
Interest Payment/Revenue Expenditure (%)	17.3	13.8
Non-Developmental Expenditure/Total Expenditure (%)	23.2	27.4
Debt Servicing/Total Expenditure (%)	40.0	18.3
Expenditure on Education/GSDP (%)	4.3	3.7
Expenditure on Health/GSDP (%)	0.9	0.8
Capital Outlay/Capital Receipts (%)	10.3	58.9
Public Finance (Figures in Rs Crore)		
GSDP	**15,826**	**77,580**
Revenue Receipts		
Tax Revenue	1,122	6,865
Non-Tax Revenue	162	678
State's Own Revenue Receipts	971	4,405
Grants from Centre	1,324	4,065
State's Share of Central Taxes	151	2,460
Total Revenue	2,608	11,608
Capital Receipts	2,019	3,148
Total Receipts	4,627	14,756
Gross Fiscal Deficit	643	1,844
Revenue Deficit	331	14
Capital Outlay	208	1,855
Primary Deficit	136	240
Outstanding Debt	4,204	19,807

(Cont'd)

Annexure 7.1 *(Cont'd)*

Parameters (Area: 53,483 sq km)	2000–01	2010–11
Non-Developmental Revenue Expenditure	1,062	4,180
Interest Payment	507	1,604
Revenue Expenditure on Social Services	1,121	5,170
Revenue Expenditure on Economic Services	692	1,864
Expenditure on Education	673	3,134
Expenditure on Health	140	688
Grants to PRIs	64	408
Revenue Expenditure	2,939	11,622
Capital Expenditure	1,637	3,095
Total Expenditure	4,576	15,232
Capital Outlay	208	1,855
Appropriations to Contingency Fund		515
Debt Servicing (Principal Amount)	1,321	1,180
Loans and Advances etc.	108	60
Discharge of Debt Obligations (Principal + Interest)	1,828	2,784
Net Debt Receipts	191	364
Recovery of Loans and Advances	4	85

Source: Please see endnote 26 in Chapter 2 for data sources.
Note: i. Using Tendulkar Methodology.

Notes

1. *The UP Forest Act, 1980,* had explicitly prohibited villagers living in the vicinity of the forests from collecting firewood or grazing of their cattle within forest areas. This had alienated the villagers in no small measure.

2. 'The BJP recognizes that regional imbalances have developed in some states because of their size. The Party would appoint a Commission to report on formation of smaller states which are economically and democratically viable. Initially BJP will have Uttarakhand, Vananchal and Union Territory of Delhi as three new States of the Indian Union.'—Election Manifesto of BJP, 1991.

3. Vinod Barthwal was the national secretary of the SP. Ramashankar Kaushik was a Cabinet Minister in the Mulayam Singh Yadav Government.

4. *Hindustan Times,* New Delhi, October 5, 1994.

5. *Hindustan Times,* New Delhi, October 6, 1994.

6. *The Observer*, New Delhi, October 8, 1994.

7. Minutes of the 49th Meeting of the National Development Council, Planning Commission, Govt. of India, New Delhi.

8. Available at http://rstolia.in/wp/what-ails-uttarakhands-economic-development/ quoting Mamgain, R P, 'Growth, Poverty and Employment in Uttarakhand', *Journal of Labour and Development*, Vol. 13, No.2 &1, June 2008.

9. *Uttarakhand Development Report*, Planning Commission, Govt. of India, 87.

10. *Uttarakhand Development Report*, Planning Commission, Govt. of India, 195–6.

11. *Uttarakhand Development Report*, Planning Commission, Govt. of India,196.

12. *Uttarakhand Development Report*, Planning Commission, Govt. of India, 92–3.

13. *Uttarakhand Development Report*, Planning Commission, Govt. of India, 93–5.

14. *Uttarakhand Development Report*, Planning Commission, Govt. of India, 105–06.

15. *Uttarakhand Development Report*, Planning Commission, Govt. of India, 447–8.

16. *Uttarakhand Development Report*, Planning Commission, Govt. of India, 415–6.

17. *Uttarakhand Development Report*, Planning Commission, Govt. of India, 119–22.

8 Evaluation of Current Socio-Economic and Developmental Parameters of Special Category States

Overall Assessment

In the foregoing chapters, the socio-economic realities of the individual special category states were discussed and the progress of their socio-economic indicators was tracked over the period since they were accorded the special category status through 2011. In these chapters, the developmental courses followed by these states were traced individually, since the problems faced by each state were unique in some way, and so were the measures devised and applied for their resolution, which may not always have worked satisfactorily. There was no way these problems and situations could have been generalized. However, it is also imperative to assess the efficacy of the policies and developmental paths followed by the individual states and evaluate their performance on a common scale. This would indicate where they are in relation to each other and also in relation to the other states outside the special category. For this purpose we select two reference points in time, 2001 and 2011, and use the all-India average as a standard of comparison.

The socio-economic parameters of the individual special category states relating to the years 2001 and 2011 have been listed out in the preceding chapters. Table 8.1 computes the growth rates as well as vertical and horizontal shifts in the values of these parameters over the decade, and also compares these shifts with corresponding shifts in the national averages pertaining to those parameters.

Table 8.1 Progress in Socio-Economic Parameters of Special Category States between 2001 and 2011

	Arunachal Pradesh	Assam	Himachal Pradesh	Jammu & Kashmir	Manipur	Meghalaya	Mizoram	Nagaland	Sikkim	Tripura	Uttarakhand	All India
A. State Income												
Annual Growth Rate of NSDP (2001–2011)[i]	17.5	11.5	12.8	12.6	11.0	13.6	13.9	13.1	22.7	12.5	18.9	**14.2**
Growth rate of Per Capita Income (Rs) (At current prices)	14.8	10.0	11.6	10.6	8.9	12.1	11.1	13.1	21.1	11.2	16.4	**12.5**
Change in the Share of Primary Sector (per cent) (2001–2011)	+7	–9	–6	–8	–6	–10	0	–6	–14	0	–15	**–10**
Change in the Share of Secondary Sector (per cent)	3	7	6	6	5	6	2	–2	39	–6	9	**1**
Change in the Share of Tertiary Sector (per cent)	-10	2	0	2	1	4	-2	8	-25	6	5	**9**

	Arunachal Pradesh	Assam	Himachal Pradesh	Jammu & Kashmir	Manipur	Meghalaya	Mizoram	Nagaland	Sikkim	Tripura	Uttarakhand	All India
Change in the percentage of people below poverty line (2001–2011)	1	−4	1	7	8	−22	2	−14	−24	−20	−29	**-4**
B. Demography												
Annual growth rate of Population (per cent)	2.4	1.4	1.2	2.2	1.6	2.7	2.0	−0.1	1.1	1.5	1.7	**1.6**
Change in the percentage of Rural Population (2001–2011) (per cent)	−3	−1	0	−2	−5	0	−3	−11	−15	−9	−4	**-3**
Change in the density of Population per sq.km.	4	57	14	24	19	29	10	−1	10	46	33	**57**

(Cont'd)

Table 8.1 (*Cont'd*)

	Arunachal Pradesh	Assam	Himachal Pradesh	Jammu & Kashmir	Manipur	Meghalaya	Mizoram	Nagaland	Sikkim	Tripura	Uttarakhand	All India
Change in the Literacy Rate (per cent)	12	10	7	14	11	13	3	14	13	15	8	**9**
Change in the sex ratio (2001-2011)	27	19	4	−17	9	14	37	22	14	13	1	**7**
Change in the percentage of Working Population	10	13	15	3	8	20	8	13	19	14	7	**12**
Growth in the number of Villages (per cent)	45	1	18	2	10	14	4	10	1	4	7	**8**
Change in the percentage of Net Irrigated Area to Net Cultivated Area	0	−2	1	1	NA	−1	−4	5	NA	9	2	**5**
Change in Infant Mortality Rate	−12	−23	−26	−4	−14	0	11	−15	−26	−20	−6	**−27**

	Arunachal Pradesh	Assam	Himachal Pradesh	Jammu & Kashmir	Manipur	Meghalaya	Mizoram	Nagaland	Sikkim	Tripura	Uttarakhand	All India
C. Infrastructure												
i. Education												
Growth in the number of Primary and Middle Schools (per cent)	69	14	29	66	–6	29	51	20	59	43	16	**33**
Growth in the number of Secondary and Higher Secondary Schools (per cent)	51	68	50	1	44	34	65	67	34	31	72	**49**
Growth in the number of Other Institutions of Higher Learning (per cent)	108	43	204	628	30	91	66	27	33	118	446	**208**

(Cont'd)

Table 8.1 *(Cont'd)*

	Arunachal Pradesh	Assam	Himachal Pradesh	Jammu & Kashmir	Manipur	Meghalaya	Mizoram	Nagaland	Sikkim	Tripura	Uttarakhand	All India
Change in the Number of Universities	1	3	11	3	0	5	1	2	4	2	10	**259**
Change in the Gross Enrollment Ratio (per cent)	53	−16	20	20	63	60	46	−4	26	25	18	**22**
Growth in Per Capita Revenue Expenditure on Education (per cent)	415	188	2625	176	80	149	158	292	345	83	149	**180**
Change in the share of Education Expenditure in Total Budget (per cent)	2	10	−4	3	−2	−1	−4	1	3	10	8	**−2**
ii. Public Health												
Growth in the number of Govt. Hospitals (per cent)	1050	9	6	21	118	333	69	45	560	88	19	**71**

	Arunachal Pradesh	Assam	Himachal Pradesh	Jammu & Kashmir	Manipur	Meghalaya	Mizoram	Nagaland	Sikkim	Tripura	Uttarakhand	All India
Growth in the number of Hospital Beds (per cent)	NA	–41	9	20	107	NA	22	–100	70	27	15	**67**
Growth in the number of Primary Health Centres and Sub-Centres (per cent)	–16	–3	1	538	14	4	5	8	–1	32	14	**4**
Growth in Per Capita Expenditure on Health (per cent)	458	266	2472	126	168	150	161	252	238	112	269	**179**
iii. Roads												
Growth in Total Road Length (per cent)	41	203	73	98	167	55	93	201	90	123	90	**42**

(*Cont'd*)

Table 8.1 *(Cont'd)*

	Arunachal Pradesh	Assam	Himachal Pradesh	Jammu & Kashmir	Manipur	Meghalaya	Mizoram	Nagaland	Sikkim	Tripura	Uttarakhand	All India
Growth in Length of Surfaced Roads (per cent)	91	269	150	25	83	NA	134	197	132	NA	NA	**53**
Change in Surfaced Road per 100 sq. km	8	11	62	1	17	NA	19	62	33	NA	NA	**25**
Increase in Total Road per 100 sq km	8	207	11	6	54	12	24	138	31	177	32	**34**
Increase in Total Road Length per 1000 Population (km)	2	5	3	1	4	1	3	12	3	5	1	**1**
iv. Electricity												
Increase in Per Capita power Consumption (kwh)	457	89	1041	697	56	321	286	88	658	240	454	**449**

	Arunachal Pradesh	Assam	Himachal Pradesh	Jammu & Kashmir	Manipur	Meghalaya	Mizoram	Nagaland	Sikkim	Tripura	Uttarakhand	All India
Increase in Generation of electricity (million kwh)	88	941	–8239	3695	15	528	90	–145	89	NA	2677	**343544**
Increase in Installed Capacity (MW)	49	-104	859	552	38	-139	56	3	11	85	463	**69786**
Increase in Percentage of Villages electrified	0	15	–13	–2	–8	14	–1	–1	5	34	11	**4**
v. Post Offices and Banks												
Growth in number of Bank Branches (per cent)	80	26	41	60	6	24	29	4	81	39	77	**39**
Change in Credit Deposit Ratio (per cent)	8	4	18	2	–6	7	19	14	24	12	9	**18**

(*Cont'd*)

Table 8.1 *(Cont'd)*

	Arunachal Pradesh	Assam	Himachal Pradesh	Jammu & Kashmir	Manipur	Meghalaya	Mizoram	Nagaland	Sikkim	Tripura	Uttarakhand	All India
D. Industry												
Growth in number of Registered Small Scale Units (per cent)	77	29	10	–1	–100	133	113	134	–29	31	148	**–100**
Growth in the Number of Persons Employed in SSIs (per cent)	292	143	86	109	–100	19	157	160	8	130	221	**54**
Growth in the Number of Registered Factories (per cent)	NA	95	336	137	63	213	NA	–28	NA	97	236	**61**
Growth in Value of Output (per cent)	NA	449	1008	1317	1428	2761	NA	353	NA	360	1421	**404**

	Arunachal Pradesh	Assam	Himachal Pradesh	Jammu & Kashmir	Manipur	Meghalaya	Mizoram	Nagaland	Sikkim	Tripura	Uttarakhand	All India
Growth in Net Value Added (per cent)	NA	418	1292	1642	1800	7757	NA	111	NA	163	2048	**391**
Growth in Profits (per cent)	NA	292	2066	26243	1823	−71267	NA	141	NA	78	53442	**993**
Growth in Gross Fixed Capita Formation (per cent)	NA	−68	1104	450	1167	4411	NA	1380	NA	614	4633	**505**
Growth in number of Persons Employed in Factories (per cent)	NA	61	297	138	461	584	NA	−24	NA	272	484	**59**

Note: i. In computing the growth rates, linear compounded growth rates have been used, as individual data for all intervening years were not available for all states over the period of about 50 years (1969–2011) used in this study.

It was pointed out that the central assistance that flowed to the special category states by virtue of this status had enabled them to survive their many geographical and historical handicaps. But then initially it was survival almost at the level of subsistence, since the slowly growing national economy could not generate enough revenues out of which to spare sufficient funds for adequate development of the special category states. This situation continued until the liberalization and economic reforms unleashed in the decade of the 1990s started producing their effects in the new millennium. These reforms pushed up growth rate to almost double digits, lifted millions of people out of poverty, and set free the enterprise, innovation, and creative energy of people, which were hitherto stifled under the oppressive command and control structure of decadent License-Permit Raj regime. As growth picked up across the country, their impact ought to have been felt across the special category states also, and the liberating process of economic reforms that was transforming the lives of citizens in almost all major states of the country ought to have benefited these states too, as forward and backward integrations of the economic reforms process should have extended their outreach to them as well. The growth generated by these reforms led to significant increases in government revenues and consequently, the flow of financial assistance to the special category states also increased substantially. But some states were in better positions to take advantage of the increased inflow of resources than others among them.

It cannot be denied that special category status had helped all these states survive the slow growth of economy in their initial years. But some among them could use the central funds to build up infrastructure and productive capacities of their economies; they were poised to take advantage of the reform process that had started affecting and altering the traditional economic relations within their territories also. Reforms had taken a decade to start producing visible results within the country. If we look for signs of development produced by these reforms within the special category states, the appropriate reference point would be the decade after the 1990s.

Development is often a function of investment in social and physical infrastructure, but mere investment is not enough if appropriate social and economic institutions and monitoring mechanisms are not created to channelize the investments properly and to oversee their effectiveness. An enabling environment is an essential prerequisite to promote a culture of entrepreneurship. Educational institutions play an important role in creating such an environment by imparting and inculcating the necessary skill-sets among the people. Side by side, the state must provide a stable political environment and reduce if not eliminate conflicts for economic activities to gather steam. Unfortunately, some of the special category states—Manipur, Nagaland, Jammu & Kashmir in particular—lacked such a stable political environment even in the new millennium due to their nagging insurgency which could not be tamed, though some other states—Tripura and Mizoram in particular and Assam to some extent—could largely extinguish the flames of anger, hatred, and distrust. The mindless violence that had raged in most of these states had already taken their toll, not only by driving away the little capital that was available within these states along with all their potential entrepreneurial talent they could have benefited from otherwise, but also by preventing the entry of any investment capital into their territories. Hence comparison with the mainstream states that did not suffer from these unusual handicaps would not be appropriate; even within the special category of states, problems faced by different states differed in their complexity, dimension, and magnitude. It is important to keep this in mind while interpreting the results of any comparison, whether within the special category states or with the rest of India. The rest of India often assumes a condescending attitude towards these states since they have to be given special assistance through this status. But it was only due to the special nature of their problems that they were accorded this status, by giving which the centre was not really obliging these states in any way. For keeping the national fabric intact, it was essential to address their uniqueness, backwardness, and developmental needs.

Comparison of Socio-Economic Indicators of Special Category States

In 2001, we note that the per capita income of most special category states was comparable to the national level of Rs 16,648 (at current prices)—only two of these states, Assam and Manipur—had per capita income levels which were significantly lower. But as many as seven of the 11 special category states were still primarily agricultural; share of their primary sector in the respective state income was more than 30 per cent as against the national average of 27 per cent; of these, the shares of the primary sector in Assam and Arunachal Pradesh were respectively 40 per cent and 35 per cent. Poverty was still widespread among these states; except Himachal Pradesh, Jammu & Kashmir, and Mizoram, all other states had higher percentage of people living below the poverty line as compared to the national average of 26 per cent (Tendulkar methodology). Poverty ratio in Uttarakhand was as high as 40 per cent, compared to 36 per cent in Assam, or 37 per cent in Sikkim.

Ten years hence (2011), this situation was dramatically reversed. The share of primary sector in the national economy had by then fallen to 17 per cent, and five out of 11 special category states had their shares of the primary sector in state income comparable to the national average (below 20 per cent), while Arunachal, Assam, Manipur, and Nagaland still retained more than a quarter of their income coming from the primary sector. In terms of per capita income, Sikkim, Tripura, Uttarakhand, and Himachal Pradesh surged much ahead of the national average, while Assam, Jammu & Kashmir, and Manipur had lagged far behind. The others had levels of per capita income comparable with the national average. It was interesting to note that while in 2001, only three states (Himachal Pradesh, Mizoram, and Nagaland) had per capita income levels above the national average; in 2011, as many as five states (Sikkim, Tripura, Uttarakhand, Himachal Pradesh, and Arunachal Pradesh) had raised their income levels above the national average, some of them substantially higher. But the most remarkable results were achieved in terms of reduction in the levels of poverty. While in 2001, only three states (Jammu & Kashmir, Himachal Pradesh, and Mizoram) had poverty ratios less than the national average, in 2011, all states except three (Assam, Arunachal Pradesh, and Manipur) had managed to reduce their poverty levels well below the national average—some had poverty ratio even lower than half the national average (Himachal Pradesh, Jammu & Kashmir, Uttarakhand). Four states had brought it down by more than 20 per cent (Uttarakhand, Sikkim, Meghalaya, and Tripura).

But despite these achievements, the ruralization of these states has not shown much change over the decade. Except for Nagaland, Sikkim, and Tripura, the percentages of rural population remained more or less the same over this period; for these three states, the level of ruralization even in 2011 was higher than the national average. Mizoram was the only one among this group of states that had a higher urban population (51 per cent) than rural. The level of literacy was far higher than the national averages in most states and comparable to the national averages in others. But in comparison to the national scenario, while in 2001, the literacy rates in four states (Assam, Meghalaya, Arunachal Pradesh, and Jammu & Kashmir) were lower than the national average, in 2011, only one of these, Meghalaya, could lift it above the national average, along with the other seven states. One reason for the rise in per capita income and consequent reduction in poverty was the significant increase in the percentage of working population for all states except Jammu & Kashmir; even for that state, the percentage of working population (49 per cent) was comparable to the national average of 51 per cent in 2011. Infant mortality rates were higher than the national average only in Assam and Meghalaya and life expectancy at birth was also comparable to the national averages in 2011.

As regards the educational infrastructure, except Manipur, there has been remarkable growth in the number of primary schools in five of the 11 states, while there has been moderate growth in respect of this in the other five states. Except Jammu & Kashmir, all other states had also registered significant growth in the number of secondary and higher secondary schools. As a result, the Gross Enrolment Ratio for classes I to VIII improved in all states except Assam and Nagaland. All states had registered moderate to significant growth in the number of institutions of higher learning, and except Manipur, all other states had also added new universities during this decade. Some states had significantly increased the per capita public expenditure on education; Himachal Pradesh had increased it more than 26 times during the past decade; except Manipur and Tripura, other states had also increased it by more than 100 per cent. In 2011, revenue expenditure on education had constituted more than 10 per cent of the state budget for nine out of the 11 states.

In respect of health infrastructure, even at the turn of the century, several states had heavily invested in creating reasonable public health infrastructure, since private players could not be expected to invest in such backward and remote regions. Among them were Assam, Himachal Pradesh, Manipur, and Uttarakhand. The other states, however, had rather poor health infrastructure in 2001. But ten years hence, most of these states had caught up with the rest. Significant growth in improving the public health infrastructure was noticed in Arunachal Pradesh, Sikkim, and Meghalaya. Himachal Pradesh had increased the per capita public expenditure on health by nearly 25 times during the last decade, way ahead of the other states, but the other states had also increased it at least twofold.

As regards physical infrastructure, four states (Assam, Manipur, Meghalaya, and Tripura) had more than doubled their total road length during this period and five states had more than doubled the length of their surfaced roads. Still by 2011, only three states (Tripura, Nagaland, and Himachal Pradesh) had surfaced roads per 100 sq kms above the national average; other states were hopelessly behind the national average in this respect. As regards electricity, in terms of the per capita power consumption, only three states (Himachal Pradesh, Jammu & Kashmir, and Sikkim) had achieved figures higher than the national average with Uttarakhand following closely behind, but states like Assam, Manipur, Mizoram, Nagaland, and Tripura had per capita electricity consumption which was not even half the national average. Except Arunachal Pradesh, other states had more than 60 per cent of their villages electrified, but in terms of adding to the installed capacity, only Himachal, Jammu & Kashmir, and Uttarakhand could record some progress over the decade. Even these states could not add 1000 MW to their installed capacity over the 10-year period.

As regards the financial infrastructure, except Assam, Himachal Pradesh, Jammu & Kashmir, and Uttarakhand, no other state had made real progress in terms of increasing the number of bank branches significantly; the growth in the number of bank branches over the decade had been modest in all states. The credit deposit ratio had also remained abysmally low in all the states, though some states (Sikkim, Mizoram, Himachal Pradesh, Nagaland, and Tripura) had increased it by more than 10 per cent over the period of 10 years. Still, with the exception of Mizoram, Himachal Pradesh, and Sikkim, the credit deposit ratio in other states had not reached even half the national average of 75 per cent; even in these three states, it was only marginally better than the others. But improvement in credit deposit ratio depends on lot of factors, like stability of economic and political climate, level of industrialization within the state, availability of physical infrastructure, especially power, as also skill, resources and market. Few of the special category states had all these in place. These are also the necessary preconditions for industrialization.

Naturally, absence of all these prerequisites had resulted in singular lack of industrialization in almost all special category states. There is hardly any medium or large scale industry worth the name in any of the special category states; the only industries that could be established were in the small scale sector, mostly informal. Reliable data on this were not available in respect of most states. Many states have resources waiting to be tapped, but the absence of viable infrastructure stands in the way of harnessing these resources. A list of the major resources available with these states is given in Table 8.2. Though there are a number of useful minerals available within these states, due to non-availability of viable all-weather roads to the sources of such minerals, lack of electricity, and absence of industrial climate as well as markets within these states, their extraction and processing were difficult, and for the same reasons, no industries could develop around these minerals within these states. The only major industries within the entire northeastern region are oil and tea in Assam.

Composite Development Index

To compare the socio-economic development performance of these states, a Composite Development Index has been developed comprising the following 10 indicators, each carrying equal weights and categorized under the following three groups:

(I) **Income, Employment, and Poverty Indicators** comprising (i) per capita income, (ii) share of primary sector in total state income (iii) percentage of main workers in total population and (iv) percentage of people below poverty line; indicators (i) and (iii) will impact the index positively and indicators (ii) and (iv) will impact the index negatively, all indicators carrying equal weights;

(II) **Socio-Economic Development Indicators** comprising (v) literacy rate (vi) infant mortality ratio (vii) percentage of villages electrified (viii) credit-deposit ratio, all indicators carrying equal weights and all indicators except (ix) contributing positively to the index; for indicators (x), the higher the value of the indicator, the less its contribution to the index; and

Table 8.2 Resources of Special Category States

States	Major Agricultural Products	Major Mineral Resources	Major Industries
Arunachal Pradesh	Rice, Pulses, Ginger, Sugarcane, Wheat, Millets, Oilseeds, Bamboo, Orchids	Dolomite, Graphite, Coal, Quartzite, Limestone, Marble	Agro-based small scale industries
Assam	Tea, Rice, Sugarcane, Maize, Pulses, Potato, Timber, Beetle nut, Banana, Bamboo	Petroleum, Natural Gas, Coal, Limestone	Oil, Tea, Silk and other Agro-based small scale industries
Himachal Pradesh	Maize, Paddy, Wheat, Potato, Apple	Limestone, Clay, Mica, Gypsum, Lead, Pyrites	Electronics and ICT, Brewing, Light Engineering, Pharmaceuticals, Wool and Textiles
Jammu & Kashmir	Paddy, Maize, Wheat, Barley, Apple, Almond, Timber	Limestone, Quartzite, Graphite, Gypsum	Machinery parts, Plastics, Chemicals and Drugs, Paper, Automobile equipment and Handicrafts, mostly in the small scale sector
Manipur	Paddy, Wheat, Pulses, Oilseeds, Pineapple, Cabbage, Bamboo	Ignite, Copper, Salt, Nickel, Asbestos, Limestone, Chromite	Handicrafts and Handloom, Cane and Bamboo based small scale industries
Meghalaya	Rice, Maize, Orange, Pineapple, Banana, Jackfruit, Potato, Turmeric, Tapioca, Areca nut, Jute, Mustard	Limestone, Coal, Granite, Kaolin, Iron Ore	Cement, Handloom and Handicrafts based industries, mostly in the small scale sector

(Cont'd)

Table 8.2 *(Cont'd)*

States	Major Agricultural Products	Major Mineral Resources	Major Industries
Mizoram	Paddy, Maize, Chilly, Ginger, Turmeric, Tobacco, Bamboo, Vegetables, Pineapple	Lignite, Sandstone, Pyrites	Agro and Forest-based industries, Handloom, Handicrafts, Electronics, mostly in the small scale sector
Nagaland	Rice, Sugarcane, Maize, Pulses, Potato, Bamboo	Coal, Limestone, Nickel, Cobalt	Agro-Forest based industries, Bio-Tech, Electronics, mostly in the small scale sector
Sikkim	Wheat, Rice, Maize, Barley, Buckwheat, Cardamom, Tea	Copper Ore, Dolomite, Graphite, Talc, Marble, Coal, Limestone	Brewing, Distilling, Tanning and Watch-making, Agro-Forest based small scale industries
Tripura	Rice, Potato, Sugarcane, Rabi Pulses, Maize, Bamboo	Hard Rock, Clay, Glass Sand, Limestone	Natural Gas, Tea, Rubber, Bamboo, Food Processing, Medicinal Plant, Handloom and Handicrafts industries, mostly in the small scale sector
Uttarakhand	Rice, Wheat, Barley, Corn, Mandua, Litchi	Limestone, Soapstone, Magnetite, Gypsum, Copper, Iron Ore	Sugar, Textiles, Paper, Agro-based industries, Pharmaceuticals, Mentha Oil, Stone Rolling

Source: Respective State Development Reports, Planning Commission, Government of India and also the web portals of the respective states.

(III) **State Intervention Indicators** comprising (xi) per capita revenue expenditure on education and (xii) per capita revenue expenditure on health, both having positive contributions to the index.

Income, employment, and poverty are all interrelated and are indicators of development, so are the socio-economic parameters listed above. State intervention is a major factor in accelerating and directing development and there are various ways in which the state intervention can be factored in any analysis. However, availability of reliable data is a major constraint to capture and reflect different aspects of state intervention; for the sake of objectivity and simplicity, we have factored the two most widely used indicators listed above. All the three groups are assigned equal weights and individual indicators within each group have also been assigned equal weights, since all the three groups are, in my opinion, equally important for the development of a state and so are the individual indicators within each group; it is difficult if not impossible to rate one above the others. The values of the indicators are then normalized using the denominator (Maximum Value–Minimum Value) for each indicator. The numerator would be (Actual Value–Minimum Value) for the positively correlated indicators like per capita income, etc. and (Maximum Value–Actual Value) for the negatively correlated indicators like IMR or percentage of BPL people. The weighted average of the ten indicators would indicate the value of the Composite Development Index for each state comprising these 10 indicators, higher the value, higher the position of the state in the development ladder. The ranking of the states according to this Composite Development Index is shown in Tables 8.3 and 8.4, for 2011 and 2001 respectively.

It would appear from these tables that even in 2001, five States, viz. Mizoram, Himachal Pradesh, Sikkim, Manipur, and Jammu & Kashmir were above the national averages and ahead of the other states in respect of these indicators. While Sikkim emerged at the top in 2011 followed by Himachal Pradesh and Mizoram, Manipur slipped way below, from fourth to eighth position. This is understandable, since by the turn of the century, Mizoram had effectively freed itself from any insurgency problem and established peace, while Manipur was still reeling from these problems that had brought most developmental programs within the state to a grinding halt. Sikkim and Himachal Pradesh has been

Table 8.3: Values of Development Indicators, 2011 and 2001

	Income, Employment and Poverty Indicators				Socio-Economic Development Indicators				State Intervention Indicators	
2011										
States	PCI (Rs)	Per cent of Primary Sector in NSDP	Per cent of Working Population	BPL per cent	Literacy per cent	IMR	per cent of Villages Electrified	CDR (per cent)	PCRE on Education (Rs)	PCRE on Health (Rs)
Arunachal Pradesh	60896	42	54	35	67	32	52	23	6500	2900
Assam	33087	27	49	32	73	55	92	36	2068	476
Himachal Pradesh	68297	20	65	8	84	38	85	40	3897	1106
Jammu & Kashmir	40089	25	40	10	69	41	96	37	2179	806
Manipur	28931	25	52	37	80	11	78	33	2107	774
Meghalaya	49261	17	62	12	76	52	73	24	2527	923
Mizoram	50956	21	60	21	92	34	80	43	5355	1582
Nagaland	55582	27	56	19	80	23	63	26	3414	1197
Sikkim	108972	08	58	13	82	26	100	38	9233	1983
Tripura	46050	24	50	14	88	29	91	35	2311	549
Uttarakhand	73819	14	44	11	80	36	93	31	2851	609
All India	54021	17	51	22	74	44	88	75	2285	457

(Cont'd)

Table 8.3 *(Cont'd)*

	2001									
States	PCI (Rs)	Per cent of Primary Sector in NSDP	Per cent of Working Population	BPL per cent	Literacy per cent	IMR	per cent of Villages Electrified	CDR (per cent)	PCRE on Education (Rs)	PCRE on Health (Rs)
Arunachal Pradesh	15260	35	44	33	55	44	60	15	1261	520
Assam	12803	42	36	36	63	78	77	32	719	130
Himachal Pradesh	22795	26	49	8	77	64	98	22	143	43
Jammu & Kashmir	14628	33	37	3	55	45	98	35	789	356
Manipur	12369	31	44	29	69	25	86	39	1168	289
Meghalaya	15657	27	42	34	63	52	59	17	1016	370
Mizoram	17826	21	53	20	89	23	81	24	2079	606
Nagaland	16253	33	43	33	67	38	64	12	870	340
Sikkim	16077	22	39	37	69	52	94	14	2077	587
Tripura	15983	24	36	34	73	49	57	23	1263	259
Uttarakhand	16232	26	37	40	72	42	82	22	1146	165
All India	16648	27	39	26	65	71	84	57	815	164

Table 8.4 Composite Development Index and Ranking of Individual States vis-à-vis All India Averages: 2011 and 2001

	2011											
	PCI (Rs)	Per cent of Primary Sector in NSDP	Per cent of Working Population	BPL per cent	Literacy per cent	IMR	Per cent of Villages Electrified	CDR (per cent)	PCRE on Education (Rs)	PCRE on Health (Rs)	Composite Development Index	Over-all Rank
Sikkim	1.00	1.00	0.72	0.83	0.60	0.66	1.00	0.29	1.00	0.62	0.77	1
Himachal Pradesh	0.49	0.65	1.00	1.00	0.68	0.39	0.69	0.33	0.26	0.27	0.57	2
Mizoram	0.28	0.62	0.80	0.55	1.00	0.48	0.58	0.38	0.46	0.46	0.56	3
Uttarakhand	0.56	0.82	0.16	0.90	0.52	0.43	0.85	0.15	0.11	0.06	0.46	4
Tripura	0.21	0.53	0.40	0.79	0.84	0.59	0.81	0.23	0.03	0.04	0.45	5
All India	**0.31**	**0.74**	**0.44**	**0.52**	**0.28**	**0.25**	**0.75**	**1.00**	**0.03**	**0.00**	**0.43**	**–**
Nagaland	0.33	0.44	0.64	0.62	0.52	0.73	0.23	0.06	0.19	0.30	0.41	6
Meghalaya	0.25	0.74	0.88	0.86	0.36	0.07	0.44	0.02	0.06	0.19	0.39	7
Manipur	0.00	0.50	0.48	0.00	0.52	1.00	0.54	0.19	0.01	0.13	0.34	8
Jammu & Kashmir	0.14	0.50	0.00	0.93	0.08	0.32	0.92	0.27	0.02	0.14	0.33	9
Arunachal Pradesh	0.40	0.00	0.56	0.07	0.00	0.52	0.00	0.00	0.62	1.00	0.32	10
Assam	0.05	0.44	0.36	0.17	0.24	0.00	0.83	0.25	0.00	0.01	0.24	11

(*Cont'd*)

Table 8.4 *(Cont'd)*

	2001											
	PCI (Rs)	Per cent of Primary Sector in NSDP	Per cent of Working Population	BPL per cent	Literacy per cent	IMR	Per cent of Villages Electrified	CDR (per cent)	PCRE on Education (Rs)	PCRE on Health (Rs)	Comp-osite Develop-ment Index	Over-all Rank
Mizoram	0.52	1.01	1.00	0.71	1.00	1.25	0.58	0.27	1.00	1.00	0.83	1
Himachal Pradesh	1.00	0.77	0.80	1.12	0.66	0.32	1.00	0.22	0.00	0.00	0.59	2
Sikkim	0.36	0.97	0.19	0.10	0.42	0.59	0.91	0.04	1.00	0.97	0.55	3
Manipur	0.00	0.53	0.49	0.40	0.42	1.20	0.70	0.60	0.53	0.44	0.53	4
Jammu & Kashmir	0.22	0.44	0.07	1.26	0.00	0.75	1.00	0.51	0.33	0.56	0.51	5
All India	**0.41**	**0.72**	**0.20**	**0.48**	**0.30**	**0.16**	**0.65**	**1.00**	**0.35**	**0.21**	**0.45**	–
Uttarakhand	0.37	0.77	0.07	0.00	0.51	0.82	0.60	0.22	0.52	0.22	0.41	6
Nagaland	0.43	0.39	0.43	0.25	0.35	0.91	0.18	0.00	0.38	0.53	0.38	7
Tripura	0.35	0.87	0.02	0.19	0.55	0.66	0.00	0.24	0.58	0.38	0.38	8
Arunachal Pradesh	0.28	0.36	0.49	0.23	0.01	0.77	0.07	0.07	0.58	0.85	0.37	9

2001												
	PCI (Rs)	Per cent of Primary Sector in NSDP	Per cent of Working Population	BPL per cent	Literacy per cent	IMR	Per cent of Villages Electrified	CDR (per cent)	PCRE on Education (Rs)	PCRE on Health (Rs)	Comp-osite Develop-ment Index	Over-all Rank
Meghalaya	0.32	0.73	0.37	0.21	0.25	0.59	0.05	0.11	0.45	0.58	0.37	**10**
Assam	0.04	0.00	0.00	0.14	0.26	0.00	0.48	0.44	0.30	0.15	0.18	**11**

Abbreviations used in the tables:

PCI = Per Capita Income at current prices; BPL= People Below poverty Line measured as per Tendulkar methodology; IMR = Infant Mortality Ratio as per census data; CDR = Credit : Deposit Ratio of Scheduled Commercial Banks as per sanction; PCRE = Per capita Revenue Expenditure of the Government; GSDP = Gross State Domestic Product at Current Prices.

peaceful throughout. It again vindicates that peace and political stability are essential for development. For the same reasons, Jammu & Kashmir had also slipped from fifth to ninth position among these states, while Tripura had moved up from eighth to fifth position in 2011, following Uttarakhand at fourth position. The middle positions in the list in 2011 were taken up by Nagaland (sixth) and Meghalaya (seventh) which had moved up from the seventh and 10th positions in 2001 respectively, while the bottom positions in 2011 were occupied by Manipur (eighth), Jammu & Kashmir (ninth), Arunachal Pradesh (10th) and Assam (11th). Assam was also at the bottom in 2001.

Lastly, we note that in 2001, Mizoram with an index of 0.83 was way ahead of Himachal Pradesh (0.59) occupying the second position in the list, while Sikkim stood third with an index score of 0.55. In 2011, Sikkim with index of 0.77 was way ahead of the state following it (Himachal Pradesh with index of 0.57), while Tripura made a remarkable transition from an index score of 0.38 in 2001 to index score of 0.45 in 2011.

9 Public Finances of Special Category States

Overview of Public Finances

Having examined the socio-economic parameters of the special category states, it is now left to us to assess the impact, if any, of the special category status on the public finances of these states. Public finance is basically about prudent management of resources and expenditure of the government while keeping the debt and deficits of the government well under control. Since government expenditure forms a very substantial part of the GSDP of the special category states, proper administration of public finance plays a crucial role in their socio-economic development.

As discussed earlier in the introduction, 'special category states' are special primarily in respect of plan assistance they receive from the Government of India. Because of their inherited disadvantages, they could not derive full benefits of the economic liberalization and reform processes set out in the country, a process that was transforming the economy in other states of India which could attract private capital by virtue of their better infrastructure and hence derive quicker benefits. We have observed that there was a marked divergence in the growth and income levels among the Indian states during both the pre- and post-reform periods and that this divergence was most noticeable within the poorer group of states which included the special category states. The liberal plan assistance to these states was meant to address precisely the disadvantages that stymied and stifled their growth, and a heavy dependence on the centre was an inevitable consequence of the special category status.

As already observed, 30 per cent of the centre's gross budgetary support for plan expenditure goes to the special category states. The per capita central assistance to these states was far higher than the general category states and the share of special category states in total central plan assistance had increased from a meagre 3.52 per cent of the total central plan assistance during the First Plan period to nearly 29.74 per cent during the Eleventh Plan period. In general, all these states were not only heavily dependent on central transfers for meeting their revenue expenditure, but also heavily indebted. In this chapter, we shall undertake a detailed analysis of the public finances of these states during the ten-year period from 2000–01 to 2010–11, covering the four major aspects of government finances, viz., (i) Resource Management; (ii) Expenditure Management; (iii) Debt Management, and (iv) Deficit Management.

One objective of this study was to assess if the special category status conferred upon these states had indeed made an impact on their finances. If so, then the values of relevant parameters observed between the beginning and the terminal years of the period 2001–11 would be markedly different, indicating an improvement over time. Since, except Uttarakhand, all the other special category states were created long ago, they also have been receiving liberal central assistance for a sustained period of time, long enough to make an impact upon their development. If so, the signature of such an impact would also be discernible in the trends and patterns of their public finances. Our attempt, then, would be to identify these signatures, as reflected in the relevant indicators which could be used to capture their performance over a period of time.

As explained in the introduction, accounts of governments are kept in three parts: Consolidated Fund, Contingency Fund, and Public Account. Here it will be necessary to discuss these in somewhat greater details.

Structure of Consolidated Fund

The Consolidated Fund is again classified into Revenue and Capital Accounts. Receipts into the revenue account of the Government come from (i) tax revenues which include the states own tax revenues and its share of the divisible pool of central taxes as determined by the Finance Commissions, (ii) non-tax revenues, and (iii) central grants for plan and non-plan purposes. The receipts into the capital account comprise the (i) public debt receipts from within the state (internal debt) as also from the centre (external debt), (ii) dividends and profits of state public sector undertakings and the proceeds of their disinvestment, if any, and (iii) recovery of principal amounts of loans and advances made by the state. The revenue and capital receipts together constitute the total receipts into the Consolidated Fund.

In government accounts, revenue and capital accounts are grouped by functions or services, which are classified following a six-tier hierarchical structure in which a major function of the government, say education, is represented by a major head and a sub-function like primary education by a sub-major head. Objectives of a function/ sub-function are achieved through various programmes which are represented by minor heads, and schemes drawn up under the programmes by sub-heads. Detailed head represents a sub-scheme and lastly, the object head represents the type and object of expenditure under each scheme/ sub-scheme.

The expenditure under the revenue account is of maintenance nature, incurred to run the day-to-day administration of the state. Such expenditure is classified under three services: General, Social, and Economic, besides expenditure for making grants and compensations to various bodies and authorities including the Panchayati Raj Institutions and Urban Local Bodies. Expenditure from the capital account is incurred for creation of capital assets under the above three services (capital outlay) and also to repay the principal amounts of loans borrowed by the state, while the interest on outstanding loans is paid from the revenue account under General Services. The major elements under the three services are shown in Table 9.1. Non-tax revenues of the state are also raised from these three services.

Structure of Public Account

There are five major heads of accounts under the Public Account: (i) small savings, provident fund, and other accounts; (ii) reserve funds; (iii) deposits and advances; (iv) suspense and miscellaneous, and

Table 9.1 Structure of Services

General Services	Social Services	Economic Services
a) Organs of State	a) Education, Sports, Arts and Culture	a) Agriculture and Allied Activities
b) Fiscal Services	b) Health and Family Welfare	b) Rural Development
i) Collection of Taxes on Property and Capital Transactions	c) Water Supply, Sanitation, Housing, and Urban Development	c) Special Area Programmes
ii) Collection of Taxes on Commodities and Services	d) Information and Broadcasting	d) Irrigation and Flood Control
iii) Other Fiscal Services	e) Welfare of SC, ST, and OBCs	e) Energy
c) Interest Payment and Servicing of Debt	f) Labour and Labour Welfare	f) Industry and Minerals
d) Administrative Services	g) Social Welfare and Nutrition	g) Transport
e) Pensions and Misc. General Services	h) Others	h) General Economic Services

Note: Expenditure under the three services is classified into development and non-development expenditure; expenditure on general services, being spent basically on the administration of the state is treated as non-developmental expenditure, while expenditure on social and economic services qualifies as developmental expenditure.

(v) remittances. Funds held in these accounts do not belong to the government which holds these funds in trust and manages the funds on behalf of their owners who can be ordinary people, government contractors, or even the government itself when it holds taxpayers' money outside of Consolidated Fund. Some of these funds are interest bearing on whose balances the government has to pay interest from the Consolidated Fund using taxpayers' money—others may not carry any interest liability.

The first three of these accounts deal with receipts and payments in respect of which the government is liable to repay the amounts received or has a claim to recover the amounts paid. In respect of these transactions, the government acts as a banker, receiving amounts which it later repays and paying out advances which it subsequently recovers. Provident funds of government employees, deposits of local funds, reserve funds deposits, departmental advances, etc. fall under this category. Balances in these accounts constitute a part of the overall financial liabilities of the government, a proposition whose logic is not beyond doubt.[1] The other two accounts—suspense and remittances—are used only for adjustment purposes; all initial debits or credits to these accounts are made pending final adjustments and cleared eventually by mutual adjustments once their final destinations are traced. Suspense temporarily accommodates all governmental/inter-governmental/departmental transactions pending availability of the requisite details in corresponding vouchers/challans that would identify their final destinations. It also includes temporary investments of cash balances in short term loans or government securities at nominal rates of interest. Remittances concern intra- and inter-governmental cash remittances between its various departments/ministries and also between the Reserve Bank of India and the various governments and government departments.

The most important of these accounts is of course the 'small savings, provident funds and other accounts' that includes a number of interest bearing obligations in respect of provident fund contributions of all government and non-government employees and some other contributions. Government has to pay interest on monies deposited in these funds at the prescribed rates, and in return can use this money for investment in specified government securities; such investments can eventually be used for development purposes for which the funds provide a ready source of capital at the disposal of the government. Because of this reason, the logic of including these balances in the government's total financial liabilities along with outstanding public debt is perhaps understandable, but the logic behind including the balances of other heads of Public Account in the government's total liability is often baffling (Bhattacharjee 2015: 6). For example, the Reserve Funds are created by debit to the Consolidated Fund to create reserves which are assets, e.g. for the renewal/replacement of assets of governments/parastatals (Depreciation Reserve Funds of Government's commercial concerns), for amortization of loans raised by the government (Sinking

Funds) and for other specific and sometimes esoteric purposes, such as Hindu Religious and Charitable Endowment Fund, Famine Relief Fund, Calamity Relief Fund, State Disaster Response Funds, etc.[2] But these are shown as government's liabilities to the respective funds. Some of these are interest bearing and some are not, and all these funds are managed by the government usually through the Secretaries/Principal Secretaries of the concerned departments/ministries. Government creates these funds out of taxpayers' money and then pays interest to these funds again by using taxpayers' money; it also controls the use of these funds through its administrators who are its own bureaucrats but without any accountability to the Legislature, as these funds are maintained outside the Consolidated Fund. Many of these funds also remain inoperative for a number of years.

The Deposit head under 'Deposits and Advances' includes sums deposited with government in the daily course of business by members of the public, e.g., deposits made in connection with revenue administration, deposits made in civil and criminal courts, security deposits taken from government servants/contractors when required, public works and earnest money deposits, deposits made by electoral candidates, etc. Like the reserve funds, some of these again carry interest liability while others do not; but all these are included in the government's total financial liabilities. Civil Advances relate to interest free temporary advances including advances of a permanent nature held by government officers to enable them to incur contingent expenditure in the day to day administration like the Permanent Cash Imprest.

It is to be understood that all these accounts stand merged in the cash balance of the government; they lose their individual identities by being part of the cash balance which represents the combined balances in the Consolidated Fund, Contingency Fund, and Public Account. Public Account balances, being part of the cash balances of the government, thus inflate them and also make the cash management of the government fraught with grave risks.

The way these accounts are maintained, especially the interest bearing ones, again defies all logic. For example, there is one fund created in 1999 under Small Savings called the National Small Savings Fund (NSSF) to which all public deposits under the Central Government's Small Savings Schemes are credited. States have to borrow 80 per cent of the accumulated balances under this fund mandatorily (and hence pay interest to the centre), with the option to go up to 100 per cent. This borrowing, strangely, is based on availability rather than requirement.[3]

In our analysis in this chapter, for reasons explained above, only the balances under small savings, provident fund, and other accounts are included in the total outstanding liability of the state governments as inclusion of other balances will distort the actual liability carried by the states. They also may not represent real liability; their net effect would result only in the accumulation of higher cash balances of the government leading to a position where it might be forced to resort to borrowings despite having a surplus cash balance.

Growth of GSDP in Special Category States

Table 9.2 shows the growth of GSDP at current prices[4] in the special category states during the decades beginning respectively with 1990–91 and 2000–01, and compares their growth rates with the growth rate of national GDP at current prices. It can be seen from this table that while the average rates of GSDP growth of three states (Arunachal Pradesh, Assam, and Manipur) during the decade of 1990s were more or less comparable to the national average of 14 per cent, all other special category states grew at much higher rates during that decade, led by Himachal Pradesh (19 per cent). But growth rates declined steeply during the next decade for most of these states, while the national average had remained unchanged. Only Sikkim and Uttarakhand, both with an average growth rate of 19 per cent, and Arunachal Pradesh with 17 per cent growth rate stand out as some of the fastest growing states in the country. We shall thus expect to find improvements in their public finances as well, and if we cannot find these, then the failure can only be attributed to issues related to governance.

Undisputedly, governance remains a vital issue for most of the special category states, with endemic corruption, inefficiency, and wastes eating into the development funds in most. For all special category states except these three, the first decade of the present century marked a period of lower growth compared to the previous one, and this was in stark contrast to most other states in India which were richly reaping the harvests of the reform process initiated during the early 1990s. This presents a paradox—in the post-reforms period, especially after 2000–01,the revenues of Central Government had increased

Table 9.2 Growth of GSDP in Special Category States between 1990–91 and 2010–11 (at Current Prices)

	Arunachal Pradesh	Assam	Himachal Pradesh	Jammu & Kashmir	Manipur	Meghalaya	Mizoram	Nagaland	Sikkim	Tripura	Uttarakhand[i]	All India
Average Growth Rate (1991–2001) per cent	13	13	19	17	14	16	18	18	16	18	11	14
Average Growth Rate (2001–11) per cent	17	12	14	13	11	14	13	13	19	12	19	14
Change in Growth Rate (1991–2001) per cent	+4	–1	–5	–3	–3	–2	–4	–5	+3	–6	+8	0

Note: i. Since Uttarakhand was created only in 2000, the growth rate of Uttarakhand for 2000–01 over the previous year has been taken as a proxy for the average annual growth rate for 1991–2001.

substantially, resulting in much higher transfers to the special category states compared to the earlier periods. It was thus to be expected that such high transfers would reflect in high growth rates of GSDP of these states, which generally was not the case. It points to a possibility that all these funds might not have been utilized productively by these states.

Resource Management

The thirteen performance indicators shown in Box 9.1 have been used in respect of resource management and their values during 2000–01 and 2010–11 are shown respectively in Tables 9.3 and 9.4. The respective contributions of tax and non-tax revenues in these two years are shown in Table 9.5.

In 2000–01, some of these states had hardly any revenue of their own; own tax plus non-tax revenues were less than or about Rs 100 crore for four states (Arunachal Pradesh, Manipur, Nagaland, and Mizoram), of which Mizoram's own revenues were only Rs 55 crore. Ten years hence, though other states had increased their own revenues substantially, Mizoram still had only Rs 277 crore from its own resources. While Nagaland (Rs 411 crore) and Manipur (Rs 527 crore) had registered

Box 9.1 Resource Management Performance Indicators

Ratios of:

1. State's Own Revenue to Total Revenue
2. Own Tax Revenue to Total Own Revenue
3. Non- Tax Revenue to Total Own Revenue
4. Central Grants to Total Revenue
5. Share of Central Taxes to Total Revenue
6. Revenue Receipts to Total Receipts
7. Capital Receipts to Total Receipts
8. Internal Debt to Total Borrowing
9. Central Loans to Total Borrowing
10. Total Revenue to Revenue Expenditure
11. Own Revenue to Revenue Expenditure
12. Total Revenue to GSDP
13. Own Tax Revenue to GSDP

Table 9.3 Important Parameters of Resource Management in Special Category States: 2000–01 (per cent)

	Arunachal Pradesh	Assam	Himachal Pradesh	Jammu & Kashmir	Manipur	Meghalaya	Mizoram	Nagaland	Sikkim	Tripura	Uttarakhand
State's Own Revenue/ Total Revenue	9	34	30	21	9	18	7	7	41	13	43
Own Tax Revenue/ Total Own Revenue	30	73	80	63	54	58	26	52	18	57	86
Non-Tax Revenue/ Total Own Revenue	70	27	20	37	46	42	74	48	82	43	14
Central Grants/ Total Revenue	82	36	59	67	76	67	83	90	51	72	51

Share of Central Taxes/ Total Revenue	8	30	11	12	16	15	11	3	8	14	6
Revenue Receipts/ Total Receipts	87	79	66	46	42	88	85	58	96	91	79
Capital Receipts/ Total Receipts	13	21	34	54	58	12	15	42	4	9	21
Internal Debt/ Total Borrowing	55	38	79	93	84	78	69	94	75	90	82
Central Loans/ Total Borrowing	45	62	21	7	16	22	31	6	25	10	18

(*Cont'd*)

Table 9.3 *(Cont'd)*

	Arunachal Pradesh	Assam	Himachal Pradesh	Jammu & Kashmir	Manipur	Meghalaya	Mizoram	Nagaland	Sikkim	Tripura	Uttarakhand
Total Revenue/ Revenue Expenditure	105	88	70	85	93	105	81	93	113	94	91
Own Revenue/ Revenue Expenditure	1	3	2	2	1	2	1	1	5	1	4
Total Revenue / GSDP	52	15	19	34	34	29	48	33	85	30	16
Own Tax Revenue/ GSDP	1	4	5	4	2	3	1	1	6	2	6

Table 9.4 Important Parameters of Resource Management in Special Category States: 2010–11 (per cent)

Ratios (per cent)– 2010–11	Arunachal Pradesh	Assam	Himachal Pradesh	Jammu & Kashmir	Manipur	Meghalaya	Mizoram	Nagaland	Sikkim	Tripura	Uttarakhand
State's Own Revenue/ Total Revenue	14	36	42	21	10	20	10	8	47	15	44
Own Tax Revenue/ Total Own Revenue	29	71	68	76	51	65	47	55	19	83	87
Non-Tax Revenue/ Total Own Revenue	71	29	32	24	49	35	53	45	81	17	13
Central Grants/Total Revenue	73	29	45	66	72	58	74	78	36	64	35

(Cont'd)

Table 9.4 *(Cont'd)*

Ratios (per cent)–2010–11	Arunachal Pradesh	Assam	Himachal Pradesh	Jammu & Kashmir	Manipur	Meghalaya	Mizoram	Nagaland	Sikkim	Tripura	Uttarakhand
Share of Central Taxes/Total Revenue	13	35	13	14	18	21	16	14	17	22	21
Revenue Receipts/Total Receipts	98	92	84	76	95	92	90	91	99	90	82
Capital Receipts/Total Receipts	2	8	16	24	5	8	10	9	1	10	18
Internal Debt/Total Borrowing	100	99	98	114	100	100	100	100	200	99	98
Central Loans/Total Borrowing	0	1	2	–14	0	0	0	0	–100	1	2

Total Revenue/ Revenue Expenditure	145	100	91	117	133	106	88	103	105	119	104
Own Revenue/ Revenue Expenditure	2	4	4	2	1	2	1	1	5	2	5
Total Revenue/ GSDP	62	20	23	39	60	29	47	44	54	29	14
Own Tax Revenue/ GSDP	2	5	6	6	3	4	2	2	5	4	5

Table 9.5 Major Contributors to States' Revenues: 2000–01 and 2010–11 (share in per cent)

2000–01											
Major Contributors to Tax Revenue	**Arunachal Pradesh**	**Assam**	**Himachal Pradesh**	**Jammu & Kashmir**	**Manipur**	**Meghalaya**	**Mizoram**	**Nagaland**	**Sikkim**	**Tripura**	**Uttarakhand**
Sales Tax Receipts/Own Tax Revenue	54	65	41	48	64	55	42	76	38	65	50
State Excise/ Own Tax Revenue (per cent)	1	10	29	40	2	35	7	4	27	16	24
Motor Vehicle tax/Own Tax revenue (per cent)	34	5	8	3	6	4	14	11	3	3	7
Stamp & Registration Fees/Own Tax Revenue (per cent)	0	3	4	3	4	3	0	2	2	5	9

Share of Above in Total Tax Revenue	**89**	**83**	**82**	**94**	**76**	**96**	**63**	**93**	**69**	**88**	**90**
Major Contributors to Non-Tax Revenue											
Receipts from Power/Non-Tax revenue	17	0	5	54	63	0	44	53	3	37	0
Royalty/Non-Tax Revenue (per cent)	6	70	7	1	0	58	0	0	0	0	11
Industry/Non-Tax Revenue (per cent)	0	0	24	0	0	0	0	0	0	6	0
Forestry & Wildlife	36		10	13	2	6		7		8	50
Water Supply & Sanitation							7				

(*Cont'd*)

Table 9.5 *(Cont'd)*

	2000–01										
Major Contributors to Tax Revenue	**Arunachal Pradesh**	**Assam**	**Himachal Pradesh**	**Jammu & Kashmir**	**Manipur**	**Meghalaya**	**Mizoram**	**Nagaland**	**Sikkim**	**Tripura**	**Uttarakhand**
Roads & Bridges			2								
Road Transport	10							16			
Lotteries									83		
Irrigation											4
Police			5								2
Interest Receipts	8	1	9	24	2	10	8	7	2	19	2
Share of Above in Total Non-Tax Revenue	**77**	**71**	**62**	**91**	**68**	**82**	**59**	**84**	**88**	**72**	**70**

2010–11											
Major Contributors to Tax Revenue	Arunachal Pradesh	Assam	Himachal Pradesh	Jammu & Kashmir	Manipur	Meghalaya	Mizoram	Nagaland	Sikkim	Tripura	Uttarakhand
Sales Tax Receipts/Own Tax Revenue	78	73	58	70	85	72	80	73	52	71	67
State Excise/ Own Tax Revenue (per cent)	14	5	15	10	3	18	2	1	26	14	17
Motor Vehicle tax/Own Tax revenue (per cent)	6	4	4	3	1	3	6	11	4	4	5
Stamp & Registration Fees/Own Tax Revenue (per cent)	1	2	4	2	1	2	0	0	2	4	10
Total Share of above taxes	**99**	**84**	**81**	**85**	**91**	**95**	**88**	**86**	**84**	**93**	**99**

(Cont'd)

Table 9.5 *(Cont'd)*

2000–01											
Major Contributors to Tax Revenue	**Arunachal Pradesh**	**Assam**	**Himachal Pradesh**	**Jammu & Kashmir**	**Manipur**	**Meghalaya**	**Mizoram**	**Nagaland**	**Sikkim**	**Tripura**	**Uttarakhand**
Major Contributors to Non–Tax Revenue											
Receipts from Power /Non–Tax revenue	53	0	64	75	34	0	50	40	8	0	2
Royalty/Non–Tax Revenue (per cent)	7	69	7	3	10	71	3	1	0	0	14
Industry/Non-Tax Revenue (per cent)	0	0	0	0	0	0	0	19	0	24	0
Forestry & Wildlife	2	6	4	4	1	7	2	5	1	6	34
Roads & Bridges			1				7				

Road Transport							2	7	2		34
Water Supply & Sanitation					5						
Irrigation					4						
Police			1							19	
Lotteries									83		
Interest Receipts	8	18	4	1	17	8	9	5	2	17	8
Total Share of Non–Tax Revenue	**70**	**92**	**81**	**84**	**71**	**87**	**72**	**78**	**96**	**66**	**92**
Buoyancy Ratios											
State's Own Tax Revenue	**1.42**	**1.10**	**2.45**	**0.85**	**3.50**	**2.00**	**1.40**	**3.47**	**1.27**	**1.30**	**1.38**
Taxes on Sales, Trade etc.	1.73	1.29	2.43	0.73	3.81	1.92	1.44	3.54	0.93	1.34	1.79
State Excise	1.49	2.05	0.72	0.82		1.10		5.50	1.21	2.91	0.42
Non Tax Revenue	**0.22**	**–0.80**	**–0.29**	**0.81**	**0.81**	**0.67**	**1.05**	**6.04**	**–0.84**	**0.37**	**0.42**

Source: Finance accounts of the respective states.

moderate growth of their own resources, Arunachal Pradesh had substantially increased its own resources to Rs 745 crore, obviously resulting from its higher growth during the period 2000–01 to 2010–11 as seen earlier. For these four states, in 2000–01, their own resources formed less than 10 per cent of their total revenues, while Uttarakhand, Sikkim, Assam, and Himachal Pradesh had raised more than 30 per cent of their total revenues from their own resources; Uttarakhand and Sikkim had in fact raised more than 40 per cent of their total revenues from their own resources. In 2010–11, Sikkim's share of its own resources reached 47 per cent, closely followed by Uttarakhand (44 per cent) and Himachal Pradesh (42 per cent). Clearly, as far as resources were concerned, these states had reaped the benefits of their higher growth. Nagaland, Mizoram, and Manipur continued to generate less than 10 per cent of their total revenues from their own resources even in 2010–11, while the share of others ranged between 14 per cent and 21 per cent.

It is interesting to note that almost all special category states continued to depend overwhelmingly on tax revenues rather than non-tax revenues for their resources, except Arunachal Pradesh and Sikkim, and to some extent Manipur and Mizoram. Sikkim raised more than 90 per cent of its resources from non-tax revenues, the bulk of it (83 per cent) coming from its highly popular state lotteries, while Arunachal Pradesh raised 71 per cent of its own revenue from non-tax sources, major receipts coming from power. In 2000–01, forestry and wildlife used to be an important source of non-tax revenues for Uttarakhand and Arunachal Pradesh, providing 50 per cent and 36 per cent respectively of their total non-tax revenues. By 2010–11, receipts from forestry and wildlife had declined to only 2 per cent for Arunachal Pradesh. Only for Uttarakhand, it still remained a major source of tax revenues and provided 34 per cent of its total non-tax revenues.

Of the tax receipts, sales tax/Value Added Tax (VAT) constituted the most important source of tax revenues for all the states, and in this respect they were no different from the general category states. Sales Tax/ VAT contributed more than two thirds to the total tax revenues of these states from their own resources in 2010–11, with the exception of Himachal Pradesh and Sikkim, in whose case state excise duty on medicine and alcohol also contributed significantly to their tax revenues. Other states that raised substantial amounts (more than 10 per cent) from their excise duties included Arunachal Pradesh, Meghalaya, Tripura, Uttarakhand, and Jammu & Kashmir. Compared to 2000–01, share of revenues from the sales tax increased significantly for most states, especially Himachal Pradesh, Jammu & Kashmir, Mizoram, and Sikkim. Motor vehicles tax contributed significantly (11 per cent) only in Nagaland. Contribution of other taxes was insignificant for all states.

Share of central taxes had never been a significant part of revenues of these states except for Assam (30 per cent and 35 per cent of total revenues in 2000–01 and 2010–11 respectively), though its share had increased over time for all these states. This is because in determining the share of individual states, the formula adopted by the Finance Commissions had always included population (and sometimes area) of the respective states and allotted higher weightage to these criteria; revenue performance (tax effort) was another important criterion for determining the states' shares. The special category states, except Assam, lost on all these counts.

Central grants, however, constituted by far the most important source of revenue for all states. But all states had over the course of the decade reduced their dependence on the central grants, except Jammu & Kashmir and Manipur. Both Uttarakhand and Sikkim received 51 per cent of their total revenues from central grants in 2000–01; by 2010–11, they had reduced their dependence on central grants by 16 per cent and 15 per cent respectively, followed by Himachal Pradesh which reduced its share of central grants in its total revenue by 14 per cent. But even in 2010–11, central Grants constituted about 60 per cent or more of the total revenues for nine of these 11 states. Only for Assam and Himachal Pradesh, the shares of central grants were significantly lower (29 per cent and 45 per cent respectively).

One significant change that occurred over these ten years was the decline in the share of capital receipts in the total receipts for all the states. Revenue receipts constituted more than 90 per cent of total receipts for eight states in 2010–11, while two states raised more than 80 per cent of their total receipts into their Consolidated Funds from revenue receipts only. This was because in the post-Twelfth Finance Commission period, most states could generate surpluses in their revenue account that reduced their need to meet the capital requirements from borrowing. Jammu & Kashmir was the only exception.

Once their revenue accounts started generating surplus, most states switched over to borrowing from the market at favourable terms only when they needed additional resources, thereby reducing the need for central loans whose share became insignificant for all states by 2010–11, in stark contrast to the situation prevailing at the beginning years of the decade. By 2010–11, except resource-scarce Mizoram and resource-rich but heavily indebted Himachal Pradesh, all other special category states had become revenue surplus. But with their own revenues, they could meet hardly five per cent of their revenue expenditure, and this situation had not changed over the decade. Central funds were still driving their economies to a large extent. As seen from Table 9.6, the average levels of Own Tax: GSDP ratios for all special category states were much lower than the corresponding ratios for general category states.

Expenditure Management

As already explained, expenditure of the governments is classified under three major categories—General Services, Social Services, and Economic Services. Apart from revenue expenditure and capital outlay on these services, the other areas of spending are grants to local bodies and autonomous institutions under the state government and repayment of loans and advances (on the capital account).

Accounts of the Government are classified under revenue and capital heads, each component being classified again under plan and non-plan expenditure, or developmental non-developmental expenditure, even though such classifications have no constitutional basis. A plan has both revenue and capital components; while the capital portion of

Table 9.6 Tax : GSDP Ratio of General and Special Category States: 2010–11

General Category State	Tax: GSDP Ratio (per cent)	Special Category State	Tax: GSDP Ratio (per cent)
Tamil Nadu	8	Himachal Pradesh	6
Madhya Pradesh	8	Jammu & Kashmir	6
Andhra Pradesh	8	Assam	5
Chhattisgarh	8	Sikkim	5
Punjab	7	Uttarakhand	5
Maharashtra	7	Meghalaya	4
Gujarat	7	Tripura	4
Uttar Pradesh	7	Manipur	3
Haryana	6	Arunachal Pradesh	2
Rajasthan	6	Mizoram	2
Bihar	5	Nagaland	2

plan expenditure of the states is mostly financed by plan loans from the centre and capital receipts, central plan grants to states normally finance their plan revenue expenditure. In the absence of any clear guideline for classification of expenditure between plan and non-plan on a rational basis, the distinction continues to remain ambiguous and sometimes irrational. The division of expenditure into plan and non-plan is indicated in the budget itself. Plan expenditure is generally made for taking up new development projects in the states, hence, the extent of expenditure on plan projects also indicates the level of new developmental projects initiated by the state during a year.

The distinction of expenditure into developmental and non-developmental is also made only for the purpose of analysis. Non-developmental expenditure is incurred for running the day to day administration of the state; it comprises the expenditure on general services. Such expenditure is not directly attributable to the state's socio-economic development, for which the expenditure on social and economic services is more relevant, which, therefore, is said to constitute development expenditure. The indicators for measuring the performance of the special category states used for this analysis are listed in Box 9.2 and the values of these parameters are indicated in Tables 9.7 and 9.8 for 2000–01 and 2010–11 respectively.

Box 9.2 Expenditure Management Performance Indicators

Ratios of:

1. Revenue Expenditure/Total Expenditure (per cent)
2. Capital Outlay/Total Expenditure (per cent)
3. Non-Plan Expenditure/Total Expenditure (per cent)
4. Developmental Expenditure/Total Expenditure (per cent)
5. Non-Developmental Expenditure/Own Revenue (per cent)
6. Revenue Expenditure on Education and Health as per cent of Total Expenditure
7. Capital Outlay/ Capital Receipts (per cent)
8. Interest Payments/Revenue Expenditure (per cent)
9. Interest Payments/Revenue Receipts (per cent)
10. Interest Payments/Own Revenue (%)
11. Own Revenue/Revenue Expenditure (%)
12. Gross Central Transfers/Total Expenditure (%)
13. Total Expenditure/GSDP (%)

Table 9.7 Expenditure Parameters of Special Category States: 2000–01 (per cent)[i]

Ratios (per cent)	Arunachal Pradesh	Assam	Himachal Pradesh	Jammu & Kashmir	Manipur	Meghalaya	Mizoram	Nagaland	Sikkim	Tripura	Uttarakhand
Revenue Expenditure/ Total Expenditure	74	50	81	85	46	76	79	82	81	81	89
Capital Outlay/Total Expenditure	22	4	10	11	6	16	13	14	16	16	6
Non-Plan Expenditure/ Total Expenditure	44	86	66	80	86	65	62	73	68	67	82
Developmental Expenditure/ Total Expenditure	69	35	60	64	31	63	66	53	53	66	60
Non–Developmental Expenditure/ Own Revenue	403	430	233	234	1844	258	810	910	127	331	118

Revenue Expenditure on Education and Health/Total Expenditure	16	18	21	15	14	21	19	17	15	23	23
Capital Outlay/ Capital Receipts	192	37	35	13	10	147	112	25	405	207	30
Interest Payments/ Revenue Expenditure	11	13	18	12	16	11	10	14	10	13	17
Interest Payments/ Revenue Receipts	10	15	26	14	17	10	12	15	9	14	19
Interest Payments/Own Revenue	107	45	88	65	195	55	185	225	22	103	45
Own Revenue/ Revenue Expenditure	10	30	21	18	8	19	5	6	46	13	38

(*Cont'd*)

Table 9.7 (*Cont'd*)

Ratios (per cent)	Arunachal Pradesh	Assam	Himachal Pradesh	Jammu & Kashmir	Manipur	Meghalaya	Mizoram	Nagaland	Sikkim	Tripura	Uttarakhand
Gross Central Transfers/Total Expenditure	78	36	46	63	49	67	63	75	54	67	48
Total Expenditure/ GSDP	64	35	34	47	78	36	74	44	94	39	21

Note: i. As in resource management, for Arunachal Pradesh, Nagaland and Uttarakhand, figures for 2001–02 have been used while for all other states 2000–01 figures have been used.

Table 9.8 Expenditure Parameters of Special Category States: 2010–11 (per cent)

Ratios (per cent)	Arunachal Pradesh	Assam	Himachal Pradesh	Jammu & Kashmir	Manipur	Meghalaya	Mizoram	Nagaland	Sikkim	Tripura	Uttarakhand
Revenue Expenditure/ Total Expenditure	69	88	83	65	67	84	78	75	85	78	79
Capital Outlay /Total Expenditure	29	8	11	21	31	12	15	20	13	19	13
Non–Plan Expenditure/ Total Expenditure	50	73	80	77	51	57	59	64	67	66	71
Developmental Expenditure/ Total Expenditure	71	65	62	56	65	68	68	58	50	58	60
Non-Developmental Expenditure/ Own Revenue	222	110	121	280	406	176	482	565	122	311	117

(*Cont'd*)

Table 9.8 *(Cont'd)*

Ratios (per cent)	Arunachal Pradesh	Assam	Himachal Pradesh	Jammu & Kashmir	Manipur	Meghalaya	Mizoram	Nagaland	Sikkim	Tripura	Uttarakhand
Revenue Expenditure on Education and Health/Total Expenditure	12	30	21	13	13	22	18	15	20	19	24
Salary Expenditure (Revenue A/c)/ Total Revenue Expenditure	40	46	42	41	41	37	43	49	30	49	41
Capital Outlay/ Capital Receipts	1322	97	72	86	639	150	205	242	1965	189	74
Interest Payments/ Revenue Expenditure	10	8	14	12	9	6	3	9	6	10	13
Interest Payments/ Revenue Receipts	7	8	15	10	7	6	4	8	6	9	13

Interest Payments/Own Revenue	54	23	37	50	69	29	38	96	13	59	29
Own Revenue/ Revenue Expenditure	19	36	38	24	13	22	9	10	49	17	44
Gross Central Transfers/Total Expenditure	82	57	44	57	80	71	62	82	47	79	45
Total Expenditure/ GSDP	65	23	30	51	67	33	69	49	61	32	18
Growth Rate of Revenue Expenditure: 2001–11	17	14	12	11	14	14	12	13	14	10	16
Growth Rate ofCapital Outlay, 2001–11	21	14	13	21	29	10	14	19	12	12	28

(Cont'd)

Table 9.8 (*Cont'd*)

Ratios (per cent)	Arunachal Pradesh	Assam	Himachal Pradesh	Jammu & Kashmir	Manipur	Meghalaya	Mizoram	Nagaland	Sikkim	Tripura	Uttarakhand
Growth Rate ofTotal Expenditure, 2001–11	17	7	12	14	10	13	12	14	14	10	18
Growth Rate of GSDP, 2001–11	17	12	14	13	11	14	13	12	19	12	20

Capital outlay represents the money spent on creation of income-generating capital assets. It is seen that during the decade beginning 2000–2001, while revenue expenditure for different states grew at annual average rates between 10 per cent and 17 per cent, the rate of growth of capital outlay was much higher for all states except Meghalaya and Sikkim. Some states like Arunachal Pradesh, Jammu & Kashmir, Manipur, and Uttarakhand had increased their capital outlay very significantly during this period. The growth rates in total expenditure for all states were generally comparable to their GSDP growth rates, except for Assam. Revenue expenditure, however, consumed bulk of the expenditure for all states, mostly on account of salaries which accounted for around 40 per cent of total revenue expenditure for most states in 2010–11. Eight out of the 11 states had spent more than 75 per cent of the total expenditure on revenue account in 2010–11, with capital outlay remaining at less than 15 per cent for six of these. Only Arunachal Pradesh and Manipur were spending about 30 per cent of their total expenditure on capital outlay in 2010–11.

For all states in India, non-plan expenditure dominates the total expenditure; special category states were no exception to this. In 2001–02, as many as eight out of 11 states were spending above two thirds of their total expenditure on non–plan account. By 2010–11, this number had come down to six, but the number of states spending more than 80 per cent of their expenditure on non-plan purposes had come down from four in 2000–01 (Assam, Jammu & Kashmir, Manipur, and Uttarakhand) to just one in 2010–11, Himachal Pradesh. Most states could maintain their proportion of developmental expenditure at more than 50 per cent throughout the decade. Assam and Manipur could spend only 35 per cent and 31 per cent of their total expenditure respectively on developmental social and economic services in 2000–01, but by 2010–11, they had caught up with the rest of the states and raised the level of developmental expenditure to 65 per cent of total expenditure. In 2010–11, five states (Assam, Himachal Pradesh, Meghalaya, Sikkim, and Uttarakhand) were spending more than 20 per cent of their total revenue expenditure on education and public health, while three others were spending between 15 per cent and 20 per cent; only Arunachal Pradesh, Jammu & Kashmir, and Manipur were spending less than 15 per cent of their total revenue expenditure on education and public health. Assam used to spend 18 per cent of its revenue expenditure on education and public health in 2000–01, but could raise this share substantially to 30 per cent by 2010–11 (25 per cent on education).

Among the non-developmental expenditure, interest payment on outstanding debt was a major consumer of revenue expenditure. It accounted for more than 10 per cent of total revenue expenditure for five states in 2010–11; only for Mizoram, it was less than five per cent. But payment obligations on account of interest had substantially reduced for all states after the Twelfth Finance Commission recommendations (discussed under Debt management); in 2000–01, interest payments amounted to more than 15 per cent of revenue expenditure for three states (Himachal Pradesh, Manipur, and Uttarakhand) and between 10 per cent and 15 per cent for all the rest. Pension was another important charge on general services; Sikkim paid more than 25 per cent of its revenue expenditure on pension and misc. general services in 2000–01 which share increased to 31 per cent by 2000–01. The rest of the states except Tripura (12 per cent) managed to keep it well within 10 per cent of their total revenue expenditure.

Comparing expenditure with revenue receipts and especially the own revenue receipts of the states would give us some idea about the extent to which these states are dependent on central resources. Gross central transfers, i.e. the aggregate of a state's share of the divisible pool of central taxes, central grants for plan and non-plan purposes, and central loans, accounted for more than three-fourths of the total expenditure of four states in 2010–11 (Arunachal Pradesh, Manipur, Nagaland, and Tripura) and between 50 per cent and 75 per cent for four more states (Assam, Jammu & Kashmir, Meghalaya, and Mizoram). Only Himachal Pradesh, Sikkim and Uttarakhand used central funds to finance less than 50 per cent of their total expenditure in 2010–11. Though the percentages vary over time for different states, on the whole, compared with the situation prevailing in 2000–01, the level of dependence on central transfers had not decreased significantly, implying that most special category states were still in need of financial support and assistance. Own revenues could finance more than 30 per cent of their revenue expenditure for four states in 2010–11 (Arunachal Pradesh [19 per cent], Manipur [13 per cent], Mizoram [9 per cent], Nagaland [10 per cent], and Tripura [17 per cent]); the situation was not much different ten years ago with only three states (Assam, Sikkim, and Uttarakhand) financing more than 30 per cent of their revenue expenditure from their own resources. Even for running their day-to-day administration, i.e. on general services alone, the expenditure needed was several times their own revenues. Even the more self-sufficient among them (Assam, Himachal Pradesh, Meghalaya, Sikkim, and Uttarakhand) would exhaust their entire own revenues for meeting only their administrative needs and still need more, and would be in no position to spend anything for socio-economic development. Interest payments on past debts alone, in fact, wiped out a substantial part of their own revenues—as much as 96 per cent for Nagaland and 69 per cent for Manipur in 2010–11. Even after the relief granted by the Twelfth Finance Commission, interest payments still took away a significant part of their revenues. If they were to secede today from the Indian Union, as some over-enthusiastic independence-seeking insurgents of the northeast or Jammu & Kashmir fancied and some still cherish those fond dreams, these states would be likely to implode sooner than later only under their financial pressure without the support of the central grants that run their economies, and would soon be forced to seek financial help from some other country. They just lack the resources to exist as independent entities.

The ratio of capital outlay to capital receipts indicates the extent to which capital receipts, i.e. borrowed funds, can be applied to create capital assets in the economy that can really drive the future growth of the state. In this regard, however, we find that many states not only utilized the whole of their capital receipts for creation of capital assets, but also invested substantial portion of their own funds for the same purpose. Remarkable among them were Sikkim, Arunachal Pradesh, Manipur, Mizoram, Nagaland, Tripura, and Meghalaya in 2010–11. Arunachal and Sikkim had been consistently doing this throughout the entire decade.

The economies of all these states are largely driven by the government activities, without many other productive economic activities. Government expenditure thus forms a significant part of the total GSDP of most of these states. In 2000–01, it used to account for 94 per cent of the GSDP for Sikkim, 78 per cent for Manipur, 74 per cent for Mizoram and 64 per cent for Arunachal Pradesh. In 2010–11, though the overall percentages had reduced for all except Arunachal Pradesh, government expenditure still formed more than 60 per cent of GSDP for all the above four states, and about 50 per cent for two more states (Jammu & Kashmir and Nagaland).

Debt Management

Public debt assuredly is one of the most powerful agents of economic transformation, provided it is utilized for the creation of productive capital assets that generate income; this income can be used for debt repayments without putting the economy into undue stress. Debt receipts and repayments are treated as capital transactions in the government accounts and are accounted for under the major head public debt in the Consolidated Fund. Since any borrowing by the government of the day imposes a burden of repayment of principal plus an annual interest burden on future generations, it is imperative that the benefits of more productive capital assets created out of the borrowed funds be passed on to posterity. Governments also borrow from the Public Account as explained earlier. For our analysis, we shall take the outstanding debt as being constituted by public debt liabilities as well as the liabilities under the Small Savings, Provident Fund, and Other Accounts only under Public Account, for reasons already explained.

It really does not make much sense to deal with debt at the absolute level—a rich state can afford a higher level of debt and hence can borrow more. Thus debt is to be linked to the flow of income of the borrower and his ability to service the additional debt liability from the net increase in his non-debt income from other sources. Debt is always related to the capacity of the borrower to pay, and for a state government, the income of the state serves as a proxy for this capacity; hence Debt: GSDP ratio is generally used in analysis as one of the most important parameters of debt sustainability. There is no hard and fast rule prescribing a tolerable limit for this ratio, but Dholakia et al.(2004: 5) in a study conducted for the Twelfth Finance Commission (TwFC) had suggested a limit of 35 per cent for the Indian states which seems reasonable, though this limit would have been breached by most special category states. The ratio of state's own tax revenue to the outstanding debt as also the ratio of debt receipts to revenue receipts may also serve as parameters to judge the ability of a state to service its debt, on the logic that debt should not grow faster than revenue receipts and that the ratio of outstanding debt to tax revenue should be bounded. But as pointed out by Vaidya (2005: 8), taking the ratio of outstanding debt to total revenue receipts may mask the structure of such receipts, since a very substantial part of the receipts for the states would come from the grants, and the grants are often tied to particular projects or specific purposes, so that the states have no liberty to use them as they would like to. Further, grants do not reflect the scale of economic activity within the states, they are variable and often political in nature. Grants are important for the special category states all of whom depend on it very heavily. Even the non-tax revenues lack the predictability and permanent nature of tax receipts. Hence we are considering only the tax revenues of the states in our analysis.

The parameters used for our analysis are indicated in Box 9.3. The results of the measurement are shown in Table 9.9. As noted earlier, historically the special category states were disadvantaged in many ways which made the cost of infrastructure creation as well as the cost of public service delivery within their territories much higher compared to the other states. Besides, all these states are extremely prone to severe natural calamities that often take them to the brink of disaster, like the one that happened in Uttarakhand in 2013, recovery from which may severely drain them out of resources, affecting their growth very seriously. These factors often combine together, forcing them to resort to heavy borrowings. Thus, they always carried a heavier debt burden compared to the general category states. In fact, as can be seen from Table 9.9, in 2010–11, seven out of 11 Special Category States had Debt: GSDP ratios exceeding 40 per cent unlike any of the 17 General Category States. For two states, the ratio exceeded even 50 per cent.

Box 9.3 Debt Management Performance Indicators

Ratios of:

1. Outstanding Debt to Gross State Domestic Product (GSDP) (per cent)
2. Net Debt Available (after repayment of principal and interest on past loans plus the net lending made by the State) to Total Debt Raised (per cent)
3. Outstanding Debt to State's Own Tax Revenues (per cent)
4. Outstanding Debt to Total Tax Revenue Receipts (per cent)

Conditions:

5. Whether Primary Balance >= 0 and Weighted Interest Rate on Outstanding Debt <= Growth Rate of GSDP (Solvency Condition);
6. Whether Quantum Spread + Primary Balance >=0.

Table 9.9 Debt: GSDP Ratios of General and Special Category States: 2010–11

General Category States	Debt: GSDP Ratio (per cent)	Special category States	Debt: GSDP Ratio (per cent)
West Bengal	37	Mizoram	61
Punjab	31	Manipur	50
Uttar Pradesh	30	Nagaland	48
Bihar	29	Jammu & Kashmir	47
Kerala	29	Arunachal Pradesh	44
Rajasthan	27	Himachal Pradesh	43
Madhya Pradesh	26	Sikkim	41
Goa	24	Tripura	33
Gujarat	22	Uttarakhand	24
Andhra Pradesh	21	Assam	23
Jharkhand	21	Meghalaya	23
Odisha	20		
Karnataka	18	**Summary**	
Tamil Nadu	18	3 States	20 per cent–30 per cent
Maharashtra	17	1 State	30 per cent–40 per cent
Haryana	16	5 States	40 per cent–50 per cent
Chhattisgarh	11	2 States	>50 per cent

Genesis of Debt Problem

The states' debt problem had worsened after the substantial hikes of salary for the central government employees recommended by the Fifth Central Pay Commission, when state governments were also forced to match the salary levels of their own employees with the central government's pay scales, without having the resources to finance this huge additional burden. As a result, all states were forced to borrow more, throwing their finances completely out of gear. The problem hit the special category states especially hard. Without any resources of their own, this hike was clearly unsustainable and they had to resort to large scale borrowings from the centre at high rates of interest.

In fact, centre's role was largely responsible for the progressive indebtedness of the states in India. Most of the central loans to states were loans for financing of plans within the states, but the plan sizes in the states were never linked with sustainable levels of debt. As pointed out by Gupta (1992),

> Legally the States are under no obligation to ask for or accept loans from the Union Government. But actually the states are not in a position to exercise their legal freedom to decline Union loans. They can, dare not, forgo to undertake the development projects in the States, and are, therefore, willingly compelled to accept the Union loans with or without strings attached to them. And once they accept the loan, the process becomes unending. This makes states dependent on the Union and, in a sense, it amounts to infraction of State autonomy. But such has become the logic of Union–State fiscal relationship that the Union can neither refuse to give loans nor can it bring a distress warrant against the States.[5]

Further, Article 293(3) of the Constitution makes it obligatory for every state indebted to the centre to seek prior permission from the centre to raise any loans from the market. Centre was often using this provision to arm-twist the states to force them to continue to borrow from the centre only. It raised the interest on loans from 7.5 per cent in 1984–85 to 13 per cent in 1995–98 and then lowered it to 10.5 per cent in 2003–04. But the market rate of interest was actually much lower. These interest rates were fixed by the centre unilaterally based on its own formula, and the states had no way to refuse these expensive loans and instead go to the market to raise cheaper loans. Consequently, the states' outstanding dues to the centre outweighed their internal loans raised from the market, with average interest rate running far higher than market rates. This was affecting their finances in two ways: first, the centre was deducting the overdue instalments of the principal amounts and interest on outstanding loans while releasing fresh loans, leaving very little in the hands of the states. Second, this was forcing the states to borrow more and by the turn of the century, most states in India were falling into a vicious debt trap where they were borrowing only to repay the debt service charges. In the process, centre itself was raising loans from the market at cheaper rates and lending to the states at higher rates, the difference being its administrative charges. The loans to the states were thus serving as sources for its own finances.

Various Finance Commissions had attempted to address the problem of increasing indebtedness of the states from time to time without much success. The Tenth Commission had introduced a scheme of debt relief linked to a state's fiscal performance, defined as improvement in its ratio of revenue receipts to revenue expenditure. The Eleventh Finance Commission introduced a debt swap scheme, allowing states to pre-pay the high interest loans owed to the centre by swapping those with market borrowings and proceeds from small savings at prevailing interest rates which were much lower. While these gave the states some temporary relief, they failed to bring about the required structural changes that would have brought back the states from the brink of impending disaster on this account. It was not only the special category states, but all states in the country were facing this problem in varying degrees, with debt servicing obligations wiping out almost the entire fresh borrowings for most states.

The Twelfth Finance Commission (TwFC) (2005–10) was given the task of suggesting the restructuring of the public finances of the states for 'restoring the budgetary balance, achieving macroeconomic stability and debt reduction with equitable growth.' It went into the structural aspects of the problems and its recommendations had far reaching effects on the finances of the states in India. They also successfully addressed the problem of unmanageable debt burden of the states.

In 2003, the centre had enacted the Fiscal Responsibility and Budget Management Act (FRBMA) to reduce its rising fiscal deficit by bringing in some semblance of fiscal and financial discipline and move towards a balanced budget, by progressively reducing and then eliminating the revenue deficit and bringing down the fiscal deficit to a manageable three per cent of the GDP by March 2008. Of course due to the 2007–08 global financial meltdown and then due to its obsession with populist policies, the landmark legislation has since been diluted by the centre itself. But it was used by the TwFC to restore the finances of the states and to eliminate the revenue deficits for most states. The TwFC recommended a debt write-off scheme linked to the reduction of revenue deficit of states. Under the scheme, the repayments due from 2005–06 to 2009–10 on central loans contracted up to 31 March 2004 were to be consolidated and considered eligible for write-off, the quantum of which was linked to the absolute amount by which the revenue deficit was reduced in each successive year during the Commission's award period (2005–06 to 2009–10), provided the state had enacted an FRBM Act. The precondition was that the reduction in the revenue deficit must be cumulatively higher than the cumulative reduction attributable to the interest relief available. Another precondition was that the fiscal deficit of the state must be contained at least to the level of 2004–05. In effect, if the revenue deficit could be brought down to zero, the entire repayment during the period could be written off.

To address the problem of high interest bearing central loans to the states, the TwFC had further recommended that the central loans to states contracted till March 2004 and outstanding at the end of March 2005 should be consolidated and rescheduled for a fresh term of 20 years at 7.5 per cent only, again subject to the state enacting the FRBMA.

The Twelfth Finance Commission's formulas brought substantial relief to the states and did indeed help most of them to lighten their debt burden. Most states took advantage of the scheme and reduced their debt burden to manageable levels. The FRBM Act 2003 at the centre also provided a target based framework for management of government finances. All special category states except Jammu & Kashmir Meghalaya, Mizoram, and Sikkim had enacted FRBMA in 2005–06, and the others except Sikkim followed suit in 2006–07. By 2009–10, as many as 26 out of 28 States had enacted FRBMA bringing in some semblance of fiscal discipline that was hitherto largely absent and this had resulted in significant fiscal correction. But only two states failed to do so—West Bengal and Sikkim—and as a result, could not take advantage of the scheme to reduce their severe debt burden. Among the special category states Sikkim lost much of the potential debt relief for its failure to enact the FRBMA until 2010–11. Its Debt: GSDP ratio that was 62 per cent in the revised estimates of 2011–12 came down to 41 per cent in the budget estimates of 2012–13.

The Thirteenth Finance Commission (2010–15) also prescribed certain modalities for reducing the debt burden of the States. The terms of the reference of the Thirteenth Finance Commission (TFC) required it to 'review the state of finance of the Union and the States keeping in view, in particular, the operation of the States' Debt Consolidation and Relief Facility (DCRF) 2005–10'. DCRF was introduced by the Union Government on the recommendation of the TwFC—providing for

(i) Consolidation of central loans contracted till 31st March 2004 and outstanding as on 31st March 2005 for a fresh tenure of twenty years at 7.5 per cent rate of interest and (ii) Debt waiver to states based on their fiscal performance as discussed in the preceding paragraphs.

Due to the tight financial circumstances following the global economic meltdown of 2008–09, during 2009–2010 and 2010–11, the process of fiscal consolidation suffered setbacks across many states in India. TwFC expected all states to eliminate their revenue deficits by 2011–12 and generate revenue surpluses by 2014–15. Most states have already eliminated their revenue deficit, barring three general category states, Kerala, Punjab and West Bengal. TwFC was very particular about the enactment/amendment of FRBM Acts by the states to lay down the required fiscal reform path prescribing the borrowing limits for individual states and enforcing fiscal correction; the state-specific grants recommended by the TwFC would be released only after complying with the conditions stipulated in their respective FRBM Acts. It suggested further debt relief in respect of loans from National Small Savings Fund (NSSF) and for dues pertaining to central plan loans other than from the Ministry of Finance and outstanding as on 1 April 2010 to be written off, both again being incumbent upon enactment of FRBM Acts, laying down a road map for fiscal correction by the state.

Thanks to the recommendations of these two Finance Commissions, most of the special category states have come out of a vicious debt trap. The amount of debt relief available to the special category states under Twelfth and Thirteenth Finance Commission recommendations are shown in Table 9.10; obviously these reliefs helped bring their finances back to health in no small measure. Sikkim was recipient of the least amount of relief because it was the last to enact the FRBMA.

Surplus Cash Problem

One related area is cash management which is very weak in most special category states. Table 9.11 shows the position of closing cash balances of the special category states at the close of FY 2011 and FY 2012. It will be apparent that the many states have been sitting on piles of cash invested at nominal rates of interest with the treasury bills of the Government of India, while the same states have been borrowing from the market, and sometimes also from centre, at much higher cost.

Table 9.10 Debt Relief under Twelfth and Thirteenth Finance Commission Recommendations (Rs Crore)

	Debt Relief Measures Extended under TFC		Debt Relief Measures Extended under FC–XIII		
	Debt consolidated	Debt waiver allowed	Debt write off of CSS/CPS	NSSF Interest relief	Projected NSSF relief during 2011–12 as per FC–XIII
Arunachal Pradesh	404	40	17	0	3
Assam	2108	422	306	5	34
Himachal Pradesh	906	118	35	12	23
Jammu & Kashmir	1525	0	57	0	22
Manipur	751	150	21	0	3
Meghalaya	298	45	12	1	2
Mizoram	259	26	28	0	1
Nagaland	317	16	23	0	1
Sikkim	113	16	0	0	1
Tripura	445	89	18	3	8
Uttarakhand	262	26	28	15	27

If they could draw up a cash budget reflecting the cash inflows and outflows during the year with higher degree of accuracy, that would have obviated much of their borrowing itself.

Sustainability of Debt

Debt sustainability is defined as the ability of the state to maintain a constant Debt: GDP ratio over a period of time and reflects its ability to service its debt. The size and growth rate of the Debt: GDP Ratio assumes importance in this context as high debt ratios are costly and will eventually become unsustainable. Fiscal sustainability is also linked to the concept of solvency and liquidity; while solvency refers to the

Table 9.11 Cash Management by Special Category States: 2011–12 (Rs Crore)

	Closing Cash Balance – 31.3.2011	Deposits with RBI 31.3.2011	Interest Received on Investment of Cash Balances (2010–11)	Interest Received on Investment of Cash Balances (2011–12)	Debt Raised during 2010–11	Interest Payment	Closing Cash Balance – 31.3.2012
Arunachal Pradesh	1904	–285	110	48	241	109	874
Assam	6748	–973	408	465	7285	885	6022
Himachal Pradesh	907	–274	50	56	2249	798	949
Jammu & Kashmir	37	0	0	11	7382	769	750
Manipur	155	96	37	20	1625	177	2
Meghalaya	844	–508	20	22	232	114	301
Mizoram	81	–	6	8	476	101	19
Nagaland	274	–603	13	6	1056	200	0
Sikkim	440	21	25	28	122	79	565
Tripura	657	–186	22	49	676	226	1104
Uttarakhand	0	334	14	10	2326	507	50
Total	**12047**	**–2378**	**705**	**723**	**23670**	**3965**	**10637**

government's ability to service its debt obligations without explicitly defaulting on them, liquidity refers to government's ability to roll over its maturing liabilities with its liquid assets and available financing. Vulnerability to such problems is related to structure of debt—short-term/long term or internal/ external.

Sustainability of debt thus refers to the sufficiency of current assets to meet current or committed obligations and the capacity to balance the cost of additional borrowings with returns from such borrowings. Borrowings are necessary to bridge the resource gap or fiscal deficit; debt sustainability implies that the increase in fiscal deficit should be accompanied by an enhanced ability to service the additional debt burden. While calculating sustainability of debt, we are thus concerned with the inter-temporal budget constraint of the government and the change in public debt ratio over time.

A necessary condition for sustainability or stabilization of Debt:GSDP ratio is that the rate of growth of GSDP should exceed the interest rate i.e. the cost of borrowed funds; Debt:GSDP ratio is then likely to be stable provided there is a sustained primary surplus (at least not a deficit in the primary account). This is known as the Solvency Condition. The determinants of sustainability are therefore the relative rates of growth between the GSDP and the cost of additional borrowings, for which the average interest rate on outstanding debt can serve as a proxy. Given the rate spread (GSDP growth rate – interest rate) and quantum spread (debt stock multiplied by the rate spread), debt sustainability condition states that if quantum spread together with primary deficit is zero, Debt:GSDP ratio would be stable or debt would be sustainable. On the other hand, if it is negative, the Debt:GSDP ratio would continue to rise and in case it is positive, Debt:GSDP ratio would eventually fall.

Looking at the Table 9.12, we see that three of the special category states (Mizoram, Sikkim, and Manipur) had more than 60 per cent Debt: GSDP ratios in 2000–01, and as many as four more states had this ratio above 50 per cent (Arunachal Pradesh, Himachal Pradesh, Jammu & Kashmir, and Nagaland). However, by 2010–11, the debt position had improved in all states and all of them had reduced their Debt: GSDP ratio, some of them remarkably, like Sikkim which had reduced the Debt: GSDP ratio by as much as 31 per cent in ten years' time, down to 41 per cent in 2010–11 from 72 per cent a decade ago,

Table 9.12 Comparison of Debt Positions: 2000–01 and 2010–11

	Arunachal Pradesh	Assam	Himachal Pradesh	Jammu & Kashmir	Manipur	Meghalaya	Mizoram	Nagaland	Sikkim	Tripura	Uttarakhand
Debt: GSDP Ratio2001 (per cent)	58	27	51	53	62	27	77	54	72	40	34
Debt:GSDP Ratio 2011 (per cent)	44	23	43	47	50	23	61	48	41	33	24
Reduction in Debt–GDSP Ratio (2001–2011) (per cent)	14	4	8	6	12	4	16	6	31	7	10
Average Growth Rate of Outstanding Liability – 2001–2011 (per cent)	**14**	**10**	**13**	**12**	**9**	**12**	**11**	**11**	**12**	**10**	**15**

Average Growth Rate of GSDP – 2001–2011 (per cent)	**17**	**12**	**14**	**13**	**11**	**14**	**13**	**12**	**19**	**12**	**20**
Net Debt Available/Total Debt Received (per cent) - 2001	21	7	27	6	14	−6	21	19	−17	33	11
Net Debt Available/Total Debt Received (per cent) -2011	−58	−9	9	2	−20	6	42	10	−17	12	31
Debt: Total Tax Revenue (per cent), 2000–01	1005	325	753	626	906	371	1305	2480	533	613	486
Debt: Total Tax Revenue (per cent), 2010–11	411	183	456	405	364	229	636	597	289	331	289

(Cont'd)

Table 9.12 *(Cont'd)*

	Arunachal Pradesh	Assam	Himachal Pradesh	Jammu & Kashmir	Manipur	Meghalaya	Mizoram	Nagaland	Sikkim	Tripura	Uttarakhand
Debt: Own Tax Revenue (per cent), 2000–01	3965	714	1094	1193	3927	885	9217	4637	1123	1765	561
Debt: Own Tax Revenue (per cent), 2010–11	1787	430	671	761	1716	588	2840	2399	845	927	450
Debt Sustainability Analysis											
Primary Balance (Rs Crore) 2001	–140	–655	–1047	–1104	–49	136	–274	–136	27	–212	–129
Primary Balance (Rs Crore) -2011	425	–79	–1213	–84	–204	84	–914	–123	–129	219	1579
Quantum Spread + Primary Balance –2011	–42	–1045	–1046	–1334	–335	124	–224	9	41	–174	–307
Quantum Spread + Primary Balance –2011	665	2325	280	2231	-105	296	-645	-153	126	551	3399

followed by Mizoram, Arunachal Pradesh, Manipur, and Uttarakhand, all of which had reduced this ratio by more than 10 per cent. The Debt: GSDP ratio was within a safe limit of 35 per cent for four states (Assam, Meghalaya, Uttarakhand, and Tripura) in 2010–11, while it was still dangerously high for Mizoram (61 per cent), Manipur (50 per cent), and Nagaland (48 per cent). But during this decade, none of the states had allowed the outstanding liabilities to rise faster than their GSDP; in fact, some of the states, like Arunachal Pradesh, Sikkim, and Uttarakhand, increased their incomes at rates much higher than the growth of their outstanding liabilities.

However, the net debt available was negligible for most states, implying that very little of the debt funds were available to the states for making productive capital investments to ensure their higher and faster future growth. In 2010–11, the net debt available was negative for as many as four states, implying that not only were they unable to discharge their debt servicing obligations with the debt funds, but had to spend some of their own resources to discharge their current debt service obligations. Performance of Arunachal Pradesh was the worst in this regard, followed by Manipur, Sikkim, and Assam. In 2000–1, only two states, Meghalaya and Sikkim, had negative net debts; Sikkim even in 2000–01 had the same 17 per cent negative net debt as in 2010–11.

In terms of the ratios of outstanding debt to both the state's own tax revenue as well as to total tax revenue including state's share of central taxes, the time series data indeed show convergence; both the ratios for all the states had declined remarkably in 2010–11 compared to 2000–01.

Lastly, coming to the sustainability of debt, it is seen that primary balance was negative for 9 out of 11 states in 2000–01, while it still remained negative for all but four states in 2010–11. Of these four states, Uttarakhand had a substantial surplus of nearly Rs 1600 crore in its primary account, followed by Arunachal Pradesh (Rs 425 crore), Tripura (Rs 219 crore), and Meghalaya (Rs 84 crore). However, the rate spread which measure the extent to which the GSDP growth rate exceeded the weighted interest rate on outstanding loans, was positive for all states in 2010–11, except Nagaland which had a negative spread only by 0.54 per cent. Ignoring this, we can say that the solvency condition was partly satisfied by all these states in 2010–11, which was a remarkable improvement compared to 2000–01. Almost all states, except Nagaland

and Manipur, in fact, had their GSDP growth rates much above their average interest rate on outstanding loans indicating their ability to service their additional debt. The surplus in primary account together with the quantum spread was also positive for all states in 2010–11 except Manipur, Mizoram, and Nagaland, suggesting that their existing debt levels might not be sustainable in the long run. But the majority of special category states had indeed been able to bring down their debt to sustainable levels.

Deficit Management

Revenue deficit and capital deficit represent the excess of expenditure over receipts under the revenue and capital accounts respectively. The conventional budget deficit is the algebraic sum of the revenue and capital deficits, but this does not actually show the total resource gap in the economy, as it includes the borrowings under the capital receipts. The overall resource gap is reflected by the Gross Fiscal Deficit (GFD) which is to be bridged by borrowings of one sort or another. Gross fiscal deficit is composed of revenue deficit, capital outlay, and net lending made by the government; it is financed by net borrowings under the Consolidated Fund, net borrowings under the Public Account, and also by drawing down the cash balance that the state governments maintain with the Reserve Bank of India.

The indicators used for measuring deficit management by the states are shown in Box 9.4 and the results of their measurement are shown in Table 9.13. It can be seen that in 2000–01, almost all special category states were running very high level of fiscal deficits;

Box 9.4 Deficit Management Performance Indicators

Deficit Ratios

1. Ratio of Gross Fiscal Deficit to GSDP (per cent)
2. Ratio of Revenue Deficit to GFD (per cent)
3. Ratio of Capital Outlay to GFD (per cent)
4. Ratio of Net Lending to GFD (per cent)
5. Ratio of Primary Deficit to GSDP (per cent)

Table 9.13 Deficit Indicators of Special Category States: 2000–01 and 2010–11

Deficit Ratios (per cent)	Arunachal Pradesh	Assam	Himachal Pradesh	Jammu & Kashmir	Manipur	Meghalaya	Mizoram	Nagaland	Sikkim	Tripura	Uttarakhand
						2000–01					
Revenue Deficit to GFD	–46	51	70	51	35	–21	51	30	–190	20	54
Capital Outlay to GFD	144	36	30	46	65	91	44	71	290	79	34
Net Lending to GFD	1	13	1	2	0	31	5	-1	0	0	12
GFD/ GSDP (per cent)	9.9	4.2	11.8	11.2	7.3	6.3	21.6	8.5	5.1	8.0	3.9
Primary Deficit/ GSDP (per cent)	4.8	1.8	6.7	6.6	1.6	3.4	15.8	3.4	–2.7	3.9	0.7

(Cont'd)

Table 9.13 *(Cont'd)*

Deficit Ratios (per cent)	Arunachal Pradesh	Assam	Himachal Pradesh	Jammu & Kashmir	Manipur	Meghalaya	Mizoram	Nagaland	Sikkim	Tripura	Uttarakhand
2010–11											
Revenue Deficit to GFD	–	–	39	–	–	–	39	–	–	–	1
Capital Outlay to GFD	–	101	56	256	337	168	60	231	143	464	101
Net Lending to GFD	–	2	5	3	0	4	0	0	2	–1	–1
GFD/ GSDP (per cent)	–0.3	1.8	5.6	4.2	6.2	2.3	16.8	4.8	5.6	1.3	2.2
Primary Deficit/ GSDP (per cent)	–4.9	0.1	2.2	0.1	2.2	0.6	15.1	1.1	2.3	–1.2	0.4

only Uttarakhand and Assam had somewhat manageable fiscal deficits. For all other states, the fiscal deficits had reached dangerous levels which clearly were unsustainable. Mizoram's fiscal deficit amounted to 21.6 per cent of its GSDP, followed by Himachal Pradesh (11.8 per cent), Jammu & Kashmir (11.2 per cent), Arunachal Pradesh (9.9 per cent), Nagaland (8.5 per cent), and Tripura (8.0 per cent). All these state were also having high levels of deficit in their primary accounts. Only three states—Sikkim, Arunachal Pradesh, and Meghalaya—were able to generate surpluses in their revenue accounts and hence could increase their capital outlays significantly; the revenue accounts of all other states were in deficits. The revenue deficits of as many as five states contributed to more than 50 per cent of their fiscal deficits. It was a sure recipe for impending disaster. But they were saved from this disaster by the TwFC, which forced the states to curtail their revenue expenditure by enacting FRBMAs. In 2010–11, i.e. one year after the end of the TwFC period, only two states (Himachal Pradesh and Mizoram) had deficits in their revenue accounts, Uttarakhand had a balanced revenue account and the rest all were generating surpluses, six of them very substantially, which surpluses they could use for making capital outlay and limit borrowing to that extent. Fiscal deficit for five states were within the FRBMA norm of 3 per cent of GSDP (Arunachal Pradesh in fact had a small fiscal surplus in 2010–11), four states had fiscal deficits ranging between 4.2 per cent and 6.2 per cent of their GSDPs and only Mizoram had very high fiscal deficit (16.8 per cent). Finances of most states were back on track.

Sustainability, Flexibility, and Vulnerability of State Finances

For development, government must expand the levels of its activities. It would then be necessary to know whether the means of financing these activities are sustainable, i.e. if they meet the increased expenditure needs of the state government without substantially adding to its debt burden. If the government wishes to expand the level of its activity, it would be pertinent to examine the flexibility of the means of financing (either by increasing the revenue or by additional borrowing) and whether the expanded level of activity makes the government vulnerable to financial risks.

Box 9.5 Flexibility, Vulnerability and Sustainability Indicators

Sustainability Indicators
1. Buoyancy of State's Own Tax Receipts w.r.t. GSDP
2. Growth in Outstanding Debt/Growth in Total Revenue Receipts
3. Growth of Outstanding Debt/Growth of GSDP

Flexibility Indicators
4. Capital Repayment/Capital Borrowings (per cent)
5. Interest Ratio = (Net Interest payment)/(Total Revenues–Interest Receipt) (per cent)

Vulnerability Indicators
6. Outstanding Guarantees/Revenue Receipts (per cent)

The indicators used for measuring the sustainability, flexibility, and vulnerability of finances of the special category states are shown in Box 9.5 and the results of measurement by applying these indicators are shown in Table 9.14. The indicators used are briefly explained in the succeeding paragraphs. Other relevant indicators like Debt: GSDP ratio or GFD: GSDP ratio, etc. which already have been discussed have not been included in this analysis.

A. Sustainability Indicators

Buoyancy of State's Own Tax Receipts with respect to GSDP: Any rise in GSDP should automatically result in the increased tax receipts. Buoyancy ratios capture the incremental increases in receipts from tax due to income growth in the economy, and hence reflect the potential to raise more revenues from these sources.

The ratio of **Growth in Outstanding Debt/Growth in Total Revenue Receipts** indicates the sustainability of the debt level of a state. A ratio less than one would indicate that tax receipts were growing faster than debt, in which case the state would be able to service the additional debt burden from its increased taxes and at the same time would be able to reduce the level of outstanding debt.

The ratio of **Growth of Outstanding Debt/Growth of GSDP** would also reflect on the sustainability of debt level. A ratio more than one would not be sustainable.

Table 9.14 Sustainability, Flexibility and Vulnerability of Finances of the Special Category States: 2010–11

Ratios	Arunachal Pradesh	Assam	Himachal Pradesh	Jammu & Kashmir	Manipur	Meghalaya	Mizoram	Nagaland	Sikkim	Tripura	Uttarakhand
Sustainability Ratios											
Buoyancy of State's Own Tax Receipts w.r.t. GSDP	1.42	1.10	2.45	0.85	3.50	2.00	1.40	3.47	1.55	1.30	1.38
Growth in Outstanding Debt/Growth in Total Revenue Receipts	0.15	0.44	0.48	0.39	0.13	-0.49	-4.66	0.18	-0.86	0.61	0.73
Growth in Outstanding Debt/Growth in GSDP	0.23	0.41	0.65	0.58	0.50	-0.82	1.12	0.84	-0.69	0.77	0.95

(Cont'd)

Table 9.14 *(Cont'd)*

Ratios	Arunachal Pradesh	Assam	Himachal Pradesh	Jammu & Kashmir	Manipur	Meghalaya	Mizoram	Nagaland	Sikkim	Tripura	Uttarakhand
Flexibility Ratios											
Capital Repayment/ Capital Borrowings (per cent)	28	31	19	43	24	27	26	17	28	18	26
Interest Ratio (per cent)	5	8	15	10	6	6	4	8	5	8	12
Vulnerability Ratios											
Outstanding Guarantees/ Revenue Receipts (per cent)	–	1	31	12	4	26	4	1	8	1	–

B. Flexibility Indicators

Capital Outlay/Capital Borrowings: This ratio indicates to what extent capital receipts are applied for capital formation. A ratio of less than 100 per cent would not be sustainable in the long run, as that would indicate that capital receipts are utilized for meeting revenue expenditure without adding to productive capacity in the economy.

Interest Ratio: This is calculated as (Interest payment–Interest receipt)/(Total revenue–Interest receipt). A higher ratio indicates a lower ability of the state government to service any fresh debt and to meet its revenue expenditure from its revenue receipts.

C. Vulnerability Indicators

Outstanding Guarantees/ Revenue Receipts (per cent): Outstanding guarantees represent the contingent liabilities of the state governments. Governments provide guarantees to their public sector undertakings for raising loans from banks and financial institutions. In the event of default by them, government has the obligation to underwrite the outstanding loans of these undertakings. These are basically unfunded debt and represent the fiscal risks that might arise in future in an uncertain manner. Since these are not backed by adequate funds, a high level of outstanding guarantees may render state government finances extremely vulnerable to future uncertainties. Most states have now created 'Guarantee Redemption Funds' in the Public Account for meeting the payment obligations arising out of the guarantees under recommendations of the TwFC; their Fiscal Responsibility Legislations have also fixed an upper limit on the guarantees to be provided.

Contingent liabilities can be explicit or implicit; explicit contingent liabilities are specific government obligations defined by a contract or a law where the government is legally bound to settle such an obligation when it's due; guarantees given to banks or financial institutions on behalf of PSUs fall into this category. In contrast, implicit contingent liabilities represent moral obligations for the government which may not be binding in the legal sense, but which governments may find difficult to ignore due to political or other reasons. Defaults by public or private entities on non-guaranteed debt funds towards their repayment obligations to citizens would fall into this category.

From Table 9.14, we see that in terms of all sustainability indicators as discussed above, finances of all special category states are very much sustainable as on 2010–11. Tax receipts were highly buoyant for all except Mizoram, revenue receipts and GSDP were growing faster than outstanding debt—in fact for some states there has actually been a decrease in the level of outstanding debt in 2010–11.

As regards flexibility of public finances, however, except for Jammu & Kashmir, capital repayments did not consume large shares of capital receipts of most states and interest ratios were also kept within reasonable limits. Outstanding guarantees constituted significant percentage of revenue receipts only in Himachal Pradesh and Meghalaya.

Ranking of States: Composite Index

There were several attempts in the past to develop composite indices to measure and analyse the fiscal performance of governments. Bhide and Pande (2002) adopted a composite index comprised of five indicators such as share of revenue and capital expenditure in total expenditure, ratio of net-tax revenue to GDP, ratio of fiscal deficit to GDP, and revenue deficit to GDP. Three indices, viz. deficit index, own revenue effort index, and expenditure and debt servicing index based on a set of eight indicators were developed by Dholakia (2005); these were then combined to make a composite index of fiscal performance. Nambiar (2005) also developed a set of three indices, viz. Revenue Effort Index, Resource Allocation Index, and Deficit Index, constructed in terms of several ratios under each, and combining these indicators by giving them equal weightage.

While the above methodologies provide valid basis for comparison among the states, the present study has attempted to construct a more broad-based composite index comprising the following four indices:

(1) **Resource Management Index** to be computed in terms of ratios of (i) Own Revenue/ Revenue Expenditure and (ii) Own Revenue/ Total Revenue (iii) Own Tax Revenue/ Gross State Domestic Product (GSDP), all of which carry equal weights;

(2) **Expenditure Management Index** to be computed in terms of ratios of (i) Development Expenditure/ Total Expenditure (ii) Plan Expenditure/ Total Expenditure and (iii) Capital Outlay/ Capital Receipts, all of which carry equal weights;

(3) **Debt Management Index** to be computed in terms of ratios of (i) Total Outstanding Liability/GSDP (ii) Interest Payments/ Revenue Expenditure and (ii) Net Debt Available/Total Debt, all of which carry equal weights; higher the values of the first two ratios, lower the values of the corresponding indices and higher the value of the third, higher the value of the corresponding index;

(4) **Deficit Management Index** to be computed in terms of ratios of (i) GFD/GSDP; (ii) Primary Deficit/GSDP and (iii) Capital Outlay/GFD, all carrying equal weights again; higher values of the ratios under (i) and (ii) will impact the index negatively and higher value of the ratio (iii) will impact the index positively.

These indices are then combined into a single composite Public Finance Performance Index by assigning equal weights to each and using the same methodology as adopted in Chapter 8, states are ranked according to this composite index.

Tables 9.15 and 9.16 show the rankings of the states for the years 2000–01 and 2010–11 respectively. From these tables, we find that in both these years, Sikkim had topped the list of special category states in respect of management of public finances, though its total index had declined from 8.91 to 7.01 between these two years. It was followed

Box 9.6 Correlation between Public Finance Management and Socio-Economic Development of the Special Category States: 2010–11

Ranking	Public Finance Performance	Socio-Economic Development
1	Sikkim	1. Sikkim
2	Arunachal Pradesh	2. Himachal Pradesh
3	Uttarakhand	3. Mizoram
4	Assam	4. Uttarakhand
5	Meghalaya	5. Tripura
6	Himachal Pradesh	6. Nagaland
7	Tripura	7. Meghalaya
8	Manipur	8. Manipur
9	Jammu &Kashmir	9. Jammu & Kashmir
10	Nagaland	10. Arunachal Pradesh
11	Mizoram	11. Assam

Table 9.15 Composite Ranking of Special Category States: 2000–01

State	Own Revenue/ Revenue Expenditure	Own Revenue/ Total Revenue	Own Tax Revenue/ Gross State Domestic Product (GSDP)	Development Expenditure/ Total Expenditure	Plan Expenditure/ Total Expenditure	Capital Outlay/ Capital Receipts
Sikkim	1.00	0.94	1.00	0.57	0.43	1.00
Uttarakhand	0.81	1.00	0.95	0.75	0.09	0.05
Meghalaya	0.34	0.31	0.39	0.83	0.50	0.35
Arunachal Pradesh	0.12	0.08	0.11	1.00	1.00	0.46
Tripura	0.18	0.19	0.26	0.91	0.45	0.50
Assam	0.61	0.75	0.54	0.09	0.01	0.07
Himachal Pradesh	0.38	0.63	0.69	0.77	0.48	0.06
Jammu & Kashmir	0.31	0.39	0.65	0.87	0.14	0.01
Nagaland	0.02	0.00	0.06	0.58	0.31	0.04
Mizoram	0.00	0.00	0.00	0.90	0.56	0.26
Manipur	0.07	0.06	0.13	0.00	0.00	0.00

Table 9.16 Composite Ranking of Special Category States: 2010–11

State	Own Revenue/ Revenue Expenditure	Own Revenue/ Total Revenue	Own Tax Revenue/ Gross State Domestic Product (GSDP)	Development Expenditure/ Total Expenditure	Plan Expenditure/ Total Expenditure	Capital Outlay/ Capital Receipts
Sikkim	1.00	1.00	0.64	0.00	0.42	1.00
Arunachal Pradesh	0.26	0.14	0.10	1.00	1.00	0.65
Uttarakhand	0.88	0.93	0.74	0.47	0.31	0.00
Assam	0.69	0.73	0.73	0.70	0.22	0.01
Meghalaya	0.33	0.32	0.43	0.85	0.76	0.04
Himachal Pradesh	0.74	0.88	1.00	0.56	0.00	0.00
Tripura	0.22	0.17	0.34	0.40	0.45	0.06
Manipur	0.11	0.04	0.21	0.72	0.98	0.29
Jammu & Kashmir	0.39	0.32	0.92	0.30	0.08	0.01
Nagaland	0.03	0.00	0.00	0.41	0.53	0.09
Mizoram	0.00	0.04	0.03	0.86	0.69	0.08

Total Outstanding Liability/ GSDP	Interest Payments/ Revenue Expenditure	Net Debt Available/ Total Debt Raised	GFD/ GSDP	Primary Deficit/ GSDP	Capital Outlay/ GFD	Index	Rank
0.09	0.96	0.00	0.93	1.00	1.00	8.91	1
0.85	0.16	1.00	1.00	0.82	0.02	7.49	2
1.00	0.92	0.13	0.86	0.67	0.24	6.54	3
0.37	0.87	0.43	0.66	0.60	0.44	6.13	4
0.72	0.63	0.61	0.77	0.65	0.19	6.05	5
0.98	0.54	0.30	0.98	0.76	0.03	5.67	6
0.51	0.00	0.54	0.55	0.49	0.00	5.11	7
0.47	0.80	0.28	0.59	0.50	0.06	5.06	8
0.46	0.52	0.33	0.74	0.67	0.16	3.90	9
0.00	1.00	0.47	0.00	0.00	0.05	3.24	10
0.29	0.31	0.39	0.81	0.77	0.14	2.96	11

Total Outstanding Liability/ GSDP	Interest Payments/ Revenue Expenditure	Net Debt Available/ Total Debt Raised	GFD/ GSDP	Primary Deficit/ GSDP	Capital Outlay/ GFD	Index	Rank
0.52	0.70	0.41	0.66	0.64	0.01	7.01	1
0.45	0.36	0.00	1.00	1.00	1.00	6.95	2
0.97	0.12	0.89	0.85	0.73	0.01	6.89	3
1.00	0.53	0.49	0.88	0.75	0.01	6.74	4
0.99	0.71	0.65	0.85	0.73	0.02	6.66	5
0.46	0.00	0.67	0.65	0.65	0.00	5.61	6
0.73	0.35	0.70	0.91	0.82	0.06	5.21	7
0.28	0.47	0.38	0.62	0.64	0.04	4.77	8
0.38	0.18	0.60	0.74	0.75	0.03	4.70	9
0.33	0.38	0.68	0.70	0.70	0.02	3.87	10
0.00	1.00	1.00	0.00	0.00	0.00	3.70	11

by Arunachal Pradesh in 2011 and Uttarakhand in 2001. Mizoram, Manipur, Nagaland, and Jammu & Kashmir shared the bottom places in both three years, though Manipur had moved up from the eleventh position in 2001 to eighth position in 2011, while the other three had slipped by one rank each between these years. Arunachal Pradesh had moved up from the fourth to the second position by successfully containing its fiscal deficit and investing substantially in capital assets, while Uttarakhand had slipped to the third position in 2011. Himachal Pradesh, despite significant improvement in its revenue performance, could only improve its position from seventh to sixth between these two years due to its heavy indebtedness that limited its capital outlay. Assam improved its position from sixth in 2001 to fourth in 2011 by its improved expenditure and debt management, while Meghalaya and Tripura had slipped by two ranks each to fifth and seventh positions respectively.

It would be interesting to compare their performance rankings in respect of public finances with those in respect of socio-economic parameters as discussed in Chapter 8. While Sikkim is at the top of both lists in 2011, and Manipur and Jammu & Kashmir occupy the eighth and ninth positions respectively in both the lists. Uttarakhand also shows some correlation, but no other state seems to have any such correlation between their socio-economic and public finance performances. The absence of such correlation may be due to many factors, like a low base of development in some states, historical and geographical factors, and of course due to issues related to governance and proper use of public funds. But we have no empirical evidence to explain the difference between these rankings. However, there is a vindication of our premise that faster growth should ordinarily translate into better public financial health of a state. Sikkim, Uttarakhand, and Arunachal Pradesh—states that had recorded highest growth rates during the decade, as seen earlier, also topped the composite index of public finance.

Notes

1. The other financial liabilities of the Government being its public debt liabilities and contingent liabilities on account of outstanding guarantees given to public sector entities and public bodies/ authorities.

2. Some of these funds— like the Sinking Fund, Calamity Relief Fund, or State Disaster Response Fund, etc.—have been created as per recommendations of the successive Finance Commissions.

3. NSSF was established in 1999 in the Public Account for crediting collections from all small savings (PPF, NSC, KVP, etc.). Balance of this fund is invested in Central and State Govt. Securities and states were allowed to borrow 80 per cent from this fund initially. Since 2002–03, the net collections are being invested only in State Govt. Securities and thus states are forced to borrow the entire proceeds. But the responsibility to repay to the investors lies with the Centre and these schemes are linked to tax deductions under Section 80C of the Income Tax Act 1961. They carry interest higher than the market rates and these rates are administered by the Centre.

4. Only current prices have been used in this study since all Government transactions are recorded only at market prices.

5. Quoted in Vaidya (2005).

Conclusion

Summary, Discussions, and a Road Map

Special Category States—Inherited Disadvantage

Having come to the end of this study, it is now time to summarize the findings and address the issues that could not be discussed earlier, especially the demands for the special category status by many states. It would also be imperative to suggest some broad road map on the future path of development of the special category states. The objective of the study was to explore the reality of the special category states, to go to the root of their backwardness, and to examine their distinct ethnic, cultural, and historical identities within a framework of asymmetric federalism in India. In the process, a lot of common traits and drawbacks as well as strengths shared by these states have emerged.

It was observed that the special category states were incapacitated in many ways—they were essentially ruralized states characterized by scarcity of natural resources, low income, low growth, and heavy dependence on agriculture. Agricultural practices were, and by and large still are, characterized by primitive methods and low productivity. Industrialization has not taken roots in these states due to the lack of viable and quality infrastructure. The difficulties of hilly terrains and the lack of connectivity increased the cost of public services manifolds, which was often the reason for their heavy indebtedness. Regular recurrence of floods and natural calamities takes a heavy toll not only on the life and property of their people but also on development. Alienation, produced by decades of economic disempowerment and sense of apparent neglect along with the perceived fear of losing the ethno-cultural identities had turned many of them into fertile breeding grounds for terrorism and insurgency that had further crippled their economic growth and in some of these states, economy has coalesced with insurgency in a bizarre symbiotic relationship. The protracted insurgency in some of these states has taken a heavy toll on their development. Problems of illegal immigration, economic backwardness, and lack of employment opportunities are increasingly driving the youth away from these states. While poor governance and widespread corruption have paralysed the administration's capacity to deliver, the ethno-cultural alienation has deepened due to inappropriate policies pursued by the centre, born out of unfamiliarity with and inadequate understanding of the problems of these states.

Inaccessibility and physical isolation were disadvantages produced by geography, but these natural deficiencies were further accentuated due to events over which these states had little control. Partition had isolated the entire northeastern region not only from the rest of the country, but also from the emerging markets in east and south east Asia by closing their gateways to traditional markets in those countries, and our uneasy relationships with these neighbours did not help matters either. In Jammu & Kashmir, the peculiar circumstances of the state's accession to India and events thereafter had embroiled the state into the power politics between two countries and turned it into a permanent trouble-spot. The attempt to address the genuine concerns of these states through inadequate asymmetrical powers and their subsequent dilution by insincere machinations contributed towards compounding an already twisted and convoluted imbroglio. Failure of governance, sometimes total abdication of responsibility by the government of the day, and collusive exploitation of the situation by the politicians-bureaucrats-contractor nexus had given way to complete breakdown of law and order machinery, creating a miasma of despair and frustration for the hapless people forcing them to live on the edge of rebelliousness. Disruption of normal life has put a brake on all economic activities, slowly driving away talent and capital, along with hope.

Special Category Status—A Flawed Mechanism

Reasons for creation of a separate 'special' category of states were political as well as economical. The political compulsions arose out of the need to strengthen cohesion in the Indian federation by attempting to address the widespread ethno-cultural, linguistic, and socio-religious diversity in these states, especially in Jammu & Kashmir and in northeast India, by providing guarantees and protection through constitutional provisions of Articles 370 and 371, besides Fifth and Sixth Schedules of the Constitution. It was an attempt to accommodate diversity through *de jure* asymmetry but this failed to improve the quality of participation in the federal process by expanding the scope for 'dignity, diversity, dissent and development'. The statutory protection can be successful only when backed by sufficiently empowering and enabling political and economic processes, but in their absence, the asymmetry proved inadequate to accommodate the existing diversities. Further, the emergence of coalition governments at the centre and subsequent weakening of the central authority had allowed Indian states more bargaining power, but the special category states were not in a position to use this increased power to their advantage in the absence of sufficient autonomy and capacity within themselves. The model of autonomy instituted within these states was an essentially top-down model, and it had all the constraints of a traditional bureaucratic system—economic centralization, overriding control, inadequate devolution of power, and limited capacity of local governance institutions, limited functional and fiscal autonomy at the local level and increasing bureaucratization of the administrative machinery. On top of it, the politics of convenience subverted the spirit of federalism, further eroding the constitutional safeguards.

The special category states suffered from a number of debilitating handicaps—geographical isolation, acute deficiency of capital, high cost structure of economy, absence of viable infrastructure including transport and communication network, poor financial inclusion, primitive state of technology use, sensitive borders, inefficiency in administrative machinery, etc. These were not addressable in the short term, and needed more than mere funds. These were other structural imbalances which made these states laggard in development, like poor capital formation, absence of adequate skill-set among people at productive age, lack of entrepreneurial and managerial talent, and consequent lack of industrial development. All these were responsible for a subsistence-level existence for most people in these states.

The mechanism of according special category status devised to address these deep-rooted structural weaknesses equally lacked imagination and understanding. By giving a preferential treatment to these states through liberal plan assistance along with tax breaks was no way to ensure their development and requisite capacity-creation. Entrenched structural incapacities produced by centuries of isolation, neglect, and derivation shaped by history and geography cannot be addressed so simplistically, by merely designing a novel pattern of funding that was again scale-neutral, without any relation to the magnitude and dimension of backwardness of the concerned states. Formulating a coherent and pragmatic strategy by addressing the structural weaknesses was essential for any development, a strategy in which funding would be just one essential element. But strategy was given a go-by and neither was the required institutional set-up created to guide, monitor and steer these states towards a predefined goal. The whole structure was thus a diffused mélange of ad-hoc, visionless, goalless, short-term plans marked by singular lack of any performance expectation or any accountability structure. Instead of empowering these peripheral, marginalized states and bringing them within the folds of the mainstream, all it had achieved was to create states overwhelmingly dependent on central funding, unable to negotiate their economic future on their own strength.

The mechanism of plan funding naturally failed to deliver optimally under these circumstances. It is, however, undeniable that giving these states special category status on their creation was to ensure their survival in the face of enormous inherited backwardness and lack of capacity. Without the financial support, they would not have survived as states, given their small sizes, inadequate resource base, and lack of productive capacity. At the time of creation, most special category states were unviable financially and also politically, because political existence was incumbent upon economic viability which was missing and hence it was imperative to usher in this viability through some mechanism. The special category status was one such mechanism. It is indeed true that without the special category status, these states would never have achieved the standards that they have achieved, with about half of them attaining levels of socio-economic development comparable to the national standards by 2010–11.

But the belief that providing liberal funding alone would address their problems of development and backwardness, was flawed *ab initio*. To the Planning Commission that contrived the entire mechanism, allotment of funds to the special category states was the ultimate fulfilment of their developmental commitments. Under these circumstances, it inevitably led to misuse and diversion of these easy funds that fed and fuelled corruption and created a separate rent-seeking class—the 'nouveau riche' special class of the special category states. Not that it was happening only within the special category states, but being within societies that were deprived more than the most, such a retrograde course of development was all the more reprehensible. As the Chinese sage Confucius had said, 'In a country well governed, poverty is something to be ashamed of. In a country badly governed, wealth is something to be ashamed of.' Most special category states, without a shadow of doubt, have been badly governed for most part of their existence, with a leadership that lacked not only vision or imagination, but also integrity.

The political leaders at the centre never sincerely tried to appreciate the nature of problems in these states and lacked pragmatism in their approach; they rather adopted a patronizing attitude towards these states due to their inadequate understanding. Where engagement with the people would have solved problems, they applied force and where force was necessary to deal with violence, they condescended. Whenever the problems seemed to get out of hand, the recipe was simple, carve out another state and accord it the special category status, as if giving this status alone was a panacea for all problems without addressing the structural weaknesses inherited by these states from their history and geography. Those structural weaknesses still remain unaddressed, despite decades of special category status enjoyed by these states.

Even the pattern of funding that was initially prescribed for the special category states was diluted substantially through the gradual incursion by an astounding number of centrally sponsored schemes and the vicious mechanism of direct transfers devised by a Planning Commission. It created a structure that diffused accountability, encouraged corruption, deepened the already entrenched bureaucratic controls, and prevented further reforms. The Planning Commission started behaving more and more like a Control Commission, enjoying its illegitimate authority to allocate increasing proportion of public funds directly to the implementing agencies of the centrally sponsored schemes, actively encouraged by a government that was delighted to discover the use such funds for electoral gains. Fortunately, the newly elected government had put an end to such arbitrary powers and abolished the anachronistic relic of an outdated and dysfunctional Nehruvian model of socialism, completely out of sync and irrelevant in an era guided by market capitalism. The criteria devised by the Planning Commission for awarding the special category status to a state were also arbitrary. That these criteria could be twisted at will to suit political convenience was amply demonstrated in the case of Bihar and Andhra Pradesh, after creation of Telengana .

With an eye to forging an electoral alliance with Nitish Kumar who had made the special category status for Bihar conditional to any such alliance, the UPA government at the centre appointed the Raghuram Rajan Committee that worked out the criteria for backwardness, according to which 10 states including Bihar were found 'least developed' among 28 states—and hence eligible for special assistance. The report generated widespread criticism as it was seeking to introduce a third tier for devolution of central funds, over and above those of the Finance Commission and the Planning Commission, and when that electoral alliance failed to work out, the centre played the same card by proposing to grant a special status to Seemandhra region after carving out Telangana from Andhra Pradesh, again with an eye upon the impending Lok Sabha elections. Seemandhra—the successor state of the erstwhile composite state of Andhra Pradesh—like Bihar, did not fulfil the Planning Commission criteria for special category status, but in the structure of illegitimacy surrounding the Planning Commission, anything was acceptable so long as it served political ends of the ruing dispensation, for which political considerations always outweighed economic considerations.

For the special category states, things actually started changing slowly after globalization and liberalization opened up the economic horizons for the country and along with it, dismantled the closed control-command based economic decision-making process. With national growth reaching almost double digits, the flow of funds into the special category states also increased significantly. Some of these additional funds were used to expand the infrastructure of education, health, power, transport and communication, and for upgradation of technology. Even in the outlying special category states, scarred by decades of violence, disruption of normal life, poverty, and misery, people were slowly realizing that economic stability was a goal worth pursuing at any cost and this realization ultimately translated into waning support for radical and separatist causes. The prospect for peace and growth now seemed not so distant, and with insurgency losing steam and opportunities opening up gradually, a change was set in motion, imperceptible initially, but slowly getting the stage ready for processes in motion for the gradual transformation of their rural agrarian economies into modern market based economies. Not all of them could derive the benefits from this process in substantial measures, but states that had built up some infrastructure and entrepreneurial capacity could utilize their synergies better to march ahead and eventually to catch up with the rest of India. These were the states where peace had prevailed and conflict and tension were kept under control, through a model of good governance and proper utilization of liberal central assistance. Others who were not that fortunate are still struggling, but stagnation and the feeling of hopelessness and despair seem to be things of the past. Special category states are now poised to make a break with the past and embark upon a new future. In the last two chapters we have seen results of these changes, with some states achieving living standards not only comparable to the national averages, but also to those in the advanced states of India.

Dependency Syndrome

This study also focused on the management of public finances by these states and on their socio-economic development, on the assumption that the former will have a bearing on the latter. No such straight correlation could be established because of factors related to governance, like institutional capacity, transparency and accountability in the use of funds, etc., which are not measurable but whose impact on development cannot be denied, though such impact could not be captured or quantified for our analytical framework. However, a few patterns did emerge from our study. It was seen that the special category status had indeed helped in bringing about some developmental transformation over the years. Though a substantial part of this transformation can be traced to the FRBMAs and recommendations of the Twelfth and Thirteenth Finance Commissions, the fact remained that the most important sources of their finances have all along been the central grants. Higher plan—and also non-plan—grants helped them not only to bridge their revenue deficits, but also to increase their spending on capital outlay. Though most of them are still far from being self-sufficient, at least some of them have attained a reasonable degree of self-sufficiency. It is to be appreciated that all special category states, like others, were revenue deficit states till the turn of the century, but now almost all of them have become revenue surplus states upon implementation of the FRBMA. The plan sizes of these states have grown substantially from plan to plan. Their own tax revenues and GSDP, and more importantly, the ratio of own tax revenues to GSDP have also been increasing over the years for most states, and some have recorded substantially higher growth of GSDP than the rest. Central grants, however, still constitute by far the most important source of revenue for all. But the most remarkable change has been in respect of their indebtedness; most of them have been able to come out of a debt trap into which they were falling irrevocably, by using the FRBMA and Finance Commission largesse. They may further consolidate the gains by efficient cash management to better manage their debt that will allow them more fiscal space. While FRBMAs have done a world of good to their finances, it should be remembered it has also limited the scope for their capital outlay that is essential for rapid growth and there might be a case for undertaking a state-specific review of these limits. These states may further reduce their fiscal deficits by cutting on unproductive subsidies and loans to their loss making public enterprises, and by winding up the unviable ones.

There are some tax concessions available to tribal people in the Sixth Schedule areas that defy all logic, like exemption from income taxation. Finance Act 1955, had first incorporated provisions for exemption of tribal people of the northeastern region from payment of income tax. Provisions relating to such exemptions were included in the Indian Income Tax Act 1961, under section 10(26). These provisions were extended to Nagaland with effect from 1 December 1963. Initially such exemption was only in respect of government servants, understandably to compensate them for less pay, but such distinctions were removed in 1970 when Parliament passed the Taxation Laws (Amendment) Act 1970. There remains no ground to continue with such exemptions any longer. Nothing prevents the concerned states to impose an equivalent amount of tax on these people by invoking their own powers of taxation under the State List—something like a tax on vocation or profession. This will augment the scarce tax revenue of these states, but the only hurdle remains that the people who have to decide upon this are also the beneficiaries of the same exemptions.

Special category states have always been getting per capita central plan assistances several times higher than those given to other states. Liberal central transfers even now are driving the economy of many of these states, especially in the northeast, where government expenditure still constitutes a very significant part of the GSDP. In 2010–11, central transfers constituted more than 50 per cent of GSDP for six special category states. This dependency is deeply entrenched in their finances, and it will be difficult if not impossible to overcome this dependency. Even for running their day-to-day administration, the expenditure needed by them are several times their own revenues from all tax and non-tax sources, and there will be no money to spend on development without central assistance. The separatist insurgents who not only survive but enjoy a cushy lifestyle from the taxes extorted by their respective outfits from the civilian population in some of these states would do well to take note of this.

Demands for More Special Category States

This should raise the *bona fide* question about the future of this category. Are they to remain in the special category for ever? Since 1969, the number of such states has increased from three to 11 and the last state to have been accorded this status was Uttarakhand that was formed in 2000. Since then, there have been demands from all these newly formed states, as well as from Bihar, Rajasthan, Odisha, and latest, from the successor state of Andhra Pradesh after separation of Telangana, for the special category status, claiming that the criteria devised by the Planning Commission were arbitrary. The criteria, as we have already seen, were indeed arbitrary and ad-hoc, by all standards.

From 1972 onwards, the creation of more special category states followed as a result of the increasing aspirations of people inhabiting these states, since the pre-existing structure was unable to accommodate their expectations and aspirations. As we have seen, a few special category states thus created have already registered even higher rates of growth than national averages—some have attained levels of development comparable to those of the advanced states. The question is would they still be treated as special category, or should they make way for other backward states to be treated as 'special'?

Chief Ministers of Bihar and Odisha have been especially vocal in raising persistent demands for this status from time to time. As reiterated by the Thirteenth Finance Commission, the definition of some states as 'special category states' addresses their low resource base and the cost disabilities due to their physical geography, sparse terrain, remoteness, and high costs of providing similar standard of public goods and services as the non-special category states, arising mainly from their historical circumstances or geopolitical constraints to development. But the problems of states which today are demanding this status don't appear to stem from difficult terrain or cost disabilities due to adverse physical geography. On the contrary, both Bihar and Odisha are resource-rich in terms of minerals; both share many geographical advantage rather than adversities. The delivery cost of public services is not because of any natural disadvantages in these states, but because of governance failure in the past. It is precisely this failure that the governments in these states are now trying to reverse.

During the 11th Plan, Bihar's share in total Normal Central Assistance was 11 per cent, the highest among all non-special category states save UP, whose share was 19.5 per cent. Among the special category states, share of individual states varied between 3.8 per cent of the funds earmarked for the special category states for Sikkim to 19.5 per cent for Assam. Even though the number of special category states has increased from only three to 11 between 1969 and now, the kitty of 30 per cent of the central plan funds has remained unchanged. As a result, the share of individual states within the category had declined.

As per the 2013–14 Budget, the total central assistance to states was Rs 1.3 lakh crore, of which the normal plan assistance was only Rs 27,636 crore, and about a third of this money was to go to the special category states. This was, however, miniscule compared to the total plan expenditure of Rs 4.2 lakh crore for central and centrally sponsored plans, of which Rs 1.4 lakh crore were earmarked for flagship welfare schemes of the centre to be implemented in states, to be spent not through their budgets, but as direct transfers to the implementing agencies in districts. As observed earlier, the increasing intrusion of centrally sponsored schemes in total plan allocations and direct transfers of plan funds have progressively diluted the Normal Central Assistance—the Gadgil transfers—from which the special category states benefit directly. As the extra-budgetary direct transfers have increased phenomenally, the Gadgil transfers have shrunk. Their share in total plan transfers has gradually fallen from 35 per cent during the Ninth Plan to only 10 per cent during the Eleventh Plan, while the share of direct transfers has increased from 20 per cent to 52 per cent over this period. Consequently the plan transfers to special category states have also contracted. The special category status has thus already lost much of its sheen and if awarded to more states would cease to have any real benefits for anyone.

During 2011–12, Rs 8958 crore, or 90 per cent of total central plan grants to Bihar—nearly one fifth of its total revenue receipts—were given as direct transfers, over which the state government had no control. This in itself would be far more than the grants Bihar would receive as a special category state, should it be accorded that status. Compared to this, the total plan grants received by the state during 2011–12 were only Rs 7320 crore. However, in the first budget presented by the newly elected NDA Government in July 2014, these direct transfers were stopped. Though the funds remained tied to the flagship schemes, they would now pass through the state budget which would get considerably expanded. By becoming a special category state, Bihar does not stand to gain much otherwise. Tax breaks wouldn't get many industries to the state, as they have not in the north eastern states even though they have been among the special category states for so many decades. Their credit deposit ratio is low, lower even than Bihar's 30 per cent because of low demand for credit by the industry. For attracting industries into a state and thereby for generating employment and income, availability of power and infrastructure are much more powerful incentives than any subsidies or tax concessions. Equally important is the availability of skill and a climate of entrepreneurship. Bihar has none of these essentials, and some additional grants are not going to help the cause of Bihar's underdevelopment.

As regards scarcity of resources, Bihar is not even able to spend whatever little resources and funds it has even now. As per the Appropriation

Accounts of the Government of Bihar prepared by the Accountant General (Audit) Bihar for the year 2010–11, the Government could not spend as much as Rs 14748 crore approved by the Legislature and appropriated from the Consolidated Fund of the State for expenditure under 44 grants related to various schemes and projects, covering both revenue and capital expenditure (Bhattacharjee 2013). Bihar's problem is not scarcity of resources, but lack of institutional capacity, infrastructure, developed market within the state, and easy and affordable access to markets outside, lack of entrepreneurial skill, and a proper industrial climate. These are impediments not addressable in the short term, and special category status will not be able to change things overnight.

As observed earlier, in case the status is awarded to Bihar, there will be other political problems as well. As *Economic Times* had pointed out on 16 May 2009, 'Singling out Bihar would be politically difficult. Moreover, if a large, mainstream state like Bihar is given special treatment, the meaning of special would blur. Uttar Pradesh could well ask for the status. Any change in the share of the central assistance pie going to the special category states would also raise controversy, within the group, and without.'

The case of Odisha is no different. During 2012–13, Odisha had received total plan grants of Rs 5355 from the Centre, of which Rs 3434 crore were meant for state plan schemes and Rs 1688 crore were meant for centrally sponsored schemes. But the amount of plan funds directly transferred to the state implementing agencies were Rs 3892 crore (42 per cent of the total plan grants including direct transfers) over which it had no control. During the year, it could not utilize Rs 5795 crore from 17 grants, which was even higher than the total amount of plan grants received by the state. Thus, like Bihar, spending capacity rather than resource availability seems to be the real problem in this case also.

The case of Andhra is, however, different. The erstwhile state of Andhra Pradesh was divided into Telangana and Andhra Pradesh with effect from 2 June 2014, by the Andhra Pradesh Reorganisation Act 2014. Of the 23 districts of undivided Andhra Pradesh, nine districts in the coastal region and four districts in the backward Rayalseema region remained with the residual state of Andhra Pradesh, while the remaining 10 districts including the most prosperous Hyderabad district with the capital city of Hyderabad and the contiguous Ranga Reddy district, also equally prosperous, went to Telangana. As per the Reorganization

Act, the total liabilities of the undivided state were shared by the two successor states in the ratio of their population, i.e. 58:42, as specified in the Act. The division of the state had already caused a great deal of resentment, and the residual state of Andhra Pradesh had indeed been left much poorer after the division due to the inequitable nature of distribution of revenues and liabilities between the two successor states.

Andhra Pradesh with its own revenue of Rs 11,627 crore and expenditure of Rs 60,750 crore inherited a total debt liability of Rs 90,910 crore, while Telengana with revenue of Rs 56,476 crore and expenditure of Rs 42,376 crore inherited debt liability of Rs 65,832 crore only, as per the 2012–13 accounts. But the asymmetry in the whole arrangement becomes shocking, once we consider that the combined revenues of the two prosperous districts of Telangana, Hyderabad, and Ranga Reddy, are Rs 51,478 crore, or 91 per cent of the total revenues of Telangana and these two districts together account for expenditure of Rs 23,302 crore or 48 per cent of the total expenditure of Telangana.[1] The result will be increasing impoverishment of Andhra Pradesh as its own revenue will be too inadequate to meet even one fifth of its expenditure requirements. The huge debt inherited in addition will impose heavy repayment burden on the poor state. This is indeed a case that certainly deserves consideration for the special category status.

Need for a Relook?

It is perhaps time to take a relook at the whole arrangement of award of the special category status to a state and its continuation in perpetuity. We have seen the existing mechanism is flawed in various respects, the most serious of these shortcomings being: (i) absence of any accountability and monitoring mechanism; (ii) absence of any performance expectation from the states linked to a definite time period; (iii) scale neutrality in relation to backwardness of individual states, and (iv) arbitrariness of selection criteria. Further, given the emphasis that is increasingly being placed upon good governance, accountability and transparency, equity and efficiency, the purpose of development is likely to be served better if the status is reviewed periodically and a target-based time-bound approach is adopted for assistance. Suitable incentive for better performance and disincentives for sub-optimal performance should also be built into the system for it to work efficiently.

There should also be a system of periodic review of the status and once the targets are fully achieved, the assistance may continue for a further term after which it may be diverted to another state that is in need of assistance. A target-oriented formula-based approach for assistance instils accountability, improves performance, removes complacency, and helps a state move rapidly forward. It also makes the field more level for all players, with open entry and exit to the special status for all.

Alternatively, since direct transfers have now been abolished and budgetary allocations have been taken out of the whims of the Planning Commission, another option would be to abolish the distinction between plan and non-plan expenditure and shift the entire responsibility of devolution of funds to states to the Finance Commission. Then there would be no need for a special group of states called 'Special Category' claiming a higher share of the total plan funds. Finance Commission can be entrusted to look into the financial requirements of each state individually according to its developmental needs and capacity, and to recommend devolution of central funds to each state accordingly, going by the objective criteria determined by it that will strike a balance between backwardness and financial performance of individual states. In the present scheme of things, population is a vital criterion for deciding upon the inter-se distribution of the proceeds of divisible pool of taxes among the states. Since all special category states stand to lose on this count, the same set of criteria cannot be applied in respect to forward and backward states and the realities and special requirements of backward states must be accommodated in an appropriate formula to be devised for the purpose. This will remove the aberrations and make the entire system of devolution based on transparency, accountability, equity, need, and ability.

Preparing for Future

The future will be shaped by the present just as the present has been shaped by the past. Hence any future path for progress must take into account the present realities of the special category states. It is needless to state that the most important prerequisites of economic development are non-economic—stable law and order situation, internal and external security, and good governance, backed by democracy at the grassroots through local self-governing institutions. Deepening of such grassroots processes of devolution of authority paves the way for accommodating the demands of various groups and enhancing participation in the growth process without which much of the fruits of growth can be frittered away. With peace reigning over the last few years in most of the troubled special category states, the conditions for such growth have already been created. But the capital base of almost all these states remains rather poor in all respects—natural, physical, social, and entrepreneurial. These ground realities are not going to change anytime soon.

Socially, special category states have some inherent advantages even over some mainstream states, as they do not suffer from caste and other impediments because of the inclusive nature of societies with their distinctive indigenous social institutions in these predominantly tribal states. As the document 'North Eastern Region Vision 2020' brought out by MDONER says, 'Inclusive growth calls for inclusive governance. The North Eastern Region has long established traditions of community-based economic and social organization. This has facilitated a smooth transition to contemporary institutions of Panchayati Raj...... Thus the North Eastern Region is well-equipped with institutions of inclusive governance to assure inclusive growth.'[2] Other special category states also have similar features in their social structures.

The unique nature of these institutions has often been used and exploited by misdirected movements to protect the vested interests entrenched in the existing power configurations in these states in the name of preservation of unique tribal culture and identity, preventing not only the entry of outsiders but also of outside capital and new ideas. In most tribal societies, power structure is often hierarchical—and a hierarchy-based system always fears invasion by new ideas and adoption of new methods of production that can upset the existing social contracts and the nature of power dynamics. The extremely irrational xenophobia created on this account in some states has led to the flight of talent and skill, scarce though they are, from within the region to outside for lack of opportunities for growth.

It must be emphasized that traditional institutions, unless guided to accept a modern outlook, to adopt modern practices and to transform themselves into modern institutions of relevance while retaining the essence of traditional culture and identity, can be highly dysfunctional. Many of the institutions in the northeast have degenerated to such a state. Identity is a strange word in the modern flat world we live in; too strong an emphasis on identity may lead to isolation, which ultimately becomes life-threatening. One must realize that we live in a world where words and ideas like existentialism, roots, or identity crisis are now almost passé. It's a world connecting continents and countries the world over by fibre-optic cables, where innovation and creativity of individuals in one part of the world travels through these wires instantaneously to other continents and countries, where they inspire people to connect with each other and collaborate, creating wealth and improving productivity to lift people out of poverty. It is bizarre that in a world yearning ever more to be connected by all means, in the northeast, when there is a proposal to extend railway line to a state which would immediately lead to development and growth, opposition is built up by stoking the old fire of hatred in the name of preserving the tribal identity which itself is in the process of transformation by assimilation of new ideas and ethos brought by increased connectivity. Sometimes, strangely, demands are raised for extending inner line permits, which itself is the relic of an old isolationist era, in a state free from any such anachronism, and saner voices are silenced by the coercive nature of such demands. Identity politics is indeed a two-way sword, it cuts both ways. A closed society, like a closed system, is doomed to extinction. The earlier this truth dawns upon the students and the youth as well as upon those who use them for their own gains—leaders and politicians, the faster would be their transition and integration into a modern economy, for which connectivity is the keyword—road, rail, waterways, and air connectivity, cyber and telecom connectivity, and connectivity of ideas and innovation and democracy, creating a far more beneficial and all-embracing identity for all.

As opportunities have gradually opened up in the rest of the country in the post- reform period, more and more people are moving out every year in search of income, jobs, and opportunities from the northeast, where life and opportunities have almost remained standstill as they were decades ago. In the other states of India, liberalization and globalization have thrown up challenges, prospects, and opened up avenues for everyone to seize and climb the ladder of individual growth and development. It is a point to ponder for the leaders of northeast as to why people belonging to this region, once forced to come out of the comfort zone of their own culture, ethnicity, or language, rarely want to go back to the region. In today's world, it is economy that is the lever for change—certainly not identity politics. As we have observed, funding alone cannot solve the problem of backwardness—it hasn't so far, despite the much higher per capita devolution of central funds to the special category states—and within this group, to the northeastern states in particular. Along with finance, the need to align with aspirations of a restless young generation impatient to live the interesting changes the country and outside world is going through, is also equally important and imperative.

Road Map for Future

As already stated, a pragmatic roadmap must take into cognizance the existing strengths and realities. Given the dependence of all special category states on agriculture and allied activities, the developmental priority must still be accorded to agriculture. As the Vision 2020 document of MDONER correctly identifies, 'it is only through a Green Revolution that the back of the Region's poverty can be broken and the people as a whole placed on the parabola of progress.'[3] Without seeming to be too prescriptive in policy areas, I may only highlight the essential elements for such a Green Revolution as identified in the Vision 2020 document itself, which are also equally applicable to the special category states outside the northeastern region:

- Increase in agriculture productivity by immediate replacement of traditional cropping patterns by short-duration, high-yielding varieties of foodgrains and vegetables, along with judicious use of soil nutrients and fertilizers
- Increase in productivity of agro-horticulture crops by using improved methods of cultivation and promotion of agro forestry, horticulture, and floriculture, as well as of medicinal and aromatic plants and herbs, including organic farming, to capture the highly remunerative niche markets abroad
- Promotion of all forms of animal husbandry, accompanied by promotion of fodder cultivation; and
- Conservation of nature, increasing forest cover, and preserving the rich bio-diversity and wildlife for sustainable development

Development can never take place in isolation, hence it is imperative that increases in agro-productivity must be complemented by development of market and monetization of rural economy, which in turn would require establishment of easily accessible markets, financial inclusion, augmentation of storage facilities, and extension of agriculture through mobilization of PRI and other local self-government institutions. This has to be supported by substantial land reforms and availability of adequate rural credit by removing the institutional, legal, and administrative roadblocks many of which are political in nature. Non-farm rural self-employment through cottage industries should at the same time be sufficiently incentivized and encouraged through appropriate policies to augment household income. These activities earn income for a substantial number of households in all special category states and they need to be better connected to markets inside and outside, through appropriate marketing and credit policies framed and implemented with government support.

Tourism has immense potential for attracting investments and generating income and employment within the special category states, all of which are scenic paradises and enjoy the liberal bounties of Mother Nature. In order to capitalize on this strength, states need to overcome the structural bottlenecks that hinder the growth of tourism industry. A stable law and order and internal security are the most important requirements for development of tourism industry, followed by creation of quality infrastructure of hotels, roads, and air-links. With peace and political stability returning to most of these states, it is now time to devise an appropriate strategy in this respect, focused on creation of quality infrastructure through a policy of offering tax breaks and other incentives to the private sector and reputed hotel chains that need to be roped in from outside. Side by side, attention should be directed towards developing all-weather roads and the transport sector in each state.

Industrial scenario remains grim in all the special category states even after decades of their special category status. The prerequisites for industrialization—capital, skill, power, resources, and markets (and land in states where there is a community ownership)—being absent in these states, a situation that is unlikely to change in the short-run, rapid large scale industrialization may not be expected or even be feasible, and the development has to be incremental. The few existing incentives are also too inadequate to attract capital from outside. This is apparent from the fact that despite having sufficient reserves of petroleum,

Assam does not have any large production facility for petrochemicals apart from four public sector refineries, and despite being the second largest producer of rubber in the country, Tripura does not have a single rubber factory. Similarly despite having large reserve of limestone, the northeast does not have a single factory with annual capacity exceeding one MT of cement.

Industrialization can take place only through gradual expansion of the existing small scale industries; these are largely in the mining and quarrying sectors, tea, food processing, paper, and printing, timber, pharmaceuticals, wool and weaving, watches and clocks, and other small scale manufacturing activities based on locally available resources. It is still feasible to enlarge the existing industrial base by achieving forward and backward integration between existing industries and creating a cluster to exploit the synergies that already exist. Rather than focusing immediately on large scale manufacturing, the states should concentrate on trade and commerce, tourism, and service sector industries including IT, ITES, and telecom services.

Most special category states have sufficient water resources with immense hydroelectric potential which have largely remained untapped as yet. Harnessing this potential is of course a big challenge, given the difficulty of terrains, besides huge investment that is beyond the capacity of most states. Negotiating all the complex environmental, ecological, and rehabilitation related issues can be extremely difficult and time consuming. A more pragmatic approach would be to create a number of small projects along the courses of different rivers, after careful assessment of the environmental and related problems—and not forgetting the lessons from the recent disaster in Uttarakhand.

Without emphasizing human resource and capacity development, there cannot be any development. As we have seen, in terms of literacy, eight of the 11 special category states rank higher above the national averages, but the educational infrastructure, especially in respect of science, technical, and vocational education, lags way behind the national standards, forcing talented students to pursue higher education outside, from where they are unlikely to return to their native states. The system of education imparted is also rather generic and does not reflect the needs and strengths of these states. There is inadequate access to technical training, skill development in IT, engineering, and medical education, and business management skills. Though effort is on to create centres of excellence through public as well as private initiatives and a few such institutions like an NIT in Tripura or an IIM in Shillong have already been established, but demand which is increasing every year far outstrips supply. These centres also suffer from want of quality teachers and shortage of skill in critical areas and these problems need to be addressed. Expanding IT infrastructure and incentivizing the application of IT are essential for creating avenues for 'sunshine industries' in the region.

Uttarakhand, and to some extent Sikkim also, have pioneered some successful experiments in converting their states to educational hubs to attract students from all over India, in the process creating excellent educational infrastructure while generating local income and employment. This has attracted substantial capital to their states and some of these institutions have emerged at the forefront of technical and health education in the country. Given the ever-increasing demands for technical education in the country, other states can benefit by emulating their examples.

It is indeed time to shake off all lethargy and embark on the road to development and progress by putting the failures of the past behind—with new hope, new zeal, and new energy for the future, for bequeathing to our children a future unmarred by the past.

I conclude by echoing the words of Kashmiri poet Dina Nath Naadim who lived in the last century: *'Mey chhum aash pagahich pagaah sholey duniya /Zameenus sosur lagi te sabzaar prezlun'*— 'I am optimistic that our tomorrow will be sunlit. Mother earth shall again bear greenery for us'. This reminds me of the eternal benediction of our ancient sages: *'Kaale varshatu paryannam prithivi shasyashalini/ Lokah santu niramayah'*—In course of time, rains will come and there will be abundance on earth. People will be free from suffering.

Notes

1. Final division of assets and liabilities and revenue and expenditure are yet to be made; figures have been worked out provisionally on the basis of accounts and allocation of common items in 58:42 ratio.
2. Vision Statement, iii.
3. Vision Statement, iii to x.

Annexure

Impact of 14th Finance Commission Recommendations on Special Category States[1]

The Fourteenth Finance Commission has since submitted its recommendations in February 2015 which are likely to alter the landscape of federal finances in India. It has recommended 42 per cent of the central divisible pool of resources for transfer to the states, as against the existing 32 per cent. States will now have much more fiscal space to accommodate their own priorities. This is precisely in line with the argument used in this book that centralized planning is a negation of the spirit of true federalism, in which centre and states are equal partners in development, not one as a giver and others as recipients of common resources.

The recommendations will have the effect of increasing the net flow of funds to the states by extra Rs 2.21 lakh crore during 2015–16 alone—the biggest ever jump in the state's share so far. During the award period of the Commission (2015–20), tax share to states will exceed Rs 44 lakh crore. Local bodies stand to gain significantly, with Rs 2 lakh crore earmarked for Gram Panchayats and Rs 87,000 crore for urban local bodies. The aggregate level of transfer of central resources, plan and non-plan combined, to the states, however, is estimated to increase only marginally by about 2 per cent over the award period, but most of it will now be based on formula rather than on discretion and not tied to plan schemes of questionable usefulness.

Every Finance Commission adopts its own criteria for determining the *inter se* share of the states in the total transfers out of the divisible pool. The fourteenth Commission's criteria, however, mark two important deviations from all previous Commissions. All previous commissions have adopted 1971 population as one of the criteria for distribution of the proceeds of taxes among the states, but for the first time, inter-state migration that has taken place since 1971 has been considered as a determinant of states' shares. Also, for the first time, by including forest cover as a new criterion while determining the transfers, environmental concerns have been given due recognition. Both these factors have significant impact upon special category states as explained in the preceding chapters and reflect the changing realities of our time. Tables A.1 and A.2 will show that the net effect of these has been a significant increase in the shares of all special category states in the total transfers.

It was noted earlier that central transfers play a very significant role in the economy of the special category states in that they contribute substantially to their GSDPs (Table A.3). They also help these states which do not have much resources of their own to generate revenue surpluses; without the transfers, most special category states would fall far short of meeting their revenue expenditure alone, as can be seen from Table A.4, which will also vindicate the argument used in the book for awarding the special category status to Andhra Pradesh. Eleven revenue-deficit states will get grants amounting to Rs 1.95 lakh crore during the Commission's award period to bridge their revenue deficits; of these, as many as eight belong to the special category (Table A.5).

Table A.1 Criteria and Weights[2]

Criteria	Weights (%)		
	14th FC	13th FC	12th FC
Population (1971)	17.5	25	25
Demographic Change since 1971	10		
Income Distance	50		50
Area	15	10	10
Forest Cover	7.5		
Fiscal Discipline		17.5	7.5
Fiscal Capacity Distance		47.5	
Tax Effort			7.5

Table A.2 *Inter se* Share of States (per cent)

	Share of Divisible Pool without Service tax			Share of Service Tax		
	14th FC	13th FC	12th FC	14th FC	13th FC	12th FC
Arunachal Pradesh	1.370	0.328	0.288	1.431	0.332	0.292
Assam	3.311	3.628	3.235	3.371	3.685	3.277
Himachal Pradesh	0.713	0.781	0.522	0.722	0.793	0.529
Jammu & Kashmir	1.854	1.551	1.297	Not Applicable		
Manipur	0.617	0.451	0.362	0.623	0.458	0.367
Meghalaya	0.642	0.408	0.371	0.650	0.415	0.376
Mizoram	0.460	0.269	0.239	0.464	0.273	0.242
Nagaland	0.498	0.314	0.263	0.503	0.318	0.266
Sikkim	0.367	0.239	0.227	0.369	0.243	0.230
Tripura	0.642	0.511	0.428	0.648	0.519	0.433
Uttarakhand	1.052	1.120	0.939	1.068	1.138	0.952
Total SCS	**11.526**	**9.600**	**8.171**	**1.431**	**0.332**	**0.292**
All States	1000	100	100	100	100	100

Table A.3 Total Transfers as States as per cent of GSDP

States	2011–12	2012–13	2013–14	2014–15 Revised Estimates
Arunachal Pradesh	45.4	42.7	50.4	58.8
Assam	13.5	14.1	18.0	20.7
Himachal Pradesh	13.1	13.0	12.7	10.5
Jammu & Kashmir	27.4	24.1	24.1	30.4
Manipur	47.4	52.2	54.1	53.1
Meghalaya	21.9	23.2	34.1	38.1
Mizoram	48.3	50.9	55.0	55.0
Nagaland	38.2	38.1	42.5	56.9
Sikkim	27.1	25.6	34.7	39.1
Tripura	25.8	24.6	27.7	32.4
Uttarakhand	7.1	6.8	9.8	10.7
All States	**4.9**	**4.8**	**5.4**	**6.5**

Table A.4 Pre- Devolution Revenue Deficit (+)/ Surplus (–) (Rs Crore)

State	2015–16	2016–17	2017–18	2018–19	2019–20
Arunachal Pradesh	4,609	5,169	5,786	6,467	7,215
Assam	21,435	23,396	25,451	27,734	30,999
Himachal Pradesh	12,150	13,010	13,832	14,593	15,264
Jammu & Kashmir	18,640	20,860	23,366	26,194	29,385
Manipur	5,645	6,227	6,865	7,564	8,328
Meghalaya	4,346	4,837	5,375	5,964	6,606
Mizoram	4,809	5,375	6,005	6,706	7,485
Nagaland	6,092	6,785	7,552	8,401	9,338
Sikkim	1,863	1,862	1,782	1,594	1,232
Tripura	4,815	5,388	6,027	6,739	7,531
Uttarakhand	5,838	4,896	3,441	1,865	700
Andhra Pradesh	**31,646**	**33,823**	**37,817**	**42,272**	**47,240**
Telangana	**–818**	**–2184**	**–3930**	**–6138**	**–8902**

Table A.5 Grants-in-aid for Revenue Deficit (2015-20) : Rs Crore

State	2015–16	2016–17	2017–18	2018–19	2019–20	2015–20
Assam	2,191	1,188	Nil	Nil	Nil	3,379
Himachal Pradesh	8,009	8,232	8,311	8,206	7,866	40,625
Jammu & Kashmir	9,892	10,831	11,849	12,952	14,142	59,666
Manipur	2,066	2,096	2,091	2,042	1,932	10,227
Meghalaya	618	535	404	213	Nil	1,770
Mizoram	2,139	2,294	2,446	2,588	2,716	12,183
Nagaland	3,203	3,451	3,700	3,945	4,177	18,475
Tripura	1,089	1,089	1,059	992	875	5,103
Andhra Pradesh	**6,609**	**4,930**	**4,430**	**3,644**	**2,499**	**22,113**
Kerala	**4,640**	**3,350**	**1,529**	**Nil**	**Nil**	**9,519**
West Bengal	**8,449**	**3,311**	**Nil**	**Nil**	**Nil**	**11,760**
Total State	**48,906**	**41,308**	**35,820**	**34,581**	**34,206**	**1,94,821**

For transfers outside the Finance Commission, the Commission has recommended setting up of a new institutional mechanism 'consistent with the overarching objective of strengthening cooperative federalism', by limiting discretion, improving design and giving adequate flexibility to the states. By recommending to exclude the states from the operations of NSSF which was forced upon them, it has given them more liberty to manage their debt. It has also urged the Centre to follow the true spirit of fiscal responsibility by discarding the concept of 'Effective Revenue Deficit', ingeniously invented by it to circumvent the 3 per cent limit on fiscal deficit. All these recommendations are likely to bring in transparency and accountability in the public finances of union as well as states, heralding a spirit of federalism this country has not seen so far. However, the higher tax devolution recommended by the Commission has been offset by merciless slashing of plan grants to the states in the budget for 2015–16. The block grants given under Normal Central Assistance has suffered the most, getting reduced to nil from Rs 26814 crore in the revised estimates of 2014–15 (Table A.6).

It is to be noted that NCA was based on the modified Gadgil Formula; providing no funds under NCA is tantamount to sacrificing the formula

Table A.6 Schemes for which no funds have been provided in Budget Estimates (BE) 2015–16 (Rs Crore)

	2014–15 RE (Review Estimates)
National Scheme for Modernisation of Police and Other Forces	1433
BRGF-State Component	3450
NCA	26814
Other ACA	1780
SCA	10150
SCA for Hill Areas	220
Special Plan Assistance	7666
BRGF	2837
NeGAP	464
Schemes for Model Schools at Block Level	1020
Central Assistance for Developing Export Infrastructure	565
Creation of Tourist Infrastructure	495
	56894

itself. The Gadgil formula gives 60 per cent weightage to population, while Fourteenth Finance Commission gives population a total weightage of only 27.5 per cent. Larger states with higher population will therefore lose on this account. Since both Gadgil and Fourteenth Finance Commission transfers are formula based, for the sake of equity, it was desirable to sacrifice non-formula based plan transfers like those linked to the CSS, rather than jettisoning the transfers based on Gadgil formula.

Notes

1. Based on author's article in the *Statesman* dated 3rd March 2015.
2. All data used in this annexure have been taken from reports of the respective finance commissions except Table A.5.

Bibliography

Agarwal, J. C. and S. P. Agarwal. 1995. *Uttarakhand: Past, Present and Future*. New Delhi: Concept Publishing Co.

Agranoff, Robert. 1999. 'Intergovernmental Relations and the Management of Asymmetry in Federal Spain', in *Accommodating Diversity: Asymmetry in Federal States*, ed. Robert Agranoff, Series of the European Centre for Research on Federalism, Tuebingen, Volume 10. Baden-Baden: Nomos Verlagsgelsellschaft.

Ahluwalia, Manjit S. 1998. *Social, Cultural and Economic History of Himachal Pradesh*. New Delhi: Indus Publishing Co.

Ahluwalia, Montek S. 2000a. 'Economic Performance of States in Post Reforms Period', *Economic and Political Weekly*, 6 May.

———. 2000b. 'State-level Performance under Economic Reforms in India'. Available at http://planningcommission.nic.in/hindi/aboutus/speech/spemsa/msa007.pdf; accessed on 1 February 2013.

Anand, Justice A. S. 1998. *The Constitution of Jammu & Kashmir: Its Development and Comments*. Colorado: Fred B. Rothman & Co.

Arora, Balveer. 1995. 'Adapting Federalism to India: Multilevel and Asymmetrical Innovations', in *Multiple Identities in a Single State: Indian Federalism in Comparative Perspective*, eds Arora, B. and D. Verney. New Delhi: Konark Publishers.

Arora, Balveer, K. K. Kailash, R Saxena and H. Kham Khan Suan. 2013. 'Indian Federalism', in *Indian Democracy*, ed. K. C. Suri, New Delhi: Oxford University Press.

Ayres, Alyssa and Philip Oldenburg. 2002. *India Briefing: Quickening the Pace of Change*. New York: M E Sharpe.

Baddeley, M., K. McNay, and R. Cassen. 2006. 'Divergence in India: Income Differentials at the State Level, 1970–97', *Journal of Development Studies*, 42 (6),

Available at http://www.econ.cam.ac.uk/faculty/baddeley/jds03.pdf; accessed on 1 February 2013.

Bahadur, Rai Pati Ram. 1916. *Garhwal, Ancient and Modern*. Simla: Simla Army Press (Reprinted edition, 2010. Nainital: Pahar Pothi).

Bajpai, Nirupam and Jeffrey D. Sachs. 1999. 'Progress of Policy Reform and Variations in Performance at the Sub-National Level in India', Development Discussion Paper No. 730, Harvard Institute for International Development, Harvard University. Available at http://www.cid.harvard.edu/ archive/india/pdfs/730.pdf; accessed on 1 February 2013.

Barua, P. C. 1992. *Planning and Development of Assam*. New Delhi: Mittal Publications.

Baruah, Sanjib. 1999. *India against Itself: Assam and the Politics of Nationality*. Philadelphia: University of Pennsylvania Press.

———. 2003a. 'Nationalizing Space: Cosmetic Federalism and the Politics of Development in Northeast India', *Development and Change*, 34(5): 915–39.

———. 2003b. 'Protective Discrimination and Crisis of Citizenship in North-East India, Alternatives for the Future', *Economic and Political Weekly*, April 26: 1624–26.

Bhagawati, Dhiren. 2007. *Meghalaya—Issues and Legacies of its Early Years*. Guwahati: DBS Publishers.

Bhal, John de. 2008. 'Malaysia's Centralised Federal System', http://aliran.com/aliran-monthly/2008/2008-4/malaysias-centralised-federal-system/ accessed on 22 June 2014.

Bhargava, Rajeev. 2012. 'Should Indian Federalism Be Called Multinational?', in *Multinational Federalism : Problems and Prospects*, eds Michel Seymour and Alain-G Gagnon. New York: Palgrave Macmillan.

Bhattacharjee, Giriraj. 2012. 'Tripura: Mopping Up', Institute for Conflict Management, New Delhi. Available at http://www.satp.org/satporgtp/sair/Archives/sair10/10_27.htm#assessment3#; accessed on 12 October 2012.

Bhattacharjee, Govind. 2013. 'Special Category Status: Will It Benefit Bihar', *Economic and Political Weekly*, 4 May, pp. 17–18.

———. 2014a. 'Reality of the Special Category States', *Economic and Political Weekly*, 4 October, Vol XLIX, No 40: 48–56.

———. 2014b. 'Disband Yojana Bhavan', *The Statesman*, July 28, New Delhi.

———. 2014c. 'Choice of Techniques', *The Statesman*, 6 October, New Delhi.

———. 2015. 'Reforms in Government Accounting: Accounts of State Governments', in *Government Accounting Reforms: An Overview*, pp. 1–16. New Delhi: Institute of Chartered Accountants of India.

Bhattacharjee, Pravas Ranjan. 1993. *Economic Transition in Tripura*. New Delhi: Vikas Publishing House.

Bhattacharya, B. 1997. *Sikkim: Land and People*. New Delhi: Omsons Publications.

Bhaumik, Subir. 2003. 'Tripura's Gumti Dam Must Go', *The Ecologist Asia*, 11 (1): 84–89.

Bhaumik, Subir. 2010. *Troubled Periphery: The Crisis of India's North East*. New Delhi: Sage Publications.

Bhide S. and M. Panda. 2002. 'Evaluating Quality of Budgets with a Composite Index', *Economic and Political Weekly*, 37(13): 1177–80.

Bora, H. N. 2008. 'A Brief Geo-Economic Setting of Arunachal Pradesh' in *The Economy of Arunachal Pradesh: Problems, Performances, Prospects*, ed. Manish Sharma. Guwahati: DVS Publishers.

Borah, S., D. Tourangbam, and A. C. Meitei. 2010. *Encyclopaedic Studies of North Eastern States of India: Vol.4: Meghalaya*. New Delhi:New Academic Publishers.

Börzel, Tanja A. 2002. *States and Regions in the European Union: Institutional Adaptation in Germany and Spain*. Cambridge: Cambridge University Press.

Bose, Sumantra. 2003. *Kashmir: Roots of Conflict, Paths to Peace*. Cambridge, Mass. and London: Harvard University Press.

Brahma, Jayanta. 2010. 'Mapping the North East on India's Foreign Policy Agenda', in *Beyond Borders: Look East Policy and North East India*, ed. Dilip Gogoi. Delhi/ Guwahati: DVS Publishers.

Brahmananda, P. R. 1977. *50 Years of Free Indian Economy*. New Delhi: IEA Trust Publications.

Burgess, Michael. 2006. *Comparative Federalism: Theory and Practice*. New York: Routledge.

Burgess, Michael and Franz Gress. 1999. 'Symmetry and Asymmetry Revisited', in *Accommodating Diversity: Asymmetry in Federal States*, ed. Robert Agranoff. Series of the European Centre for Research on Federalism, Tuebingen, Volume 10. Baden-Baden: Nomos Verlagsgelsellschaft.

Chakravarti, Anjan. 2009. *Economic Development and Employment in Sikkim*. New Delhi: Authorspress.

Chandra, Bipan, Mridula Mukherjee, and Aditya Mukherjee. 2000. *India After Independence: 1947 to 2000*. New Delhi: Penguin.

Datta, PS. 1991. *Economic Development of Arunachal Pradesh: A Case Study of North-Eastern Council's Role*. New Delhi: Har-Anand Publications in association with Vikas Publishing House.

Debnath, Jagadish Chandra. 2009. *Economic History and Development of Sikkim Before and After Independence*. Delhi: Abhijeet Publications.

Delmartino, Frank, Dumont Hugues, and Sébastien Van Drooghenbroeck. 2010. 'Kingdom of Belgium', in *A Global Dialogue on Federalism, Volume VII: Diversity and Unity in Federal Countries*, eds Luis Moreno and César Colino. Quebec:McGill-Queen's University Press.

Dholakia, Archana. 2005. 'Measuring Fiscal Performance of States: An Alternative Approach', *Economic and Political Weekly*, July 30: 3421–28.

Dholakia, Ravindra H., T. T. Ram Mohan and Navendu Karan. 2004. 'Fiscal Sustainability of Debt of States', Report Submitted to the Twelfth Finance

Commission, IIM, Ahmedabad, May. Available at http://www.iimahd.ernet.in/assets/upload/faculty/dr2.pdf; accessed on 12 October 2013

Duchacek Ivo D. 1971. *Comparative Federalism: The Territorial Dimension of Politics*. New York: Holt, Rinehart and Winston.

Fernandes, Walter. 2012. 'Politics of Tribal Land in Northeast India', *Journal of North East India Studies*. Available at http://www.jneis.com/?p=279; accessed on 31 December 2014.

Fernandes, Walter and Gita Bharali. 2008. 'Customary Law-Formal Law Interface: Impact on Tribal culture' in *Christianity and Change in Northeast India*, eds, T. N. Subba, Joseph Puthenpurackal and Shaji Joseph Puykunnel. New Delhi: Concept Publishing Company.

Fernandes, Walter and Sanjoy Barbora (eds). 2008. 'Tribal Land Alienation in the Northeast: An Introduction' in *Land, People and Politics: Contest over Tribal Land in Northeast India*.Guwahati: North Eastern Social Research Centre.

Fernandes, Walter and Vijay Paranjpye (eds). 1997. *Rehabilitation Policy and Law in India: A Right to livelihood*. New Delhi: Indian Social Institute.

French, Patrick. 2004. *Tibet, Tibet: A Personal History of a Lost Land*. London: Harper Perennial.

Funk, Alixandra. 2011. 'Asymmetrical Federalism: A Stabilizing or Destabilizing Factor in the Multinational Federation?', Thesis, Institut European des Hautes Etudes Internationale, Nice.

Gagnon, Alan-G and Charles Gibbs. 1999. 'The Normative Basis of Asymmetrical Federalism', in *Accommodating Diversity: Asymmetry in Federal States*, ed. Robert Agranoff. Series of the European Centre for Research on Federalism, Tuebingen, Volume 10. Baden-Baden: Nomos Verlagsgelsellschaft.

Gagnon, Alain-G and Richard Simeon. 2010. 'Canada', in *A Global Dialogue on Federalism, Volume VII: Diversity and Unity in Federal Countries*, eds Luis Moreno and César Colino. Montreal: McGill Queen's University Press, pp. 109–38.

Garg, Subhas Chandra. 2006. 'Transformation of Central Grants to State: Growing Conditionality and Bypassing State Budgets', *Economic and Political Weekly*, 2 December, 41 (48).

George, K. K. and I. S. Gulati. 16 February 1985. 'Centre-State Resource Transfers, 1951-84', *Economic and Political Weekly*. Available at http://www.epw.in/special-articles/centre-state-resource-transfers-1951-84-appraisal.html; accessed on 10 February 2013.

Gopalakrishnan, R. 1995. *Meghalaya: Land and People*. New Delhi: Omsons Publications.

Goswami, M. P. 2007. 'Emerging Trends and Issues in Centre State Financial Relation' in *Indian Public Finance and Twelfth Finance Commission*, eds Anil Kumar Thakur and Md. Abdus Salam. New Delhi: Deep and Deep Publications.

Guha, Ramachandra. 1990. *The Unquiet Woods: Ecological Change and Peasant Resistance in the Himalaya*. Berkeley: University of California Press.

Gupta, R. K. 1992. *Centre-State Financial Relations under Indian Constitution*. New Delhi: Deep and Deep Publications.

Hausing, Kham Khan Suan. 2009. 'Identities, Autonomy and Patriotism: Asymmetric Federalism in North-East India', Unpublished, PhD Dissertation, Centre for Political Studies, Jawaharlal Nehru University, New Delhi, quoted in Arora *et al.* (2013: 131–2).

———. 2014. 'Asymmetric Federalism and the Question of Democratic Justice in Northeast India', *India Review*, 13 (2).

Huat, Wong Chin and James Chin. 2011. 'Malaysia: Centralized Federalism in an Electoral One-Party State', 208–231, in *Varieties of Federal Governance—Major Contemporary Models*, ed. Rekha Saxena.New Delhi: Foundation Books.

Iralu, Kaku D. 2002. 'Is Underdevelopment the Cause of Insurgency in Nagaland', in *Dimensions of Development in Nagaland*, eds Thomas, C. Joshua and Gurudas Das. New Delhi: Regency Publications.

Ivanov, Georgi. 2011. *Asymmetrical Pluralism in Spain: A Multidimensional Analysis, Carlton University, Canada*. Available at https://carleton-ca.academia.edu/GeorgiIvanov; accessed on 20 June 2014.

Jagmohan. 2011. 'The Politics of Maximum Autonomy' in *A Tangled Web: Jammu & Kashmir*, ed. Ira Pande. New Delhi: HarperCollins Publishers.

Jasaal, Comdt. R. S. 2011. *Militancy and Conflict Resolution in Manipur*. New Delhi: Akansha Publishing House.

Jayal, Niraja Gopal. 2000. 'Uttaranchal: Same Wine, Same Bottle, New Label', *Economic and Political Weekly*, 2 December.

Kak, Sanjay. 2011. 'What Are Kashmir's Stone-pelters Saying to US' in *Until My Freedom Has Come: The New Intifada in Kashmir*, ed. Sanjay Kak. New Delhi: Penguin.

Khemani, S. 2003. 'Partisan Policies and Intergovernmental Transfers in India', Policy Research Working paper 3016, The World Bank, Washington DC. Available at http://www-wds.worldbank.org/external/default/WDSContentServer/IW3P/IB/2003/05/13/000094946_03050104011126/Rendered/PDF/multi0page.pdf; accessed on 10 Februrary 2013.

Krishna, Sridhar. 2002. 'Economic Profile of Uttaranchal', *Economic and Political Weekly*, May 11.

Kumar, Girindra. 2012. *Dynamics of Development and Planning: Mizoram: A Comprehensive, Regional Analysis*. Delhi: Kalpaz Publications.

Kumar, N. V. R. Jyoti. 2008. 'India's North East Region and Border Trade in the Context of Emerging Borderless World: The Mizoram Experience' in *Mizoram, Dimensions and Perspectives*. New Delhi: Concept Publishing Company.

Kumar, Pradeep. 2000. *The Uttarakhand Movement: Construction of a Regional Identity*. New Delhi: Kanishka Publishers Distributors.

Kurian, N. J. 2000. 'Widening Regional Disparities in India – Some Indicators', *Economic and Political Weekly*, Vol. XXXV, No. 7. Available at http://www.epw.in/special-articles/widening-regional-disparities-india.html; accessed on 6 February 2013.

Lama, Mahendra P. 1994. 'Sikkim: Agenda for Priorities and Resource Management', in *Sikkim: Society, Polity, Economy, Environment*. New Delhi: Indus Publishing Company.

Lianzela. 1994. *Economic Development of Mizoram*. Guwahati: Spectrum Publications.

Loh, Francis. 2008. 'Malaysia's Centralised Federal System'. Available at http://aliran.com/aliran-monthly/2008/2008-4/malaysias-centralised-federal-system/; accessed on 23 June 2014.

Majumdar, R. C., H. C. Raychaudhury, and K. K. Datta. 1978. *An Advanced History of India*, New Delhi: Macmillan.

Mawdsley, Emma. 2002. 'Redrawing the Body Politic: Federalism, Regionalism and the Creation of New States in India', *Commonwealth and Comparative Politics*, 40 (3): 34–54.

McGarry, John. 2005. 'Asymmetric Federalism and the Plurinational State' in *Third International Conference on Federalism: Speeches, Contributions and Conclusions*, March 3–5, eds Frank Geerkens and ICF Management Team. Brussels: European Parliament.

Mehta, Pratap Bhanu. 2011. 'Kashmir as a Syndrome' in *A Tangled Web: Jammu & Kashmir*, ed. Ira Pande. New Delhi: HarperCollins Publishers.

Menon, V. P. 1956. *The Story of the Integration of the Indian States*. London: Longmans, Green & Co.

Moreno, Luis and César Colino. 2010a. 'Introduction', in *A Global Dialogue on Federalism, Volume VII: Diversity and Unity in Federal Countries*, Montreal: McGill Queen's University Press.

———. 2010b. 'Kingdom of Spain' in *A Global Dialogue on Federalism: Volume VII: Diversity and Unity in Federal Countries*. Montreal: McGill Queen's University Press.

Nambiar, A. C. K. 2010. 'Fiscal Performance of States: An Alternative Approach to Measurement', *The IUP Journal of Public Finance*, VIII (3): 7–25.

Paranjape, H. K. 17 September 1988. 'Task of the Ninth Finance commission: The Planning Commission Tangle', *Economic and Political* Weekly, pp. 1953–55.

Patnaik, Jagadish K., and Lalthakima. 2008. 'Mizoram: A Profile' in *Mizoram: Dimensions and Perspectives*. New Delhi: Concept Publishing Company.

Peer, Basharat. 2009. *Curfewed Night*. New Delhi: Random House India.

Prasad, R. N. 2004. 'Sixth Schedule and Working of the District Councils in North-Eastern States', *Dialogue*, October–December, 6 (2). Available at http://www.asthabharati.org/Dia_Oct04/R.N.Pras.htm; accessed on 11 July 2014.

Pudaite, Lal Thanzaua. 2010. *Mizoram and Look East Policy*. New Delhi: Akansha Publishing House.

Puri, Balraj. 2011. '5000 Years of Kashmir', in *A Tangled Web: Jammu & Kashmir*, ed. Ira Pande. New Delhi: HarperCollins Publications.

Raizada, Dr Shefali. 2012. *Merger of Sikkim—A New Perspective*, Delhi: Swati Publications.

Rangarajan, C. and D. K. Srivastava.2011. *Federalism and Fiscal Transfers in India*. New Delhi:OUP.

Ray, Animesh. 1993. *Mizoram*. New Delhi: National Book Trust.

Ray, Ashok Kumar. 1994. 'Territorial Issues and Manipur', in *Reorganisation of North East India since 1947*, eds Datta Ray, B and S P Agarwal. New Delhi: Concept Publishing Company.

Routray, Bibhu Prasad. 2008. 'Tripura: The Peace Consolidates', Institute for Conflict Management. Available at http://www.satp.org/satporgtp/sair/Archives/sair9/9_26.htm#assessment2.

Roy Chaudhury, Dipanjan. 2005. 'Autonomous District Councils and Panchayati Raj Institutions in North-East India', *Dialogue*, July–September, Volume 7, No. 1. Available at http://www.asthabharati.org/DiaJul% 2005/dip.htm; accessed on 11 July 2014.

Roy, Subroto. 2009. *Encyclopaedia of Tripura*, New Delhi: Anmol Publications.

Rudolph, Lloyd I. and Susanne Hoeber Rudolph. 2001. 'Living with Difference in India: Legal Pluralism and Legal Universalism in Historical Context', in *Religion and Personal Law in Secular India: A Call to Judgment*, ed. Gerald James Larson, pp. 36–55. Bloomington: Indiana University Press.

Sachdeva, Gulshan. 2000a. 'Economy of the North-East: Policy, Present Conditions and Future Possibilities'. New Delhi: Centre for Policy Research.

———. 2000b. 'India's Northeast: Rejuvenating a Conflict-Driven Economy', *Faultlines*, Vol. 6.

Sachs, Jeffrey D., Nirupam Bajpai and Ananthi, Ramiah. 2002. 'Understanding Regional Economic Growth in India', Center for International Development, Harvard University, Working Paper No. 88, March. Available at http://www.hks.harvard.edu/var/ezp_site/storage/fckeditor/file/pdfs/centers-programs/centers/cid/ publications/faculty/wp/088.pdf; accessed on 9 February 2013.

Sahaya, D. N. 2011. 'How Tripura Overcame Insurgency', *The Hindu*, September 19. Available at http://www.thehindu.com/opinion/lead/article2465348.ece; accessed on 12 October 2012.

Sahni, Ajai and Bibhu Prasad Routray. 2005. 'Tripura: Counter-insurgency Success', Institute for Conflict Management. Available at http://www.satp.org/satporgtp/sair/ Archives/4_7.htm#assessment1; accessed on 15/10/2012.

Sanz, Ixone Alonso. 2010. 'Spanish Decentralization and the Current autonomous State: A Budgetary View', *International Journal of Public Budget*, XXXVIII

No. 72. Available at http://www.asip.org.ar/en/content/72-international-journal-public-budget-3; accessed on 21 June 2014.

Sashinungla. 2005. 'Nagaland: Insurgency and Factional Intransigence'. Available at http://www.satp.org/satporgtp/publication/faultlines/volume16/Article4.htm; accessed on 12 October 2013.

Sati, V. P. and Kamlesh Kumar. 2004. *Uttaranchal—Dilemma of Plenties and Scarcities*. New Delhi: Mittal Publications.

Sharma, H. Isworchandra. 2010. 'Economic Liberalisation in Manipur: A Critical Understanding' in *Perspectives on the Economy of Manipur*, eds Singh, Bijoykumar and Damodar Nepram, pp. 310–15. New Delhi: Akansha Publishing House.

Singh, Ch. Priyoranjan. 2010. 'Institutional Impediments to Development of Manipur', in *Perspectives on the Economy of Manipur*, eds Singh, Bijoykumar and Damodar Nepram. New Delhi: Akansha Publishing House.

Singh, N. Bhupendro. 2010. 'Border Trade at Moreh-Tamu Sector: Boon or Bane for Manipur?' in *Perspectives on the Economy of Manipur*, eds Bijoykumar Singh and Damodar Nepram. New Delhi: Akansha Publishing House.

Singh, Th. Priyokumar. 2010. 'Trade and Industrialisation in Manipur: The Post-Liberalisation Scenario' in *Perspectives on the Economy of Manipur*, eds, Singh, Bijoykumar and Damodar Nepram. New Delhi: Akansha Publishing House.

Singh, N. Joykumar. 2005. *Revolutionary Movements in Manipur*. New Delhi: Akansha Publishing House.

Singh, N. Lokendra. 1998. *Unquiet Valley*. New Delhi: Mittal Publications.

Singh, N. and G. Vashishtha. 2004. 'Patterns in Centre-State Fiscal Transfers: An Illustrative Analysis', *Economic and Political Weekly*, November 6. Available at http://escholarship.org/uc/item/1r02k470; accessed on 10 February 2013.

Sinha, Amitabha and Kiran Sankar Chakraborty. 2010. *Reflections on Economy and Society of Tripura*. New Delhi: Akansha Publishing House.

Sinha, Nirmal C. 1966. 'Was the Simla Convention not signed?', Bulletin of Tibetology, Gangtok Sikkim, Vol III No, 1. 21 February. Available at http://www.thlib.org/static/reprints/bot/bot_03_01_04. pdf; accessed on 10 November 2013.

Stepan, Alfred. 1999. 'Federalism and Democracy: Beyond the U.S. Model,' *Journal of Democracy*, 10 (4), October.

Swenden, Wilfried. 2006. *Federalism and Regionalism in Western Europe: A Thematic and Comparative Analysis*. New York: Palgrave Macmillan.

Tarapot, Phanjoubam. 2003. *Bleeding Manipur*. New Delhi: Har-Anand Publication.

Tarlton, Charles D. 1965. 'Symmetry and Asymmetry as Elements of Federalism: A Theoretical Speculation', *The Journal of Politics*, 27 (4).

Tillin, Louise. 2007. 'United in Diversity? Asymmetry in Indian Federalism', *Publius: The Journal of Federalism*, 37 (1): 45–67.

———. 2008. 'Politics in a New State: Chhattisgarh', *Seminar*, no. 591, pp. 23–33.

Upadhyay, R. 2005a. 'Naga Insurgency - A Confusion of War or Peace!', Paper no. 1256, South Asian Analysis Group. Available at http://www.southasiaanalysis.org/%5cpapers13%5cpaper1256.html; accessed on 12 February 2013.

———. 2005b. 'Manipur–In a strange whirlpool of Cross-Current Insurgency', South Asia Analysis Group, 2005. Available at http://www.southasiaanalysis.org/papers13/paper1210.html; accessed on 10 December 2010.

Vaidya, Rajendra R. 2005. 'Borrowing: Debt Management and Contingent Liabilities: A Study of Indian State Governments', paper presented before the Final Technical Workshop of Policy Research Networking to Strengthen Policy Reform, (ADB) at Hyderabad. Available at http://www2.adb.org/Documents/Reports/Consultant/TAR-IND-4066/GovtBudget/vaidya.pdf, accessed 09/02/2013.

Verma, A. K. 2003. 'Uttar Pradesh: Politics of Social Polarisation and its Limits', *Journal of Indian School of Political Economy*, Jan–June: 255–58.

Verma, V. 1995. *The Emergence of Himachal Pradesh*. New Delhi: Indus Publishing Co.

Vithal, B. P. R. and M. L. Sastry. 2001. *Fiscal Federalism in India*. New Delhi: Oxford University Press.

———. 2002. *The Gadgil Formula*. New Delhi: Manohar.

Watts, Ronald L. 1999. 'Theoretical and Practical Implications of Asymmetric Federalism' in *Accommodating Diversity: Asymmetry in Federal States*, ed. Robert Agranoff. Series of the European Centre for Research on Federalism, Tuebingen, Volume 10. Baden-Baden: Nomos Verlagsgelsellschaft.

———. 2005. 'A Comparative Perspective on Asymmetry in Federations', *Asymmetry Series* 2005(4): Institute of Intergovernmental Relations, School of Policy Studies, Queen's University. Available at http://www.queensu.ca/iigr/ WorkingPapers/asymmetricfederalism/Watts2005.pdf; accessed on 5 June 2014.

Weiner, Myron. 1978. *Sons of the Soil: Migration and Ethnic Conflict in India*. Princeton: Princeton University Press.

Yeoh, Tricia. 2010. 'Revisiting the Federalist System: Federal-State Relations in Malaysia', *Penang Economic Weekly*, April 23. Available at http://egalitaria.wordpress.com/2010/04/23/federal-state-relations-in-malaysia/; accessed on 23 June 2014.

Index

About the Author

Govind Bhattacharjee is a civil service officer, currently serving as Director General at the Office of the Comptroller and Auditor General of India in New Delhi. During his long service career, he has held many important positions in India and abroad.

Bhattacharjee is a prolific writer on many issues ranging from physics to economics to photography. He has been a regular contributor to national newspapers and academic journals on socio-economic and developmental issues. He has published books on public finance and popular science. His areas of interest include public finance, developmental economics, public policy, and international relations, besides popular science.